Explaining Individual Differences in Reading

New Directions in Communication Disorders Research: Integrative Approaches

Rhea Paul, Series Editor

Rhea Paul (Ed.)
Language Disorders from a Developmental Perspective: Essays in Honor of Robin S. Chapman

Elena L. Grigorenko and Adam J. Naples (Eds.)
Single-Word Reading: Behavioral and Biological Perspectives

Marilyn A. Nippold and Cheryl M. Scott (Eds.)
Expository Discourse in Children, Adolescents, and Adults: Development and Disorders

Amy L. Weiss (Ed.)
Perspectives on Individual Differences Affecting Therapeutic Change in Communication Disorders

Susan A. Brady, David Braze, and Carol A. Fowler (Eds.)
Explaining Individual Differences in Reading: Theory and Evidence

Explaining Individual Differences in Reading

Theory and Evidence

Edited by
Susan A. Brady
David Braze
Carol A. Fowler

Psychology Press
Taylor & Francis Group
New York Hove

Psychology Press
Taylor & Francis Group
270 Madison Avenue
New York, NY 10016

Psychology Press
Taylor & Francis Group
27 Church Road
Hove, East Sussex BN3 2FA

Psychology Press is an imprint of Taylor & Francis Group, an Informa business

Printed in the United States of America on acid-free paper
10 9 8 7 6 5 4 3 2 1

International Standard Book Number: 978-1-84872-936-0 (Hardback)

Library of Congress Cataloging-in-Publication Data

Explaining individual differences in reading : theory and evidence / [edited by] Susan A. Brady, David Braze, Carol A. Fowler.
p. cm. -- (New directions in communication disorders research)
Summary: "Research into reading development and reading disabilities has been dominated by phonologically guided theories for several decades. In this volume, the authors of 11 chapters report on a wide array of current research topics, examining the scope, limits and implications of a phonological theory.The chapters are organized in four sections. The first concerns the nature of the relations between script and speech that make reading possible, considering how different theories of phonology may illuminate the implication of these relations for reading development and skill. The second set of chapters focuses on phonological factors in reading acquisition that pertain to early language development, effects of dialect, the role of instruction, and orthographic learning. The third section identifies factors beyond the phonological that may influence success in learning to read by examining cognitive limitations that are sometimes co-morbid with reading disabilities, contrasting the profiles of specific language impairment and dyslexia, and considering the impact of particular languages and orthographies on language acquisition. Finally, in the fourth section, behavioral-genetic and neurological methods are used to further develop explanations of reading differences and early literacy development.The volume is an essential resource for researchers interested in the cognitive foundations of reading and literacy, language and communication disorders, or psycholinguistics; and those working in reading disabilities, learning disabilities, special education, and the teaching of reading"-- Provided by publisher.
Includes bibliographical references and index.
ISBN 978-1-84872-936-0 (hardback)
1. Reading disability. 2. Reading--Physiological aspects. 3. Phonology. I. Brady, Susan A. II. Braze, David. III. Fowler, Carol A.

LB1050.5.E97 2011+
418'.4019--dc22 2010048562

Visit the Taylor & Francis Web site at
http://www.taylorandfrancis.com

and the Psychology Press Web site at
http://www.psypress.com

To Don Shankweiler
Scholar, Scientist, Mentor, Friend

Photograph by Harold Shapiro

Contents

Part III Sources of Individual Differences Beyond Phonological Deficits

Part IV Unraveling the Biology of Reading and Reading Differences

Foreword

I was very pleased to be asked to write the foreword to this book in honor of my longtime friend and colleague, Don Shankweiler. The pioneering theoretical and empirical contributions to reading research by Don and his colleagues at Haskins Laboratories, and the many interactions I have had with Don over the years, have been enormously helpful to me in my own work and for that I am personally very grateful.

Explaining Individual Differences in Reading: Theory and Evidence is a collection of chapters by leading scientists in the field of reading research. The volume provides an excellent overview of theory and research on sources of individual differences in reading acquisition, describes recent research on the questions of how children learn to read and why some don't, and draws attention to several unresolved questions regarding the causes of reading problems in children. The chapters were written as a tribute to Don, who, along with his colleagues at Haskins Laboratories, was responsible for the groundbreaking research supporting the crucial role of phonological processing skills in learning to read, especially phonemic awareness. The broad range of topics covered in the volume reflects the great diversity of Don's contributions to reading theory and research.

An expression that I have heard Don use many times is that "phonemic awareness does not come free with language acquisition," an expression that, in my view, captures one of the most important insights into the reading acquisition process of the past half century. In a seminal study, Don and his colleagues (I. Y. Liberman, Shankweiler, Fischer, & Carter, 1974) reported data indicating that preliterate children and many beginning readers find it extraordinarily difficult to detect phonemic sequences in spoken words, even though they are clearly capable of discriminating between speech sounds and using phonemic contrasts to signal meaning differences. The reason, Don and his colleagues argued, is that using a phonemic contrast to signal a meaning difference (e.g., *pig* versus *big*), which is done intuitively and at a subconscious level, is not the same as the metalinguistic act of consciously reflecting on and manipulating the phonemic elements of speech. Gaining conscious access to phonemic segments is much more difficult for children because there is no simple physical basis for recognizing phonemes in speech, as researchers at Haskins Laboratories had earlier demonstrated (A. M. Liberman, Cooper, Shankweiler, & Studdert-Kennedy, 1967).

These research findings also provided an explanation for why many children who have begun formal reading instruction fail to benefit from either letter–name or letter–sound knowledge in learning to recognize words. As Isabelle Liberman and Don often pointed out (e.g., I. Y. Liberman & Shankweiler, 1985), the strategy of simply "sounding out" a word like *drag* will result in "duh-ruh-ah-guh," a nonsense word comprising four syllables. Because there is no one-to-one correspondence between phonemes and segments of the acoustic signal, most letter sounds and letter names are only imprecise physical analogues of the phonemes in spoken words. Whether children learn to associate the sound "duh" or the name "dee" or both with the letter *d*, they must still be able to segment the sound or name to make the connection between *d* and the abstract phoneme */d/*, which cannot be pronounced in isolation. In support of these claims is a considerable amount of research inspired by the groundbreaking discoveries of the Haskins group indicating that training in phonemic awareness during or before reading instruction produces significant experimental group advantages in reading achievement, especially when combined with letter–sound training.

Another expression that I have often heard Don use is "weak representation and access," which conveys the essence of the phonological deficit hypothesis, the idea that deficient phonemic awareness in poor readers is one manifestation of an underlying weakness in the phonological component of language (Shankweiler, 1999). The phonological deficit hypothesis proposes that persistent reading difficulties stem from weak phonological representations that result in deficits in one or more aspects of phonological processing, which include encoding phonological information (phonetic perception), gaining access to and performing mental operations on phonological information (phonological awareness), retrieving phonological information from semantic memory (lexical retrieval), retaining phonological information in working memory (short-term verbal recall), and translating letters and letter patterns into phonological forms (phonological recoding).

During the past four decades many explanations of reading disorders have been put forward, including theories that have attributed literacy learning problems to deficits in visual processing, auditory discrimination, cross-modal transfer, eye movements, serial memory, attention, association learning, or rule learning. Most of these theories were eventually rejected due to a lack of supportive evidence and/or the failure to satisfy the assumption of specificity, the notion that the child diagnosed with dyslexia has a deficit that is reasonably specific to the literacy learning task (Stanovich, 1991).

In contrast, the phonological deficit hypothesis has clearly stood the test of time, so much so that a colleague and I recently put forward a definition of dyslexia that explicitly states that the condition is due to an impairment in the phonological processing skills required to learn to read and write (Tunmer & Greaney, 2010). We argued that dyslexia should be viewed as a hypothetical construct embedded within a broader theory of reading and reading difficulties, a theory that may eventually be rejected by scientific evidence that favors an alternative theory. But, in the interests of scientific parsimony, we suggested that our proposed conceptualization of dyslexia should focus on the causal explanation of the condition for which there is the greatest amount of supportive evidence. In support of our view, a considerable amount of research indicates that with very rare exceptions, students diagnosed with dyslexia have a history of deficits in phonological processing skills, especially phonological awareness and phonological recoding (Snowling, 2000; Vellutino, Fletcher, Snowling, & Scanlon, 2004).

Although the arguments and evidence in support of the account of reading problems proposed by Don and his colleagues appears to be strong, their theory has not gone unchallenged. The theory predicts that not only does phonemic awareness not come free with language acquisition, but that it also does not come free with exposure to print (Shankweiler, 1999). Support for this claim comes from Byrne (1992), who found that even when examples of print were arranged to make induction of simple letter–sound relations as transparent as possible, pre-readers with no knowledge of reading or the sounds or individual letters failed to infer the alphabetic principle, confirming earlier research that pre-readers are largely ignorant of phonological segments in spoken words. But some researchers have recently suggested that implicit induction of letter–sound mappings can be part of children's earliest contributions to reading development before they have acquired an explicit awareness of the alphabetic principle. Fletcher-Flinn and Thompson (2004), two New Zealand researchers, claimed that the nonconscious induction of sublexical relations occurs almost from the outset of learning to read, arguing that this is what must have occurred for successful readers in New Zealand, where until recently, beginning reading instruction did not include the teaching of explicit phonics or any other systematic instruction in letter–sound relations. However, this view assumes that children who learn to read in a whole language setting and who acquire letter–sound relations through implicit learning do not have explicit knowledge of the alphabetic principle when this may not be the case (I. Y. Liberman & Liberman, 1992).

Supporting the Libermans' position is research carried out in New Zealand by James Chapman and myself (Tunmer & Chapman, 2002) examining the relation of beginning readers' reported strategies for identifying unknown words in text to future reading achievement. Five-year-old beginning readers participating in a 3-year longitudinal study were divided into two groups according to their responses to the following question: "When you are reading on your own and come across a word that you don't know, what do you do to try to figure out what the word is?" The majority of children reported using word-based strategies (e.g., "sound it out," "think of the sounds," "hear all the letters," "do the sounds of it") rather than text-based strategies (e.g., "think, guess what the word is," "read it over again," "have a look at the picture," "keep on going, then go back and see what the word is"). From these results, we concluded, as did Isabelle and Al Liberman, that the instructional approach to teaching reading followed in the classroom (i.e., whole language) is not necessarily reflected in the word identification strategies that the vast majority of children actually use in learning to read. Consistent with this suggestion, the results further showed that children whose responses indicated a conceptual awareness of the alphabetic principle became the better readers. The beginning readers who reported using word-based strategies outperformed the children who reported using text-based strategies on all reading and reading-related measures taken in the middle of year 3. Moreover, these children were six times less likely to require reading recovery in year 2 than the children who relied on text-based strategies in year 1 (6% versus 37%)!

An important feature of the explanatory model of reading acquisition and reading disabilities developed by Don and his colleagues is its capacity to generate corollary hypotheses and new avenues of research that ultimately lead to further refinements of the theoretical framework. A set of interrelated research questions that my colleagues and I are currently investigating relates to a point that Don made in the paper he presented when accepting the prestigious award from the Society for the Scientific Study of Reading (SSSR) for Outstanding Scientific Contributions to the Study of Reading (Shankweiler, 1999). Don stated that "decoding is the use of phonological awareness and letter knowledge to make informed guesses about the identity of new words" (p. 118). While certainly agreeing with this suggestion, Don's claim raises the question of what is the specific mechanism by which phonological awareness contributes to the process of successfully making informed guesses.

Most of what children learning to read in English come to know about the orthography is acquired through implicit learning (Bryant, 2002; Gough & Hillinger, 1980; Venezky, 1999). Because of the nature of English orthography, Venezky claimed that an essential skill that children must acquire to learn to read in English is what he called *set for variability*, the ability to determine the correct pronunciation of approximations to spoken English words. He suggested that in acquiring this skill, children learn to use their developing knowledge of letter–sound relations to produce partial decodings for unknown words in text, especially those containing irregular, polyphonic, or orthographically complex spelling patterns. The phonological representations then provide the basis for generating alternative pronunciations of target words until one is produced that matches a word in the child's lexical memory and makes sense in the context in which it appears. The orthographic representations of successfully identified target words are stored in lexical memory, thus contributing to the database from which additional letter–sound patterns can be induced. An important question posed by Venezky was this: If set for variability is so important in acquiring decoding patterns (the use of which is essential for developing automaticity in word recognition), then why do some children acquire this skill so easily, whereas others only do so with great difficulty? Venezky stated that the answer to this question "remains a mystery" (p. 232).

The aims of a study that my colleagues and I recently completed were to explore possible answers to this question and to investigate Venezky's claims empirically (Tunmer & Chapman, in press). Set for variability was operationalized as the ability to determine the correct pronunciation of mispronounced spoken English words derived from regularized pronunciations of irregularly spelled words (e.g., *stomach* pronounced as "stow-match"), the incorrect pronunciation of words containing polyphonic spelling patterns (e.g., *glove* pronounced like "clove"), and approximations to correct pronunciations based on the application of context-free spelling rules (e.g., *kind* pronounced like "pinned"). Regarding the latter, research reported by Don and his colleagues (Zinna, Liberman, & Shankweiler, 1986) indicates that beginning readers initially acquire relatively simple one-to-one letter–sound correspondences that are, for the most part, insensitive to position-specific constraints or the presence of other letters.

We hypothesized that set for variability should contribute to the development of both decoding skills and word recognition ability by enabling children to identify words based on partial decodings from which additional letter–sound patterns could be induced. We further hypothesized that vocabulary knowledge and phonemic awareness would be the two key factors contributing to individual differences in set for variability among beginning readers. Vocabulary was proposed because children would be expected to have difficulty identifying approximations to spoken words if the target words are not in their listening vocabulary or if the phonological representations of the words are weakly established in lexical memory (Perfetti, 2007). Phonemic awareness was hypothesized to be required in performing a component operation of set for variability in which children vary one or more of the sounds in approximations to spoken words in an effort to find a match to a word that is in their listening vocabulary and is appropriate to the sentence context (Venezky, 1999).

Data from a 3-year longitudinal study of beginning reading development were analyzed to test these predictions. In support of our hypotheses, the results of hierarchical regression and path analyses indicated that vocabulary and phonemic awareness each made independent contributions to variance in set for variability; that phonemic awareness directly influenced decoding and indirectly influenced both decoding and word recognition through set for variability; that vocabulary directly influenced reading comprehension and indirectly influenced decoding and word recognition through set for variability; and that set for variability influenced reading comprehension indirectly through both decoding and word recognition, controlling for autoregressive effects.

Overall, the results strongly support Venezky's claim that set for variability plays an essential role in learning to read in English. In terms of the explanatory model of reading acquisition developed by Don and his colleagues, set for variability may lead to further refinements of the model by providing the basis for specifying linkages between vocabulary knowledge, phonological processing skills, and word recognition. Such linkages might help to allay a major concern expressed by Perfetti (this volume) about the model, namely, that it does not accord word meaning the same critical status in learning to read as phonology and decoding.

Before closing, I wish to congratulate Susan Brady, Dave Braze, and Carol Fowler for putting together such an outstanding volume celebrating the accomplishments of someone we all have come to greatly admire and respect, our good friend and colleague, Donald Shankweiler. As we say in the part of the world in which I live, "Good on ya, Don!"

William Tunmer
Distinguished Professor of Educational Psychology
Massey University
Palmerston North, New Zealand

REFERENCES

Bryant, P. (2002). Children's thoughts about reading and spelling. *Scientific Studies of Reading*, *6*, 199–216.

Byrne, B. (1992). Studies in the acquisition procedure for reading: Rationale, hypotheses, and data. In P. B. Gough, L. Ehri, & R. Treiman (Eds.), *Reading acquisition* (pp. 1–34). Hillsdale, NJ: Lawrence Erlbaum Associates.

Fletcher-Flinn, C. M., & Thompson, G. B. (2004). A mechanism of implicit lexicalized phonological recoding used concurrently with underdeveloped explicit letter-sound skills in both precocious and normal reading development. *Cognition*, *90*, 303–335.

Gough, P. B., & Hillinger, M. L. (1980). Learning to read: An unnatural act. *Bulletin of the Orton Society*, *30*, 179–196.

Liberman, A. M., Cooper, F. S., Shankweiler, D. P., & Studdert-Kennedy, M. (1967). Perception of the speech code. *Psychological Review*, *74*, 431–461.

Liberman, I. Y., & Liberman, A. M. (1992). Whole language versus code emphasis: Underlying assumptions and their implications for reading acquisition. In P. Gough, L. Ehri, & R. Treiman (Eds.), *Reading acquisition* (pp. 343–366). Hillsdale, NJ: Lawrence Erlbaum Associates.

Liberman, I. Y., & Shankweiler, D. P. (1985). Phonology and the problems of learning to read and write. *Remedial and Special Education*, *6*, 8–17.

Liberman, I. Y., Shankweiler, D. P., Fischer, F. W., & Carter, B. (1974). Explicit syllable and phoneme segmentation in the young child. *Journal of Experimental Child Psychology*, *18*, 201–212.

Perfetti, C. A. (2007). Reading ability: Lexical quality to comprehension. *Scientific Studies of Reading*, *11*, 357–383.

Shankweiler, D. (1999). Words to meanings. *Scientific Studies of Reading*, *3*, 113–127.

Snowling, M. (2000). *Dyslexia*. Oxford: Blackwell.

Stanovich, K. E. (1991). Discrepancy definitions of reading disability: Has intelligence led us astray? *Reading Research Quarterly*, *26*, 7–29.

Tunmer, W. E., & Chapman, J. W. (2002). The relation of beginning readers' reported word identification strategies to reading achievement, reading-related skills, and academic self-perceptions. *Reading and Writing*, *15*, 341–358.

Tunmer, W. E., & Chapman, J. W. (in press). Does set for variability mediate the influence of vocabulary knowledge on the development of word recognition skills? *Scientific Studies of Reading*.

Tunmer, W. E., & Greaney, K. T. (2010). Defining dyslexia. *Journal of Learning Disabilities, 43*, 229–243.

Vellutino, F. R., Fletcher, J. M., Snowling, M. J., & Scanlon, D. M. (2004). Specific reading disability (dyslexia): What have we learned in the past four decades? *Journal of Child Psychology and Psychiatry*, *45*, 2–40.

Venezky, R. L. (1999). *The American way of spelling: The structure and origins of American English orthography*. New York: Guilford Press.

Zinna, D. R., Liberman, I. Y., & Shankweiler, D. (1986). Children's sensitivity to factors influencing vowel reading. *Reading Research Quarterly*, *21*, 465–480.

Preface

Don Shankweiler has made major contributions to research and theory on reading for four decades. Together with Isabelle Liberman and other colleagues at Haskins Laboratories, Don was a pivotal figure in the development of the phonological deficit hypothesis (PDH), marshalling evidence that both disconfirmed earlier theories about the bases of reading difficulties (e.g., the idea that reversal errors and deficits in visual function are causative) and supported the critical role of phonological factors in individual differences in reading. With groundbreaking research on the development of phonological awareness and its association with reading problems, Don worked toward identifying the major phenotype of reading weaknesses. The chief barrier to reading acquisition was found to stem from difficulties dealing with words and their components as phonological entities, both in terms of awareness deficits and in basic reading skills encompassed by decoding, spelling, and word recognition. Focusing on the then-emerging evidence that speech coding is widely used in short-term memory, Don investigated whether phonological weaknesses in reading skills and phonological awareness for poor readers were associated with verbal memory deficits. Finding positive associations, in *The Speech Code and Learning to Read* (Shankweiler, Liberman, Mark, Fowler, & Fischer, 1979) Don and his coauthors hypothesized that "the primary problem (for poor readers) is the availability of a phonetic representation (p. 542)" and proposed that reading difficulties may be "the result of some deficiency in the use of a speech code (p. 542)." Testing the limits of the PDH, Don extended his research to examine whether individuals with reading difficulties have deficits in other underlying phonological processes such as speech perception and lexical retrieval, and further probed the scope of phonological memory difficulties, including the consequences for sentence processing and comprehension.

As evidence accrued that phonological abilities are normally distributed in the population and that dyslexia, rather than entailing a qualitatively different way of reading, represents the tail end of the distribution, the PDH was gradually supplanted by a broader phonological theory of reading. Don has advocated the principle that an adequate theory would explain why learning to read in an alphabetic system is somewhat difficult for the average child in addition to being extremely difficult for some: (a) it would reflect elements of the writing system that are implicated by learners' reading performance (e.g., by their errors in reading and spelling), identifying those features of script that are central to the requirements of linguistic and cognitive processing; (b) it would account for variation in the difficulty of learning to read different types of orthographies; and (c) it would have practical implications for the teaching of reading. In addition, to achieve an understanding of the neurobiology of reading, the behavioral aspects of reading development, reading difficulties, and advanced reading skills would be evaluated for genetic and environmental contributions and corresponding features of brain organization. In his long and illustrious career, Don has engaged in research on all of these, as well as on topics pertaining to other aspects of the psychology of language.

Today, in no small part because of Don's contributions to reading research, it is generally understood that beginning readers must attain awareness of the phonological composition of words and that readers in an act of reading must extract and engage phonological structures. The authors of chapters for this volume, who also took part in a symposium honoring Don that was sponsored by the Society for the Scientific Study of Reading in 2008, all respect and value the extent of Don's contributions to the reading field. As Nicole Terry and Hollis Scarborough remark at the beginning of their chapter, "A hallmark of strong theories is their capacity to inspire corollary hypotheses that impel research along new paths." The phonological theory has certainly done that. The authors of the following chapters take on new research questions, as they continue to examine sources of individual differences in reading skills (both phonological and otherwise), discuss current findings, and consider their implications for theory and practice. The manner and extent that phonology is implicated in individual differences in reading skills is a common thread running through these chapters.

The chapters are organized in four parts. Part I concerns the nature of the relations between script and speech that make reading possible. Carol Fowler (Chapter 1) notes that central to the phonological theory of reading is an understanding that reading is "parasitic" (Liberman, 1968; Mattingly, 1972) on the spoken language. Readers at all levels of proficiency access the spoken forms of words when they read (e.g., Frost, 1998). Accordingly, it is important for understanding reading to understand the language forms that readers access. Theories of phonology address the nature of spoken language forms. Fowler suggests that different phonological theories vary in their characterization of language forms, but each may offer distinct and valuable insights into challenges confronting the reading learner. She discusses the hypothesized phonological language forms and the possible relevance to learning to read and to reading disability suggested by three theoretical perspectives: descriptive linguistics, generative phonology, and articulatory phonology.

Part II focuses on research questions related to phonological factors in reading acquisition. First, David Braze, Gerald McRoberts, and Colleen McDonough (Chapter 2) argue that a complete understanding of reading-relevant phonological skills requires an account of their developmental trajectories from the earliest stages. Braze et al. review existing work relating to the developmental progression in toddlers and preschoolers of phonological awareness and underlying phonological capacities (e.g., phonological memory, phonological/articulatory fluency, and efficiency of lexical access). They then summarize their recent research with very young children in which they have modified auditory preference procedures to assess individual differences in sensitivity to phonological structures and have designed memory paradigms to study emerging phonological abilities. These studies provide evidence for developmental trends in both phonological domains, indicating the promise of their assessment methods for further exploring development of these key language abilities and studying the potential predictive value of early individual differences for later reading acquisition.

In his chapter (Chapter 3), David Share addresses the compelling issue of how orthographic learning comes about, focusing on his hypothesis of a self-teaching mechanism that stems from successful decoding of written words. Share documents that this self-teaching function has an early onset when children have minimal knowledge of how the code works and that the self-teaching is item specific, building orthographic representations of individual words that in turn lay the foundation for skilled readers' word recognition expertise. Further, he proposes that the skills for this process increase over time as phonological recoding skills further develop. Pertinent studies, conducted with a variety of reading conditions, indicate that orthographic learning is closely tied to levels of decoding success. Instruction on orthographic detail and spelling appears to augment orthographic learning, whereas learning in the context of text can reduce attention to letter detail and word-specific spelling–sound relations.

Susan Brady (Chapter 4) likewise targets instructional issues, reviewing research conducted since publication of the report of the National Reading Panel (NRP) on the value of phonics instruction for reading acquisition (National Institutes of Health, 2000). The NRP report determined that children are more successful at learning to read when systematic, explicit instruction on the code is provided. Both grapheme-level instruction and methods using larger onset-rime patterns were found to be effective, with no significant advantage for one over the other. Brady notes the aftermath to the report: Educational leaders have heavily endorsed the use of larger phonological units for teaching phonics and have recommended providing multifaceted literacy instruction involving authentic text and a focus on comprehension. She concludes that subsequent research instead underscores the value of more explicit phonics methods targeting grapheme–phoneme correspondences, but also supports the benefits of explicit phonics instruction in the context of a comprehensive literacy program.

The final chapter in this part (Chapter 5), by Nicole Terry and Hollis Scarborough, examines two phonological factors, phonological awareness and phonological precision, which might contribute to explanations of the observed relationship between children's use of nonmainstream speech patterns and reading achievement. They pose two alternative hypotheses regarding the basis for this association: (a) the linguistic interference or mismatch hypothesis (i.e., that children who speak a nonmainstream dialect experience more frequent interference between written and spoken language than do children whose oral dialect aligns more closely with the printed forms) and (b) the linguistic awareness/flexibility hypothesis (i.e., that reading weaknesses of children who speak nonmainstream American English stem from a general insensitivity to language variation with regard to both structure and usage). The authors report on the findings of a study designed to investigate how much nonmainstream and mainstream speakers know about both dialect and mainstream phonological features of words. They found that phonological awareness abilities fully mediated the role of dialect differences in the prediction of reading achievement, supporting the linguistic awareness/flexibility hypothesis.

The three chapters in Part III identify factors beyond the phonological that may influence success in learning to read. In the first (Chapter 6), Maggie Snowling looks critically at the notion that reading disorder (RD) stems solely from a specifically phonological deficit. In doing so, she points to the occurrence of co-morbidity of dyslexia with other developmental conditions, drawing upon data from two research samples. In one, children were selected for co-morbidities of RD and these other cognitive limitations. For the second sample, children were chosen based on family risk of dyslexia. Examining the roles of a spectrum of cognitive processes in the development of reading skills, Snowling concludes that while phonological abilities do play a causal role in the acquisition of reading, non-phonological components of language may serve to modulate the impact of phonological weaknesses on reading difficulties. Moreover, she infers that specific reading disability occurs on a gradient rather than as a categorical syndrome, with no clear boundary between afflicted and typical readers.

Hugh Catts and Suzanne Adlof (Chapter 7) also review evidence of partial dissociations among phonological deficits, oral language weaknesses, and reading ability. Studying a sample biased toward the incidence of language impairment (LI), they identify subgroups of relatively pure dyslexia, pure LI, and co-morbid dyslexia+LI. Reviewing the contrasting profiles of these subgroups, they aver distinct etiologies for LI and dyslexia, noting that children with similar LI profiles may vary greatly in their phonological skills. While affirming the causal role of phonological deficits in reading disability, Catts and Adlof point to other factors that may moderate the relationship between phonological skills and reading difficulties. They frame their discussion of reading disability within the risk-resilience approach to psychopathology (Rolf, Masten, Cicchetti, Nuechterlein, & Weintraub, 1990). Among potential protective factors, they include motivation and quality of instruction or intervention.

Chuck Perfetti's chapter (Chapter 8) begins by reviewing reasons for the dominance of phonologically grounded explanation in models of disordered reading development and in those of skilled adult reading. He asserts that the weight of evidence implicates phonological processes strongly because the phonological level of language maps to the printed word, whether the orthography is alphabetic or character based, as in Chinese. Perfetti proposes that although phonological deficits may lead to reading disability among Chinese learners, these may be less debilitating than for learners of alphabetic orthographies. Probing further, he notes that morphemic elements are also functionally useful units for word identification, and that writing systems vary in terms of how explicitly they represent morphological structure. Perfetti concludes that knowledge of morphological units and word meanings are additional factors contributing to reading skill, their importance depending on the reader's cognitive profile and the demands of the particular language and orthography.

Chapters in Part IV are concerned with evaluating the role of phonological factors in explaining reading differences and early literacy development through the twin lenses of behavior genetics and neurobiological approaches that relate reading behavior to the brain.

The chapters by Brian Byrne (Chapter 9) and Dick Olson (Chapter 10) note that the PDH has motivated much of the research on genetic and environmental etiology of reading differences and evaluations of methods of remediation. Byrne reminds us that the awareness of segmental phonology needed to grasp the alphabetic principle does not come free with exposure to the spoken language or from exposure to print without also a "helping hand" from instruction. Instruction, if it is to be effective, has to be tailored to surmount another obstacle: the child's natural focus on word meaning rather than sound. Studies of reading development from the perspective of behavior genetics have shown that individual differences in reading and spelling are subject to substantial genetic variation. Some of this variation is related to phonological awareness, but genes that affect phonological awareness independent of other precursors of reading (such as letter knowledge) have a limited role. Further, some of the genes that influence reading outcomes seem to be having their influence by affecting the rate of learning. It is not yet known how specific or general their effects may be. Olson also stresses that the PDH needs modification to take account of the repeated finding of third variable influences on the correlations between phonological awareness, word decoding, and reading comprehension, and of the evidence that the genetic influences on word recognition and reading comprehension are partially independent. While the importance of phonological factors is sustained, these caveats remind us that reading comprehension draws on both print-specific and general language and cognitive abilities, the general abilities being shared between reading processes and those relating to comprehension of spoken language. From this perspective, it makes sense that the discovery of genes that influence phonological factors takes us partway but not all the way to an understanding of reading differences.

Joshua Diehl and his colleagues (Stephen Frost, Einar Mencl, and Kenneth Pugh) (Chapter 11) examine the guiding role that a phonological theory of reading has played in the development of brain-mapping studies in normal and disabled readers. Originally, the discovery of brain sites implicated in abnormal reading development was derived from postmortem study of the brains of dyslexic individuals. Physiological methods based on EEG and functional imaging techniques opened a new era by enabling researchers to obtain information regarding neural circuitry in normal readers, as well as in cases of reading disability. As Diehl et al. show, these developments provided new opportunities to assess the role of phonological processing in reading skill and its development across languages and orthographies, and new ways to sensitively assess the effects of intervention. Cross-language comparisons show substantial commonality in reading circuits among learners from different language communities (e.g., difficulties in learning to read are everywhere associated with abnormal reliance on portions of the right hemisphere). Some differences across languages and writing systems are also found that reflect the level at which the orthography maps the phonology and other aspects of language structure.

In closing, we know that Don is delighted with this book and the achievements it documents, and that he is touched and honored by this acknowledgment of his contributions. We are pleased to offer this tribute to him.

Susan Brady
David Braze
Carol Fowler

REFERENCES

Frost, R. (1998). Toward a strong phonological theory of visual word recognition: True issues and false trails. *Psychological Bulletin*, *123*, 71–99.

Liberman, A. M. (1970). The grammars of speech and language. *Cognitive Psychology*, *1*, 301–323.

Mattingly, I. G. (1972). Reading, the linguistic process, and linguistic awareness. In J. F. Kavanagh & I. G. Mattingly (Eds.), *Language by ear and by eye: The relationships between speech and reading*. (pp. 133–147). Cambridge, MA: MIT Press.

Rolf, J., Masten, A., Cicchetti, D., Nuechterlein, K., Weintraub, S. (1990). *Risk and protective factors in development of psychopathology*. Cambridge: Cambridge University Press.

Shankweiler, D., Liberman, I. Y., Mark, L. S., Fowler, C. A., & Fischer, F. W. (1979). The speech code and learning to read. *Journal of Experimental Psychology: Learning, Memory, and Cognition*, *5*, 531–545.

The Publications of Donald P. Shankweiler

(IN CHRONOLOGICAL ORDER)

Shankweiler, D. P. (1959). Effects of success and failure instructions on reaction time in patients with brain-damage. *Journal of Comparative and Physiological Psychology, 52*, 546–559.

Shankweiler, D. P. (1961). Performance of brain-damaged patients on two tests of sound localization. *Journal of Comparative and Physiological Psychology, 54*, 375–381.

Shankweiler, D. P. (1964a). Some critical issues in the study of developmental dyslexia. In A. W. Franklin (Ed.), *Word blindness or specific developmental dyslexia* (pp. 51–56). London: Pitman.

Shankweiler, D. P. (1964b). A study of developmental dyslexia. *Neuropsychologia, 1*, 267–286.

Shankweiler, D. P. (1964c). Developmental dyslexia: Critique and review of recent evidence. *Cortex, 1*, 53–62.

Shankweiler, D. P. (1966). Effects of temporal-lobe damage on perception of dichotically presented melodies. *Journal of Comparative and Physiological Psychology, 62*, 115–119.

Shankweiler, D. P., & Harris, K. S. (1966). An experimental approach to the problem of articulation in aphasia. *Cortex, 2*, 277–292.

Liberman, A. M., Cooper, F. S., Shankweiler, D. P., & Studdert-Kennedy, M. (1967). Perception of the speech code. *Psychological Review, 74*, 431–461.

Shankweiler, D. P., & Studdert-Kennedy, M. (1967). Identification of consonants and vowels presented to left and right ears. *Quarterly Journal of Experimental Psychology, 19*, 59–63.

Shankweiler, D. P., Harris, K. S., & Taylor, M. L. (1968). Electromyographic studies of articulation in aphasia. *Archives of Physical Medicine and Rehabilitation, 49*, 1–8.

Shankweiler, D. (1970). Recovery of speech after stroke: Comments on a paper by F. L. Darley. In A. L. Benton (Ed.), *Recovery from stroke*. New York: Harper & Row.

Studdert-Kennedy, M., & Shankweiler, D. (1970). Hemispheric specialization for speech perception. *Journal of the Acoustical Society of America, 48*, 579–594.

Studdert-Kennedy, M., Shankweiler, D., & Schulman, S. (1970). Opposed effects of a delayed channel on perception of dichotically and monotonically presented CVC syllables. *Journal of the Acoustical Society of America, 48*, 599–602.

Liberman, I., Shankweiler, D., Orlando, C., Harris, K., & Berti, F. (1971). Letter confusions and reversals of sequence in the beginning reader: Implications for Orton's theory of developmental dyslexia. *Cortex, 7*, 127–142.

Shankweiler, D. P. (1971). Laterality effects in speech perception. In D. L. Horton, & J. J. Jenkins (Eds.), *Perception of language* (pp. 185–200). Columbus, OH: Chas. E. Merrill.

Shankweiler, D., & Liberman, I. Y. (1972). Misreading: A search for causes. In J. Kavanagh, & I. G. Mattingly (Eds.), *Language by eye and by ear: The relationships between speech and reading* (pp. 293–317). Cambridge, MA: MIT Press.

Studdert-Kennedy, M., Shankweiler, D., & Pisoni, D. (1972). Auditory and phonetic processes in speech perception: Evidence from a dichotic study. *Journal of Cognitive Psychology*, *2*, 455–466.

Liberman, I. Y., Shankweiler, D., Fischer, F. W., & Carter, B. (1974). Explicit phoneme and syllable segmentation in the young child. *Journal of Experimental Child Psychology*, *18*, 201–212.

Shankweiler, D., & Studdert-Kennedy, M. (1975). A continuum of lateralization for speech perception? *Brain and Language*, *2*, 212–225.

Shankweiler, D., & Liberman, I. Y. (1976). Exploring the relations between reading and speech. In R. M. Knights, & D. J. Bakker (Eds.), *Neuropsychology of learning disorders*: *Theoretical approaches* (pp. 297–313). Baltimore, MD: University Park Press.

Fowler, C. A., Liberman, I. Y., & Shankweiler, D. (1977). On interpreting the error pattern in beginning reading. *Language and Speech*, *20*, 162–175.

Liberman, I. Y., Shankweiler, D., Liberman, A. M., Fischer, F. W., & Fowler, C. (1977). Phonetic segmentation and recoding in the beginning reader. In A. S. Reber, & D. L. Scarborough (Eds.), *Toward a psychology of reading*: *The proceedings of the CUNY conferences* (pp. 207–225). New York: Erlbaum.

Mark, L. S., Shankweiler, D., Liberman, I. Y., & Fowler, C. A. (1977). Phonetic recoding and reading difficulty in beginning readers. *Memory & Cognition*, *5*, 623–629.

Shankweiler, D., Strange, W., & Verbrugge, R. (1977). Speech and the problem of perceptual constancy. In R. Shaw, & J. Bransford (Eds.), *Perceiving, acting, and knowing*: *Toward an ecological psychology* (pp. 315–345). New York: Erlbaum.

Strange, W., Verbrugge, R. R., Shankweiler, D. P., & Edman, T. R. (1977). Consonantal environment specifies vowel identity. *Journal of the Acoustical Society of America*, *60*, 213–224.

Verbrugge, R. R., Strange, W., Shankweiler, D. P., & Edman, T. R. (1977). What information enables a listener to map a talker's vowel space? *Journal of the Acoustical Society of America*, *60*, 198–212.

Fischer, F. W., Liberman, I. Y., & Shankweiler, D. (1978). Reading reversals and developmental dyslexia: A further study. *Cortex*, *14*, 496–510.

Liberman, I. Y., Mark, L. S., & Shankweiler, D. (1978). Reading disability: Methodological problems in information-processing analysis. *Science*, *200*, 801–802.

Shankweiler, D., & Liberman, I. Y. (1978). Reading behavior in dyslexia: Is there a distinctive pattern? *Bulletin of the Orton Society*, *28*, 114–123.

Fowler, C. A., Shankweiler, D., & Liberman, I. Y. (1979). Apprehending spelling patterns for vowels: A developmental study. *Language and Speech*, *22*, 243–252.

Liberman, I. Y., & Shankweiler, D. (1979). Speech, the alphabet and teaching to read. In L. B. Resnik, & P. A. Weaver (Eds.), *Theory and practice of early reading* (Vol. 2, pp. 109–134). Hillsdale, NJ: Erlbaum.

Shankweiler, D., Liberman, I. Y., Mark, L. S., Fowler, C. A., & Fischer, F. W. (1979). The speech code and learning to read. *Journal of Experimental Psychology*: *Learning, Memory, and Cognition*, *5*, 531–545.

Liberman, I. Y., Liberman, A. M., Mattingly, I. G., & Shankweiler, D. (1980). Orthography and the beginning reader. In J. F. Kavanagh, & R. Venezky (Eds.), *Orthography, reading, and dyslexia* (pp. 137–153). Baltimore, MD: University Park Press.

Liberman, I. Y., Shankweiler, D., Camp, L., Blachman, B., & Werfelman, M. (1980). Steps toward literacy: A linguistic approach. In P. Levinson & C. Sloan (Eds.), *Auditory processing and language*: *Clinical and research perspectives*. New York: Grune & Stratton.

Mann, V., Liberman, I. Y., & Shankweiler, D. (1980). Children's memory for sentences and word strings. *Memory & Cognition*, *8*, 329–335.

Katz, R., Shankweiler, D., & Liberman, I. Y. (1981). Memory for item order and phonetic coding in the beginning reader. *Journal of Experimental Child Psychology*, *32*, 474–484.

Studdert-Kennedy, M., & Shankweiler, D. (1981). Hemispheric specialization for language processes. *Science*, *211*, 960–961.

Liberman, I. Y., Mann, V. A., Shankweiler, D., & Werfelman, M. (1982). Children's memory for recurring linguistic and nonlinguistic material in relation to reading ability. *Cortex*, *18*, 367–375.

Shankweiler, D., Liberman, I. Y., & Mark, L. S. (1982). Phonetic coding in dyslexics and normal readers, by Hall, Ewing, Tinzmann and Wilson: A reply. *Bulletin of the Psychonomic Society*, *19*, 78–79.

Brady, S., Shankweiler, D., & Mann, V. (1983). Speech perception and memory coding in relation to reading ability. *Journal of Experimental Child Psychology*, *35*, 345–367.

Hanson, V. L., Shankweiler, D., & Fischer, F. W. (1983). Determinants of spelling ability in deaf and hearing adults: Access to linguistic structure. *Cognition*, *14*, 323–344.

Katz, R. B., Healy, A. F., & Shankweiler, D. (1983). Phonetic coding and order memory in relation to reading proficiency: A comparison of short-term memory for temporal and spatial order information. *Applied Psycholinguistics*, *4*, 229–250.

Hanson, V. L., Liberman, I. Y., & Shankweiler, D. (1984). Linguistic coding by deaf children in relation to beginning reading success. *Journal of Experimental Child Psychology*, *37*, 378–393.

Katz, R. B., Healy, A. F., & Shankweiler, D. (1984). On accounting for deficiencies on order memory associated with reading difficulty: A reply to Tallal. *Applied Psycholinguistics*, *5*, 170–174.

Mann, V. A., Shankweiler, D., & Smith, S. (1984). The association between comprehension of spoken sentences and early reading ability: The role of phonetic representation. *Journal of Child Language*, *11*, 627–643.

Rakerd, B., Verbrugge, R. R., & Shankweiler, D. (1984). Monitoring for vowels in isolation and in a consonantal context. *Journal of the Acoustical Society of America*, *76*, 27–31.

Shankweiler, D., Smith S. T., & Mann, V. A. (1984). Repetition and comprehension of spoken sentences by reading disabled children. *Brain and Language*, *23*, 241–257.

Fischer, F. W., Shankweiler, D., & Liberman, I. Y. (1985). Spelling proficiency and sensitivity to word structure. *Journal of Memory and Language*, *24*, 423–441.

Liberman, I. Y., & Shankweiler, D. (1985). Phonology and the problems of learning to read and write. *Remedial and Special Education*, *6*, 8–17.

Katz, R. B., & Shankweiler, D. (1985). Repetitive naming and the detection of word-retrieval deficits in the beginning reader. *Cortex*, *21*, 617–625.

Shankweiler, D., & Crain, S. (1986). Language mechanisms and reading disorder: A modular approach. *Cognition*, *24*, 139–168.

Smith, S., Mann, V. A., & Shankweiler, D. (1986). Sentence comprehension by good and poor readers: A study with the token test. *Cortex*, *22*, 627–632.

Zinna, D., Liberman, I. Y., & Shankweiler, D. (1986). The development of children's sensitivity to factors influencing vowel reading. *Reading Research Quarterly*, *21*, 465–480.

Cossu, G., Shankweiler, D., Liberman, I. Y., Tola, G., & Katz, L. (1988). Reading and awareness of phonological segments in Italian children. *Applied Psycholinguistics*, *9*, 1–16.

Crain, S., & Shankweiler, D. (1988). Syntactic complexity and reading acquisition. In A. Davison, & G. M. Green (Eds.), *Linguistic complexity and text comprehension: Readability issues reconsidered*. Hillsdale, NJ: Erlbaum.

Lukatela, K., Crain, S., & Shankweiler, D. (1988). Sensitivity to inflectional morphology in agrammatism. *Brain and Language*, *33*, 1–15.

Liberman, I. Y., & Shankweiler, D. (1989). Phonology and the beginning reader: A tutorial. In L. Rieben & C. A. Perfetti (Eds.), *L'Apprenti Lecteur—Apports experimentaux et implications pedagogiques* (pp. 3–17). Neuchatel: Delachaux et Niestle. Trans. 1991. *Learning to read: Basic research and its implications*. Hillsdale, NJ: Erlbaum.

Liberman, I. Y., Shankweiler, D., & Liberman, A. M. (1989). The alphabetic principle and learning to read. In D. Shankweiler, & I. Y. Liberman (Eds.), *Phonology and reading disability: Solving the reading puzzle*, IARLD Monograph Series. Ann Arbor, MI: University of Michigan Press.

Macaruso, P., Bar-Shalom, E., Crain, S., & Shankweiler, D. (1989). Comprehension of temporal terms by good and poor readers. *Language and Speech*, *32*, 45–67.

Shankweiler, D. (1989). How problems of comprehension are related to difficulties in decoding. In D. Shankweiler, & I. Y. Liberman (Eds.), *Phonology and reading disability: Solving the reading puzzle*, IARLD Monograph Series. Ann Arbor, MI: University of Michigan Press.

Shankweiler, D., Crain, S., Gorrell, P., & Tuller, B. (1989). Reception of language in Broca's aphasia. *Language and Cognitive Processes*, *4*, 1–33.

Shankweiler, D., & Liberman, I. Y. (Eds.). (1989). *Phonology and reading disability: Solving the reading puzzle*, IARLD Monograph Series. Ann Arbor, MI: University of Michigan Press.

Smith, S. T., Macaruso, P., Shankweiler, D., & Crain, S. (1989). Syntactic comprehension in young poor readers. *Applied Psycholinguistics*, *10*, 429–454.

Crain, S., & Shankweiler, D. (1990). Modularity and learning to read. In I. G. Mattingly (Ed.), *Modularity and the motor theory of speech perception*. Hillsdale, NJ: Erlbaum.

Crain, S., & Shankweiler, D. (1990). Explaining failures in spoken language comprehension by children with reading disability. In D. Balota, G. B. Flores d'Arcais, & K. Rayner (Eds.), *Comprehension processes in reading*. Hillsdale, NJ: Erlbaum.

Crain, S., Shankweiler, D., Macaruso, P., & Bar-Shalom, E. (1990). Working memory and comprehension of spoken sentences: Investigations of children with reading disorder. In G. Vallar, & T. Shallice (Eds.), *Neuropsychological impairments of short-term memory* (pp. 477–508). Cambridge, England: Cambridge University Press.

Brady, S. A., & Shankweiler, D. (Eds.). (1991). *Phonological processes in literacy: A tribute to Isabelle Y. Liberman*. Hillsdale, NJ: Erlbaum.

Shankweiler, D. (1991a). Starting on the right foot. A review of *Beginning to Read: Thinking and Learning About Print* by M. J. Adams. *Educational Researcher*, *20*(4), 33–35.

Shankweiler, D. (1991b). The contribution of Isabelle Y. Liberman. In S. Brady & D. Shankweiler (Eds.), *Phonological processes in literacy: A tribute to Isabelle Y. Liberman*. Hillsdale, NJ: Erlbaum.

Shankweiler, D., Crain, S., Brady, S., & Macaruso, P. (1992). Identifying the causes of reading disability. In P. B. Gough, L. Ehri, & R. Treiman (Eds.), *Reading acquisition*. Hillsdale, NJ: Erlbaum.

Shankweiler, D., & Lundquist, E. (1992). On the relations between learning to spell and learning to read. In R. Frost, & L. Katz (Eds.), *Orthography, phonology, morphology, and meaning* (pp. 179–192). Amsterdam: Elsevier.

Bar-Shalom, E., Crain, S., & Shankweiler, D. (1993). A comparison of comprehension and production abilities of good and poor readers. *Applied Psycholinguistics*, *14*, 197–227.

Macaruso, P., Shankweiler, D., Byrne, B., & Crain, S. (1993). Poor readers are not easy to fool. Comprehension of adjectives with exceptional properties. *Applied Psycholinguistics*, *14*, 285–298.

Fletcher, J. M., Shaywitz, S. E., Shankwiler, D. P., Katz, L., Liberman, I. Y., Stuebing, K. K., et al. (1994). Cognitive profiles of reading disability: Comparisons of discrepancy and low achievement definition. *Journal of Educational Psychology*, *86*, 6–23.

Shankweiler, D. (1994). A review of *Beginning to Spell by Rebecca Treiman*. New York: Oxford University Press, 1993. *Language & Speech*, *37*(1), 77–79.

Cossu, G., Shankweiler, D., Liberman, I. Y., & Gugliotta, M. (1995). Visual and phonological determinants of misreadings in a transparent orthography. *Reading and Writing: An Interdisciplinary Journal*, *7*, 237–256.

Lukatela, K., Carello, C., Shankweiler, D., & Liberman, I. Y. (1995). Phonological awareness in illiterates: Observations from Serbo-Croatian. *Applied Psycholinguistics*, *16*, 463–487.

Lukatela, K., Shankweiler, D., & Crain, S. (1995). Syntactic processing in agrammatic aphasia by speakers of a Slavic language. *Brain & Language*, *49*, 50–76.

McRoberts, G. W., Studdert-Kennedy, M., & Shankweiler, D. P. (1995). The role of fundamental frequency in signaling linguistic stress and affect: Evidence for a dissociation. *Perception & Psychophysics*, *57*, 159–174.

Milekic, S., Boskovic, Z., Crain, S., & Shankweiler, D. (1995). Comprehension of non-lexical categories in agrammatism. *Journal of Psycholinguistic Research*, *24*(4), 299–311.

Shankweiler, D., Crain, S., Katz, L., Fowler, A. E., Liberman A. M., Brady, S. A., et al. (1995). Cognitive profiles of reading-disabled children: Comparison of language skills in phonology, morphology, and syntax. *Psychological Science*, *6*(3), 149–156.

Shaywitz, B. A., Pugh, K. R., Constable, R. T., Shaywitz, S. E., Bronen, R., Fulbright, R. K., et al. (1995). Localization of semantic processing using functional magnetic resonance imaging. *Human Brain Mapping*, *2*, 149–158.

Shaywitz, B. A., Shaywitz, S. E., Pugh, K. R., Constable, R. T., Skudlarski, P., Fulbright, R. K., et al. (1995). Sex differences in the functional organization of the brain for language. *Nature*, *373*, 607–609.

Brady, S., Scarborough, H. S., & Shankweiler, D. (1996). A perspective on two recent reports in *Science* (by Merzenich et al. and Tallal et al., January 5, 1996). *Perspectives*, International Dyslexia Association, *22*(3), 5–8. Reprinted in *Advance*, American Speech and Hearing Association, *6*, 16–17.

Crain, S., Ni, W., Shankweiler, D., Conway, L., & Braze, D. (1996). Meaning, memory and modularity. In C. Schütze (Ed.), *Proceedings of the NELS 26 sentence processing workshop*, MIT Occasional Papers in Linguistics, Vol. 9, pp. 27–44.

Fletcher, J. M., Francis, D. J., Stuebing, K. K., Shaywitz, B. A., Shaywitz, S. E., Shankweiler, D. P., et al. (1996). Conceptual and methodological issues in construct definition. In G. R. Lyon, & N. A. Krasnegor (Eds.), *Attention, memory and executive function*. Baltimore, MD: York Press.

Fodor, J. D., Ni, W., Crain, S., & Shankweiler, D. (1996). Tasks and timing in the perception of linguistic anomaly. *Journal of Psycholinguistic Research*, *25*(1), 25–57.

Ni, W., Crain, S., & Shankweiler, D. (1996). Sidestepping garden paths: Assessing the contribution of syntax, semantics and plausibility in resolving ambiguities. *Language and Cognitive Processes*, *11*, 283–334.

Pugh, K. R., Shaywitz, B. A., Shaywitz, S. E., Constable, R. T., Skudlarski, P., Fulbright, R. K., et al. (1996). Cerebral organization of component processes in reading. *Brain*, *119*, 1221–1238.

Pugh, K. R., Shaywitz, B. A., Shaywitz, S. E., Fulbright, R. K., Byrd, D., Skudlarski, P., et al. (1996). Auditory selective attention: An fMRI investigation. *NeuroImage*, *4*, 159–173.

Shankweiler, D., Lundquist, E., Dreyer, L. G., & Dickinson, C. C. (1996). Reading and spelling difficulties in high school students: Causes and consequences. *Reading and Writing*, *8*, 267–294.

Pugh, K. R., Shaywitz, B. A., Shaywitz, S. E., Shankweiler, D. P., Katz, L., Fletcher, J. M., et al. (1997). Predicting reading performance from neuroimaging profiles: The cerebral basis of phonological effects in printed word identification. *Journal of Experimental Psychology: Human Perception and Performance*, *23*(2), 299–318.

Morris, R. D., Stuebing, K. K., Fletcher, J. M., Shaywitz, S. E., Lyon, G. R., Shankweiler, D. P., et al. (1998). Subtypes of reading disability: Variability around a phonological core. *Journal of Educational Psychology*, *90*, 347–373.

Ni, W., Fodor, J. D., Crain, S., & Shankweiler, D. (1998). Anomaly detection: Eye-movement patterns. *Journal of Psycholinguistic Research*, *27*, 515–539.

Shaywitz, B., Shaywitz, S., Pugh, K., Fulbright, R., Constable, T., Mencl, E., et al. (1998). Functional disruption in the organization of the brain for reading in dyslexia. *Proceedings of the National Academy of Sciences*, *95*, 2636–2641.

Shankweiler, D. (1999). Words to meanings. *Scientific Studies of Reading*, *3*, 113–127.

Shankweiler, D., Lundquist, E., Katz, L., Steubing, K., Fletcher, J., Brady, S., et al. (1999). Comprehension and decoding: Patterns of association in children with reading difficulties. *Scientific Studies of Reading*, *3*, 95–112.

Ni, W., Constable, R. T., Mencl, W. E., Pugh, K., Fulbright, R., Shaywitz, S., et al. (2000). An event-related neuroimaging study distinguishing form and content in sentence processing. *Journal of Cognitive Neuroscience*, *12, 120–133*.

Pugh, K., Mencl, W. E., Shaywitz, B. A., Shaywitz, S. E., Fulbright, R. K., Skudlarski, P., et al. (2000). The angular gyrus in development dyslexia: Task-specific differences in functional connectivity in posterior cortex. *Psychological Science*, *11*, 51–56.

Crain, S., Ni, W., & Shankweiler, D. (2001). Grammatism. *Brain and Language*, *77*, 294–304.

Braze, D., Shankweiler, D. P., Ni, W., & Palumbo, L. C. (2002). Reader's eye movements distinguish anomalies of form and content. *Journal of Psycholinguistic Research*, *31*, 25–44.

Constable, R. T., Pugh, K. R., Berroya, E., Mencl, W. E., Westerveld, M., Ni, W., et al. (2004). Sentence complexity and input modality effects in sentence comprehension: An fMRI study. *NeuroImage*, *22*, 11–21.

Fletcher-Flinn, C. M., Shankweiler, D., & Frost, S. J. (2004). Coordination of reading and spelling in early literacy: An examination of the discrepancy hypothesis. *Reading and Writing: An Interdisciplinary Journal*, *17*, 617–644.

Shankweiler, D., & Fowler, A. E. (2004). Questions people ask about the role of phonological processes in learning to read. *Reading and Writing: An Interdisciplinary Journal*, *17*, 483–515.

Hindson, B., Byrne, B., Fielding-Barnsley, R., Newman, C., Hine, D., & Shankweiler, D. (2005). Assessment and early instruction of preschool children at risk for reading disability. *Journal of Educational Psychology*, *94*, 687–704.

LeVasseur, V. M., Macaruso, P., Palumbo, L. C., & Shankweiler, D. (2006). Syntactically cued text facilitates oral reading fluency in developing readers. *Applied Psycholinguistics*, *27*, 423–445.

Braze, D., Tabor, W., Shankweiler, D. P., & Mencl, W. E. (2007). Speaking up for vocabulary: Reading skill differences in young adults. *Journal of Learning Disabilities*, *40*, 226–243.

Byrne, B., Shankweiler, D., & Hine, D. W. (2008). Reading development in children at risk for dyslexia. In M. Mody, & E. Silliman (Eds.), *Language impairment and reading disability: Interactions among brain, behavior, and experience*. New York: Guilford.

LeVasseur, V. M., Macaruso, P., & Shankweiler, D. (2008). Promoting gains in reading fluency: A comparison of three approaches. *Reading and Writing: An Interdisciplinary Journal, 21*, 205–230.

Shankweiler, D., Mencl, W. E., Braze, D., Tabor, W., Pugh, K. R., & Fulbright, R. (2008). Reading differences and brain: Cortical integration of speech and print in sentence processing. *Developmental Neuropsychology, 33*(6), 745–776.

Macaruso, P., & Shankweiler, D. (2010). Expanding the simple view of reading in accounting for reading skills in community college students. *Reading Psychology, 31*(5), 454–471.

Shankweiler, D., Conway Palumbo, L., Fulbright, R. K., Mencl, W. E., Van Dyke, J., Kollia, B., et al. (2010). Testing the limits of language production in long-term survivors of major stroke: A psycholinguistic and anatomic study. *Aphasiology, 24*(11), 1455–1483.

Braze, D., Mencl, W. E., Tabor, W., Pugh, K. R., Constable, R. T., Fulbright, R. K., et al. (in press). Unification of sentence processing via ear and eye: An fMRI study. *Cortex*.

Magnuson, J. S., Kukona, A., Braze, D., Johns, C. L., Van Dyke, J. A., Tabor, W., et al. (in press). Phonological instability in young adult poor readers: Time course measures and computational modeling. In P. McCardle, J. Ren, & O. Tzeng (Eds.), *Dyslexia across languages: Orthography and the brain-gene-behavior links*. Baltimore, MD: Paul H. Brookes.

Shankweiler, D. (in press). Reading and phonological processing. In V. S. Ramachandran (Ed.), *Encyclopedia of human behavior* (2nd ed., chap. 279). Amsterdam: Elsevier.

Acknowledgments

This book, and the symposium it is based on, was made possible through support from the Society for the Scientific Study of Reading, Haskins Laboratories, and the National Science Foundation (grant # BCS-0747677). We especially thank the participants for generously giving their time and expertise to both the symposium and the chapters within this volume. In addition, we are very grateful to Bill Tunmer for his thoughtful foreword to the book and to Rhea Paul for her support as editor of the series on New Directions in Communications Disorders Research. Lastly, we thank Karen Aicher for assistance with preparation of the manuscript and Yvonne Manning for help with formatting the figures.

Contributors

Suzanne Adlof
Learning Research and Development Center
University of Pittsburgh
Pittsburgh, Pennsylvania

Susan A. Brady
Psychology Department
University of Rhode Island
Kingston, Rhode Island

and

Haskins Laboratories
New Haven, Connecticut

David Braze
Haskins Laboratories
New Haven, Connecticut

Brian Byrne
School of Behavioural, Cognitive and Social Sciences
University of New England
Armidale, New South Wales, Australia

Hugh W. Catts
Department of Hearing and Speech
University of Kansas
Lawrence, Kansas

Joshua John Diehl
Haskins Laboratories
New Haven, Connecticut

and

Department of Psychology
Center for Children and Families
University of Notre Dame
Notre Dame, Indiana

Carol A. Fowler
Haskins Laboratories
New Haven, Connecticut

and

Psychology Department
University of Connecticut
Storrs, Connecticut

Stephen J. Frost
Haskins Laboratories
New Haven, Connecticut

Colleen McDonough
Psychology Department
Neumann University
Aston, Pennsylvania

Gerald W. McRoberts
Haskins Laboratories
New Haven, Connecticut

W. Einar Mencl
Haskins Laboratories
New Haven, Connecticut

Richard Olson
Department of Psychology
University of Colorado
Boulder, Colorado

Charles Perfetti
Learning Research and Development Center
University of Pittsburgh
Pittsburgh, Pennsylvania

Kenneth R. Pugh
Haskins Laboratories
New Haven, Connecticut

and

Psychology Department
University of Connecticut
Storrs, Connecticut

Hollis S. Scarborough
Haskins Laboratories
New Haven, Connecticut

David L. Share
Department of Learning Disabilities
University of Haifa
Haifa, Israel

Margaret J. Snowling
Department of Psychology
Center for Reading and Language
University of York
Heslington, United Kingdom

Nicole Patton Terry
Department of Educational
Psychology and Special Education
Georgia State University
Atlanta, Georgia

and

Haskins Laboratories
New Haven, Connecticut

Photograph by Donald Compton

Back row, left to right: Charles Perfetti, David Share, Dick Olson, Hugh Catts, Maggie Snowling, Brian Byrne, and Dave Braze

Front/middle row, left to right: Ken Pugh, Hollis S. Scarborough, Ruth Millikan, Don Shankweiler, Carol Fowler, and Susan Brady

Part I

Theoretical Foundations

Phonology and Reading

1 How Theories of Phonology May Enhance Understanding of the Role of Phonology in Reading Development and Reading Disability

Carol A. Fowler
Haskins Laboratories
and
University of Connecticut

INTRODUCTION

A theory of *phonology* characterizes the systematic ways in which language communities use basic language forms (for present purposes, consonants and vowels) to encode linguistic meanings. *Phonology* contrasts with *phonetics*, the study of the physical articulatory and acoustic properties of those language forms. In most approaches, the contrast between phonology and phonetics is between the cognitive or mental, and the physical (e.g., Pierrehumbert, 1990). Phonological language forms are held to be discrete, symbolic components of a language user's linguistic competence; phonetic language forms are its continuous, articulatory, and acoustic realizations. This is not the conceptualization with which I will end this chapter, but it is one that pervades most linguistic perspectives on the sound systems of languages.

Understanding the nature of phonology is relevant to understanding reading, reading acquisition, and reading impairments. This is in part because humans are biologically adapted to spoken language, whereas reading and writing are too new (and insufficiently widespread) in human history to have shaped human evolution.

The adaptation of humans to the spoken language is evidenced by specializations of the human brain, not only for language, but, specifically, also for the spoken language, not the written language. Lieberman (1984) also suggests that the human vocal tract is adapted to speech (but see, Fitch & Reby, 2001, for another point of view). The human vocal tract differs from that of other primates in a way (a lowered larynx) that permits the production of a wide array of consonantal and vocalic gestures. The range of sounds producible by other primates is considerably more limited. A lowered larynx, other than conferring this advantage in sound production, appears maladaptive in permitting accidental choking on food; accordingly, Lieberman suggests that it must be an adaptation to speech.

That the spoken language is an evolutionary achievement of humans is also indicated by its universality. It is universal across human cultures and is nearly universally acquired within cultures. Unless children are prevented by severe hearing loss or severe mental deficiency, they learn a spoken language and learn it without explicit instruction. Literacy contrasts with the command of the spoken language in all of these respects. Many human cultures lack a writing system, and, within cultures, literacy is not universal. Children almost always have to be explicitly taught to read, and many, even when given apparently adequate instruction, fail to learn to read well.

A second reason why understanding phonology should foster understanding of reading, here particularly reading acquisition, is that the vast majority of children begin reading instruction when they are already highly competent users of a spoken language. Moreover, the language they will learn to read is typically the language they speak, albeit generally a different dialect of it. If beginning readers can learn to map printed forms of words onto the words' phonological forms, they can take advantage of their competence in the spoken language when they read.

Both of these observations, that the spoken language, but not the written language, is an evolutionary achievement of the human species and that most novice readers already know by ear the language of which they are becoming readers, suggests that reading should be "parasitic" on the spoken language (Mattingly & Kavanagh, 1972) during reading acquisition and thereafter. Research on skilled readers bears out the latter expectation. Skilled readers access the phonological forms of words very soon after seeing the printed form (e.g., Frost, 1998); this occurs among readers of writing systems that vary considerably in the transparency with which the writing system signals the pronounced form of words.

In short, a language user's phonological competence appears to provide an entryway or interface by which readers can access their knowledge of the spoken language, and, perhaps, their biological adaptation to the spoken language. Understanding phonology, then, may provide insights into reading, reading acquisition, and reading difficulties. In the following, I will offer some speculative insights that the study of phonology may provide into the latter two domains.

DIVERSITY AMONG THEORIES OF PHONOLOGY

There are, and there have been, many different theoretical approaches to the study of phonology. In some instances, new approaches emerged from the identification of deficiencies in an existing approach, for example, when generative approaches to phonology (beginning with Chomsky & Halle, 1968) superseded descriptive (also known as structural) approaches (e.g., Gleason, 1961; Trager & Smith, 1951). However, in some cases, approaches have coexisted (e.g., autosegmental theories beginning with Goldsmith, 1976, and metrical approaches, beginning with M. Liberman & Prince, 1977), focusing on largely, but not entirely, distinct phonological domains.

In each case, issues of special interest in one approach recede in relevance or even disappear in others. For example, a central construct for descriptive linguists was that of the "phoneme," an abstract category characterized by its role in capturing the phenomenon of linguistic contrast (see section "Descriptive linguistics"). When Halle (1959) and Chomsky (1964) identified inadequacies in the outcomes of the procedural system by which descriptive linguists partitioned the phones of a language into phoneme classes, they (Chomsky & Halle, 1968) abandoned the concept of the phoneme altogether. Their generative phonology set aside the notion of contrast, focusing instead on systematic processes that hold across the lexicons of languages (see section "The generative phonology of Chomsky and Halle (1968)").

I will take the view here that the successes and failures of different theories of phonology, past and present, shed valuable light on different aspects of the phonologies of languages, which, in turn, may provide insight into reading. In the following, I will discuss three different phonological theories: descriptive linguistics, generative phonology, and articulatory phonology (e.g., Browman & Goldstein, 1986), and discuss the possible insights that an examination of them may provide on reading acquisition and difficulties in learning to read.

Descriptive Linguistics

The aim of descriptive linguists in the domain of phonology was to classify the consonantal and vocalic phonetic segments of the given languages into phonemes. Phonemes are classes of phonetic segments used by members of a language community. Community members use phonemes contrastively to distinguish words; they do not use phonetic segments within a phoneme class contrastively. Examples in English of phoneme classes are /p/, /t/, and /k/. Roughly, each of these phonemes has two variants, an aspirated variant [p^h] that occurs in stressed syllable-initial position (*pill*, *till*, *kill*) and an unaspirated version [p] that occurs elsewhere (*spill*, *still*, *skill*). There are no words of English that differ just in whether the unvoiced stop is aspirated or not. So, for example, there is no word [pɪl] that differs from [p^hɪl] in having an unaspirated [p], but otherwise differs in no other way from *pill* in its form. ([p] differs from the initial segment of *bill* in having a devoicing gesture.) Thus, the different variants or "allophones" of a phoneme do not contrast. This is different from the relation of either allophone of /p/ relative to /b/. We have word pairs such as *pill* and *bill* that differ only in the first consonant and that have different meanings. /p/ and /b/ are contrastive in English.

In descriptive linguistics, phonemes are represented in terms of their featural attributes. Figure 1.1 provides an example. In the word *tab*, the first consonant is an unvoiced, alveolar stop, the vowel is a front, low, unrounded vowel, and the

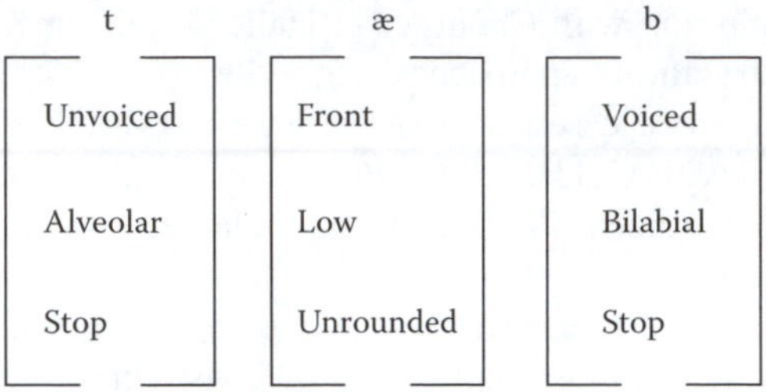

FIGURE 1.1 One way of representing word forms as sequences of consonants and vowels characterized by their featural attributes. The word is *tab*.

final consonant, /b/, is a voiced bilabial stop consonant. (There are many feature systems. I have chosen a simple one for Figure 1.1.)

In these representations, consonant and vowel phonemes are discrete from one another and are invariant in their featural attributes. Entities with these characteristics are what the letters of an alphabetic writing system represent more or less directly depending on the writing system.

When consonants and vowels are represented by feature columns, time is absent except as serial order. Therein lies a difficulty for this way of describing phonological or phonetic segments. There are some indications that time is inherent in the consonantal and vocalic segments of languages. For the present, I will present just some of the evidence. Its relevance to reading, however, may not be obvious. After all, alphabetic writing systems have the same character. Time is absent in their representations except as serial order. In the following, I will suggest that the relevance to reading has to do with the attainment of phonemic awareness. It is not always clear whether a set of features constitute one segment or two.

Ewan (1982) offers several examples of the so-called complex segments in which there is ambiguity as to whether a phonological "segment" is really one segment or two. One compelling kind of example comes from languages that will be unfamiliar to most readers. Some languages have consonants that are identified as "prenasalized stops." These are segments that begin as nasalized segments, but end as oral consonants. An example is from the language Nyanga, the disyllable /^{m}bale/. In this language, prenasalized stops have the duration of single segments. In some languages, they also have the distributional characteristics of single segments. That is, they occur in the contexts that single segments occur in. In Nyanga, they contrast with trisyllabic sequences such as /mbale/ in which the /m/ is syllabic (Herbert, 1977, cited in Ewan).

Although at least one phonologist proposed retaining the featural representation of segments, despite the existence of complex segments, by allowing a feature (here nasality) to change state within a feature column (Anderson, 1976), it violates the fundamental nature of this representation type.

Other examples come from English. English has two affricate consonants, the phone at the beginning and end of the word *church* and the phone at the beginning and end of *judge*. Like prenasalized stops, they are characterized by a dynamic change. At onset, they have a stop-like character, but this gives way to a fricative-like character subsequently. Relatedly, two notations are used to represent these phones. In one, they are /ʧ/ and /ʤ/, respectively, whereas in the other they are /č/ and /ǰ/. One segment or two?

A final, surprising set of examples consists of the /s/-stop clusters in English. The clusters /sp/, /st/, and /sk/ appear to be sequences of two consonants. But there are reasons to question whether they are. As consonant sequences they are the only clusters in English that violate the "sonority constraint" that is commonplace in languages. The constraint is that consonants closer to the vowel nucleus in syllables must be more "sonorous" (roughly more vowel-like) than those farther away. So, if /p/ and /r/ precede the vowel in a syllable, the order must be /pr/ (as in *pram*, for example), with the continuant consonant /r/ closer to the vowel than the noncontinuant /p/. If the same two consonants follow the vowel in a syllable, the order has to be /rp/ (as in *harp*). But continuant /s/ precedes /p/, /t/, and /k/, both before (*spill, still, skill*) and after (*rasp, last, ask*) the vowel. The order violates the sonority constraint before the vowel. But if s-stop "clusters" are, in fact, single segments, then there is no violation. Fudge (1969) points out also that, in English, a statement about what consonants can occur in clusters is simpler (because no three-consonant clusters can occur) if /s/-stop clusters are considered single segments.

I will show shortly that the shortcomings of the featural representations in handling dynamic change can be overcome to a large extent by using a different representational system, that of articulatory phonology (e.g., Browman & Goldstein, 1986, 1992). However, the central message here is not that featural systems are inadequate. It is that word forms are only approximately composed of sequences of discrete consonants and vowels. Some consonants (e.g., prenasalized stops and affricates) and vowels (e.g., diphthongs) have properties of single segments and some properties of sequences of segments. There may be no right answer to the question whether affricates are single segments or else are sequences of segments. They have properties consistent and inconsistent with both solutions.

That is the nature of natural languages. The properties of languages emerge and change as people talk to one another. The properties that work (i.e., that enable communicative exchanges to succeed) have to be mostly systematic, but they do not have to be wholly formal. When phonological analyses fail to capture all of the relevant facts about a language's phonological system (e.g., when Chomsky and Halle's (1968) trisyllabic laxing rule has to predict that *obesity* should be pronounced *obehsity*), that is just a fact about living languages. There are exceptions to most of the generalizations that can be drawn about the sound systems of language.

What does any of this have to do with reading? For one thing, it offers yet another reason why achieving phonemic awareness is difficult. Phonemic awareness is difficult for children to achieve because, quite rightly, they are inclined to think about what word forms mean, not what they sound like (e.g., Byrne, 1996). If A. M. Liberman (1996) was right that speech perception is served by a brain "module," then phonemic awareness is also difficult to achieve because language users cannot introspect on the workings of the module (Fodor, 1983) that produces consonants and vowels and extracts them from spoken input. But, thirdly, it is difficult to achieve because there is sometimes no clear answer to the question of how many segments compose a word. How many segments are there in *church*? Are there three, the two affricates and the /r/ colored vowel? Are there five, because the affricates are each really two segments? Are there six, because the vowel is not /r/ colored, it is a vowel coarticulating with /r/? There may be no right or wrong answer. Because even spoken languages with very regular and consistent alphabetic writing systems will have these ambiguous segmental properties, the letters of the alphabet only can come close to mapping in a one-to-one way to the basic phonological entities of the spoken language.

The Generative Phonology of Chomsky and Halle (1968)

Analysis of the phonetic segments of a language community into phoneme classes was shown not to work in all cases by Halle (1959) for Russian and by Chomsky (1964) for English. In some cases, violation of principles used to associate phones with phoneme classes occurred. For example, a violation of the "absolute invariance condition" (that the phoneme class to which a particular phonetic segment belongs has to be determinable independently of the context in which it occurs) happens in the words *writer* and *rider* when the /d/ and /t/ phonemes are both realized as the flap [ɾ]. Because of occurrences like this, the flap appears to be an allophone of both phonemes, and the phoneme class to which the phonetic segment belongs cannot be determined independently of its context (in the example, the preceding vowel length).

This violation and others might have been interpreted as yet another indication that language forms are only almost formalizable. However, for Chomsky and Halle (1968), they necessitated a radical change in approaches to phonology, in which the concept of phoneme was banished. Although the notion of abstract cognitively represented segments, as in Figure 1.1, was retained, the property of *contrast* as the defining characteristic of those segments was abandoned. Instead, Chomsky and Halle focused their attention on distinguishing properties of words that are systematic across the lexicon from those that are idiosyncratic to a word. They proposed that lexical forms should represent just the idiosyncratic properties. Systematic properties could be generated by rules applied in the transformation of cognitively represented lexical forms to physically realizable phonetic forms. The difficulty discussed earlier that time needs to be incorporated into linguistic representations of word forms was not addressed, and so lexical representations resembling that of Figure 1.1 continued to be part of the phonology.

For example, in the English word *tab* of Figure 1.1, the fact that the initial consonant is aspirated is not indicated, because aspiration can be generated by a general rule of the language that voiceless stops are aspirated in stressed, syllable-initial position. Likewise, that the vowel is long (as compared to its length in *tap*) is not represented, because increased vowel length can be generated by a general rule that vowels are lengthened before voiced obstruents. Only properties of *tab* that are idiosyncratic to it (e.g., that the first phonological segment is /t/, the next one /æ/, and the final one /b/) are represented in the lexicon.

This approach ran into its own difficulties. One concerned determining what should count as a systematic property. Many phonological regularities are true of most relevant words but not of all of them. Chomsky and Halle had a rather low threshold for identifying a property as systematic. A consequence of pulling lots of "systematicities" from lexical representations of words is that the representations can become quite abstract. Whereas that of *tab* in Figure 1.1 is not abstracted very far from its surface pronunciation [tʰæ:b], that proposed for the word *right* was /rīxt/ a representation that is both far from the actual pronunciation /rayt/, and that contains a phonological segment (the voiceless velar fricative /x/) that no longer appears in surface pronunciations in English. Considerable attention was devoted then to the issue of how to set limits on the abstractness of proposed lexical forms (see, e.g., Kenstowicz & Kisseberth, 1979).

Interestingly, the abstract lexical forms of Chomsky and Halle (1968) often conformed to the spellings of words more closely than did the surface phonetic forms (witness *right* and /rīxt/ versus the surface pronunciation [rayt]). This was notably true for words that are morphologically related, with same-spelled stems, but different surface pronunciation of the stems (e.g., such forms as *serene-serenity, divine-divinity, profane-profanity*). In turn, this led to speculation that spelling in English mapped onto lexical ("deep") phonological forms, whereas writing systems such as those for Turkish or Serbo-Croatian mapped onto shallow phonetic forms (I. Y. Liberman, A. M. Liberman, Mattingly, & Shankweiler, 1980). It also led to the conjecture (by Chomsky & Halle, among others; see also Klima, 1972) that, in some ways, English spelling is close to optimal because it maps transparently to lexical forms. However, an alternative view is that some of the systematicities that Chomsky and Halle were identifying were not alive in the language use of present-day speaker/hearers, but rather were regularities in historical sound change (e.g., /x/ was at one time pronounced in *right*). Because English has not reformed its spelling recently, spellings sometimes map more simply onto historically older pronunciations, and these were being approximated by the lexical representations of Chomsky and Halle's generative phonology. (Chomsky and Halle themselves discounted this idea, however.)

Of course, in some ways, it does not matter why English spellings frequently contain both morphological and phonological information (i.e., are "morphophonemic"). Possibly, English spellings do map onto deep representations of lexical forms. Perhaps they do not. Even if they do not, Chomsky and Halle's phonology shows that English spellings do reflect phonological (near-) systematicities across the lexicon, with the result that spellings tend to be morphophonemic. Can reader-spellers take advantage of that information?

Two fairly clear cases of an advantage of morphophonemic spellings are provided by the inflectional suffixes spelled *s* and *ed*. Even though each suffix is associated with three different pronunciations (unvoiced, voiced, and schwa-C forms), they look the same in print. This must facilitate picking them out. This facilitation comes early. Byrne (1996) trained prereading children to distinguish singular and plural spellings of words in which the plural *s* was pronounced [s]. First they learned to associate such word pairs as *book* and *books* to different pictures. Then they learned to identify each word by its spelling alone. After reaching criterion on "reading" *book* and *books* and *hat* and *hats*, they were tested for generalization to discover what the children had learned about the final *s*. They might have learned the mapping of *s* to [s], in which case they should be successful identifying which of two words was *bike* and which *bikes*, but also which of *bug* and *bus* had the pronunciation [bʌs]. Alternatively, they might have learned that *s* was the spelling of the plural morpheme, in which case they should fail on *bug-bus*, but succeed at *dog-dogs*, in which *s* is pronounced [z]. The latter was the outcome. Prereading children are disposed to expect letters to map onto something meaningful, and it can only be helpful that letters do that in the case of *s* and *ed*.

As Mann and Singson (2003) point out, there is also something that readers can learn about derivational suffixes. Some suffixes are "neutral" in that when they are added to a word, the pronunciation of the stem is unchanged. Examples are *ness* and *ment*. Others are non-neutral in that they do change the pronunciation of the stem. Examples are *ic* (compare *magic, magician)* and *ity*. Readers who know how to pronounce a base form (say, *excite*) can know how to pronounce it in a morphologically complex form with a neutral suffix (*excitement*). In addition, if they are very morphologically aware, they may learn how non-neutral suffixes change the pronunciation of base forms. Then if they know how to pronounce *magic*, they can know how to implement "velar softening" (Chomsky & Halle, 1968) and a stress shift to pronounce *magician*.

Relatedly, in a recent study of third grade children, Jarmulowicz, Hay, Taran, and Ethington (2008) measured "morphophonological accuracy" as well as phonemic and morphological awareness, to determine both the developmental pattern of their emergence and their relation to word decoding and reading comprehension. Morphophonological accuracy was assessed by having participants add a non-neutral suffix to a base form and pronounce the complex form. A model emerged from a path analysis suggesting that morphophonological accuracy emerges after morphological and phonemic awareness and that it is a strong predictor of word decoding, but affects reading comprehension only indirectly through the effect of decoding on comprehension.

Addressing the issue most directly of whether the morphophonemic spelling of English is helpful to readers seems to require a near impossible kind of experiment. Required are comparisons between readers of a variety of skill levels, some of whom are readers of English and some of whom are readers of a shallow orthography (in which such words as *heal* and *health* have different stem spellings). The problem, however, is that, unless the shallowly spelled spoken language is English, the languages are bound to differ morphologically in ways that would affect the salience of morphological information to language users for reasons unrelated to the writing system.

However, there are some less-direct indications that the knowledge of morphology and morphophonology is related to reading and spelling. First, a number of studies have shown that morphological awareness is related to reading skill (see, Carlisle, 2003, for a review), and some (e.g., Fowler & I. Y. Liberman, 1995) have shown that this is especially so for tasks involving morphologically complex words in which derivational suffixes are non-neutral. It is also known that morphological awareness grows in importance as a predictor of word recognition as phonological awareness declines. Mann and Singson (2003) found in a regression analysis predicting a z score combining word and nonword reading performance that phonological awareness explained 60% of the variance among third graders. However, it gradually declined over the succeeding grades until it explained only about 10% of the variance in sixth grade. In contrast, morphological awareness explained no variance among third graders, but it did contribute significant variance in fifth and sixth grade. Like other studies, however, this one showed that the percentage of variance explained by morphological awareness is modest, at least in the grades examined. In sixth grade it explained approximately 10% of the variance. A subsequent experiment showed that, with vocabulary and phonological awareness entered into a regression analysis, tests of morphological awareness only explained significant variance if the morphologically complex words tested had non-neutral suffixes. Mann and Singson comment that this kind of outcome has been interpreted (e.g., Fowler & I. Y. Liberman) as evidence that these tests of morphological awareness are really assessing phonological skills; however, they suggest alternatively that they may be assessing awareness of non-neutral suffixes and the morphophonological systematicities associated with their attachment to base forms.

Morphological knowledge should also help with spelling. Knowing that *equality* contains *equal*, can help spellers spell the stem correctly in the complex form. Carlisle (1987) found that this apparent spelling approach (spelling the stem in the same way in the simple and complex form) was more characteristic of typically reading fourth graders than of a group of ninth grader dyslexic readers matched to the fourth graders on spelling accuracy. However, Bourassa, Treiman, and Kessler (2006) found that both dyslexic children (aged 9–14 years) and spelling-matched typically reading children were more likely to spell both consonants of a final consonant cluster in inflected words such as *tuned* (/tund/) than in monomorphemic words such as *brand*. This implies that both groups of readers were able to take advantage of their knowledge of the base form *tune* to overcome the difficulty that final clusters can cause for young spellers.

In a second experiment, Bourassa et al. (2006) found that both dyslexic readers and typical readers were more likely to represent accurately the *t* in inflected forms such as *waiting* and the *d* in words such as *louder* than in monomorphemic words such as *daughter* and *spider*. In all of these words, the internal *t* and *d* are flapped and indistinguishable in American English. This finding, compatible with the previous one, suggests that both groups of readers can take advantage of their knowledge of stem forms such as *wait* and *loud* in spelling the morphologically complex forms. However, both groups of readers were less accurate in spelling the *t* or *d* in the complex forms than in simple forms such as *wait* and *loud*. This signifies that the children were not taking full advantage of their morphological knowledge.

In turn, this implies that morphological awareness should predict spelling accuracy. It appears that it does. For example, Deacon and Bryant (2006) gave 7–9-year-old children a spelling test like that of Bourassa et al. (2006) in which they compared their accuracy on inflected forms such as *turning* and on matched monomorphemic words such as *turnip*. As Bourassa et al. had found, children were able to use their knowledge of base forms to assist in their spelling of the morphologically complex form. In a regression analysis with age partialed out, variance in scores on the spelling test was significantly predicted by performance on a test of morphological awareness (adding inflections to base forms).

In short, the generative phonology of Chomsky and Halle (1968) draws attention to the observations that English spellings tend to map in a straightforward way to the abstract lexical phonological representations that their theory proposed for English speakers. Whether or not lexical forms have that abstract character has proven controversial. However, even so, it remains the case that English spelling preserves information about morphology more so than do shallower writing systems with more consistent spelling-sound mappings. Readers and spellers have been shown to make use of this information.

Articulatory Phonology

Browman and Goldstein's articulatory phonology (e.g., Browman & Goldstein, 1986, 1992; Goldstein & C. A. Fowler, 2003) offers a way to address the problem of time noted earlier. Conceptualizations of phonological segments as discrete and timeless collections of featural attributes do not have a good way to represent dynamic properties of phonological elements, including those of complex segments.

Articulatory phonology is revolutionary and unique in two important and related ways. First, time is inherent to phonological entities in the theory. Second, phonological forms are public things. In my view, it is ironic that in all theoretical accounts of phonology except articulatory phonology, phonological language forms are held to be categories in the mind. It is ironic because language forms are the means that languages provide to make communicative messages public. Why would language communities develop forms that are fundamentally covert, and, that, due to coarticulation in speech, remain so as talkers speak? In the view of Browman and Goldstein (e.g., 1986), phonological forms are not covert.

In articulatory phonology, uniquely, language forms are linguistically significant actions of the vocal tract. This is not to say that minds do not know something about language forms. It is to say that, just as minds know something about elephants, but elephants do not reside in knowers' minds, phonological language forms are known to language users, but do not reside in language knowers' minds. They are public actions.

In this approach to phonology, then, there is no separation between the mental (phonological) and the physical (phonetic) aspects of the spoken language as there is in other phonological theories, and hence no need for the supposition of other phonological theorists that a translation must occur between a symbolic and a physical domain of linguistic representation. Rather, the

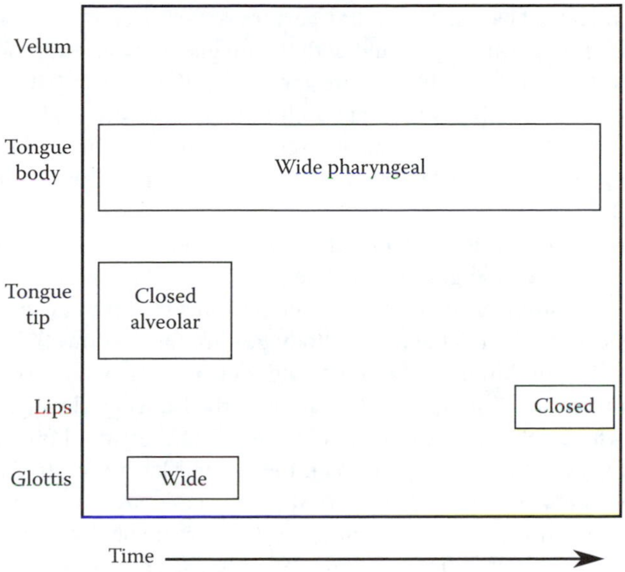

FIGURE 1.2 A gestural score for the word *tab*.

phonology–phonetic contrast (Gafos & Benus, 2006) is between a low- and a high-dimensional characterization of the same speech system.

In articulatory phonology, word forms are represented by "gestural scores." Figure 1.2 shows a gestural score for the word *tab*. A gestural score represents the linguistically significant actions, or *gestures*, of the vocal tract as they unfold over time for the production of a word. Linguistic gestures create and release constrictions in the vocal tract, and the constrictions are characterized by two parameters: constriction location and constriction degree. For the /t/ in *tab*, for example, a constriction is created at the alveolar ridge of the palate by the tongue tip. The constriction degree is complete closure. Accordingly, the constriction location is alveolar; the constriction degree is closed. Overlapping with that gesture is a gesture of the larynx in which the vocal folds open. The constriction location is glottal. The constriction degree is wide. The vocalic gesture of the tongue body spans the entire duration of the word. Its location is pharyngeal for the vowel /æ/. The final consonantal gesture at the lips begins during the vowel. Its constriction degree is closed.

In the approach of Browman and Goldstein (1992), contrast is a focus of the theory. The presence or absence of a gesture can create contrast. For example, omission of the laryngeal gesture at the beginning of the word *tab* creates the word *dab*. The laryngeal gesture is contrastive.

For present purposes, a notable characteristic of the gestural score is that segments are not in any apparent way discrete; rather, the gestures for different segments overlap in time. Nor is it obvious that the gestures of multiple-gesture segments, such as initial /t/ in *tab*, are any more cohesive than are gestures for different segments. That is, the glottal gesture for /t/ overlaps temporally both with the tongue tip gesture for /t/ and with the tongue body gesture for the vowel. Moreover, nothing in the gestural score shows that the glottal gesture somehow belongs more with the tip gesture than with the body gesture. Indeed, Browman and Goldstein (1990) wrote of phonemic segments that they are more a practical tool than they are entities that correspond to important informational units of the phonological system.

In contrast to this, in the view of Saltzman and Byrd (2000), there is evidence that coupling between the gestures of a segment (e.g., the tongue tip and glottal gestures of /t/) is stronger than that between gestures of different segments (e.g., the glottal gesture of /t/ and the tongue body gesture for the vowel). For example, they cite findings by Munhall, Löfqvist, and Kelso (1994) who show that when the lip gesture for the first /p/ in /ipip/ is perturbed during closing, lip closure occurs, but with a delay that is mirrored by a delay in the glottal opening gesture for /p/. This suggests a coupling between the lip and larynx gestures. However, the glottal gesture and therefore the period of devoicing are not terminated early to preserve its relation to the oral opening gesture for the next vowel.

However, the study by Munhall et al. (1994) had literate adult talkers as subjects. Would this finding hold for prereading children and illiterate adults? Is it possible that literacy has an impact on language users' "gestural scores" such that before a language user learns to read, the coupling inhomogeneities that reflect formation of multigesture segments are absent or at least are less marked than they are in readers of alphabetic writing systems? If so, then we might also see differences in the phonological forms of words of poor readers, which are consequences of poor reading. These would augment effects of the poor reader's hypothesized weak phonological systems (I. Y. Liberman, Shankweiler, & A. M. Liberman, 1989) in fostering a poor fit between units of spoken and written word forms.

We know that there are, in some sense, links between spoken and written word forms in memory such that skilled readers access phonological word forms when they read (e.g., Frost, 1998) and orthographic word forms when they listen (e.g., Seidenberg & Tanenhaus, 1979; Slowiaczek, Soltano, Wieting, & Bishop, 2003). This means that there is the possibility of orthographic representations having an impact on phonological representations (and vice versa).

There is also evidence that literacy affects performance on spoken language tasks in other ways. For example, Castro-Caldas, Petersson, Reis, Stone-Elander, and Ingvar (1998) found that illiterate adults had much more difficulty repeating pseudo-words than matched literate individuals.

It is well-known that there is a bidirectional causal relationship between phonemic awareness and reading. Phonemic awareness is a strong predictor of reading in the early grades (e.g., Mann & Singson, 2003, described earlier). In addition, however, literacy fosters phonemic awareness. For example, Morais, Cary, Alegria, and Bertelson (1979) found that illiterate adults performed very poorly on a task in which they were to delete or add consonants to words and non-words, averaging 36% correct on words and 19% correct on nonwords. Matched literate participants performed the tasks more successfully (averaging 89% and 72% correct on word and nonwords, respectively).

Moreover, the kind of literacy that fosters phonemic awareness appears to be literacy in an alphabetic writing system. Navas (2004) used a deletion task and an oddity task (in which participants indicated which of three words started with a different sound) to test the phonemic and syllabic awareness of three groups of bilingual Japanese–Portuguese speakers. One group was literate only in Japanese, a syllabic and logographic system; one only in Portuguese, an alphabetic system; and the final group was literate in both languages. Individuals who were literate only in Japanese performed very poorly on the consonant deletion and oddity tasks in comparison to individuals who were literate in Portuguese.

Why does literacy in an alphabetic writing system foster phonemic awareness? Two kinds of reasons have been proposed for why prereaders lack phonemic awareness (see Fowler, 1991, for a discussion). One is that children perceive consonants and vowels when they hear words, and represent the consonants and vowels lexically, but they cannot introspect on what they know (I. Y. Liberman, 1973). The other possibility, raised by Fowler is that, initially, phonemes are not extracted from spoken input, and words in the lexicon have a more holistic representation. This is suggested by a variety of findings that she summarizes. For example, Studdert-Kennedy (1986) notes that Ferguson and Farwell's (1975) list of attempts by a 15-month old to say the word *pen* shows that the attempts characteristically retain many of the features of that word, but in a variable order. Sometimes she gets very close to the mark as in [p^hɪn]. Sometimes she misses a gesture as in [hɪn]; in this production, the bilabial constriction gesture is missing so that the devoicing gesture for /p/ sounds like word-initial [h]. That one gesture of a two-gesture segment is missing may signify that, for this child, the two gestures do not cohere into a segment. Sometimes she is farther away still as in [mã$^\text{ə}$] in which the velum lowering gesture for the final nasal appears at the beginning of the word along with the bilabial constriction gesture for /p/ and persists into the vowel. However, in all cases, gestures that should be there are there; often they are improperly phased with respect to one another. In other instances, just one gesture of a two-gesture segment is preserved. This kind of evidence may signify that gestures have not coalesced into segments for this young preliterate speaker. Compatibly, perhaps, Stemberger's (1989) corpus of his two prereading daughters' spontaneous errors of speech production show twice as many feature errors ("I got that gall for Pristmas"—"I got that ball for Christmas") than whole segment errors. This contrasts with (literate) adults who show more segment than feature errors. Both of these findings may imply lexical representations in which gestures or features are present but are not organized segmentally.

Compatibly on the side of reception, Treiman and Breaux (1982) asked adults and 4-year-olds to put together which two of the three consonant–vowel–consonants were more similar. In a free sorting condition, there was a trend for adults to sort based on shared phonemes (/bɪs/ and /bun/, not /diz/), and a trend for children to sort based on global featural similarity (e.g., /bɪs/ and /diz/, not /bun/). When children and adults were trained to sort in one way or the other, children trained to sort on shared phonemes showed a significantly higher error rate than children trained to sort on featural similarity. (Adult performance was at ceiling.) In a final free sort, children who had been trained to sort on phonemes did so on under half the trials, whereas adults did so on more than three quarter of the trials. Children trained to sort on similarity did so on over half the trials on the free sort; they sorted on phonemes just a third of the time. Adults trained on similarity sorted on phonemes and similarity about equally often.

It is presumed that a segmental structure emerges in the lexicon as it grows in size (e.g., Fowler, 1991). But does it for illiterate language users? As noted earlier, they persist in their failure to exhibit phoneme awareness. How would they fare on Treiman and Breaux's (1982) sorting task? Would their feature errors outstrip their segment errors? The answers to these questions are unknown to date.* It is possible, then, that one way in which their phonological representations are weak or are unsuited for an appreciation of an alphabetic writing system is that their "gestural scores" remain unorganized or incompletely organized into segmental chunks.

CONCLUDING REMARKS

Different approaches to a linguistic understanding of phonology offer different insights into challenges presented by the task of learning to read. I have offered three. The assumption of descriptive and many generative phonologists that words are composed of discrete, countable consonants and vowels appears to be almost true. That the assumption is close to reality ensures the viability of alphabetic writing systems. But that it is not quite accurate for complex segments and other segments that undergo dynamic change over time adds to the prereader's difficulty in achieving phonemic awareness.

Articulatory phonologists do not all make the assumption even that "gestural scores" have a segmental structure. Phonetic gestures are coupled one to the other so that their phasings are appropriate. However, Browman and Goldstein (1990), as noted, did not suppose that couplings between gestures that compose conventional segments are stronger than those of different segments. There is a little evidence that they do for literate speakers. However, this leaves open the possibility that literacy itself has an impact on gestural organization.

Insights from the earliest version of generative phonology, finally, have to do with the value of the morphophonemic nature of English spelling. Chomsky and Halle (1968) derived underlying word forms that are abstract with respect to surface pronunciation by distinguishing systematic from idiosyncratic properties of words. Doing

* In her study of bilingual Japanese–Portuguese speakers who were or were not literate in the alphabetic writing system of Portuguese, Navas (2004) did elicit speech errors in a tongue twister repetition task. She found no difference in the relative frequency of different error types depending on literacy in Portuguese. However, she did not distinguish feature from segment errors and probably could not do so. This is because her tongue twisters were such pairs as *sopa-shapa* in which the target consonants differed in just one feature. Accordingly, an expected error such as *sopa-sapa* or *shopa-shapa* might be either a segment or a feature/gesture error.

that led to a finding that the same morpheme tends to be represented phonologically identically in different lexical forms despite surface pronunciation differences. This in turn fostered an idea that there is an advantage to morphophonemic spelling. I identified some evidence for this.

REFERENCES

Anderson, S. (1976). Nasal consonants and the internal structure of segments. *Language*, *52*, 326–344.

Bourassa, D., Treiman, R., & Kessler, B. (2006). Use of morphology in spelling by children with dyslexia and typically developing children. *Memory & Cognition*, *34*, 703–714.

Browman, C., & Goldstein, L. (1986). Towards an articulatory phonology. *Phonology Yearbook*, *3*, 219–252.

Browman, C., & Goldstein, L. (1990). Representation and reality: Physical systems and phonological structure. *Journal of Phonetics*, *18*, 411–424.

Browman, C., & Goldstein, L. (1992). Articulatory phonology: An overview, *Phonetica*, *49*, 155–180.

Byrne, B. (1996). The learnability of the alphabetic principle: Children's initial hypotheses about how print represents spoken language. *Applied Psycholinguistics*, *17*, 401–426.

Carlisle, J. F. (1987). The use of morphological knowledge in spelling derived forms by learning-disabled and normal students. *Annals of Dyslexia*, *27*, 90–108.

Carlisle, J. F. (2003). Morphology matters in learning to read: A commentary. *Reading Psychology*, *24*, 291–322.

Castro-Caldas, A., Petersson, K. M., Reis, A., Stone-Elander, S., & Ingvar, M. (1998). The illiterate brain: Learning to read and write during childhood influences the functional organization of the adult brain. *Brain*, *121*, 1053–1063.

Chomsky, N. (1964). *Current issues in linguistic theory*. The Hague, The Netherlands: Mouton.

Chomsky, N., & Halle, M. (1968). *The sound pattern of English*. New York: Harper & Row.

Deacon, F. H., & Bryant, P. (2006). This turnip's not for turning: Children's morphological awareness and their use of root morphemes in spelling. *British Journal of Developmental Psychology*, *24*, 567–575.

Ewan, C. (1982). The internal structure of complex segments. In H. van der Hulst & N. Smith (Eds.), *The structure of phonological representations (Part II)* (pp. 27–67). Dordrecht, The Netherlands: Foris Publications.

Ferguson, C., & Farwell, C. (1975). Words and sounds in early language acquisition. *Language*, *51*, 419–439.

Fitch, W. T., & Reby, D. (2001). The descended larynx is not uniquely human. *Proceedings of the Royal Society of London Series B-Biological Sciences*, *268*, 1669–1675.

Fodor, J. A. (1983). *Modularity of mind*. Cambridge, MA: Bradford Books.

Fowler, A. E. (1991). How early phonological development might set the stage for phoneme awareness. In S. A. Brady & D. P. Shankweiler (Eds.), *Phonological processes in literacy: A tribute to Isabelle Y. Liberman* (pp. 97–117). Hillsdale, NJ: Lawrence Erlbaum Associates.

Fowler, A. E., & Liberman, I. Y. (1995). The role of phonology and orthography in morphological awareness. In L. B. Feldman (Ed.), *Morphological aspects of language processing* (pp. 157–188). Hillsdale, NJ: Lawrence Erlbaum Associates.

Frost, R. (1998). Toward a strong phonological theory of visual word recognition: True issues and false trails. *Psychological Bulletin*, *123*, 71–99.

Fudge, E. (1969). Syllables. *Journal of Linguistics*, *5*, 253–286.

Gafos, A., & Benus, S. (2006). Dynamics of phonological cognition. *Cognitive Science*, *30*, 905–943.

Gleason, H. A. (1961). *An introduction to descriptive linguistics* (Rev. ed.). New York: Holt, Rinehart and Winston.

Goldsmith, J. (1976). *Autosegmental phonology*. Bloomington, IN: Indiana University Linguistics Club.

Goldstein, L., & Fowler, C. A. (2003). Articulatory phonology: A phonology for public language use. In N. O. Schiller & A. S. Meyer (Eds.), *Phonetics and phonology in language comprehension and production* (pp. 159–207). Berlin, Germany: Mouton de Gruyter.

Halle, M. (1959). *The sound pattern of Russian: A linguistic and acoustical investigation*. The Hague, The Netherlands: Mouton.

Herbert, R. K. (1977). *Language universals, markedness theory, and natural phonology: The interaction of nasal and oral consonants*. PhD dissertation, Ohio State University, Columbus, OH.

Jarmulowicz, L., Hay, S., Taran, V., & Ethington, C. (2008). Fitting derivational morphophonology into a developmental model of reading. *Reading and Writing*, *21*, 275–297.

Kenstowicz, M., & Kisseberth, C. (1979). *Generative phonology*. New York: Academic Press.

Klima, E. (1972). How alphabets might reflect language. In J. F. Kavanagh & I. G. Mattingly (Eds.), *Language by ear and by eye: The relationship between speech and reading* (pp. 57–80). Cambridge, MA: MIT Press.

Liberman, A. M. (1996). Some assumptions about speech and how they changed. In A. M. Liberman (Ed.), *Speech: A special code* (pp. 1–44). Cambridge, MA: MIT Press.

Liberman, I. Y. (1973). Segmentation of the spoken word and reading acquisition. *Bulletin of the Orton Society*, *23*, 65–77.

Liberman, I. Y., Liberman, A. M., Mattingly, I. G., & Shankweiler, D. P. (1980). Orthography and the beginning reader. In J. Kavanagh & R. Venezky (Eds.), *Orthography, reading, and dyslexia* (pp. 137–153). Baltimore, MD: University Park Press.

Liberman, I. Y., Shankweiler, D. P., & Liberman, A. M. (1989). The alphabetic principle and learning to read. In D. P. Shankweiler & I. Y. Liberman (Eds.), *Phonology and reading disability: Solving the reading puzzle* (pp. 1–33). Ann Arbor, MI: The University of Michigan Press.

Liberman, M., & Prince, A. (1977). On stress and linguistic rhythm. *Linguistic Inquiry*, *8*, 249–336.

Lieberman, P. (1984). *The biology and evolution of language*. Cambridge, MA: Harvard University Press.

Mann, V., & Singson, M. (2003).The little suffix that could: Linking morphological knowledge to English decoding ability. In E. Assink & D. Sandra (Eds.), *Morphology and reading: A cross-linguistic perspective* (pp. 1–26). Amsterdam, The Netherlands: Kluwer Publishers.

Mattingly, I. G., & Kavanagh, J. F. (1972). The relationships between speech and reading. *The Linguistic Reporter*, DHEW Publication No. NIH 73-475.

Morais, J., Cary, L., Alegria, J., & Bertelson, P. (1979). Does awareness of speech as a sequence of phones arise spontaneously. *Cognition*, *7*, 323–331.

Munhall, K. G., Löfqvist, A., & Kelso, J. A. S. (1994) Lip-larynx coordination in speech: Effects of mechanical perturbations to the lower lip. *Journal of the Acoustical Society of America*, *95*, 3605–3616.

Navas, A. P. G. (2004). Implications of alphabetic instruction in the conscious and unconscious manipulations of phonological representations in Portuguese-Japanese bilinguals. *Written Language and Literacy*, *7*, 119–131.

Pierrehumbert, J. (1990). Phonological and phonetic representation. *Journal of Phonetics*, *18*, 375–394.

Saltzman, E., & Byrd, D. (2000). Task-dynamics of gestural timing: Phase windows and multifrequency rhythms. *Human Movement Science*, *19*, 499–526.

Seidenberg, M. S., & Tanenhaus, M. K. (1979). Orthographic effects on rhyme monitoring. *Journal of Experimental Psychology: Human Learning and Memory*, *5*, 546–554.

Slowiaczek, L. M., Soltano, E. G., Wieting, S. J., & Bishop, K. L. (2003). An investigation of phonology and orthography in spoken word recognition. *The Quarterly Journal of Experimental Psychology A: Human Experimental Psychology*, *56A*, 233–262.

Stemberger, J. (1989). Speech errors in early child language production. *Journal of Memory and Language*, *28*, 164–188.

Studdert-Kennedy, M. (1986). Sources of variability in early speech development. In J. Perkell & D. Klatt (Eds.), *Invariance and variability in speech processes* (pp. 58–76). Hillsdale, NJ: Lawrence Erlbaum Associates.

Trager, G. L., & Smith H. L. (1951). *An outline of English structure*. Norman, OK: Battenburg Press.

Treiman, R., & Breaux, A. (1982). Common phoneme and overall similarity relations among spoken syllables: Their use by children and adults. *Journal of Psycholinguistic Research*, *11*, 569–598.

Part II

Phonological Factors in Learning to Read

2 Early Precursors of Reading-Relevant Phonological Skills

David Braze and Gerald W. McRoberts
Haskins Laboratories
Colleen McDonough
Neumann University

INTRODUCTION

There is a great deal of evidence that phonological awareness is a prerequisite for reading an alphabetic orthography (McCardle, Scarborough, & Catts, 2001; NICHD Early Child Care Research Network, 2005; Scarborough, 1998, 2005; Walley, Metsala, & Garlock, 2003). Phonological awareness at the level of the phoneme, the aspect most relevant to learning to recognize words in print, does not develop spontaneously, but depends on specific learning and instruction (e.g., Byrne, 1998; Goswami, 2002). Other aspects of phonological awareness, such as rhyme sensitivity and the associated factor of phonological memory, do develop spontaneously in preschool children, but the nature of their relationship to phoneme awareness and reading readiness is not clear. Moreover, connections between phonological awareness in preschool and school-aged children and the early phonological sensitivities of infants and toddlers have not been systematically studied. Further, there are sizable gaps in our understanding of relationships between early preliterate phonological sensitivities, individual variation in vocabulary development, and language development more generally.

Broadly speaking, phonological awareness is the ability to reflect on the building blocks of word forms (Liberman, 1999; Mattingly, 1972). It is a species of metalinguistic awareness, other types of which include morphological, syntactic, and pragmatic awareness (Chaney, 1992; Tunmer, Herriman, & Nesdale, 1988). Performance on metalinguistic "awareness" tasks relies on at least two factors. First, the relevant level of structure (e.g., *phonemes*) must be present in the child's cognitive organization (Fowler, 1991; Metsala & Walley, 1998; Walley et al., 2003). Second, the child must be able to consciously access those same elements of linguistic structure (Vygotsky, 1962). Certainly, at about the same time that infants' phonological and lexical systems are beginning to develop toward an adult-like state, their domain-general memory and cognitive abilities are also beginning to take shape (Diamond, 1985; Lalonde & Werker, 1995; Tomlinson-Keasey, Eisert,

Kahle, Hardy-Brown, & Keasey, 1979). Indeed, some reading researchers have suggested that the developmental progression in meta-cognitive function, apart from the details of phonological representations themselves, may be a cornerstone of phonological awareness (e.g., Tunmer et al.). From this perspective, the relationship of phonological awareness to reading readiness may have more to do with the meta-cognitive features of the skill than with phonology as such.

In this chapter we argue, as others have before us (e.g., Fowler, 1991; Walley, 1993; Walley et al., 2003), that a complete understanding of reading-relevant phonological skills, including phonological awareness, requires an account of their developmental trajectory from the earliest stages. An improved understanding of the development of these abilities should lead to more effective and earlier identification of children at risk for reading disability, and would inform the development of age-appropriate early intervention and prevention. However, investigation of these issues, especially among the youngest individuals, has been suboptimal for two key reasons. First, research targeting the emerging language skills of infants and toddlers has tended to rely on cross-sectional rather than longitudinal research designs. There are well-known problems with the use of aggregated cross-sectional data to make inferences about change over time. These include the fact that such data do not permit inferences about individual differences in rates of development, or for the examination of (potentially) changing relationships among cognitive factors within individual learners. Certainly, the tendency to rely on cross-sectional studies is not universal, and we will review a few of the promising longitudinal studies in the literature. A second limitation of research in this area stems from the relative lack of assessments for the various levels of phonologically grounded abilities with established relevance to early literacy that are appropriate for very young children (much before the age of 3 years). A related problem is the lack of measures that can be used across a wide span of development, from infancy through preschool for example. We will discuss some of the challenges to development of reliable measurement across this age span and will summarize work from our own laboratory that we believe holds the promise of addressing these challenges.

LEXICAL REORGANIZATION AND LEXICAL QUALITY HYPOTHESES

Phonological awareness has proved to be a powerful explanatory factor with regard to group and individual variation in reading achievement, but the developmental etiology of phonological awareness itself has remained elusive, including its relationship to the earliest phonological abilities of infants and toddlers. Beginning with the earliest point at which phonological awareness can be measured using conventional awareness tasks, there is individual variation (e.g., Chaney, 1992; MacLean, Bryant, & Bradley, 1987). Some have argued that this variation is linked more or less directly to differences in the developmental state of underlying phonological representations (Anthony & Francis, 2005; Carroll & Snowling,

2001; Elbro, 1996; Fowler, 1991; Storkel, 2002; Walley, 1993). While proposals differ somewhat in detail, the basic idea underlying these *lexical reorganization hypotheses*, is that the need to keep representations distinct in a growing lexicon forces phonological word forms from initial global or holistic representations toward finer-grained, ultimately phonemic, representations. An explicit assumption of these proposals is that the observable phonological sensitivities of infants (as reflections of their emerging lexical representations) are continuous with and causally related to individual differences in subsequent meta-phonological awareness; developmental and skill-related changes in the degree of meta-phonological ability are driven, at least in part, by growth of the lexicon.

The *lexical quality hypothesis*, spelled out in Perfetti and Hart (2002; Perfetti, 2007; also see Ehri, 1992; Nation & Snowling, 1998) and elaborated in Braze, Tabor, Shankweiler, and Mencl (2007) incorporates the following premises: (a) knowledge of word forms can be partial; (b) word learning is an incremental process so that the quality of representations, both phonological and semantic attributes, changes over time; and (c) activation of stored lexical representations is a graded function of (at least) the perceptual quality of speech or print tokens. Thus, the hypothesis is consonant with dynamical models of lexical representation and access (e.g., Plaut, McClelland, Seidenberg, & Patterson, 1996; Seidenberg & McClelland, 1989). Seen in this light, a further implication of the lexical quality hypothesis is that weak knowledge about one aspect of a word's representation (ranging at least over phonology and semantics, as well as orthography in literate individuals), may be compensated for if a reader/hearer's knowledge of another aspect of the word is relatively strong. Thus, during the apprehension of speech (or print) the accessibility of word knowledge is a function of both the quality of that knowledge and the quality of the signal. A key feature of this hypothesis is that poor quality representations may provide insufficient support for linguistic apprehension in the context of particularly demanding circumstances such as reading, speech perception in noise, or simply decontextualized word recognition.

Perfetti and Hart (2002) have termed this a matter of the "functional identifiability" of words. This entails that aspects of word knowledge that are accessible and usable in some contexts may be inaccessible in other, more challenging, contexts. Functional identifiability may provide the foundation for an explanation of why the same child can more easily demonstrate phoneme awareness in some contexts than in others (e.g., Byrne & Fielding-Barnsley, 1989, experiment 5, 1990, experiment 3). Similarly, it suggests an explanation for why infants are able to discriminate phoneme level detail in some situations and yet fail to use that same level of detail for distinguishing lexical items where comprehension is at issue (e.g., Stager & Werker, 1997; Swingley, 2003). Offering a different explanation, the lexical reorganization hypothesis was put forward in part to explain the developmental progression of phonological awareness, moving from lexical to syllabic to subsyllabic (onset, rhyme and ultimately phoneme) constituents. At present, it is not clear whether the lexical reorganization hypothesis can be subsumed by the lexical quality hypothesis.

In addition to phonological awareness, other reading-related abilities have been identified which, when measured in preliterate children, correlate 1 to 3 years later with reading achievement (typically indexed as decoding skill) at least as well as does phonological awareness (see Scarborough, 1998, 2005, for reviews). These include verbal memory, rapid automatized naming and vocabulary knowledge. Moreover, a few recent studies point to predictive relationships between early phonological development, as gauged by speech perception in infancy, and later language development, including vocabulary knowledge (Espy, Molfese, Molfese, & Modglin, 2004; Leppanen, Pihko, Eklund, & Lyytinen, 1999; Lyytinen et al., 2001; D. L. Molfese, 2000). It is desirable to have a unified theoretical framework able to capture empirically established connections among these constructs, and we will use the Lexical Quality Hypothesis and the Lexical Reorganization Hypothesis to structure our discussion.

Our goals for the remainder of this chapter are first, to selectively review existing work relating to the developmental progression of individual differences in reading-related phonological awareness and underlying phonological capacities (phonological memory, phonological/articulatory fluency, and efficiency of lexical access) in the age range of toddlers and early preschool-aged children; second, to discuss measures of cognitive capacities that have the greatest potential relevance to informing a theory of the development of reading relevant language skills from infancy through maturity. We will then summarize work in our laboratory that we believe holds promise for early identification of individual differences in memory for phonologically structured material and in sensitivity to aspects of phonological structure, in particular, rhyme, in toddlers and infants (Clark, McRoberts, Van Dyke, & Braze, under review; McRoberts & Braze, under review; McRoberts, McDonough, & Lakusta, 2009).

OVERVIEW OF LONGITUDINAL STUDIES OF EARLY LANGUAGE POINTING TOWARD LITERACY

Despite a consensus about the central role of phonological awareness in attaining literacy (Ehri, 2004; Ehri et al., 2001; National Reading Panel, 2000; Scarborough, 1998, 2005; also see Adams, 1990; Anthony & Lonigan, 2004; Share & Stanovich, 1995), little is known about its earliest development or the specific nature of its relationship to other phonologically grounded capacities among the very youngest preliterate children. In fact, most longitudinal studies of precursors to reading ability begin tracking children not much more than a year or so before the onset of formal education, in part because the conventional tests of phoneme awareness and other school-age associates of reading skill are too difficult for toddlers and early preschool-aged children. Because our emphasis here is on potential literacy precursors in toddlerhood and infancy, we will touch but briefly on two longitudinal studies of preschool to grade-school literacy development; both of which are notable for the relatively early initial measurement point, and for the inclusion of children at genetic risk for reading disability. The remainder of this section will survey several studies that relate speech perception in infancy to later language development.

From Preschool Language Skills to Grade-School Literacy

Scarborough (1990) tracked the development of literacy-related skills in children from 30 months to 8 years of age. In an innovative design, two groups of children were recruited according to whether or not they carried family risk of reading disability, operationalized as having a parent or older sibling with poor reading skills despite adequate IQ. In retrospective analyses, Scarborough found that at-risk children who were subsequently identified as reading disabled showed early difficulties with syntactic performance and also made more speech production errors at 30 months of age than their at-risk but non-dyslexic peers. By the third year of life they had also fallen behind in vocabulary development. By 5 years of age, these children showed deficits in phonological awareness and picture naming skills relative to both the at-risk but non-dyslexic group and the control group. There are two remarkable design features of Scarborough's seminal study. The first is the risk-group/non-risk-group aspect of the design, and the second is the early age of the initial measurement point. Other studies using similar risk/non-risk designs have followed, but few have tracked children from such an early age. An exception is the Jyväskylä Longitudinal Study; we will discuss findings from that study in a following section.

Maggie Snowling and colleagues also employed this type of design, collecting three waves of data at about 2-year intervals beginning relatively early at 45 months of age (Snowling, Gallagher, & Frith, 2003). This allowed retrospective comparisons of fairly early preliterate profiles for three groups: at-risk children who ultimately achieved reading skill in the normal range (about 40% of the at-risk sample), at-risk children ultimately diagnosed as reading disabled, and a control group. Those comparisons revealed that, at 45 months of age, at-risk children who later achieved reading skill in the normal range were indistinguishable from controls on most measures, except for an early measure of phonological awareness (rhyme), whereas the at-risk impaired group's performance was below that of the controls (and the unimpaired group) on measures of receptive vocabulary, picture naming, verbal memory, and phonological awareness. By 6 years of age, the at-risk unimpaired group lagged behind controls in verbal memory, but not other factors, while the at-risk impaired group lagged behind both unimpaired and control groups on all measures. Therefore, the results of Snowling and colleagues are consistent with those of Scarborough (1990). An important feature of the Snowling et al. study is its clear demonstration that children who were at risk for reading disability but whose reading abilities fell within the normal range, still showed real impairments in phonologically grounded capacities (verbal memory and phonological awareness) relative to the control group. From their findings, they argued that individuals who express clinically significant levels of reading disability fall in the extreme range of a multivariate continuum, rather than bearing a categorically distinct syndrome. The work of Snowling and colleagues also lent support to earlier proposals of Nation and Snowling (1998) whose research had focused on children with poor reading comprehension despite adequate decoding skill. For this population, they proposed that relative strength or weakness in semantic aspects of word knowledge can serve to moderate individual differences in lexical access via the visual route. Based on their own work, as well as on earlier results such as Scarborough's, Snowling et al. concluded that, rather than a specific consequence of phonological limitations, reading disability is a result of multi-componential deficits, whose early developmental expressions include limitations in vocabulary and grammatical skills. This proposal is very much in accord with our own conceptualization of the lexical quality hypothesis (Braze et al., 2007), and conforms well with a dynamical systems approach to lexical representation and access (e.g., Plaut et al., 1996; Seidenberg & McClelland, 1989).

Predicting Toddler and Preschool Language From Infancy

A few recent studies point to predictive relationships between early phonological development, as gauged by speech perception in infancy, and later language development. These studies have shown that both neurophysiological (Espy et al., 2004; Lyytinen, Ahonen, et al., 2004; Lyytinen et al., 2001; D. L. Molfese, 2000; D. L. Molfese & Molfese, 1997; V. J. Molfese, Molfese, & Modgline, 2001) and behavioral measures (Fernald, Perfors, & Marchman, 2006; Kuhl, Conboy, Padden, Nelson, & Pruitt, 2005; Newman, Ratner, Jusczyk, Jusczyk, & Dow, 2006) of speech perception in the first year to 24 months of life predict a variety of indices of language development in later childhood.

Electrophysiological Studies

Among the more intriguing results in the literature are reports from two longitudinal studies that demonstrate the capacity of electroencephalographic recordings from newborn infants in response to (synthetic) speech signals to predict subsequent language and literacy skills in the preschool and early grade-school years.

In the first of these, Heikki Lyytinen and colleagues (summarized in Lyytinen, Aro, et al., 2004) related both behavioral and neurophysiological measures of speech perception in infancy to reading-related skills in the early grade-school years in the Jyväskalä Longitudinal Study of Dyslexia. Following the work of Scarborough (1990) on American-English-speaking children, this project recruited two groups of Finnish children to participate in the study; those with and those without family risk for dyslexia. Starting at birth, and continuing into the grade-school years, linguistic abilities of participating children were assessed on a number of dimensions, including speech perception in infancy and many acknowledged correlates of reading achievement from early preschool into grade-school. Here, we focus primarily on the relationship of the early neurocognitive measures of speech perception and their associations with subsequent reading-relevant capacities.

As part of the Jyväskalä study, Guttorm and colleagues (Guttorm, Leppanen, Richardson, & Lyytinen, 2001; Guttorm, Leppanen, Tolvanen, & Lyytinen,

2003) measured electroencephalographic (EEG) responses of newborn infants (1–7 days old) exposed to synthetic /ba/, /da/, and /ga/ syllables. These studies identified components of the speech-evoked EEG waveform that distinguished infants at risk for reading disability from those without family risk. The most prominent of these was a pronounced right-hemisphere-positive response to /ga/ syllables from at-risk infants. A follow-up study investigated whether differences in the lateralization of these early EEG waveforms would predict language skills in the preschool years. Guttorm et al. (2005) assessed expressive and receptive language skills at 2.5, 3.5, and 5 years of age; these yielded composite scores that loaded primarily on the lexical and somewhat on the syntactic aspects of comprehension and production. Additionally, measures of verbal memory capacity were collected at 3.5 and 5 years of age. The study found that poorer receptive language skills at 2.5 years of age were associated with increases in the right-hemisphere-positive response to /ga/ syllables in infancy, and that poor verbal memory capacity at 5 years of age was negatively associated with the magnitude of the left-hemisphere-positive response to /ga/ syllables. Regression analyses confirmed that these associations held for both risk groups. The fact that the associations hold for both risk and non-risk groups is consistent with the argument of Snowling and colleagues that RD is not a discrete syndrome.

In another EEG study, Dennis Molfese and Victoria Molfese (D. L. Molfese, 2000; D. L. Molfese & Molfese, 1997; V. J. Molfese et al., 2001; also see D. L. Molfese & Molfese, 1985) identified EEG responses in infants that distinguished between those with good and poor language skills at 3, 5, and 8 years of age. Children were recruited at birth based on their family's willingness to participate and as being either full term and healthy, or as having perinatal complications that required admission to intensive care but of a nature deemed unlikely to produce long-term cognitive difficulties (V. J. Molfese et al.); family risk of reading disability was not assessed in this study. When participating infants were less than 2 days old, they were exposed to synthetically produced syllables, similar to those of the Guttorm study, while EEG responses were recorded. The Molfese stimuli parametrically combined the consonants /b/, /d/, /g/ with the vowels /a/, /i/, /u/, creating nine syllables altogether (D. L. Molfese & Molfese, 1997). Based on a measure of verbal IQ at 5 years of age, children were classified as either high (≥100) or low (<100) language skill. In a discriminant function analysis (DFA), the factors derived from neonatal EEG responses that contributed most to reliable identification of subsequent language skill category fell within two overlapping temporal windows ranging from 70 to 320 ms post-stimulus. Difference scores for the evoked responses to consonants (e.g., the evoked response to syllables beginning with /b/ minus the evoked response to syllables beginning with /g/) at bilateral temporal and right parietal recording sites were most salient in the best fitting DFA, although evoked responses to vowel contrasts also played a role. Ultimately, classification accuracy exceeded 95% for the best model (D. L. Molfese & Molfese).

By 8 years of age, a number of children from this study were observed to meet standard diagnostic criteria for dyslexia whereas two other groups of children were identified either as typically performing readers, or as garden-variety poor readers (D. L. Molfese, 2000). Again, DFA was used to test the accuracy with which 8-year-old children could be identified as typical, poor, or disabled readers based on neonatal EEG components. The best model was able to categorize children with better than 80% accuracy. A third study used hierarchical regression analysis to predict second grade reading skill in a partially overlapping sample of children (V. J. Molfese et al., 2001). In addition to neonatal EEG components, regression models included indicators of socioeconomic status, home environment, IQ, and preschool language abilities, all collected at 3 years of age. For present purposes, the most important finding was that neonatal speech-evoked brain responses were among the significant predictors of second-grade reading skill, even after controlling for measures of environment and language skill collected at age 3.

Behavioral Studies

Several recent studies utilizing behavioral measures of speech perception in infancy have also demonstrated links between early perceptual abilities and later language development. These studies point to relations between several indices of infants' speech perception and later language development, both in the late infancy/toddler period and later into early childhood.

Pat Kuhl and her colleagues (Kuhl et al., 2005; Tsao, Liu, & Kuhl, 2004) report that infants' speech discrimination performance at 7 months is related to word knowledge from 13 to 30 months of age. A developmental decrease in the ability to discriminate phonetic contrasts that are not phonemically relevant in the child's native (or ambient) language is an established feature of the perceptual abilities of infants from about 6 to 12 months of age (e.g., Best & McRoberts, 2003); concordant increases in the ability to discriminate phonetic detail that is relevant to native language phonemic contrasts are not as well established (but see, e.g., Jusczyk, Luce, & Charles-Luce, 1994). Kuhl and colleagues found that discrimination of both native and nonnative speech contrasts as assessed through a conditioned head-turn procedure predicted expressive vocabulary growth through the second and into the third year of life. Specifically, native speech discrimination was positively correlated with vocabulary growth, while nonnative discrimination was negatively correlated with growth in vocabulary.

In two experiments, Newman et al. (2006) related infants' performance on speech perception tasks in their first year of life to later language development. In the first, three tests of infants' speech preferences in the first year of life were used to predict later vocabulary development: (a) preference for passages from a novel language; (b) preference for passages containing words previously familiarized in isolation (i.e., testing infants ability to segment known words from a novel speech stream); and (c) preference for prosodic markers of syntactic structure consistent with familiarized utterances. Results showed that performance on the segmentation test, but not the other two tests, was related to expressive vocabulary at the end of the second year. In a follow-up experiment, a subset of participants was retested on a variety of language and cognitive measures at

4–6 years of age. Newman et al. reported that subjects who had been judged to be successful segmenters as infants had higher overall language quotient scores (including both syntactic and semantic abilities) and higher communicative ability scores (based on parental report). However, there was no difference on a measure of general cognitive ability, indicating that the effect was specific to language development.

Finally, Anne Fernald and her colleagues (e.g., Fernald, McRoberts, & Swingley, 2001; Fernald, Pinto, Swingley, Weinberg, & McRoberts, 1998) examined the development of infants' lexical recognition using both accuracy and speed of processing measures. One important finding from this research is that infants recognize words embedded in sentences incrementally, in the sense that meaning is rapidly extracted from the speech signal, even in advance of it being unambiguously determined. To demonstrate this, Fernald and colleagues measured infants' eye gaze shifts from a distracter picture (e.g., *doggie*) to a target picture (e.g., *baby*), beginning with the onset of a spoken target word (*baby*, in this case). The time to shift gaze to the target image, measured from the onset of the target word provides a reaction time measure of speech processing (Cooper, 1974). When presented with familiar words and target images (e.g., *doggie* versus *baby*), the shift from distracter image to target image can occur within 300 ms for 2-year-old children. This is often before the end of the target word (spoken with prosody typical of child directed speech) and has been interpreted as demonstrating rapid and incremental extraction of meaning from speech. In a subsequent longitudinal study, Fernald et al. (2006) related infants' speech processing efficiency at 25 months, operationalized as time to shift gaze to a target word, with both retrospective and concurrent measures of language development in the second year of life. Correlations between processing speed at 25 months and language measures from 12 to 25 months were generally between $r = -.35$ and $-.48$ (with shorter RTs predicting better language development). Both speed and accuracy measures of spoken word recognition at 25 months were associated with the rate of vocabulary growth between 12 and 25 months. This result provides a link between vocabulary size and the functional identifiability of known words (e.g., Perfetti & Hart, 2002).

Together, these neurobiological and behavioral studies are consistent in showing that infants' speech perception capabilities are related to both concurrent and later language development, especially the rate of expressive vocabulary growth.

STEPS TOWARD EXPLORING LINKS BETWEEN EARLY SPEECH AND SUBSEQUENT LITERACY

In the remainder of this chapter, we will describe work from our own laboratory that we believe moves toward addressing limitations in the ability to track early developmental precursors of literacy-relevant phonological memory and sensitivity to phonological structure.

Sensitivity to Rhyme in Infants and Toddlers

The first study from our own laboratory used a version of the auditory preference procedure to gauge phonological (rhyme) sensitivity in infants and toddlers (McRoberts & Braze, under review). Our study builds on the work of Jusczyk, Goodman, and Baumann (1999), who used the auditory preference procedure (Cooper & Aslin, 1990; McRoberts et al., 2009; Pinto, Fernald, McRoberts, & Cole, 1998) to investigate whether infants categorize consonant—vowel—consonant (CVC) syllables based on shared initial phonemes (consonant or consonant–vowel) or shared final vowel–consonant patterns. They found that 9-month-old infants listened longer to syllable sequences that shared initial consonant or consonant–vowel sequences when compared to sequences with unrelated initial consonant or consonant–vowel sequences. However, they did not find a listening preference for shared final vowel–consonant sequences (i.e., no preference for rhyming syllables). This indicates that 9-month-old infants' attention is drawn to syllable onset information. In turn, the results are compatible with the interpretation that relevant memory traces of CVC syllables include representations of syllable-initial consonants, but that such traces may not be sufficiently detailed to support detection of rhyme similarity (also see Swingley, 2005; Vihman, Nakai, DePaolis, & Halle, 2004).

McRoberts and Braze (under review) investigated the emergence of sensitivity to rhyme in infants and toddlers, also using an auditory preference procedure (described below). We compared childrens' looking times to contrasting sets of rhyming and non-rhyming words. Word lists from six rhyme families (/ɪŋ/, /ɛt/, /ʌn/, /æk/, /an/, /og/) were used, with the words organized into rhyming and non-rhyming sets (as shown in Table 2.1). The non-rhyming sets were made up of one word from each of the rhyming families. Thus, on each trial, children heard a list of words all from one of six rhyming families (e.g., *king*, *ring*, *sing*, *thing*), or from a list of the same words used to form the rhyming lists, but containing only one word from each of the six rhyming families (e.g., *king*, *pet*, *fun*, *pack*).

In the auditory preference procedure used in our laboratory, infants sit on a parent's lap in a small testing booth, facing a computer monitor that displays a checkerboard that serves as a fixation target. At the beginning of each trial, the checkerboard flashes to attract the infant's attention. When the infant fixates on the checkerboard, an observer monitoring the infant's gaze via a video link from a separate room presses a "looking" key on a computer keyboard, initiating the

TABLE 2.1
Examples of Rhyming and Non-Rhyming Trials

Rhyming Trials	Non-Rhyming Trials
1. king, ring, ding, sing, etc.	1. king, hat, run, cake, etc.
2. cat, sat, mat, rat, etc.	2. sat, fun, ding, bake, etc.
3. fun, sun, run, nun, etc.	3. nun, rake, mat, sing, etc.
4. rake, take, cake, bake, etc.	4. take, sun, hat, ring, etc.

trial, and continues to press the "looking" key as long as the child maintains fixation. During the trial, a digitized audio file (in this case, a series of words that either rhyme or do not rhyme) is presented via the computer. The computer also monitors and records the amount of time the "looking" key is pressed. When the "looking" key is up (i.e., the infant is not looking at the checkerboard) for more than 1 s, the trial ends; the sound file stops and the checkerboard is removed. After a brief inter-trial interval, the checkerboard returns, signaling the availability of the next trial. Trials alternate between rhyme and non-rhyme word lists. Accumulated looking times are recorded and averaged across trials to provide mean looking times for each condition.

We used this procedure to test two groups of children for rhyme preference: infants aged 8–9 months and toddlers aged 20–24 months. Each child heard 12 trials, 6 rhyming and 6 non-rhyming, in alternating order. Each child's listening times to the rhyming and non-rhyming trials were entered into a repeated measures ANOVA, with age group as a between-subjects factor and rhyme condition (rhyming, non-rhyming) as a within-subjects factor.

Results indicated a significant Age × Listening Time interaction, readily apparent in Figure 2.1. Further, toddlers listened significantly longer to the rhyming words than to the non-rhyming words, while infants showed no preference. Examination of individual listening times confirmed that almost all the toddlers listened longer to the rhyming trials, but listening times for infants did not differ consistently by trial type (i.e., half listened more to trials in one condition, half to trials in the other). These results are consistent with those of Jusczyk et al. (1999) in showing no sensitivity to word-final VC patterns at

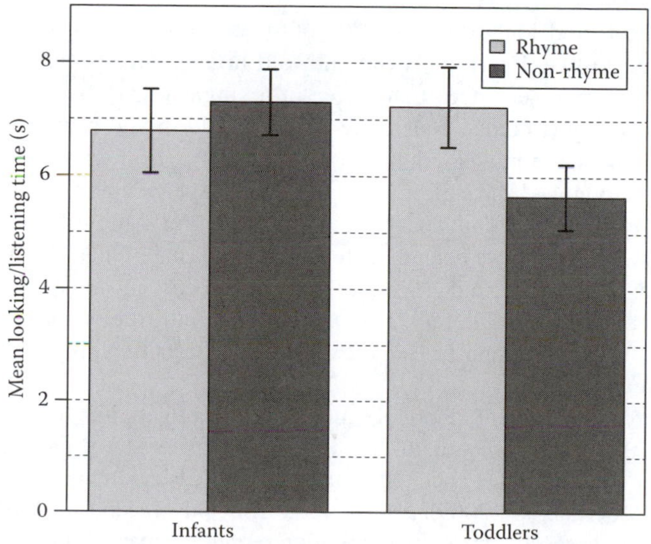

FIGURE 2.1 Mean listening times to rhyming and non-rhyming word lists by 8- to 9-month-old infants and 20- to 24-month-old toddlers.

8–9 months, but suggest that sensitivity to rhyme emerges sometime between 9 and 24 months of age.

Recently, we have begun to pinpoint the age at which rhyme preference typically emerges by testing infants and toddlers between 12 and 24 months of age. Preliminary results suggest that as infants pass 20 months of age, they show a consistent preference for rhyme. Those children who had had a rhyme preference when first tested at a younger age, continued to show a rhyme preference when retested; other toddlers who had not had a preference on initial testing showed a rhyme preference when retested after 20 months. This result holds the promise of a means to assess the early emergence of an aspect of phonological sensitivity and a possible precursor to subsequent phonological awareness abilities.

Verbal Memory in Very Young Children

Infants' emergent phonological systems and their acquisition of a lexicon are likely to be at least partially dependent on the development of memory abilities that provide both short-term and longer term retention of information from the speech signal. Although the early course of development for speech-related memory has not been extensively studied, it is clear that at least rudimentary short-term and even longer term memory for auditory stimuli, including speech, exists prenatally. Fetuses can be habituated to auditory stimuli from 36 weeks of gestation (Hepper & Shahidullah, 1992). Postnatal preferences for speech to which infants were exposed in utero demonstrate relatively long-term retention of some speech information (Decasper & Fifer, 1980; DeCasper & Spence, 1986; Moon, Cooper, & Fifer, 1993).

Both short- and long-term retention of speech information is also evident in the early postnatal period. Two-month-old infants have been shown to discriminate between sentences that differ in a single word after a 2-min post-habituation delay (Mandel, Nelson, & Jusczyk, 1996), and 6-week-old infants who heard the same nursery rhyme over a 12-day period showed evidence of retention as long as 3 days after familiarization (Spence, 1996). These studies provide evidence that infants have the ability to retain some information about speech to which they have been repeatedly exposed (habituated or familiarized) during the perinatal period. However, speech processing must eventually be done online (e.g., Fernald et al., 1998), and these indications from habituation studies fall short of demonstrating the ability to extract meaning from a speech signal in real-time.

Recent results from our laboratory move significantly in that direction by demonstrating that by 5–6 months of age infants have short-term memory for sentences they had heard just once (McDonough, 2003; McDonough & McRoberts, 2003; McRoberts et al., 2009). Using infant-directed speech (i.e., 2–4 syllables, infant-directed prosodic style) in a repetition preference paradigm, infants at 5–6 months showed a preference for immediately repeated utterances over the same utterances arranged without repetition. By 9 months, infants preferred utterances

TABLE 2.2
Examples of Repetition Conditions

I. No Repetition		II. Immediate Repetition		III. Delayed Repetition	
A	Is that funny?	A	Is that funny?	A	Is that funny?
B	Get that fishy.	A′	Is that funny?	B	Get that fishy.
C	Where do these go?	B	Get that fishy.	C	Where do these go?
D	Don't chew on that.	B′	Get that fishy!	A′	Is that funny?
E	Pick up the cup.	C	Where do these go?	D	Don't chew on that.
F	You're OK.	C′	Where do these go?	C′	Where do these go?
G	Turn the page.	D	Don't chew on that.	E	Pick up the cup.
H	Almost done.	D′	Don't chew on that.	D′	Don't chew on that.

that were repeated after two intervening utterances over both no-repetition, and immediate-repetition, conditions.

Sentence material used in this study was selected from transcripts of mother–infant interactions. The utterances were then recorded by a female speaker using prosody typical of infant-directed speech. Multiple tokens of each utterance were produced using different F0 contours identified as common in infant-directed speech (Fernald & Simon, 1984). After acoustic analysis of F0 and duration, final tokens of each utterance were selected and organized into two types of sound files.

One type was made up of non-repeated patterns (e.g., A B C, etc.; Table 2.2, No Repetition pattern). The second type was made up of repeated patterns of utterances, in which different tokens (e.g., A and A′) of the same utterance with different prosodic patterns (e.g., Almost done! and Almost done?) were arranged in repeated patterns (e.g., A A′ B B′ C C′; See Table 2.2, Immediate Repetition Pattern). For example, a series of utterances (e.g., A B C D E F G H) were arranged into two repeated trials in which four utterances were each repeated immediately (e.g., A A′ B B′ C C′ D D′, and E E′ F F′ G G′ H H′) for a total of eight utterances per trial. Later in the session, the same utterances were presented in two control trials (e.g., A B′ C D′ E F′ G H′, and E′ F G′ H A′ B C′ D). Thus, each token of each utterance served as its own control by occurring in both repeated trials and non-repeated trials.

McRoberts et al. (2009) used these stimuli to study preferences of 4- and 6-month-old infants for trials with repeated utterances versus ones without repetition. A significant Age × Repetition Condition interaction indicated that 6-month-old infants had a preference for repeated utterances, demonstrated by longer listening on trials with repetition than on trials without. The younger infants showed no preference for either condition. The fact that the 6-month-old infants detected repeated patterns despite the utterances having different prosodic patterns means they were retaining at least some information about the repeated segmental pattern, and recognized it as familiar after a single presentation. Thus, one factor involved in the emergence of a preference for verbal repetition (between 4 and 6 months of age) might be improvements in speech-related short-term memory.

The role of memory is suggested in another study (McDonough, 2003; McDonough & McRoberts, 2003) in which infants at 5, 7, and 9 months of age were tested for their detection of utterances repeated after a delay. The hypothesis was that older infants would have better short-term verbal memory, which would be seen in a preference for utterances repeated after a delay. Stimuli were prepared as described above, with two tokens of each utterance produced with different prosodic patterns typical of infant-directed speech. A third condition was added to the *no repetition* and *immediate repetition* conditions from the previous experiment. This third condition incorporated *delayed repetition* with two intervening utterances (A B C A′ D C′ E D′). The same tokens of each utterance occurred in all conditions (see Table 2.2).

Infants at each age were tested on all three repetition conditions in a single session. The results showed that 5-month-olds had a significant preference only for the immediately repeated utterances, 7-month-olds had no significant preference, and 9-month-olds had a preference only for utterances repeated after a delay of two intervening utterances. In those age groups showing a preference, 90% of 5-month-olds and 79% of 9-month-olds expressed the preferences characteristic for their age cohort. Within each of those age cohorts, there was a significant correlation between exact infant age and looking times to immediate repetition targets (r =.37) or long delay repetition (r =.21). In a follow-up experiment, 7-month-olds showed a preference for utterances repeated after a short delay of one intervening utterance (A B A′ B′ C D C′ D′, etc.) versus non-repeated utterances. Together, results from these studies point to a means of assessing individual differences in short-term memory for speech in infancy, a significant step beyond assessment of perceptual discrimination.

The experiments just described provide evidence for developmental trends in memory for verbal material. Further, they hold out hope that with an appropriately designed longitudinal study we might be able to connect the surmised developmental trajectory just described to individual differences in verbal memory in the preschool to early grade-school years. At those ages, individual differences on verbal memory measures have been associated with vocabulary acquisition (Avons, Wragg, Cupples, & Lovegrove, 1998; Gathercole & Adams, 1993; Gathercole & Baddeley, 1993; Gathercole, Service, Hitch, Adams, & Martin, 1999), other reading relevant skills, and reading itself (Lonigan, Schatschneider, & Westberg, 2008; Scarborough, 2005).

A recent study from our laboratory measured verbal working memory in preschool children between the ages of 37 and 57 months and demonstrated concurrent associations with emerging phonological awareness. Clark et al. (under review) assessed verbal memory using a novel pseudo-word repetition task and measured phonological awareness using the phonological awareness subtests of the Test of Preschool Early Literacy (TOPEL; Lonigan, Wagner, Torgesen, & Rashotte, 2007). Stimuli for the pseudo-word repetition task were built from two-syllable sequences of trochaic feet (strong–weak syllable combinations). Constituent syllables were

TABLE 2.3
Pseudo-Word Items Consisting of Two Trochaic Feet

Rhyming Items	Non-Rhyming Items
/'bog.zə'hog.zə/	/'mɔit.sə'teiv.də/
/'paif.pə'daif.pə/	/'wig.zə'fum.zə/
/'tiv.bə'kiv.bə/	/'botʃ.tə'deip.sə/

selected to satisfy two sets of constraints. First, in order to minimize articulatory challenges of pseudo-word items their segmental make-up was controlled by excluding consonant phonemes identified by Shriberg and Kwiatkowski (1994) as late acquired (/s/, /z/, /l/, /ɹ/, /ʃ/, /ʒ/, /θ/, /ð/) from items consisting of three or fewer trochees. Strong syllables were paired with weak CV syllables to build trochaic feet. Concatenated sequences of trochaic feet were used to construct two classes of pseudo-words: rhyming and non-rhyming (see Table 2.3). Trochees of rhyming items differed only in the onset of the strong syllable (e.g., /'tiv.bə'kiv.bə/), whereas non-rhyming items differed throughout the first syllable (e.g., /'wig.zə'fum.zə/). Further, because pseudo-word recall is influenced by the wordlikeness of test items (e.g., Gathercole, 1995; Treiman, Goswami, & Bruck, 1990), pseudo-words were matched on this dimension across rhyme conditions by controlling the neighborhood size and summed neighborhood frequency of the strong syllable elements (Rastle, Harrington, & Coltheart, 2002). The test set included items of both rhyme-types starting at a length of two trochaic feet and increasing to a length of six.

Pseudo-words were presented to the children in the context of learning words from a "space language" spoken by a birdlike puppet named "Glerk." Glerk, described as a recent arrival from a distant planet who wants to make friends on Earth, does not speak English, so a translator helps Glerk teach the child some words from his space language. The translator introduces the pseudo-word, a puppeteer for Glerk repeats it, and finally the participating child is asked to say the pseudo-word. (A child's repetitions were accepted as correct if at least the onset consonant in each stressed syllable was produced correctly.) The stimuli became progressively longer on subsequent items. After three consecutive repetition failures in a rhyme condition (rhyme or non-rhyme), that condition was discontinued. Testing in the alternate condition continued until the stop condition was met there. Performance on the two conditions were analyzed; the pertinent result for the present discussion was a significant correlation between pseudo-word repetition and performance on the phonological awareness task ($r = .53$). Although Clark et al. found no difference in memory for rhyming versus non-rhyming pseudo-words in this preschool-aged sample, there is a considerable body of work suggesting that rhyme interference effects do emerge in the grade-school years and that the relative magnitude of these effects is associated with reading skill (e.g., Mark, Shankweiler, Liberman, & Fowler, 1977; Olson, Davidson, Kliegl, & Davies, 1984; Shankweiler, Liberman,

Mark, Fowler, & Fischer, 1979). The availability of controlled pseudo-word materials incorporating a rhyme contrast, together with a delivery protocol suited to very young children opens the door to a more thorough investigation of the earliest developmental trajectory of rhyme interference effects.

In summary, the results from these studies examining verbal memory from infancy through preschool hold the promise for measurement of this and other literacy-related constructs across an age span that encompasses preliterate development and the earliest onset of print knowledge. Of course, verbal memory is not the only prerequisite for reading. Normal oral language development, vocabulary, and phonological awareness are also prerequisites. More research is necessary to attain a complete understanding of the patterns within early language development that presage differences in these skills among preschool-aged and early school-aged children. In future work we will ask whether the language development of children as young as 6 months of age reveals the seeds of individual differences in preschool childrens' readiness for reading instruction and in school-age children's reading skills. For example, we have the tools to ask whether and how development of memory for verbal repetition in the first year of life, and sensitivity to rhyme in the second are related to similar skills in the preschool years, and even to the development of reading skills in grade-school.

CONCLUSIONS

The main goal of this chapter was to sketch evidence that a full understanding of reading-relevant phonological skills requires an account of their development from the earliest stages. We are motivated in this by our conviction that the earliest verbal abilities of infants are continuous with subsequent reading-related phonological abilities of older children. Elucidating the emergence of the phoneme as a functional unit is an important part of the ultimate goal of providing a better account of the development of reading readiness and all features of its foundation. Certainly, other aspects of phonological awareness may be relevant, possibly as stepping stones to phoneme awareness, just as other phonologically grounded capacities like verbal memory certainly play some role. Ultimately, reading readiness is likely the result of a rather definite interweaving of phonologic and cognitive abilities. The challenges of research in this area are real, but not insurmountable. By attending to lessons from both speech research in infancy and toddlerhood and literacy research in the preschool years and beyond, we believe that an improved understanding of the development of these abilities is both possible and worthwhile. The hope is that empirical and theoretical developments in this area will open the door to earlier identification of children at risk for reading failure and inform the development of age-appropriate early interventions.

ACKNOWLEDGMENT

This work was supported in part by National Institutes of Health grants R01 HD40353 and R15 DC005947 to Haskins Laboratories.

REFERENCES

Adams, M. J. (1990). *Beginning to read: Thinking and learning about print*. Cambridge, MA: MIT Press.

Anthony, J. L., & Francis, D. J. (2005). Development of phonological awareness. *Current Directions in Psychological Science*, *14*(5), 255–259.

Anthony, J. L., & Lonigan, C. J. (2004). The nature of phonological awareness: Converging evidence from four studies of preschool and early grade school children. *Journal of Educational Psychology*, *96*(1), 43–55.

Avons, S. E., Wragg, C. A., Cupples, L., & Lovegrove, W. J. (1998). Measures of phonological short term memory and their relationship to vocabulary development. *Applied Psycholinguistics*, *19*(4), 583–601.

Best, C. C., & McRoberts, G. W. (2003). Infant perception of non-native consonant contrasts that adults assimilate in different ways. *Language and Speech*, *46*, 183–216.

Braze, D., Tabor, W., Shankweiler, D. P., & Mencl, W. E. (2007). Speaking up for vocabulary: Reading skill differences in young adults. *Journal of Learning Disabilities*, *40*(3), 226–243.

Byrne, B. (1998). *The foundation of literacy: The child's acquisition of the alphabetic principle*. East Sussex: Psychology Press.

Byrne, B., & Fielding-Barnsley, R. (1989). Phonemic awareness and letter knowledge in the child's acquisition of the alphabetic principle. *Journal of Educational Psychology*, *81*(3), 313–321.

Byrne, B., & Fielding-Barnsley, R. (1990). Acquiring the alphabetic principle—A case for teaching recognition of phoneme identity. *Journal of Educational Psychology*, *82*(4), 805–812.

Carroll, J. M., & Snowling, M. J. (2001). The effects of global similarity between stimuli on children's judgment of rime and alliteration. *Applied Psycholinguistics*, *22*(3), 327–342.

Chaney, C. (1992). Language-development, metalinguistic skills, and print awareness in 3-year-old-children. *Applied Psycholinguistics*, *13*(4), 485–514.

Clark, N. B., McRoberts, G. W., Van Dyke, J. A., Shankweiler, D. P., & Braze, D. (under review). *Immediate memory for pseudowords and phonological awareness are associated in adults and pre-reading children*. Unpublished manuscript, New Haven, CT.

Cooper, R. M. (1974). The control of eye fixation by the meaning of spoken language: A new methodology for the real-time investigation of speech perception, memory, and language processing. *Cognitive Psychology*, *6*(1), 84–107.

Cooper, R. P., & Aslin, R. N. (1990). Preference for infant-directed speech in the first month after birth. *Child Development*, *61*(5), 1584–1595.

Decasper, A. J., & Fifer, W. P. (1980). Of human bonding—Newborns prefer their mothers voices. *Science*, *208*(4448), 1174–1176.

DeCasper, A. J., & Spence, M. J. (1986). Prenatal maternal speech influences newborns' perception of speech sounds. *Infant Behavior and Development*, *9*(2), 133–150.

Diamond, A. (1985). Development of the ability to use recall to guide action, as indicated by infants' performance on A-not-B. *Child Development*, *56*(4), 868.

Ehri, L. C. (1992). Reconceptualizing the development of sight word reading and its relationship to recoding. In P. B. Gough, L. C. Ehri, & R. Treiman (Eds.), *Reading acquisition* (pp. 107–144). Hillsdale, NJ: Lawrence Erlbaum Associates.

Ehri, L. C. (2004). Teaching phonemic awareness and phonics: An explanation of the national reading panel meta-analyses. In P. McCardle, & V. Chhabra (Eds.), *The voice of evidence in reading research* (pp. 153–186). Baltimore, MD: Paul H Brookes Publishing.

Ehri, L. C., Nunes, S. R., Willows, D. M., Schuster, B. V., Yaghoub-Zadeh, Z., & Shanahan, T. (2001). Phonemic awareness instruction helps children learn to read: Evidence from the National Reading Panel's meta-analysis. *Reading Research Quarterly*, *36*(3), 250–287.

Elbro, C. (1996). Early linguistic abilities and reading development: A review and a hypothesis. *Reading and Writing*, *8*(6), 453–485.

Espy, K. A., Molfese, D. L., Molfese, V. J., & Modglin, A. (2004). Development of auditory event-related potentials in young children and relations to word-level reading abilities at age 8 years. *Annals of Dyslexia*, *54*(1), 9–38.

Fernald, A., McRoberts, G. W., & Swingley, D. (2001). Infants' developing competence in understanding and recognizing words in fluent speech. In J. Weissenborn, & B. Hoehle (Eds.), *Approaches to bootstrapping in early language acquisition* (pp. 97–123). Amsterdam, Benjamins.

Fernald, A., Perfors, A., & Marchman, V. A. (2006). Picking up speed in understanding: Speech processing efficiency and vocabulary growth across the 2nd year. *Developmental Psychology*, *42*(1), 98–116.

Fernald, A., Pinto, J. P., Swingley, D., Weinberg, A., & McRoberts, G. W. (1998). Rapid gains in speed of verbal processing by infants in the 2nd year. *Psychological Science*, *9*(3), 228–231.

Fernald, A., & Simon, T. (1984). Expanded intonation contours in mothers' speech to newborns. *Developmental Psychology*, *20*(1), 104–113.

Fowler, A. E. (1991). How early phonological development might set the stage for phoneme awareness. In S. A. Brady, & D. P. Shankweiler (Eds.), *Phonological processes in literacy: A tribute to Isabelle Y. Liberman* (pp. 97–117). Hillsdale, NJ: Erlbaum.

Gathercole, S. E. (1995). Nonword repetition: More than just a phonological output task. *Cognitive Neuropsychology*, *12*(8), 857–861.

Gathercole, S. E., & Adams, A. M. (1993). Phonological working memory in very young children. *Developmental Psychology*, *29*(4), 770–778.

Gathercole, S. E., & Baddeley, A. D. (1993). Phonological working memory: A critical building block for reading development and vocabulary acquisition? *European Journal of Psychology of Education*, *8*(3), 259–272.

Gathercole, S. E., Service, E., Hitch, G. J., Adams, A. M., & Martin, A. J. (1999). Phonological short-term memory and vocabulary development: Further evidence on the nature of the relationship. *Applied Cognitive Psychology*, *13*(1), 65–77.

Goswami, U. (2002). Phonology, reading development, and dyslexia: A cross-linguistic perspective. *Annals of Dyslexia*, *52*, 141–163.

Guttorm, T. K., Leppanen, P. H., Richardson, U., & Lyytinen, H. (2001). Event-related potentials and consonant differentiation in newborns with familial risk for dyslexia. *Journal of Learning Disabilities*, *34*(6), 534–544.

Guttorm, T. K., Leppanen, P. H. T., Poikkeus, A.-M., Eklund, K. M., Lyytinen, P., & Lyytinen, H. (2005). Brain event-related potentials (ERPs) measured at birth predict later language development in children with and without familial risk for dyslexia. *Cortex*, *41*(3), 291–303.

Guttorm, T. K., Leppanen, P. H. T., Tolvanen, A., & Lyytinen, H. (2003). Event-related potentials in newborns with and without familial risk for dyslexia: Principal component analysis reveals differences between the groups. *Journal of Neural Transmission*, *110*(9), 1059–1074.

Hepper, P. G., & Shahidullah, S. (1992). Habituation in normal and Down's syndrome fetuses. *The Quarterly Journal of Experimental Psychology Section B: Comparative and Physiological Psychology*, *44*(3), 305–317.

Jusczyk, P. W., Goodman, M. B., & Baumann, A. (1999). Nine-month-olds' attention to sound similarities in syllables. *Journal of Memory and Language*, *40*(1), 62–82.

Jusczyk, P. W., Luce, P. A., & Charles-Luce, J. (1994). Infants' sensitivity to phonotactic patterns in the native language. *Journal of Memory and Language*, *33*(5), 630–645.

Kuhl, P. K., Conboy, B. T., Padden, D., Nelson, T., & Pruitt, J. (2005). Early speech perception and later language development: Implications for the "critical period." *Language Learning and Development*, *1*(3), 237–264.

Lalonde, C. E., & Werker, J. F. (1995). Cognitive influences on cross-language speech perception in infancy. *Infant Behavior and Development*, *18*(4), 459–475.

Leppanen, P. H., Pihko, E., Eklund, K. M., & Lyytinen, H. (1999). Cortical responses of infants with and without a genetic risk for dyslexia: II. Group effects. *Neuroreport*, *10*(5), 969–973.

Liberman, A. M. (1999). The reading researcher and the reading teacher need the right theory of speech. *Scientific Studies of Reading*, *3*(2), 95–111.

Lonigan, C. J., Schatschneider, C., & Westberg, L. (2008). Identification of children's skills and abilities linked to later outcomes in reading, writing, and spelling. In The National Early Literacy Panel (Ed.), *Developing early literacy: Report of the national early literacy panel* (pp. 55–106). Washington, DC: The National Institute for Literacy.

Lonigan, C. J., Wagner, R. K., Torgesen, J. K., & Rashotte, C. (2007). *TOPEL: Test of Preschool Early Literacy*. Austin, TX: Pro-Ed, Inc.

Lyytinen, H., Ahonen, T., Eklund, K., Guttorm, T., Kulju, P., Laakso, M. L., et al. (2004). Early development of children at familial risk for dyslexia—Follow-up from birth to school age. *Dyslexia*, *10*(3), 146–178.

Lyytinen, H., Ahonen, T., Eklund, K., Guttorm, T. K., Laakso, M. L., Leinonen, S., et al. (2001). Developmental pathways of children with and without familial risk for dyslexia during the first years of life. *Developmental Neuropsychology*, *20*(2), 535–554.

Lyytinen, H., Aro, M., Eklund, K., Erskine, J., Guttorm, T., Laakso, M.-L., et al. (2004). The development of children at familial risk for dyslexia: Birth to early school age. *Annals of Dyslexia*, *54*(2), 184–220.

MacLean, M., Bryant, P., & Bradley, L. (1987). Rhymes, nursery rhymes, and reading in early-childhood. *Merrill-Palmer Quarterly-Journal of Developmental Psychology*, *33*(3), 255–281.

Mandel, D. R., Nelson, D. G., & Jusczyk, P. W. (1996). Infants remember the order of words in a spoken sentence. *Cognitive Development*, *11*(2), 181–196.

Mark, L. S., Shankweiler, D., Liberman, I. Y., & Fowler, C. A. (1977). Phonetic recoding and reading difficulty in beginning readers. *Memory and Cognition*, *5*, 623–629.

Mattingly, I. G. (1972). Reading, the linguistic process, and linguistic awareness. In J. F. Kavanagh, & I. G. Mattingly (Eds.), *Language by ear and by eye* (pp. 133–147). Cambridge, MA: MIT Press.

McCardle, P., Scarborough, H. S., & Catts, H. W. (2001). Predicting, explaining, and preventing children's reading difficulties. *Learning Disabilities Research & Practice*, *16*(4), 230–239.

McDonough, C. (2003). *Preference for verbal repetition: Evidence of auditory short-term memory in 5- to 9-month old infants*. Unpublished master's thesis, Lehigh University, Bethlehem, PA.

McDonough, C., & McRoberts, G. W. (2003). *The development of auditory–verbal short-term memory*. Paper presented at the Society for Research in Child Development.

McRoberts, G. W., & Braze, D. (under review). *Infants' sensitivity to rhyming words: The emergence of phonological awareness*. Unpublished manuscript, New Haven, CT.

McRoberts, G. W., McDonough, C., & Lakusta, L. (2009). The role of verbal repetition in the development of infant speech preferences from 4 to 14 months of age. *Infancy*, *14*(2), 162–194.

Metsala, J. L., & Walley, A. C. (1998). Spoken vocabulary growth and the segmental restructuring of lexical representations: Precursors to phonemic awareness and early reading ability. In J. L. Metsala, & L. C. Ehri (Eds.), *Word recognition in beginning literacy* (pp. 89–120). Mahweh, NJ: Erlbaum.

Molfese, D. L. (2000). Predicting dyslexia at 8 years of age using neonatal brain responses. *Brain and Language*, *72*(3), 238–245.

Molfese, D. L., & Molfese, V. J. (1985). Electrophysiological indices of auditory discrimination in newborn infants: The bases for predicting later language development? *Infant Behavior and Development*, *8*(2), 197–211.

Molfese, D. L., & Molfese, V. J. (1997). Discrimination of language skills at five years of age using event-related potentials recorded at birth. *Developmental Neuropsychology*, *13*(2), 135–156.

Molfese, V. J., Molfese, D. L., & Modgline, A. A. (2001). Newborn and preschool predictors of second-grade reading scores: An evaluation of categorical and continuous scores. *Journal of Learning Disabilities*, *34*(6), 545–554.

Moon, C., Cooper, R. P., & Fifer, W. P. (1993). 2-Day-olds prefer their native language. *Infant Behavior and Development*, *16*(4), 495–500.

Nation, K., & Snowling, M. J. (1998). Semantic processing and the development of word-recognition skills: Evidence from children with reading comprehension difficulties. *Journal of Memory and Language*, *39*(1), 85–101.

National Reading Panel. (2000). *Teaching children to read: An evidence-based assessment of the scientific research literature on reading and its implications for reading instruction* (NIH Publication No. 00-4769). Washington, DC: National Institutes of Health.

Newman, R., Ratner, N. B., Jusczyk, A. M., Jusczyk, P. W., & Dow, K. A. (2006). Infants' early ability to segment the conversational speech signal predicts later language development: A retrospective analysis. *Developmental Psychology*, *42*(4), 643–655.

NICHD Early Child Care Research Network. (2005). Pathways to reading: The role of oral language in the transition to reading. *Developmental Psychology*, *41*(2), 428–442.

Olson, R. K., Davidson, B. J., Kliegl, R., & Davies, S. E. (1984). Development of phonetic memory in disabled and normal readers. *Journal of Experimental Child Psychology*, *37*(1), 187–206.

Perfetti, C. A. (2007). Reading ability: Lexical quality to comprehension. *Scientific Studies of Reading*, *11*(4), 357–383.

Perfetti, C. A., & Hart, L. (2002). The lexical quality hypothesis. In L. Verhoeven (Ed.), *Precursors of functional literacy* (pp. 189–213). Philadelphia, PA: John Benjamins.

Pinto, J. P., Fernald, A., McRoberts, G. W., & Cole, S. (1998). Reliability and validity in infant auditory preference procedures. In C. Rovee-Collier, L. P. Lipsitt, & H. Hayne (Eds.), *Advances in infancy research* (Vol. 12, pp. 221–236). Stamford, CT: Ablex.

Plaut, D. C., McClelland, J. L., Seidenberg, M. S., & Patterson, K. (1996). Understanding normal and impaired word reading: Computational principles in quasi regular domains. *Psychological Review*, *103*(1), 56–115.

Rastle, K., Harrington, J., & Coltheart, M. (2002). 358,534 nonwords: The ARC nonword database. *Quarterly Journal of Experimental Psychology: Human Experimental Psychology*, *55A*(4), 1339–1362.

Scarborough, H. S. (1990). Very early language deficits in dyslexic children. *Child Development*, *61*(6), 1728–1743.

Scarborough, H. S. (1998). Early identification of children at risk for reading disabilities. In B. K. Shapiro, P. J. Accardo, & A. J. Capute (Eds.), *Specific reading disability: A view of the spectrum* (pp. 75–119). Timonium, MD: York Press.

Scarborough, H. S. (2005). Developmental relationships between language and reading: Reconciling a beautiful hypothesis with some ugly facts. In H. W. Catts, & A. G. Kamhi (Eds.), *The connections between language and reading disabilities* (pp. 3–24). Mahwah, NJ: Lawrence Erlbaum.

Seidenberg, M. S., & McClelland, J. L. (1989). A distributed, developmental model of word recognition and naming. *Psychological Review*, *96*(4), 523–568.

Shankweiler, D., Liberman, I. Y., Mark, L. S., Fowler, C. A., & Fischer, F. W. (1979). The speech code and learning to read. *Journal of Experimental Psychology: Human Learning and Memory*, *5*(6), 531–544.

Share, D. L., & Stanovich, K. E. (1995). Cognitive processes in early reading development: Accommodating individual differences into a model of acquisition. *Issues in Education*, *1*(1), 1–57.

Shriberg, L. D., & Kwiatkowski, J. (1994). Developmental phonological disorders I: A clinical profile. *Journal of Speech and Hearing Research*, *37*(5), 1100–1128.

Snowling, M. J., Gallagher, A., & Frith, U. (2003). Family risk of dyslexia is continuous: Individual differences in the precursors of reading skill. *Child Development*, *74*(2), 358–373.

Spence, M. J. (1996). Young infants' long-term auditory memory: Evidence for changes in preference as a function of delay. *Developmental Psychobiology*, *29*(8), 685–695.

Stager, C. L., & Werker, J. F. (1997). Infants listen for more phonetic detail in speech perception than in word-learning tasks. *Nature*, *388*(6640), 381.

Storkel, H. L. (2002). Restructuring of similarity neighbourhoods in the developing mental lexicon. *Journal of Child Language*, *29*(2), 251–274.

Swingley, D. (2003). Phonetic detail in the developing lexicon. *Language and Speech*, *46*(2/3), 265–294.

Swingley, D. (2005). 11-Month-olds' knowledge of how familiar words sound. *Developmental Science*, *8*(5), 432–443.

Tomlinson-Keasey, C., Eisert, D. C., Kahle, L. R., Hardy-Brown, K., & Keasey, B. (1979). The structure of concrete operational thought. *Child Development*, *50*(4), 1153–1163.

Treiman, R., Goswami, U., & Bruck, M. (1990). Not all nonwords are alike—Implications for reading development and theory. *Memory & Cognition*, *18*(6), 559–567.

Tsao, F.-M., Liu, H.-M., & Kuhl, P. K. (2004). Speech perception in infancy predicts language development in the second year of life: A longitudinal study. *Child Development*, *75*(4), 1067–1084.

Tunmer, W. E., Herriman, M. L., & Nesdale, A. R. (1988). Metalinguistic abilities and beginning reading. *Reading Research Quarterly*, *23*(2), 134–158.

Vihman, M. M., Nakai, S., DePaolis, R. A., & Halle, P. (2004). The role of accentual pattern in early lexical representation. *Journal of Memory and Language*, *50*(3), 336–353.

Vygotsky, L. S. (1962). *Thought and language* (E. Hanfmann & G. Vakar, Trans.). Cambridge, MA: MIT Press.

Walley, A. C. (1993). The role of vocabulary development in children's spoken word recognition and segmentation ability. *Developmental Review*, *13*(3), 286–350.

Walley, A. C., Metsala, J. L., & Garlock, V. M. (2003). Spoken vocabulary growth: Its role in the development of phoneme awareness and early reading ability. *Reading and Writing*, *16*(1), 5–20.

3 On the Role of Phonology in Reading Acquisition
The Self-Teaching Hypothesis

David L. Share
University of Haifa

INTRODUCTION

First, I would like to ask the reader to read the following short passage:

> In the middle of Australia is the hottest town in the world. This town is called Sloak and it's right in the middle of the desert. In Sloak, the temperature can reach 60 degrees Celsius. It's so hot that even the flies drop dead and the rubber tires on the cars start to melt. You can even fry an egg on the roof of your car. The houses in Sloak are under the ground, far away from the heat of the sun. The people also dig for gold deep under the ground. In Sloak, they drink lots of beer to stay cool. They drink beer in the morning, in the afternoon, and in the evening. The beer in Sloak is very strong. If you're not used to drinking beer you'd better watch out!
>
> Would you like to live in Sloak?

Without looking back at the text, look carefully at the following two spellings—*SLOAK/SLOKE*. Which do you think was the name of the town in the story? It turns out that skilled adult readers and young inexperienced readers alike demonstrate a surprisingly strong preference for the original spelling. This occurs despite the fact that both spellings can be shown to be equally "wordlike." And even when the alternative spelling *Sloke* replaces *Sloak* as the original spelling in the story, the advantage for this alternative spelling remains just as strong (Share, 1999).

The evidence reviewed in this chapter shows that, not only are able readers remarkably adept at recognizing the original spelling, but this newly acquired knowledge is manifest in a variety of tasks including regular pen-and-paper spelling, and also naming times—the original spelling is consistently pronounced more quickly and with fewer errors than the alternate unseen spelling.

This learning also seems to occur surprisingly rapidly; there were only six occurrences of the "target" word (*Sloak*) in the passage presented previously, but even a single presentation may be sufficient to get the learning process underway (Share, 2004).

No less remarkable is the durability of this learning. The data collected in a variety of languages (including English, Dutch, and Hebrew) clearly show that if the spelling choice task had been delayed until after the reader had finished reading this chapter, the choices would be no less impressive. In fact, in another week (or even another month) the reader would probably still be able to recognize the original spelling well above chance levels. A growing number of studies now indicate that this process of picking up these so-called visual-orthographic forms of new words, "orthographic learning," is a surprisingly rapid and resilient process.

In this chapter, I ask how this learning comes about, focusing on a particular theory of orthographic learning, the self-teaching hypothesis. In the first section, I provide an exposition of the theory. This is followed by a review of the empirical studies that I and others have undertaken to test the hypothesis. But why all the fuss about spellings in an age where "correct" spelling seems out of vogue? What difference does it make if we remember *Sloak* rather than *Sloke*? The answer is that it is not really about spelling but about *reading*, indeed, the very foundations of skilled reading, text understanding, and ultimately literacy.

The Crucial Role of Orthographic Learning in the Acquisition of Skilled Reading

Perhaps the single most distinctive characteristic of skilled reading is the sheer speed and apparent effortlessness with which readers identify printed words. Such accomplished word recognition depends on the accumulation of a large mental store of printed word forms ("representations"), each encapsulating the knowledge that a particular configuration of letters such as *Sloak* (as opposed to other similar-looking ones such as *Slook*, *Slack*, *Stork*, etc.) is the written form of a word identified in speech as "sloak" and referring to the name of a mythical outback Australian town. The skilled reader has at his or her disposal thousands of these so-called internal orthographic representations, not to mention a good general knowledge of orthographic (spelling) conventions. There is a broad consensus that orthographic representations specifying the identity and order of a word's letters (Ehri, 1992; Perfetti, 1992) and tightly linked to word identity—a word's phonology, meaning (and more)—are crucial to skilled reading and that compiling this orthographic knowledge is one of the main challenges for the novice reader. Orthographic learning, therefore, is one of the cornerstones of print processing.

But how do readers manage to compile such impressive repositories of orthographic knowledge? This brings us to the self-teaching hypothesis—a theory about the role of phonology in learning to read.

THE SELF-TEACHING THEORY OF ORTHOGRAPHIC LEARNING

According to the self-teaching hypothesis (Firth, 1972; Jorm & Share, 1983; Share, 1995), the ability to translate newly encountered unfamiliar printed words into their spoken equivalents ("phonological recoding" or simply "decoding") is the central means by which readers acquire orthographic representations.* Each successful decoding of a new word is assumed to provide an opportunity to acquire the word-specific orthographic information that is the foundation of skilled visual word recognition. Exhaustive phonological recoding is assumed to be critical for the formation of well-specified orthographic representations because it draws the reader's attention to the graphemic detail, the order and identity of the letters, and how they map onto the phonological representation, that is, the spoken form (see Ehri, 1992, 2005; Perfetti, 1992). In this way, phonological recoding functions as a self-teaching mechanism or built-in teacher enabling a child to independently develop the word-specific orthographic knowledge necessary for skilled reading.

The self-teaching idea is a little unconventional in that the process of orthographic learning is assumed to take place unintentionally, as a by-product of the process of decoding. It is important to note too that the available evidence (see Share, 1995, for detailed discussion) disputes the claim that a meaningful proportion of the identities of the many thousands of new printed words can be directly taught or can be guessed on the basis of contextual information. Only decoding seems to offer a sufficiently reliable means for identifying novel letter strings thereby providing the opportunities for (incidental) learning of the visual-orthographic form of these items.

SOME HISTORICAL BACKGROUND AND A PARADOX

At the time when the self-teaching notion was first conceived (see Firth, 1972), the importance of phonology and phonological recoding in reading and reading acquisition was largely unappreciated (but see Shankweiler & Liberman, 1972). Phonological recoding was seen by most solely as a back-up mechanism for word recognition when "direct" visual recognition failed (e.g., Coltheart, 1978; McCusker, Hillinger, & Bias, 1981). The dominant conceptual framework at the time was the classic "either-or" dual-route notion of two independent routes (now eschewed by Coltheart in favor of a more synergistic "two-hoses-filling-a-bucket" notion, see Coltheart, 2005). Because the focus of traditional dual-route theorizing was the skilled reader who already possessed extensive orthographic knowledge, this back-up route clearly had only a subsidiary status in skilled word

---

* In the present chapter (see also Share, 1995, footnote 1, p. 152), the term phonological recoding does *not* imply any particular procedure but is used as an umbrella term for the process of print to sound conversion by whatever means this is accomplished. This covers various possibilities including (but not necessarily limited to) explicit letter-by-letter application of grapheme–phoneme correspondence rules, an analogical activation-synthesis mechanism (see, e.g., Glushko, 1979), an implicit statistical learning mechanism, or automatic activation of a distributed (connectionist) network of simple neuron-like units. Although often misinterpreted in this way, the self-teaching hypothesis does *not* imply that orthographic learning is solely the product of the first of these procedures. Furthermore, the nature of this process will undoubtedly vary developmentally and across orthographies.

recognition, although there was a broad agreement that, for the beginning reader, phonology was somehow more important (e.g., Barron, 1986; Doctor & Coltheart, 1980) because, among less experienced readers, many more words were familiar by sound, but unfamiliar by sight. But, even here, the few developmental studies that had been undertaken did not provide convincing evidence for a major role for phonology among young readers (e.g., Barron & Baron, 1977; Condry, McMahon-Rideout, & Levy, 1979; Rader, 1975).

The self-teaching notion was originally conceived by a doctoral student named Ian Firth, one of a long line of researchers (both preceding and succeeding him) to discover, or rather rediscover, the remarkable power of pseudo-word naming to discriminate good from poor readers. Firth proposed that the ability to convert letters into sound as a means to pronounce unfamiliar words (phonological recoding) was the way a child built up the range of words recognized by "sight." Thus, decoding was the key to reading acquisition and the development of a child's sight or reading vocabulary. At this point in the history of developmental reading research, the phonological deficit hypothesis was virtually unknown, and visual/perceptual theories (eventually laid to rest some years later by Vellutino, 1979) were preeminent. Firth's pseudo-word naming data, therefore, was an unexpected finding that needed explanation in an era of visual/perceptual theories of reading difficulties.

Developing the self-teaching notion, Jorm and Share (1983) pointed to a growing body of findings indicating a major role for print-to-sound translation in written language processing, and, more generally, the processing of spoken language (perception, learning, and memory for speech-based information; see also Jorm, 1983). Like Firth, Jorm and Share (1983) were puzzled by the apparent contradiction, or paradox, between predominantly visual/non-phonological skilled word recognition favored at the time (Coltheart, 1978; Glushko, 1979; Kay & Marcel, 1981; McCusker et al., 1981) and a growing body of developmental evidence pointing to a central role for phonology in reading (e.g., Bradley & Bryant, 1983; Goldstein, 1976; Liberman, Shankweiler, Fischer, & Carter, 1974). The self-teaching idea was a way to resolve this (apparent) paradox. It was conceded that visual word recognition, at least among skilled readers, and at least for familiar words, was largely if not exclusively a visual process* but that the acquisition of this knowledge base was largely the result of decoding encounters with new words, that is, of phonological recoding. Jorm and Share stressed that children continually encounter unfamiliar words, and consequently require a means for independently identifying these orthographic newcomers, which are too abundant to be taught on a one-by-one rote-learning basis (the "direct instruction" option) and could not be guessed accurately enough on the basis of contextual information (for reasons elaborated in Share, 1995). This left only the recoding mechanism to fulfill the "self-teaching" function of enabling children to independently decipher novel letter strings and, in the spirit of paired-associate learning, permit bonding of the visual form of the word to its spoken and semantic forms.

* Today, the pendulum seems to have swung back toward a much stronger phonological position (see, e.g., Frost, 1998; Perfetti, 2003; Van-Orden, Pennington, & Stone, 1990).

At first, the proposed self-teaching process was conceptualized in rather mechanistic/behavioristic terms as a "learning trial" in which successful decoding of a printed word permitted associative pairing of the new visual form with its spoken form and meaning (see Jorm & Share, 1983). This paired-associate learning process, like the dominant dual-route model, was rather vague about what actually was acquired. The emphasis was on the *how* of orthographic learning, rather than *what* was actually learned. Jorm and Share were at pains to point out that natural text is replete with low-frequency words not only for beginning readers but also for more experienced readers (see also Foorman, Francis, Davidson, Harm, & Griffin, 2004). Share (1995), however, noted that, at some point, *every* printed word, even a child's own name, is unfamiliar visually.* Thus, self-teaching, it was argued, was relevant to the process of learning almost *every* printed word.†

A subsequent conception of the self-teaching idea recast the self-teaching function of phonological recoding within the broader more universalistic framework of a transition from initial identification (decoding) of unfamiliar words to their rapid recognition as familiar units (see Share, 2008b). I argued that this "unfamiliar-to-familiar" transition (seen from the perspective of individual items) or (from the reader's perspective) "novice-to-expert" transition represents a fundamental and overarching duality in word reading that applies to *all* words in *all* possible orthographies.

On the one hand, because *all* words are novel at some point in reading development, the reader must possess some algorithm, albeit imperfect, yet nonetheless functional, for *independently* identifying words encountered for the first time in everyday reading. On the other hand, and again a literacy universal, the reader must eventually be able to achieve a high degree of automatization in word recognition, that is, rapid and effortless recognition of familiar words and morphemes (LaBerge & Samuels, 1974; Logan, 1997, 2002; Perfetti, 1985; Rayner, 1998; van der Leij & van Daal, 1999) perceived as whole units via a direct-retrieval mechanism (see Ans, Carbonnel, & Valdois, 1998; Weekes, 1997). Here is where the well-specified "autonomous" orthographic representations discussed previously are crucial (Perfetti, 1992). This ability to automatize or "modularize" word identification (Adams, 1990; Stanovich, 1990, 2000) is probably the quintessence of reading *skill* (Perfetti, 1985, 1994). As with the decoding algorithm, this high-speed direct-retrieval mode applies to *all* words in *all* orthographies.

This universalistic dualism has several advantages over the traditional Coltheart/Baron dual-route approach (Baron, 1977; Coltheart, 1978) that focuses primarily on the distinction between regular and irregular words rather than familiar and unfamiliar words. First, it merges the study of reading with the study of human skill learning across a range of domains (see, e.g., Anderson, 1981;

---

* Until recently my own name, printed in the original Czech, complete with haček-Šer, was visually unfamiliar.

† This is almost but not quite correct. The most frequent 100 or so words in printed English (*was, is, are, to, of*) are extraordinarily irregular but pop up in almost every phrase—hence may best be learned or taught whole-word rote style.

Goldstone, 1998; Karni, 1996; LaBerge & Brown, 1989; Logan, 1988; Newell & Rosenbloom, 1981; Shiffrin & Schneider, 1977; Siegler, 1988; Venezky, 2006). The dualism common to all skill learning is a contrast between, or transition from, slow, deliberating, step-by-step unskilled performance to rapid automatized one-step or "unitized" skilled performance without which the "skill" of reading would probably never have made so profound an impact on modern knowledge-based cultures (D. R. Olson, 1994). Second, this broader "novice/expert" or "unfamiliar/familiar" dualism also converges with the dualistic nature of an efficient orthography. Specifically, an efficient script can be conceptualized as a compromise between the often competing needs of the novice and the expert reader (Rogers, 1995; Venezky, 2007). This orthographic dualism might be termed the "decipherability/automatizability" criterion.

An effective orthography must first provide the reader with a means for deciphering new words *on their own*. This applies to both the young child new to the world of print and to the skilled reader encountering a new or unfamiliar word. Furthermore, and this is crucial to skill learning in all domains, this algorithmic process must lay the foundations for the rapid direct-retrieval mechanism. This "do-it-yourself" or "self-teaching" function of decoding is probably the chief virtue of alphabetic scripts, supplying not only an economical means for identifying new words (via print to sound translation), but, critically, establishing the detailed orthographic representations on which rapid fully unitized skilled word recognition is founded. Secondly, a successful script must also answer to the needs of the expert by providing visually distinctive word-specific (or morpheme-specific) visual-orthographic configurations required for the unitization and automatization of skilled word recognition. Ideally, each morpheme should have one and only one representation (morpheme "constancy") without showing morphophonemic variation (e.g., *electric/electricity/electrician*), with different morphemes represented differently (morpheme "distinctiveness") (Rogers, 1995).[*,†]

A script catering primarily to the needs of skilled readers, such as the pre-communist Chinese characters (and in many respects English orthography; see Chomsky & Halle, 1968) will pose enormous challenges for the novice. Conversely, a script providing maximum decipherability for the novice, for example, Korean hangul, Japanese kana, or highly regular teaching alphabets such as Pitman's Initial Teaching Alphabet will often fail (as a stand-alone script) to meet the needs of the skilled reader, primarily owing to homophony. (Consider the problems incurred if *site* and *sight* shared the same spelling.)

---

* English is faithful to the distinctiveness principle in its heterographic homophones (blue/blew) but not in the large numbers of polysemous (homographic) homophones (*well*(of water)/*well* (adverbial good)/*well* (tears welled up)) or the relatively rare heterophonic homographs (*wind/wind*).

† There are clearly advantages for a script that also maintains morpheme "constancy," that is, the same morpheme always written the same way, but it may be morpheme *distinctiveness* that is crucial for the automatization of word recognition. In other words, it's not that the *w* in *two* is important for revealing morphemic relations (e.g., *twelve, twice, twilight*), a highly doubtful assumption for the young reader, but that this etymological quirk provides distinct spellings for potentially confusable homophones (*too/two/to*).

To sum up, the alphabetic code furnishes the necessary algorithm—a self-teaching mechanism permitting independent identification by means of decoding that lays the foundations for the skilled reader's word recognition expertise via the establishment of autonomous orthographic representations. Four central features of the self-teaching theory are reviewed in the following sections.

Self-Teaching Is Item Based, Not Stage Based

In their earlier review of the (inconclusive) evidence for and against ("phonological" versus "visual") stage models of word recognition development of the sort reviewed by Barron (1986), Jorm and Share (1983) proposed that many of the conflicting findings might be resolved by considering item familiarity—high-frequency words can be rapidly recognized visually (with minimal phonology) but unfamiliar items depend more on phonology. They suggested that the pertinent question was not how children identify words, but how they identify *which* words. Because word-specific orthographic knowledge is acquired so quickly (Hogaboam & Perfetti, 1978; Reitsma, 1983; Share, 1999, 2004), even among inexperienced readers, words seem to be rapidly assimilated to a child's reading or so-called sight vocabulary. This implies that at any one point, a child will be reading some words (the most common) rapidly via primarily direct visual/orthographic recognition, whereas other less familiar words are processed primarily phonologically.*

Furthermore, this item-based learning appears to begin very early (consistent with the early onset hypothesis, described subsequently) and may well be a never-ending process because unfamiliar printed words are continually being encountered even by skilled readers. The unfamiliar-to-familiar transition discussed previously implies experiential item-by-item learning. This aligns well with instance-based theories of learning such as Logan's (1988) and the multi-trace computational model of skilled reading of Ans et al. (1998), which see the process of learning as highly dependent on "episodic" encounters with specific stimuli. In the Ans et al. model, for example, the "default" mode of word recognition for familiar words is global (whole word or lexical), but for unfamiliar words is analytic (either at the syllable or letter level). (It remains to be seen to what extent this global/analytic dichotomy aligns with the phonological/orthographic dichotomy.) Once again, the key element in this learning process, as with all skill learning, is the unfamiliar-to-familiar, unskilled-to-skilled transition. Of course, recognition strategies at the level of individual words could, if one insists, be conceived of as a "stage-like" progression from one strategy or mode to another (see the below footnote), but not at the level of reading in general as

* More recent evidence suggests that phonology is an ever-present aspect of word recognition even among skilled readers (Frost, 1998; Perfetti, 2003). It appears that the "dichotomous" thinking inherent in stage models (either visual or phonological) is less accurate than a conceptualization that sees both processes (phonological and visual/orthographic) simultaneously involved in word recognition but with different relative weights depending on item familiarity (Coltheart, 2005; Frost, 1998).

in traditional stage theories (see, e.g., Frith, 1985). The emphasis on item-level changes, however, does not preclude developmental changes in the process of deciphering new words—these are captured by the concept of "lexicalization" described in the next section.

Lexicalization

Many discussions of the reading process seem to imply that phonological recoding is a single unvarying routine or set of routines (e.g., Barron, 1986; Coltheart, 1978, 2005). In contrast, the notion of lexicalization regards phonological recoding as a developmental process, particularly among English-language speakers/readers for whom this learning process probably stretches on indefinitely. The evidence reviewed by Share (1995) indicates that most English-language readers start out with a relatively simple set of one-to-one letter–sound correspondences that are relatively insensitive to orthographic and morphemic context (see, e.g., Zinna, Liberman, & Shankweiler, 1986). These initial correspondences are often invariant and therefore strictly speaking, incorrect. Yet, they offer the novice a manageable set of correspondences capable of generating an approximation to an identifiable pronunciation that can be checked for contextual "goodness of fit." With increased print exposure, these "beginner" letter–sound correspondences become "lexicalized," that is, modified in the light of lexical constraints imposed by a growing body of orthographic knowledge. The growing print lexicon alerts the child to regularities beyond the level of simple one-to-one correspondences, such as context-sensitive (soft and hard *g* and *c*), positional (final versus initial *y*), and morphemic constraints (*missed* rather than *misst*). Thus, contrary to the prevailing opinion (e.g., Coltheart, 2005), this view posits no single decoding procedure or routine, but an ever-changing and self-refining process that at first appears to be very "bottom-up," with little sensitivity to higher-order regularities, but over the course of print experience becomes increasingly attuned (lexicalized) to the given orthography in a two-way interplay between decoding abilities and orthographic knowledge.

Early Onset

A second key feature of self-teaching is early onset; beginning reading is assumed to be beginning self-teaching. Several studies suggest that some decoding skills may exist at the very earliest stages of learning to read, even before a child possesses any decoding skill in the conventional sense of being able to sound out and blend even simple pseudo-words. The early onset hypothesis proposes that even some rudimentary decoding ability may be sufficient for the establishment of primitive or incomplete orthographic representations of the kind discussed by Ehri (1992) and Perfetti (1992). This early self-teaching depends on three factors: letter–sound knowledge, some minimal phonological sensitivity in the form of awareness of initial sounds or initial and final sounds, and the ability to utilize contextual information to determine the intended word and its pronunciation when the product of decoding is incomplete or inaccurate.

Two Components to Self-Teaching: Phonology Is Primary and Orthography Is Secondary

The process of self-teaching through phonological recoding seems to involve at least two component processes: phonological and orthographic. Both components are assumed to make independent contributions to printed word learning although the phonological component is regarded as primary, accounting for the largest portion of the variance in individual differences in reading ability among beginning readers. The orthographic component represents an additional, independent but *secondary* component. The phonological component is the use of spelling–sound relationships to identify unfamiliar words. Phonological recoding skill is assumed to reflect environmental factors such as teaching method and print exposure as well as basic underlying cognitive capacities such as phonological memory and phonological awareness. The ability to translate print to speech is a necessary but not sufficient condition for orthographic learning. Decoding skill creates opportunities for self-teaching but does *not* guarantee that orthographic learning will take place. Over and above the ability to decode unfamiliar words, there exist individual differences in the speed and accuracy with which word-specific (and general) orthographic knowledge is assimilated.* Thus, visual/orthographic ability is seen not merely as a second source of variance, but as a secondary source of individual differences in printed word learning, hence the "phonology-primary/orthography-secondary" rubric.

EMPIRICAL FINDINGS

A modest number of studies have now been undertaken on the general topic of orthographic learning; some of the more recent work has focused specifically on the self-teaching hypothesis addressing issues raised in the previous section. Some of the findings have proven surprisingly robust, others remain intriguing puzzles; many more are merely research questions awaiting investigation.

Although no direct test of the self-teaching hypothesis was carried out until the study by Share (1999), a small number of pioneering studies of orthographic learning reported experimental data consistent with the hypothesis (see, e.g., Hogaboam & Perfetti, 1978; Reitsma, 1983). Typically, pseudo-words (or unfamiliar real words) are presented (or directly taught) either in isolation or in short sentences then, after a delay, retention is tested either by comparing naming times for the original spellings to times for homophonic spellings or by spelling choice. Collectively, these early studies demonstrated impressive convergence,

* The source of individual differences in this assimilation process (orthographic learning) largely remains a black box for reading researchers (but see Bosse, Tainturier, & Valdois, 2007; Breznitz, 2006; Facoetti et al., 2006; Whitney & Cornelissen, 2005).

a rare phenomenon in pioneering work, yet one indicative of highly robust effects: Surprisingly, few presentations were found to be sufficient for the acquisition of word-specific orthographic information among normal readers (but not disabled readers). The fact that training/learning effects revealed in these investigations were uniformly item-specific and did not extend to untrained control items represents strong support for the item-based view of orthographic learning espoused previously.

Summing up, the outcomes from the early "pre-self-teaching" investigations were certainly consistent with the hypothesis that word-specific orthographic representations are acquired *by virtue of the self-teaching opportunities afforded by successful decoding*. These data are nonetheless inconclusive on the self-teaching issue for reasons that will become apparent in the presentation of the next set of studies, all of which examined orthographic learning through the lens of the self-teaching hypothesis.

Studies of Orthographic Learning Within the Self-Teaching Framework

The first experimental study within the self-teaching framework was carried out in Hebrew by Share (1999). In contrast to earlier studies of orthographic learning in which target words were presented either in isolation or in isolated sentences (read and often reread), this study aimed to present targets in as natural a setting as possible by constructing short "stories" like the one at the beginning of this chapter. Children were specifically instructed to read for meaning and told they would be questioned about the content of the story following reading. A second innovation was the switch to unassisted reading. Previous work had either explicitly taught the pronunciation of target strings or had corrected errors, often asking the child to repeat the corrected pronunciation. In this first direct test of the self-teaching hypothesis, no mention was made of the target words either before or after text reading. This study also addressed a second shortcoming of the pioneering word learning studies mentioned above. Orthographic learning may be attributable to mere visual attention to the target strings rather than to the decoding process per se. The visual inspection hypothesis was directly investigated by Share (1999, Experiments 2, 3, and 4), and, subsequently by Kyte and Johnson (2006).

The targets in Share (1999) were all novel letter strings (pseudo-words) embedded in passages such as the one at the beginning of this chapter. These pseudowords each appeared in two homophonic spellings: one-half of the sample saw one version in the relevant text (e.g., *Sloak*) whereas the other half saw the alternate spelling (*Sloke*). According to the self-teaching hypothesis, even when unassisted, children will apply their knowledge of letter–sound correspondences in order to derive the pronunciation of these unfamiliar words and, if successful, will begin to acquire knowledge of their orthographic forms such that the correct form will be recognized and recalled beyond chance on future occasions. As predicted, 3 days later, readers were able to recognize the original target spellings more often than the unseen homophonic spelling, write these using the spelling they had seen rather than the homophonic spelling, and also name the target spelling more rapidly than a homophonic spelling.

These results replicate the pioneering work on orthographic learning and indicate that very few exposures (four or even less) to a target spelling are sufficient for orthographic learning to occur. This study also extends this finding to unassisted (oral) reading of the connected text.

Experiment 2 examined the alternative visual exposure hypothesis by presenting target strings under conditions designed to allow visual inspection but minimize phonological processing. Children performed a lexical decision task (deciding whether a letter string is a real word or not) with irrelevant concurrent vocalization (saying the pseudo-word *dubba* over and over) with target exposure times limited to 300 ms. Second graders showed themselves quite capable of performing this task. However, many children spontaneously commented that some items were appearing on the screen again and again, while several children actually supplied the correct pronunciation. In addition, an error analysis revealed that incorrect spellings and orthographic choices that matched the sound of the target (but were incorrect orthographically) outnumbered spellings that were similar visually but did not preserve sound. Thus, it seems likely that phonological processing was not "eliminated" but merely reduced by the experimental procedures.

A brief visual inspection was sufficient to produce reliable orthographic learning in orthographic choice and spelling, but there was no significant advantage for original spellings in naming accuracy or times. The levels of orthographic learning were significantly inferior to the levels observed in Experiment 1 with unlimited exposure to orthographic targets. There still remained the possibility that the attenuated but significant orthographic learning in this second experiment might be attributable to visual inspection alone, but learning was diminished owing either to brief visual exposure and/or presentation without supporting context. Experiment 3 evaluated this possibility by asking children to name (i.e., phonologically recode) the same briefly presented items. Results showed that phonological recoding of the same targets under conditions similar to those of Experiment 2 produced significantly greater orthographic learning than orthographically irrelevant vocalization in Experiment 2, pointing to a unique contribution of phonological recoding and indicating that the results of Experiment 1 could not be attributed solely to visual exposure. Comparison of the outcomes of Experiments 2 and 3, that is, comparison of effects of orthographically *relevant* pronunciation (Experiment 3) versus *irrelevant* articulation under the same conditions (brief decontextualized exposure in Experiment 2) provided a relatively clean test of the contribution of phonology to orthographic learning. These results were subsequently replicated in a more rigorous fully within-subject design by Kyte and Johnson (2006).

The basic findings from Share's first experiment, with targets appearing in short texts, were replicated and extended to the English language by Cunningham, Perry, Stanovich, and Share (2002). Using the same procedure and materials adapted from Hebrew to English, the experiment showed that overall decoding accuracy among second graders was 74%. Replicating Share (1999, Experiment 1), the original target spellings were correctly recognized more often than the unseen homophonic spelling, reproduced with greater accuracy and named more rapidly than homophonic foils.

Confirming a key prediction of the self-teaching hypothesis, Cunningham et al. reported a significant correlation ($r = .52$) between children's orthographic learning and the number of target words correctly decoded during story reading. Significant positive correlations have also been reported by Kyte and Johnson (2006) and Cunningham (2006). To complete the picture, Share (2008a) found a correlation of .43 between Hebrew target word decoding and a composite measure of orthographic learning (orthographic choice and spelling production of targets versus homophonic foils) that remained significant (.31) even after controlling for age, general intelligence, and two measures of phonological recoding ability: Shatil's (1997) test of pointed Hebrew pseudo-word naming accuracy, and a time-limited phonological choice task adapted from R. K. Olson, Kliegl, Davidson, and Foltz (1985) in which a child must decide which of the two pseudo-words sounds like a real word. This latter finding is especially important because it shows that these decoding–orthographic learning correlations do not merely reflect a general association between decoding and orthographic skills but an item-specific relationship as specified by the self-teaching hypothesis.

Orthographic Learning Is Rapid and Durable

The evidence reviewed thus far suggests that orthographic learning is both rapid and highly robust. Only a few presentations of an unfamiliar word are sufficient to produce detectable orthographic learning. The tantalizing possibility that a single learning trial is sufficient to produce significant orthographic learning was investigated by Share (2004). In this study, targets were presented (again in meaningful text) either once, twice, or four times. This study also pursued the question of durability by comparing orthographic learning after 3, 7, and 30 days. Even a single exposure produced significant posttest orthographic learning. And remarkably, this newly acquired orthographic knowledge was retained for up to 30 days after exposure. However, a study by Nation, Angells, and Castles (2007) produced inconsistent findings regarding single-trial orthographic learning, in that only the outcome (four-alternative orthographic choice) for the 1-day posttest delay (41%) but not the 7-day delay (30%) was beyond chance (25%) performance.

Silent and Oral Reading

Bowey and Muller (2005) raised an important concern regarding the use of oral reading. When a child engages in unassisted oral reading before an adult, there is an implicit obligation to read all the text. Truly independent reading, however, is a private activity not performed either in a dyadic or public setting and furthermore is typically silent rather than oral at least among young readers who are no longer "beginners." Accordingly, Bowey and Muller examined self-teaching during silent reading among third graders. They found that children read lists containing spellings that had appeared in the initial passages faster than lists containing non-target homophonic spellings (with no difference in accuracy), and orthographic choices for the original spelling far outnumbered selections of homophonic foils. Bowey and Muller argued that their findings provide "a strong case for self-teaching through phonological recoding" (p. 218), because the presence of rapid orthographic learning not only in the orthographic choice task but also in the list-reading tasks indicated that rapid orthographic learning must have involved phonological recoding during silent reading of stories. de Jong and Share (2007) also found evidence of significant orthographic learning in silent reading in a Dutch study designed to directly compare the two reading modes, oral and silent. Significant and similar levels of orthographic learning were obtained in both modes.

Individual and Group Differences in Self-Teaching Among Dyslexics and Other Poor Readers

As with the enormous variability in acquired skills such as reading, orthographic learning also encompasses profound individual differences. Although some children just keep decoding new words laboriously over and over as if seen for the first time, for others orthographic learning seems virtually instantaneous. What are the sources of these individual differences? This question has been pursued in a variety of research designs including group-wise comparisons of high-ability and low-ability readers (or diagnosed dyslexics) as well as correlational approaches examining the full spectrum of variability.

Turning first to comparisons between designated groups of good and poor (or dyslexic) readers, both Hogaboam and Perfetti (1978) and Reitsma (1983) found significant orthographic learning, but results were similar for above-average readers and below-average readers. In contrast, Reitsma (1983, 1989) found no evidence of orthographic learning (even after six exposures) either in naming speed or in accuracy among a group of diagnosed dyslexics. Similar results for disabled readers have also been reported by Manis (1985) and Ehri and Saltmarsh (1995).

All of these data are consistent with the self-teaching hypothesis, which holds that poor decoding skill should impair orthographic learning. Hence, disabled readers, who have well-known decoding deficits, would be expected to demonstrate inferior orthographic learning. In contrast, it is often claimed that disabled readers, particularly older ones, have "compensatory" abilities in non-phonological aspects of reading such as visual-orthographic skills. If this is more than just a reflection of greater print exposure among more experienced disabled readers and constitutes an acquired processing strategy, then orthographic learning tested in an experimental paradigm in which the amount of print exposure is fixed should be better than expected on the basis of decoding ability alone.

This compensatory hypothesis was examined in a study by Share and Shalev (2004) comparing the self-teaching of four groups of children: dyslexics in Grades 4, 5, and 6, non-dyslexic (so-called garden-variety) poor readers, age-matched normal readers, and a younger group of normal readers matched to the garden-variety poor readers on both reading skill and mental age. Decoding deficits were expected to impair identification of target words leading to inferior orthographic learning but, if the compensatory hypothesis is correct, disabled readers' orthographic learning was predicted to be somewhat *less* impaired than that of non-disabled readers. Consistent with their preexisting levels of reading ability, target decoding levels were highest for the non-disabled (normal) readers and lowest for the dyslexics with the garden-variety sandwiched in between. Contrary to the English and Dutch data, however, the Hebrew data revealed lower but reliable levels of orthographic choice and spelling among the disabled readers that were closely tied to levels of target decoding. This remarkably close match between overall (group-wise) levels of target decoding and orthographic learning reinforces the differences reported by Share (1999) and also Kyte and Johnson (2006) using experimental procedures (such as articulatory suppression) to manipulate levels of target decoding accuracy. As regards the "compensatory processing" hypothesis, there was no hint of evidence that either group of poor readers was able to compensate for poor decoding via "superior" orthographic skills. It would seem that experiential factors such as print exposure rather than inherent or cultivated processing skills may be the source of the so-called orthographic advantage enjoyed by poor readers when compared to younger children matched on reading level (see, e.g., Siegel, Share, & Geva, 1995).

The next group of studies examined the individual difference issue by using correlational or regression-based approaches surveying the full range of ability rather than selected groups or subgroups differing in overall reading ability.

Cunningham et al. (2002) found that Woodcock-Johnson Word Attack performance (like target decoding) correlated well with orthographic learning in a sample of second graders. Rapid naming of a series of letters or digits ("RAN") correlated weakly, but general cognitive ability did not. Hierarchical regression also established that after target decoding accuracy was partialed out, neither cognitive ability nor RAN contributed additional unique variance to orthographic learning. In contrast, orthographic knowledge as measured by R. K. Olson et al.'s (1985) spelling choice test (in which a child sees two alternate (homophonic) spellings of the same word (one correct and one incorrect) and is asked to select the correct spelling) contributed a significant and substantial 20% of variance. This pattern of findings was replicated in a subsequent study with first graders (Cunningham, 2006).

In their study of self-teaching in silent reading, Bowey and Miller (2007) also found a significant correlation (.42) between phonological recoding efficiency and orthographic choice, but no evidence for a relation between rapid naming and orthographic learning, an accuracy measure in this study. A significant but weak (.30) association between orthographic knowledge and orthographic learning was also obtained, but after partialing out general phonological recoding efficiency, orthographic knowledge only explained a marginal 6% of the variance.

The contribution of RAN to orthographic learning was also evaluated in a study of the role of decoding fluency in orthographic learning by Lurie and

Share (2008). This study examined the relations between several phonological processing tasks (RAN included), target decoding accuracy and speed, and orthographic learning (a composite of spelling production and orthographic choice) in a sample of Hebrew-speaking third graders. Instead of the conventional RAN, which usually requires rapid serial naming of single digits and letters, this study presented sub-syllabic CV units for rapid naming, combinations of a consonantal letter, and an appended vowel diacritic, which are the basic phonic building blocks of printed Hebrew words. Whereas non-RAN tasks such as pseudo-word repetition (accuracy) correlated more with target decoding accuracy than target decoding speed, Lurie and Share's RAN measure correlated more with decoding speed than accuracy. Turning to the decoding–orthographic learning relation, the RAN task correlated significantly with orthographic learning, and, furthermore, this relation was sustained even after partialing out target decoding *accuracy*. However, when target decoding *speed* was partialed out, the RAN measure was no longer significant, indicating that the RAN task contributes to orthographic learning via its contribution to decoding speed. This finding supports the view that RAN contributes unique variance to orthographic learning by tapping the speed dimension of phonological processing not tapped in traditional untimed measures. The Lurie and Share data affirm that for self-teaching to operate effectively, the constituent elements of novel letter strings must not only be decoded accurately but also sufficiently fast for the establishment of word-specific orthographic representations.

Share (2008a) followed up the Cunningham et al. (2002) study with a wide-ranging battery of predictors aimed at comparing sources of individual differences in orthographic learning in two scripts, shallow pointed Hebrew and the deeper unpointed script. One of the aims of this study was to test the phonology-primary/orthography-secondary hypothesis outlined previously. In addition to multiple measures of phonology and orthography, potential predictors of orthographic learning included general intelligence, working memory, cognitive style (Kagan's test of reflectiveness-impulsivity), morphological knowledge, semantics, and syntax. Eighty third graders proficient in reading both pointed and unpointed text read a series of short passages (half pointed, half unpointed) each containing a target pseudo-word. Posttest measures (orthographic choice and spelling production) were administered 1 week later.

Levels of consonantal decoding accuracy for the two types of targets (pointed and unpointed) as well as posttest orthographic choice and spelling were very similar. To test the phonology-primary/orthography-secondary hypothesis, hierarchical regression was employed by first entering age and general intelligence followed by a block of phonological variables and a block of orthographic variables each entered in turn at Steps 2 and 3. Two mirror images emerged; the phonological block was the strongest predictor of orthographic learning in shallow pointed script, but the visual-orthographic block the foremost predictor of unpointed orthographic learning. Thus, the phonology-primary/orthography-secondary hypothesis was upheld in the case of Hebrew's highly regular fully voweled (pointed) orthography, but rejected for the deeper unpointed text. Replicating previous findings, conventional RAN digits and letters did not contribute reliably to orthographic learning, nor did meaning or syntax although it should be kept in mind that all targets were pseudo-words. On the positive side, there was evidence that greater working memory capacity and a more reflective cognitive style were associated with superior orthographic learning.

How Early Is the Onset of Self-Teaching?

How early does self-teaching begin? Studies by Ehri in English (e.g., Ehri & Roberts, 1979) and by Reitsma in Dutch (e.g., Reitsma, 1983) have both observed significant orthographic learning among first graders, but in both of these studies children were either taught the target words or had their misreadings corrected, something foreign to independent reading.

Share (2004, Experiments 2 and 3) examined the issue of self-teaching in beginning readers' *unassisted* (oral) reading of pointed Hebrew, which, unlike Dutch and English, is an extremely regular orthography. Both studies found a surprisingly uniform lack of evidence for reliable orthographic learning. The same result emerged in yet another study with beginning readers (Share & Shalev, 2004). Two alternative hypotheses may account for this unexpected result. First, the near-perfect one-to-one letter–sound relations in Hebrew may induce a highly "bottom-up" letter-by-letter decoding ("surface") strategy that is relatively insensitive to higher-order word-level orthographic information. A second explanation relates to the often-neglected dimensions of decoding *speed* and *efficiency.* The characteristically laborious, letter-by-letter decoding reported among beginning readers of shallow orthographies may simply be too slow to support orthographic learning.

Beyond Decoding Accuracy: The Role of Decoding Fluency in Orthographic Learning

The role of decoding fluency in orthographic learning over and above decoding accuracy was directly addressed by Lurie and Share (2008). Among third grade Hebrew readers, accuracy of target decoding correlated only weakly with orthographic learning ($r = .24$), but decoding times as measured from target presentation onset through to pronunciation *offset* were much more strongly related to orthographic learning ($r = .52$).* This study also examined the relation between decoding speed and orthographic learning in light of the evidence showing that the phonological store (i.e., the "phonological loop") in working memory is time limited, specifically, that memory span is limited to the number of items that subjects can articulate in a 2-s time window (e.g., Baddeley, Thomson, & Buchanan, 1975). Consistent with the 2-s notion, children who took longer than approximately 2 s to decode and pronounce target words displayed significantly

* Target onset times were also correlated significantly with orthographic learning but not quite as strongly.

poorer orthographic learning. Splitting the sample into two using a pronunciation time (offset) cutoff of 2.14 s there was a significant difference in the orthographic choice between groups whose average naming times fell either above or below this value. No significant differences in orthographic learning emerged, however, when the sample was split according to a range of pronunciation times below this value. For spelling, this "critical" point was located at a similar value of 2.2 s.

These data support the hypothesis that slow laborious letter-by-letter decoding that is characteristic of novice readers of shallow orthographies may impair orthographic learning in the same way that slow word recognition can impair text integration processes (Perfetti, 1985). If correct, this decoding fluency hypothesis would explain the lack of orthographic learning among novices.

Other Self-Teaching Mechanisms?

Context

Ever since Goodman's (1967) pioneering study, in which he claimed that better readers make greater use of context in word identification, the issue of context in word reading has remained controversial. Contemporary investigations into the role of context in orthographic learning continue this tradition of controversy.

Early studies by Ehri and Roberts (1979) and Ehri and Wilce (1980) found that learning new printed words in context reduced memory for word-specific orthographic detail compared to an isolation condition whereas the context-trained group was better at identifying the target words' meanings. Archer and Bryant (2001) also found that, although first graders were more successful reading words in context than in isolation, the experience of words in meaningful context and in isolation led to equivalent improvements in later reading. Unlike these studies, Cunningham (2006) examined the role of context in *unassisted* reading of target words selected to be familiar in spoken but not in the printed form. Once again, context helped (English-speaking) first graders to decode these items, but no advantage emerged in posttest orthographic learning.

Landi, Perfetti, Bolger, Dunlap, and Foorman (2006) also reasoned that learning new words in a meaningful context draws attention away from orthographic detail thereby detracting from long-term retention. Words were identified more successfully by first and second graders when read in meaningful passages compared to isolated presentation, but there was no overall difference in overall posttest reading accuracy. That is, a greater proportion of those words that were identified correctly in isolation (69%) than in context (47%) were retained a week later.

Martin-Chang, Levy, and O'Neill (2007) threw a spanner in the works by arguing that, in all of these studies, the measurements of practice and retention are confounded. Whereas words practiced and posttested in isolation had been recalled under the same conditions, context-trained words were tested under different conditions (i.e., transfer from context to isolation). In their study, words were trained either in context or in isolation, followed by a delayed retention task in which trained items were presented under the *same* conditions, isolation or context, respectively, as well as a transfer task (trained words presented again in a novel story). Words were read more accurately in context than in isolation and this advantage was maintained at posttest. When children read the test items in a novel passage in the transfer task, they exhibited a much larger advantage for words previously read in context compared to words presented in isolation. Confirming the authors' "congruency" hypothesis, a second study found a clear advantage at transfer for words practiced *in isolation* when posttest transfer was tested in a novel *isolated* word reading task. Martin-Chang et al. concluded that transfer is greatest when congruency of training and transfer is maximized.

Several general comments about all of these studies are pertinent. With the exception of Cunningham (2006), all of the studies involved explicit teaching or corrective feedback. This qualifies any conclusions regarding independent (unassisted) reading/self-teaching. The studies' use of words selected, not on the basis of ascertained unfamiliarity, but because they present decoding difficulties, is also problematic because such items may necessitate greater reliance on context than words that are not difficult to decode. In order to reach generalizable conclusions regarding orthographic *learning*, it is paramount that researchers ensure that test items are unfamiliar. Also crucial is the level of predictability of the sentences or passages which, in several of these studies, is often far beyond the norm for connected text (e.g., Archer & Bryant, 2001; Landi et al., 2006). Natural text has very low predictability (Share, 1995). These reservations notwithstanding, results from these investigations seem to converge in showing that contextual support for identifying hard-to-decode words is helpful, but at the expense of attention to orthographic detail. Hence, when only the print is available on a later encounter, reading suffers.

The study by Martin-Chang et al. (2007) raises an important concern: To which context do we wish to generalize the findings of printed word learning studies? Meaningful text is indisputably the most common context in which new words are first encountered and subsequently read, and, of course, is the most important context for expanding knowledge of word meaning and syntactic function (Ehri & Roberts, 1979; Ehri & Wilce, 1980). Ultimately, however, we want children to be able to read and understand words in all possible circumstances. This includes both context *and* isolation. But we want readers who are writers too. Therefore, spelling facility is also a crucial element of word learning. Here context is inconsequential. Whereas context detracts from attention to orthographic detail, spelling obliges close and thorough attention to orthography and sub-lexical print-to-sound correspondence, probably even more than does decoding.

Spelling as a Self-Teaching Mechanism

In a study focusing specifically on the role of spelling in orthographic learning, Shahar-Yames and Share (2008) presented third grade Hebrew-speaking children with target pseudo-words in three conditions: reading, spelling (actually reading-plus-spelling), and in a control condition in which the pseudo-words were unseen. In the spelling condition, participants first read meaningful sentences containing the target word and were then asked to write down the target from memory with the sentences removed from sight. Spelling was predicted to produce superior orthographic learning compared to reading owing to the additional processing demands invoked, and, furthermore, this advantage was expected to be greatest for letters appearing toward the end of a word in view of the fact that spelling obliges the writer to process each and every letter in a word on every occasion whereas decoding encounters, although likely to be quite exhaustive initially, are probably less exhaustive on subsequent occurrences, particularly in connected text.

Reading led to significant orthographic learning (relative to control pseudowords), but spelling led to more powerful and more consistent learning outcomes. The difference between reading and spelling in the case of non-initial letters was almost twice the difference for the initial letter (9.5% versus 5.0%) although, formally, this interaction failed to reach significance, possibly because many of the non-initial letters were not word-final.

SUMMARY, CONCLUSIONS, AND THE WAY AHEAD

A good deal has been learned about the basic parameters of orthographic learning, but less is known about *how* this learning comes about. It is encouraging to see that much of this work has offered support for the self-teaching hypothesis. This can be seen in several sets of findings. First, levels of orthographic learning appear to be closely tied to levels of decoding success whether induced experimentally (Kyte & Johnson, 2006; Share, 1999) or naturally occurring (Ehri & Saltmarsh, 1995; Manis, 1985; Reitsma, 1983, 1989; Share & Shalev, 2004). Second, at the individual level, the data have been quite consistent in showing a significant positive association between target decoding success and later orthographic learning for these same targets, a relation furthermore that does not appear to be simply the offshoot of the general relation between preexisting decoding skills and target-specific orthographic learning (Cunningham, 2006; Cunningham et al., 2002; Kyte & Johnson; Lurie 2007; Share, 2008a; but see Nation et al., 2007). And third, the role of context in reducing attention to orthographic detail and spelling in enhancing it also confirms the basic self-teaching premise that phonological recoding contributes to orthographic learning by drawing attention to letter detail and word-specific spelling-sound relations.

Much work in this field lies ahead. The orthographic learning function needs to be systematically mapped for both normal and disabled readers. Most studies to date have understandably used a small number of selected points on the learning curve, and although more exposures tend to elicit stronger outcomes, only a comprehensive mapping effort can determine whether orthographic learning adheres to the standard power function common to a wide variety of learned skills. Share's (2004) finding of single-trial learning needs replicating in view of the inconsistencies in Nation et al.'s (2007) single-exposure findings.

Yet another important but untouched topic in the study of orthographic learning is the acquisition of knowledge of general orthographic conventions. To date, all the work referred to in this chapter has dealt exclusively with word-specific knowledge. More general insights into orthographic conventions concerning grammatical and derivational (typically bound) morphemes is another critical dimension of orthographic learning.

Research into the determinants of individual differences in orthographic learning has only just begun. Some intriguing and puzzling findings will remain enigmas until further research offers clarification. The early onset issue provides cause for optimism: Conflicting outcomes in English and Hebrew have helped point the way to several fascinating new research directions on the question of decoding fluency.

Studies of context effects showing high levels of word identification success that do not translate into superior orthographic learning, as well as the initial Hebrew first grade data indicating negligible orthographic learning despite near-ceiling levels of decoding accuracy, all provide a warning to researchers regarding the value of using crude measures of decoding accuracy that overlook the *nature* of decoding. The "how" of decoding promises to be a painstaking but crucial avenue for future research.

To conclude, the subject of orthographic learning offers researchers a field of study lying at the very heart of one of the most important and challenging skills that children are expected to master. It is a promising young field replete not only with fresh discoveries, enigmatic and contradictory findings but brimming with research questions awaiting investigation.

ACKNOWLEDGMENTS

A number of the Hebrew studies reviewed here were supported by grants from the Israel Science Foundation and the Israeli Ministry of Education, Office of the Chief Scientist. Special thanks to Liat Butbul for his assistance in preparing this manuscript.

REFERENCES

Adams, M. J. (1990). *Beginning to read.* Cambridge, MA: Bradford.

Anderson, J. R. (1981). *Cognitive skills and their acquisition.* Hillsdale, NJ: Erlbaum.

Ans, B., Carbonnel, S., & Valdois, S. (1998). A connectionist multiple-trace memory model for polysyllabic word reading. *Psychological Review, 105*, 678–723.

Archer, N., & Bryant, P. (2001). Investigating the role of context in learning to read: A direct test of Goodman's model. *British Journal of Psychology, 92*, 579–591.

Baddeley, A. D., Thomson, N., & Buchanan, M. (1975). Word length and the structure of short-term memory. *Journal of Verbal Learning and Verbal Behavior, 14*, 575–589.

Baron, J. (1977). Mechanisms for pronouncing printed words aloud: Use and acquisition. In D. LaBerge & S. J. Samuels (Eds.), *Basic processes in reading: Perception and comprehension* (pp. 175–216). Hillsdale, NJ: Erlbaum.

Barron, R. W. (1986). Word recognition in early reading: A review of the direct and indirect access hypotheses. *Cognition, 24*, 93–119.

Barron, R. W., & Baron, J. (1977). How children get meaning from printed words. *Child Development, 48*, 587–594.

Bosse, M.-L., Tainturier, M. J., & Valdois, S. (2007). Developmental dyslexia: The visual attention span deficit hypothesis. *Cognition, 104*, 198–230.

Bowey, J. A., & Miller, R. (2007). Correlates of orthographic learning in third-grade children's silent reading. *Journal of Research in Reading, 30*, 115–128.

Bowey, J. A., & Muller, D. (2005). Phonological recoding and rapid orthographic learning in third-graders' silent reading: A critical test of the self-teaching hypothesis. *Journal of Experimental Child Psychology, 92*, 203–219.

Bradley, L., & Bryant, P. E. (1983). Categorizing sounds and learning to read: A causal connection. *Nature, 301*, 419–421.

Breznitz, Z. (2006). *Fluency in reading: Synchronization of processes*. Mahwah, NJ: Erlbaum.

Chomsky, N., & Halle, M. (1968). *The sound pattern of English*. New York: Harper & Row.

Coltheart, M. (1978). Lexical access in simple reading tasks. In G. Underwood (Ed.), *Strategies of information processing* (pp. 151–216). London, U.K.: Academic Press.

Coltheart, M. (2005). Modeling reading: The dual-route approach. In M. Snowling & C. Hulme (Eds.), *The science of reading: A handbook* (pp. 6–23). Oxford, U.K.: Blackwell.

Condry, S. M., McMahon-Rideout, M., & Levy, A. A. (1979). A developmental investigation of selective attention to graphic, phonetic and semantic information in words. *Perception & Psychophysics, 25*, 88–94.

Cunningham, A. E. (2006). Accounting for children's orthographic learning while reading text: Do children self-teach? *Journal of Experimental Child Psychology, 95*, 56–77.

Cunningham, A. E., Perry, K. E., Stanovich, K. E., & Share, D. L. (2002). Orthographic learning during reading: Examining the role of self-teaching. *Journal of Experimental Child Psychology, 82*, 185–199.

de Jong, P. F., & Share, D. L. (2007). Orthographic learning during oral and silent reading. *Scientific Studies of Reading, 11*, 55–71.

Doctor, E. A., & Coltheart, M. (1980). Children's use of phonological encoding when reading for meaning. *Memory & Cognition, 8*, 195–209.

Ehri, L. C. (1992). Reconceptualizing the development of sight word reading and its relationship to recoding. In P. B. Gough, L. C. Ehri, & R. Treiman (Eds.), *Reading acquisition* (pp.107–144). Hiilsdale, NJ: Erlbaum.

Ehri, L. C. (2005). Development of sight word reading: Phases and findings. In M. S. Snowling & C. Hulme (Eds.), *The science of reading: A handbook* (pp. 135–154). Oxford, U.K.: Blackwell.

Ehri, L. C., & Roberts, K. T. (1979). Do beginners learn printed words better in contexts or in isolation? *Child Development, 50*, 675–685.

Ehri, L. C., & Saltmarsh, J. (1995). Beginning readers outperform older disabled readers in learning to read words by sight. *Reading and Writing, 7*, 295–326.

Ehri, L. C., & Wilce, L. S. (1980). The influence of orthography on readers' conceptualization of the phonemic structure of words. *Applied Psycholinguistics, 1*, 371–385.

Facoetti, A., Zorzi, M., Cestnick, L., Lorusso, M. L., Molteni, M., Paganoni, P., et al. (2006). The relationship between visuo-spatial attention and nonword reading in developmental dyslexia. *Cognitive Neuropsychology, 23*, 841–855.

Firth, I. (1972). *Components of reading disability*. Unpublished doctoral dissertation, University of New South Wales, Sydney, Australia.

Foorman, B. R., Francis, D. J., Davidson, K. C., Harm, M. W., & Griffin, J. (2004). Variability in text features in six grade 1 basal reading programs. *Scientific Studies of Reading, 8*, 167–197.

Frith, U. (1985). Beneath the surface of developmental dyslexia. In K. E. Patterson, J. C. Marshall, & M. Coltheart (Eds.), *Surface dyslexia* (pp. 301–322). London, U.K.: Lawrence Erlbaum Associates.

Frost, R. (1998). Toward a strong phonological model of reading: True issues and false trails. *Psychological Bulletin, 123*, 71–99.

Glushko, R. J. (1979). The organization and activation of orthographic knowledge in reading aloud. *Journal of Experimental Psychology: Human Perception and Performance, 5*, 674–691.

Goldstein, D. M. (1976). Cognitive-linguistic functioning and learning to read in preschoolers. *Journal of Educational Psychology, 68*, 680–688.

Goldstone, R. L. (1998). Perceptual learning. *Annual Review of Psychology, 49*, 585–612.

Goodman, K. S. (1967). Reading: A psycholinguistic guessing game. *Journal of the Reading Specialist, 6*, 126–135.

Hogaboam, T. W., & Perfetti, C. A. (1978). Reading skill and the role of verbal experience in decoding. *Journal of Educational Psychology, 70*, 717–729.

Jorm, A. F. (1983). Specific reading retardation and working memory: A review. *British Journal of Psychology, 74*, 311–342.

Jorm, A. F., & Share, D. L. (1983). Phonological recoding and reading acquisition. *Applied Psycholinguistics, 4*, 103–147.

Karni, A. (1996). The acquisition of perceptual and motor skills: A memory system in the adult human cortex. *Cognitive Brain Research, 5*, 39–48.

Kay, J., & Marcel, T. (1981). One process, not two, in reading aloud: Lexical analogies do the work of nonlexical rules. *Quarterly Journal of Experimental Psychology, 33A*, 397–413.

Kyte, C. S., & Johnson, C. J. (2006). The role of phonological recoding in orthographic learning. *Journal of Experimental Child Psychology, 93*, 166–185.

LaBerge, D., & Brown, V. (1989). Theory of attentional operations in shape identification. *Psychological Review, 96*, 101–124.

LaBerge, D., & Samuels, J. (1974). Toward a theory of automatic information processing in reading. *Cognitive Psychology, 6*, 293–323.

Landi, N., Perfetti, C. A., Bolger, D. J., Dunlap, S., & Foorman, B. R. (2006). The role of discourse context in developing word representations: A paradoxical relation between reading and learning. *Journal of Experimental Child Psychology, 94*, 114–133.

Liberman, I. Y., Shankweiler, D., Fischer, F. W., & Carter, B. (1974). Explicit syllable and phoneme segmentation in the young child. *Journal of Experimental Child Psychology, 18*, 201–212.

Logan, G. D. (1988). Toward an instance theory of automatization. *Psychological Review, 95*, 492–527.

Logan, G. D. (1997). Automaticity and reading: Perspectives from the instance theory of automatization. *Reading and Writing Quarterly, 13*, 123–146.

Logan, G. D. (2002). An instance theory of attention and memory. *Psychological Review, 109*, 376–400.

Lurie, S. (2007). *Decoding fluency and orthographic learning*. Unpublished MA thesis, University of Haifa.

Manis, F. R. (1985). Acquisition of word identification skills in normal and disabled readers. *Journal of Educational Psychology, 77*, 78–90.

Martin-Chang, S. L., Levy, B. A., & O'Neil, S. (2007). Word acquisition, retention, and transfer: Findings from contextual and isolated word training. *Journal of Experimental Child Psychology, 96*, 37–56.

McCusker, L. X., Hillinger, M. L., & Bias, R. G. (1981). Phonological recoding and reading. *Psychological Bulletin, 89*, 217–245.

Nation, K., Angells, P., & Castles, A. (2007). Orthographic learning via self-teaching in children learning to read English: Effects of exposure, durability, and context. *Journal of Experimental Child Psychology, 96*, 71–78.

Newell, A., & Rosenbloom, P. S. (1981). Mechanisms of skill acquisition and the law of practice. In J. R. Anderson (Ed.), *Cognitive skills and their acquisition* (pp. 1–55). Hillsdale, NJ: Erlbaum.

Olson, D. R. (1994). *The world on paper*. Cambridge, MA: Cambridge University Press.

Olson, R. K., Kliegl, R., Davidson, B. J., & Foltz, G. (1985). Individual and developmental differences in reading disability. In D. Besner, T. G. Waller, & G. E. Mackinnon (Eds.), *Reading research: Advances in theory and practice* (Vol. 5, pp. 2–65). New York: Academic Press.

Perfetti, C. A. (1985). *Reading ability*. New York: Oxford University Press.

Perfetti, C. A. (1992). The representation problem in reading acquisition. In P. B. Gough, L. C. Ehri, & R. Treiman (Eds.), *Reading acquisition* (pp. 145–174). Hillsdale, NJ: Erlbaum.

Perfetti, C. A. (1994). Psycholinguistics and reading ability. In M. A. Gernsbacher (Ed.), *Handbook of psycholinguistics* (pp. 849–894). San Diego, CA: Academic Press.

Perfetti, C. A. (2003). The universal grammar of reading. *Scientific Studies of Reading, 7*, 3–24.

Rader, N. (1975). *From written words to meaning: A developmental study*. Unpublished doctoral dissertation, Cornell University, New York.

Rayner, K. (1998). Eye movements in reading and information processing: 20 years of research. *Psychological Bulletin, 124*, 372–422.

Reitsma, P. (1983). Printed word learning in beginning readers. *Journal of Experimental Child Psychology, 36*, 321–339.

Reitsma, P. (1989). Orthographic memory and learning to read. In P. G. Aaron & R. M. Joshi (Eds.), *Reading and writing disorders in different orthographic systems* (pp. 51–73). New York: Kluwer Academic/Plenum Publishers.

Rogers, H. (1995). Optimal orthographies. In I. Taylor & D. R. Olson (Eds.), *Scripts and literacy: Reading and learning to read alphabets, syllabaries and characters* (pp. 31–44). New York: Kluwer.

Shahar-Yames, D., & Share, D. L. (2008). Spelling as a self-teaching mechanism in orthographic learning. *Journal of Research in Reading, 31*, 22–39.

Shankweiler, D. P., & Liberman, I. Y. (1972). Misreading: A search for causes. In J. F. Kavanagh & I. G. Mattingly (Eds.), *Language by ear and by eye: The relationship between speech and reading* (pp. 293–317). Cambridge, MA: MIT Press.

Share, D. L. (1995). Phonological recoding and self-teaching: Sine qua non of reading acquisition. *Cognition, 55*, 151–218.

Share, D. L. (1999). Phonological recoding and orthographic learning: A direct test of the self-teaching hypothesis. *Journal of Experimental Child Psychology, 72*, 95–129.

Share, D. L. (2004). Orthographic learning at a glance: On the time course and developmental onset of self-teaching. *Journal of Experimental Child Psychology, 87*, 267–298.

Share, D. L. (2008a). Sources of individual differences in orthographic learning: A comparison of deep and shallow scripts. Unpublished manuscript, University of Haifa, Haifa, Israel.

Share, D. L. (2008b). On the Anglocentricities of current reading research and practice: The perils of over-reliance on an "outlier" orthography. *Psychological Bulletin, 134*, 584–616.

Share, D. L., & Shalev, C. (2004). Self-teaching in normal and disabled readers. *Reading and Writing*, 17, 769–800.

Shatil, E. (1997). *Predicting reading ability: Evidence for cognitive modularity*. Unpublished doctoral dissertation, University of Haifa, Haifa, Israel.

Shiffrin, R. M., & Schneider, W. (1977). Controlled and automatic human information processing: II. Perceptual learning, automatic attending, and a general theory. *Psychological Review, 84*, 127–190.

Siegel, L. S., Share, D. L., & Geva, E. (1995). Evidence for superior orthographic skills in dyslexics. *Psychological Science, 6*, 250–254.

Siegler, R. S. (1988). Strategy choice and the development of multiplication skill. *Journal of Experimental Psychology: General, 117*, 258–275.

Stanovich, K. E. (1990). Concepts in developmental theories of reading skill: Cognitive resources, automaticity, and modularity. *Developmental Review, 10*, 72–100.

Stanovich, K. E. (2000). *Progress in understanding reading: Scientific foundations and new frontiers*. New York: Guilford.

van der Leij, A., & van Daal, V. H. P. (1999). Automatization aspects of dyslexia: Speed limitations in word identification, sensitivity to increasing task demands, and orthographic compensation. *Journal of Learning Disabilities, 32*, 417–428.

Van-Orden, G. C., Pennington, B. F., & Stone, G. O. (1990). Word identification in reading and the promise of subsymbolic psycholinguistics. *Psychological Review, 97*, 488–522.

Vellutino, F. R. (1979). *Dyslexia: Theory and research*. Cambridge, MA: MIT Press.

Venezky, R. (2006). Foundations for studying basic processes in reading. In R. M. Joshi & P. G. Aaron (Eds.), *Handbook of orthography and literacy* (pp. 735–758). Mahwah, NJ: Erlbaum.

Venezky, R. (2007). In search of the perfect orthography. *Written Language and Literacy, 7*, 139–163.

Weekes, B. S. (1997). Differential effects of number of letters on word and nonword naming latency. *The Quarterly Journal of Experimental Psychology A: Human Experimental Psychology, 50A*, 439–456.

Whitney, C., & Cornelissen, P. (2005). Letter-position encoding and dyslexia. *Journal of Research in Reading, 28*, 274–301.

Zinna, D. R., Liberman, I. Y., & Shankweiler, D. (1986). Children's sensitivity to factors influencing vowel reading. *Reading Research Quarterly, 21*, 465–479.

4 Efficacy of Phonics Teaching for Reading Outcomes

Indications from Post-NRP Research

Susan A. Brady
University of Rhode Island
and
Haskins Laboratories

Ten years ago, the National Reading Panel* (NRP) assembled available research from 1970 to 2000 to investigate whether systematic phonics instruction helps children learn to read alphabetic writing systems more effectively than either unsystematic phonics or instruction teaching no phonics. This question was one of several addressed by the panel regarding efficacy of components of reading instruction: Other domains included phoneme awareness, fluency, vocabulary, and comprehension, as well as the need to address teacher preparation to teach research-based methods. With respect to phonics, after a rigorous selection process, the findings from 38 studies were analyzed and from these 66 treatment-control group comparisons were obtained. The authors of the resulting report of the NRP (National Institute of Child Health and Human Development, 2000) were careful to acknowledge the limitations of the meta-analytic study and not to overstate the findings (also see Ehri, Nunes, Stahl, & Willows, 2001; McCardle & Chhabra, 2004). Even so, the case for the value of systematic, explicit phonics instruction was quite compelling. The convergence of the body of research indicated that code-based instruction is beneficial for pupils, particularly in the early grades. The report also noted the need for changes in the content of college and university teacher preparation programs if teachers were to have the knowledge

* The National Reading Panel was commissioned by the U.S. Congress to examine the effectiveness of instructional approaches to reading. The panel developed a methodology regarding which studies to review, restricting those that were included to experimental and quasi-experimental studies. They then reviewed, analyzed, and synthesized the evidence, conducting meta-analyses when possible. In the ensuing report, Part II of the section on Alphabetics presents results pertaining to phonics.

and skills to apply the lessons from research on reading instruction. In the 10 years since, changes in teacher preparation and classroom activities have begun, but the shifts generally have been limited and substantial impediments to effective implementation of systematic phonics persist. Some of the difficulties in implementation have stemmed from inadequate representations of what is entailed by phonics and/or from resistance to using systematic and explicit methods of phonics instruction.

The goals of this chapter are (a) to provide a brief delineation of the parameters of phonics instruction that vary across studies and instructional programs, (b) to summarize the key findings of the NRP report regarding phonics instruction, (c) to note federal efforts after the report was published and responses to the report in the field of education, and (d) to present findings from subsequent research on phonics. In the final section, this chapter aims to examine whether research conducted in the last decade upholds and extends the main findings of the NRP regarding phonics instruction or, alternatively, shows them to be unsupported.

DIMENSIONS OF PHONICS INSTRUCTION

Beyond the finding by the NRP that systematic phonics instruction is beneficial, one of the key issues targeted by the panel, and persisting as a point of debate, concerns whether the particular method of teaching systematic phonics makes a difference in student progress in learning to read. Among other variations, methods vary in size of phonological or orthographic units, how explicitly patterns are identified, systematicity of sequencing, the extent of phonics concepts covered, and the types of activities employed. To set the stage for the topics in this chapter, these parameters of phonics instruction are described briefly.

Unit Size

Approaches using larger units generally focus on onsets and rimes in word families, whereas methods using smaller linguistic units target all of the individual grapheme–phoneme correspondences (GPCs) in words.*

Degree of Explicitness

More explicit programs provide explanations for children, fostering the discovery of orthographic patterns and/or giving clear descriptions of when a particular pattern is used. Instruction about the main types of vowel syllable patterns (closed,

* Syllables can be subdivided into onsets and rimes. The onset is the portion preceding the vowel, whereas the vowel and the remainder of the syllable are called the rime. The onset and/or rime may be a single phoneme (e.g., me: the onset is m and the rime is e). Yet often, the onset and rime are made up of more than one speech sound, as in the word plant (i.e., pl is the onset and ant is the rime). In reading instruction targeting onsets and rimes, word families often are employed that share an orthographic rime pattern (e.g., c-ake, b-ake, m-ake, br-ake, fl-ake, and sh-ake). In this approach, words are not segmented into all of the component phonemes as they are for methods targeting complete grapheme–phoneme analysis (e.g., bed: b-e-d).

open, silent-e, vowel team, r-controlled, and consonant-le) is one such method that gives children contextual strategies for knowing how to spell or read words (Shankweiler & Fowler, 2004). Approaches that are less explicit provide examples of phonics patterns in text but do not direct students' attention to the nature of the pattern or to the context in which it occurs (i.e., *implicit phonics*).

Degree of Systematicity

More systematic phonics programs take children through a planned set of lessons that generally start with regular spelling and decoding patterns, first introducing a set of consonants (selected on the basis of frequency and regularity), and regular, single-letter, vowel patterns. High-frequency words are taught in tandem with phonics to support reading of connected text. Patterns are added to the literacy activities in a way that builds on what has been learned, increasing accuracy and automaticity. Systematic sequencing is not restricted to grapheme level instruction. For example, a word family approach (e.g., Santa & Hoien, 1999) also can follow a planned sequence that fosters expertise in a cumulative way. Programs with a less systematic approach are more haphazard in the presentation of patterns, with teachers often providing a pattern incidentally when a child has difficulty reading a word. In this version of phonics, sometimes coming under the labels *embedded phonics* or *phonics in context*, a phonics cue might be given after encouraging the use of other strategies (i.e., to guess based on the context, to look at the picture).

Scope and Duration

A further variation is the scope and duration of the phonics program. Illustrating a minimal scope, traditional whole-language programs typically teach children many of the consonant letter–sound correspondences in kindergarten and first grade but do not focus on vowel patterns: Those are to be acquired through exposure to authentic text (i.e., children's literature). An example of a broader scope of phonics instruction would be the one that extends beyond consonant graphemes to vowel graphemes with continued instruction in orthographic patterns (e.g., vowel syllable types, syllable division strategies, and more advanced spelling rules such as when to double consonants and when to drop "e" when adding a suffix), extending throughout the second grade or later.

Types of Activities

The final dimension to be noted pertains to the types of activities employed to support student learning. A division often has been made between so-called *synthetic phonics* and *analytic phonics*. In the former, children are encouraged to identify the sounds represented by the letter in each position of the word and then to blend those sounds to arrive at the word. Analytic phonics fosters awareness of sound segments by teaching students sets of words that share beginning (onset) or ending letter sequences (rimes) with a common pronunciation. The analytic approach (also linked with *analogy phonics* in which the child is encouraged to think of how to read a word with the same rime pattern) is conducive to teaching only the onset and larger units, thereby avoiding decomposing words into all of the individual graphemes.

The particular attributes of phonics instruction often cluster, with more systematic instruction also tending to be more explicit, focusing on the grapheme level and using synthetic methods. Less systematic instruction tends to utilize more embedded approaches that target onset-rime elements and analytic activities.

MAIN FINDINGS OF THE NRP: EFFECTS OF PHONICS INSTRUCTION

Overall, research reviewed in the NRP report indicates that students taught with systematic phonics instruction have better reading scores, whether measured at the end of the training period or at the end of the school year of instruction (Cohen's d = .44).* Systematic phonics instruction was found to produce better reading growth than all of the types of nonsystematic or nonphonics instruction (i.e., basal programs, whole-language approaches, regular curriculum, whole word curriculum, and miscellaneous programs). Further, systematic phonics was found to be effective whether taught through individual tutoring (d = .57), through small groups (d = .43), or to the whole class (d = .39).

At the same time, comparisons of three different types of phonics instruction did not yield significant differences in the reading gains of students. The three types of phonics instruction compared were (a) synthetic phonics programs that emphasized teaching students to convert letters (graphemes) into sounds (phonemes) and then to blend the sounds to form words, (b) larger-unit phonics programs that emphasized the analysis and blending of larger phonological subparts of words (e.g., onsets and rimes in word families), and (c) miscellaneous programs that taught phonics in other ways than the other two or that were not sufficiently clear about the nature of the approach. The effect sizes for the three programs were all significantly greater than zero (synthetic phonics, d = .45; larger-unit programs, d = .34; miscellaneous programs, d = .27) but as noted did not differ significantly from each other.

The largest impact on student reading achievement was documented for students who had received phonics instruction during the early grades. Phonics instruction had its biggest effect on reading achievement when conducted in kindergarten (d = .56) and first grade (d = .54). Positive results also were documented for phonics instruction provided in the later grades, though the mean effect size was smaller (d = .27).

In addition to facilitating reading acquisition for normally achieving students, noteworthy benefits of systematic phonics instruction were documented for

* The effect size measures how much the mean of a treatment group exceeds the mean of a comparison group. Conventionally, an effect size of d = .20 is small, that of d = .50 is moderate, and that of d = .80 or higher is large (Cohen, 1988). In the present case, the larger the effect size difference, the more likely that the difference in instructional methods is educationally meaningful.

students in a variety of circumstances: (a) Phonics instruction was found to yield strong growth in reading for kindergarten children at risk of having future reading difficulties ($d = .58$) and for first-grade students at risk ($d = .74$). (b) Instruction in phonics also raised the reading performance of disabled readers (defined as students with average IQ but low reading achievement) ($d = .32$) but did not exert a significant effect on the reading achievement of low-achieving readers in grades 2–6 (i.e., students with reading difficulties who may have other cognitive weaknesses contributing to their low achievement). (c) Children at all SES levels made greater gains in reading when provided with systematic phonics instruction (low SES students, $d = .66$; middle-class students, $d = .44$).

The validity of the NRP findings is underscored by the fact that the positive effects of systematic instruction were equally robust when only the best designed experiments in the set of studies were examined, suggesting that the overall pattern of findings could not be attributed to other factors such as preexisting differences between the treatment and control groups.

The panel members concluded that the results of the analysis indicate the positive value of including systematic phonics programs in today's classrooms. At the same time, they made sensible cautionary remarks about implementing phonics: (a) Children also need to be aware of the phonemes in spoken words (i.e., to have phoneme awareness) in order to grasp the significance of letter–sound correspondences. (b) Phonics programs need to have an appropriate balance between teaching letter–sound relations and practice implementing those concepts in daily reading and writing activities. (c) Further research is needed to investigate critical parameters of phonics instruction concerning the optimal duration and extent of phonics instruction and regarding the ideal combination of practice with connected text and writing activities. They also acknowledged that the role of the teacher needs to be understood further in terms of motivational factors, consistency of program implementation, degree of scripting, and requisite teacher knowledge.

The results of this careful scientific analysis of the value of code-based instruction converged with earlier large-scale studies examining the merits of different approaches to reading instruction, as discussed in two important books synthesizing the prior findings (Adams, 1990; Chall, 1967). Subsequent major reviews have targeted research on how to reduce children's reading difficulties (National Research Council, 1998) and on how research informs the teaching of reading (McCardle, Chhabra, & Kapinus, 2008; Rayner, Foorman, Perfetti, Pesetsky, & Seidenberg, 2001; Vellutino, Fletcher, Snowling, & Scanlon, 2004).

AFTERMATH OF THE NRP: SUPPORT AND PUSHBACK FOR TEACHING EXPLICIT, SYSTEMATIC PHONICS

In the years since the NRP report was released, widely varying responses to the publication have occurred. At the U.S. federal level, major initiatives were designed to ameliorate the reading weaknesses of American students, especially for economically disadvantaged children. Toward that goal, under the legislation for the No Child Left Behind (NCLB) Act of 2001 (PL 107-110), the Reading First program was launched with the aim to foster implementation of evidence-based reading practices* in the early grades in phonics as well as in the other areas identified by the NRP, in low-performing schools in each state and U.S. territory. It is important to underscore that this enterprise did not constitute a research project to further test the efficacy of systematic, explicit instruction, as some thought. Rather, the purpose was to facilitate the implementation of research-based practices in the classrooms of disadvantaged pupils. States were given latitude in choosing measures, training models, type of data recorded, instructional materials, and other features of implementation. This flexibility was intended in part to allow decision making at state and local levels while still building experience with the process of documenting student progress and student outcomes. However, it led to considerable variation in states' Reading First programs and contributed to difficulties ascertaining the effects of Reading First. As such, the questions that can be asked regarding the outcomes pertain to the conditions under which it was more or less successful (e.g., quality/extent of professional development for the teachers, extent to which assessment data were used to inform instruction, level of state, and local administrative commitment to scientifically based instructional methods). Consequently, instead of allowing nationwide evaluation of the project, it primarily has been possible to examine outcomes on a more restricted scale and to explore ingredients influencing magnitude of gains for particular approaches to implementation.

A case in point is Reading First in Alabama, which has been recognized for having positive implementation procedures and outcomes. The educational leadership in that state embraced the content and goals of Reading First, seeking to disseminate the NRP findings not just to a small number of disadvantaged schools or school districts but on a statewide level, together with professional development and teacher support for how to use evidence-based methods. In addition to effective leadership, there was an ongoing focus on data and on how to continually use the data to identify and refine the necessary elements for successful implementation (K. Mitchell, personal communication, 2008; RMC Research Corporation, 2007). Following this multiyear effort, unusually large gains were obtained by minority fourth-grade students in Alabama on the 2007 National Assessment of Educational Progress (National Center for Education Statistics, 2007): African American students increased their reading scores by 13 points—an extraordinary outcome.

When more formal evaluation of Reading First was undertaken focusing on a set of states (Gamse, Jacob, Horst, Boulay, & Unlu, 2008), the results indicated that teachers spent more time on reading instruction and that students performed significantly better on a word reading task, but not on a comprehension measure.

* If a program is developed based on research that demonstrated the effectiveness of a type of instruction, then it can be called *research-based*. When research evidence is available to show that a particular program or approach is effective, one can call that program or approach *evidence-based*, a stronger level of assurance that it is worthwhile to use with students (McCardle et al., 2008). Of course, it is important in either case that the research conducted meets scientific standards (e.g., with appropriate assessment instruments, with a control or comparison group). Despite the technical difference between the terms, in nonresearch settings they often are used interchangeably.

This research endeavor was criticized for having methodological weaknesses (e.g., sharing of training resources in experimental and control sites) that limited accurate evaluation of Reading First outcomes (Francis, 2008; Mitchell et al., 2008). Related to this point, a study by Wong-Ratcliff, Powell, and Holland (2010) indicated that Reading First practices helped produce positive reading outcomes in both Reading First and non-Reading First schools. Nonetheless, the results of the Gamse et al. study have lead to mixed responses to Reading First in political and educational circles, and hence have been interpreted by some within mainstream education as lessening the impetus to emphasize phonics and other elements of scientifically based instruction at the core of Reading First (Cassidy & Cassidy, 2010).

A second development with implications for the use of systematic, explicit phonics instruction has been the increasing shift toward the use of response to intervention (RTI) methods to identify and treat reading difficulties, instead of classifying students as reading disabled based on a specified discrepancy score between aptitude and achievement measures (e.g., Fletcher, Lyon, Fuchs, & Barnes, 2006; Haager, Klinger, & Vaughn, 2007; Lyon et al., 2001; U.S. Department of Education, Office of Special Education and Rehabilitative Services, 2002; U.S. Department of Education, Office of Elementary and Secondary Education, 2002). This change in classification procedures has been included as an option in the current version of the Individuals with Disabilities Education Improvement ACT (IDEA) of 2004 (PL 108-446). The goals of the RTI method are to provide optimal, evidence-based classroom instruction for all students (Tier 1), with timely provision of early intervention, as needed. For students demonstrating weak responses to Tier 1 instruction, the intervention shifts from whole class to small-group instruction (Tier 2), with progression to more intensive delivery of instructional services as needed (Tiers 3 and higher, depending on the version of RTI). The model entails regular assessment of student progress and establishment of short-term educational goals selected to ameliorate identified areas of weakness. Because the majority of students encountering difficulty in learning to read have weaknesses with word reading skills both in decoding and in rapid word identification, knowing how to effectively teach the continuum of phonics concepts and to foster automaticity in word recognition is among the necessary mainstays of an RTI approach.

However, as the authors of the NRP report concluded, that the pertinent body of knowledge to teach phonics and word level skills has not been part of teacher preparation (see also Brady & Moats, 1997; National Research Council, 1998), with implications for the effectiveness of RTI efforts (B. F. Foorman, Carlson, & Santi, 2007). In the years since the NRP report, two studies have examined syllabi of reading-methods courses in teacher preparation programs, concluding that this shortcoming has not yet changed notably. In these studies, few education departments appear to have incorporated the body of knowledge identified by the NRP report as important for teaching students to read (Steiner & Rozen, 2004; Walsh, 2006). Likewise, a review of textbooks used in reading education courses found inadequate, and sometimes incorrect, coverage of the five components of literacy instruction recommended by the NRP report (Joshi, Binks, Graham, et al., 2009).

Correspondingly, in a study of instructors responsible for the training of preservice and in-service teachers, many were not well informed about the concepts pertinent to phonics instruction (Joshi, Binks, Hougen, et al., 2009). In turn, it follows that studies conducted both before and after the NRP report consistently have documented weaknesses in practicing teachers' knowledge of concepts central to code-based instruction (e.g., Bos, Mather, Dickson, Podhajski, & Chard, 2001; McCutchen et al., 2002; L. C. Moats, 1994; Spear-Swerling, Brucker, & Alfano, 2005), whether the teachers are recent graduates or not (e.g., Brady et al., 2009; Cunningham, Perry, Stanovich, & Stanovich, 2004).

The underpreparation of teachers in the area of code instruction is thought to be a consequence, in part, of the prevalence of meaning-emphasis programs for teaching reading, most commonly in accord with the whole-language philosophy (Liberman & Liberman, 1990; Pressley, 2006; Rayner et al., 2001). This approach, still permeating mainstream reading instruction, relies heavily on the child's experience with language: Motivation is central and children are encouraged to guess words that would fit in the context of the text. Proponents advocate the use of authentic children's literature, rather than decodable text. They suggest that children naturally acquire the knowledge necessary for skilled reading without direct instruction, much in the same way that spoken language develops. Indeed, key figures in this approach, Goodman (1970, 1993) and Smith (1979, 2003) maintain that phonics should not be taught. A central theme in whole-language approaches incorporates a constructivist perspective: Based on early research in cognitive psychology that described memory in terms of schemata and highlighted the importance of learners' prior knowledge, children are to be encouraged to construct meaning from text, connecting what they are reading with their background knowledge. A second theme emphasizes respect for experiential differences, including cultural influences, that would contribute to varying interpretations of an author's message.

These views are apparent in a recent study of teacher preparation for reading instruction. Risko et al. (2008) reviewed and critiqued 82 studies conducted in the United States on teacher preparation for reading instruction between 1990 and 2006. Most frequently, the studies were located within undergraduate programs preparing teachers for elementary and upper-grades teaching certification and targeted methods classes, asking whether the programs were successful in changing prospective teachers' knowledge and beliefs. In 73% of the studies, the researchers represented a cognitive or constructivist orientation, described as considering the "impact of prior knowledge and situated events in the teacher education program on learning to teach" (p. 258). Twenty-two percent of the studies were described as representing a sociocultural perspective: "Researchers in this category drew attention to the importance of learning about multicultural and social inequities issues and the use of this information on cultural responsive pedagogy" (p. 258). The remaining 5% were described as having a positivist/behavioral approach. Changes in knowledge and beliefs were reported for prospective teachers for the various approaches; however, the lack of focus on the specifics of the content and professional knowledge in the studies reviewed was striking, as Risko et al. noted. Further, the kinds of questions that might have reflected appreciation of the importance of current research on reading acquisition and reading instruction from the NRP report or earlier publications (e.g., Adams, 1990) were absent. The review by Risko et al. augments concern about a persisting gap between the in-service professional development goals articulated in the NRP report and the approaches to preparation of future teachers typically practiced in education departments.

In light of the theoretical backdrop of whole language and indications about teacher preparation practices, it is understandable that the recommendations in the NRP report regarding the merit of systematic, explicit instruction in phonics would have been met with discomfort. The underlying assumptions driving phonics instruction—that learning to read is not natural and that learning the alphabetic writing system is aided by direct teaching of graphemes and key orthographic patterns (Liberman, 1989)—clearly run counter to the core beliefs of whole-language approaches. Thus, it is not surprising that the response to recommendations regarding the use of phonics by individuals and organizations with this perspective has been tempered. A few of the influential responses will be summarized here to represent the degree of acceptance of phonics instruction and how the NRP findings are being interpreted within the education field. First, I will focus on the International Reading Association (IRA), a major organization for teachers of reading that has been aligned with the whole-language philosophy. In 1997, the organization released a position paper regarding the role of phonics in a total reading program (International Reading Association, 1997). While acknowledging the merit of phonics, no discussion of the key features of phonics was provided. In 2002, International Reading Association published *Evidence-Based Reading Instruction: Putting the National Reading Report into Practice*, a compilation of articles from *The Reading Teacher* (International Reading Association, 2002). In the section addressing phonics instruction, four articles were included, prefaced by an emphasis on the finding in the NRP report that there were no differences between different types of systematic phonics instruction. Three of the articles (Santa & Hoien, 1999; Stahl, 1992; Wagstaff, 1997) endorsed using phonological units larger than the phoneme (i.e., onsets and rimes) to teach phonics, and the fourth (Morrow & Tracey, 1997) was positive about incidental instruction. Although many cogent points were made, such as the importance of integrating phonics in a total reading program, the set of articles sends a mixed message about the teaching of phonics, communicating that phonics instruction above the level of the phoneme will suffice.

A second prominent source, *Best Practices in Literacy Instruction* (Gambrell, Morrow, & Pressley, 2007) has a chapter by P. Cunningham entitled "Best practices in teaching phonological awareness and phonics." Once again, there is an emphasis on the finding in the NRP report about the lack of significant differences found between different approaches to teaching phonics, with attention drawn to the fact that three studies using different methods all had positive student results (Davis, 2000; Juel & Minden-Cupp, 2000; McCandliss, Beck, Sandak, & Perfetti, 2003). In the chapter, Cunningham provides no discussion of the content or sequencing of systematic phonics instruction. Instead, she presents three phonics activities to illustrate "best practices in action" (p. 162). One (labeled Making Words) is an enjoyable review activity for students who already have learned a broad array of orthographic patterns, rather than a systematic means for teaching those patterns (i.e., words with short vowels, r-controlled vowels, vowel teams, and two syllables were included in the sample activity). The second (Using Words) presents an analogy strategy for figuring out how to spell words ("if ice is spelled i-c-e, twice is probably spelled t-w-i-c-e," p. 172). The third (Word Detectives) is suggested for students in the upper grades, focusing on morphemes (prefixes, suffixes, and roots). While each of these activities has merit if offered at appropriate points, a teacher seeking specific guidance on how, when, and how much to implement explicit, systematic instruction would not gain it from this chapter, despite the title. No mention of synthetic phonics methods was made, regardless of the fact that in the NRP report synthetic phonics had the largest effect size on reading outcomes. The absence of this more fine-grained method of phonics instruction is noteworthy. In the study mentioned earlier regarding the knowledge base of instructors teaching methods' courses in departments of education, Joshi, Binks, Hougen, et al. (2009) reported that the instructors did not cite synthetic phonics as suitable for beginning reading instruction, instead listing balanced instruction, whole language, or language experience approaches.

It is also notable that a second chapter in the volume by Gambrell et al. (2007), advocating balance in comprehensive literacy instruction (Pearson, Raphael, Benson, & Madda, 2007), conveyed two concerns regarding instruction in phonics. The first is reflected in a diagram included from Au and Raphael (1998) consisting of two dimensions: one indicating the person who is responsible for the learning process (i.e., teacher-controlled or student-controlled learning) and the second charting the level of engagement by the pupil (i.e., on a passive to active continuum). Explicit instruction is linked with teacher-led instruction and passive learning on the part of the child. This representation carries a negative valence with the attribution that explicit instruction has to entail passive learning rather than being engaging, varied, and discovery oriented as most phonics experts would maintain. The second concern by Pearson et al. was that in the wake of the NRP report, too much attention might be given to phonics, short-changing the many other topics relevant to literacy achievement and not providing adequately balanced literacy instruction. While the representation of pertinent areas of literacy was heavily skewed to depict sound/symbol learning as only 1 of 24 areas of literacy development, with no other components of word-level skills included, the problem of having sufficient time for all aspects of literacy instruction is a dilemma widely recognized by educators.

One other influential publication, *Reading Instruction That Works: The Case for Balanced Teaching* by Pressley (2006), will be mentioned here. Pressley wrestled with the same issues vexing those cited in the previous paragraph (i.e., the appropriate unit size for phonics instruction and the relative emphasis to be given to phonics in the literacy curriculum). Although he did so in a way that acknowledged the substantial body of research on the importance of word reading skills for reading success and the value of systematic phonics instruction, he reached similar conclusions. In the section on learning to read words, Pressley strongly endorsed the positive effects of explicit teaching of the alphabet, letter–sound associations, and sounding out of words, noting the consistently favorable evidence associated with synthetic phonics. Nonetheless, he went on to recommend teaching children to read by using word families and teaching students to decode by analogy, while allowing flexibility of methods as needed and providing balanced literacy instruction. Drawing on his own research (e.g., Pressley et al., 2001), Pressley emphasized that outstanding first-grade teachers provide a good balance of explicit skills instruction together with whole-language reading and writing activities.

The challenge for combined approaches, of course, is how to define the appropriate mix. Pressley attests to the "real variety out there among teachers who call themselves whole-language instructors" (p. 175), noting there are those who are very resistant to skills instruction (and do little), while others attempt to balance skills and whole-language components. A recent study by Cunningham, Zibulsky, Stanovich, and Stanovich (2009) collected responses from 121 first-grade teachers regarding what instructional practices they would propose for a 2-hr language arts block. Almost one in five teachers specified literature-based instruction in the relative absence of phonics instruction. The opposite subgroup, teachers who chose to emphasize phonics (27% of the sample), incorporated a relatively balanced collection of literature- and skills-based instructional experiences. This asymmetry may be predictable: The assumptions underlying explicit phonics instruction are not at odds with appreciation of the other components critical for becoming a skilled reader, whereas a corresponding acceptance of phonics does conflict with the assumptions central to a strong whole-language perspective.

In sum, as of 2000 when the NRP report was published, the convergence of a body of research indicated that systematic, explicit code-based instruction is beneficial for pupils, particularly in the early grades. Since that time extensive federal programs (No Child Left Behind; Reading First) were put in place, with mixed outcomes, to support the implementation of evidence-based practices on phonics and other elements of reading acquisition in schools. Likewise, the expansion of the RTI model for providing services for students encountering reading difficulties has increased focus on the assessment and intervention of subskills of reading, though numerous challenges remain for the reliable implementation of RTI, such as the need for professional development of preservice and in-service educators. At the same time, in the field of education, one of the main responses to NRP recommendations about phonics instruction has been to advocate using onset-rime units in the context of word family patterns, analytic approaches, and decoding by analogy, thus avoiding completely decomposing words into individual phonemes or using synthetic phonics activities. A second response has been to promote balanced instruction that, in genuine versions, incorporates direct instruction in phonics as part of a comprehensive literacy program.

By and large, the call in the NRP report for changes in the content of college and university teacher preparation programs has not been met. Indications from research studies on teacher knowledge and teacher preparation point to little focus on phonemic or orthographic units or on explicit, systematic ways of teaching phonics, most notably synthetic phonics methods. This may follow from the favor given to word-family approaches that do not utilize smaller units and generally do not address more advanced orthographic patterns. In turn, changes in teacher knowledge may not be seen as necessary. Stahl (1992), cited earlier, suggested that exemplary phonics instruction should focus on having children read words, not learn rules. Although he added that pointing out rules to students might be helpful in some instances, his stance may be perceived as undercutting the need for teachers to acquire knowledge of the spelling patterns of English.

Much of what has transpired in the last 10 years in educational practices regarding phonics hinges on the outcome reported in the NRP report that there were no significant differences in student outcomes between different methods of systematic phonics instruction. That finding has provided a rationale for avoiding a detailed focus on complete GPC in words with an emphasis instead on rime approaches. A second development has been the growing call for balanced instruction, sometimes troubling because the loose description of this approach has permitted resistors to give lip service to teaching phonics (L. Moats, 2007), while not providing any form of systematic instruction. In looking at the research from the subsequent decade, it is interesting to examine whether subsequent research sheds light on the issues of unit size in phonics instruction and whether, when done appropriately, a broader literacy program promotes reading acquisition better than a narrower focus on phonics.

POST-NRP RESEARCH ON PHONICS

In reviewing research on phonics published since the release of the NRP report, two main points emerge. First, the findings build the case for the benefits of teaching phonics systematically and explicitly, with advantages evident for complete analysis of the grapheme–phoneme composition of one-syllable words. As corollaries, this benefit is evident beyond the beginning of first grade and not just for struggling readers. Second, better literacy outcomes generally occur as a result of teaching other reading components in addition to phonics.

Phonics Instruction: Effects of Unit Size and Systematicity

Studies published in the last decade have continued to document the benefits of phonics instruction with most using methods that include explicit instruction of grapheme–phoneme units. For example, Connelly, Johnston, and Thompson (2001) reported that 6-year-old beginning readers taught to read by a synthetic phonics approach scored better in phoneme segmentation and on nonword reading tasks than students in a nonphonics group, as might be predicted given the attention to the alphabetic principle and decoding in phonics approaches. Although the students in the nonphonics group read known words more rapidly, those in the phonics group produced more contextually appropriate errors, made more attempts at reading unknown words, and had higher reading comprehension. Likewise, Jeynes (2008) published a meta-analysis documenting the positive relationship between phonics instruction and achievement for urban elementary school students.

More relevant to questions regarding the relative efficacy of different component of phonics instruction, Johnston and Watson (2004) compared reading achievement for 5-year-old new school entrants in Scotland who each were taught by one of the three different early reading programs. One group of students received synthetic phonics instruction with a grapheme–phoneme focus, whereas two groups were taught via analytic phonics using a word family method. (One of the analytic phonics cohorts received training in phoneme awareness in addition, whereas it was not included for the other two groups.) Instruction for all groups took place for 20 min per day for 16 weeks. Within each group, the classes participating represented both socially deprived and comparatively advantaged groups, although the synthetic phonics group came from relatively more deprived backgrounds. Nonetheless, the children who received synthetic phonics instruction had significantly better reading, spelling, and phoneme awareness at the end of the study than the children in the two groups taught analytic phonics. Further, those in the synthetic phonics group were the only ones who could read by analogy, and they also demonstrated significantly better reading of both irregular words and nonwords. A second experiment controlled for differences in the pace of letter learning across conditions; once again students in the synthetic phonics group read better than those in the analytic phonics condition. It was concluded that synthetic phonics is a more effective method than analytic phonics, and that with the former technique it is not necessary to carry out supplementary training in phoneme awareness.

Another study comparing synthetic and analytic methods reported equivalent gains with both methods (P. D. Walton, Walton, & Felton, 2001). However, the researchers seem to have used a synthetic method that minimized direct instruction. Words occasionally were sounded out while students were reading text, but the words that were selected for instruction did not build on structural redundancies that could help establish phonics knowledge (e.g., an example of words used on a single day were *hat* and *bed*, rather than words, for this condition of the study, that avoid word families, but still systematically progress [e.g., *hat/had* or *hat/hit*]). A second study by these authors (P. D. Walton & Walton, 2002) reported better results for beginning readers taught both rime analogy strategies and limited phonological knowledge (rhyming, initial phoneme identity, and letter–sound knowledge), rather than either alone. The combined method gave more opportunities for children to discern the structures of spoken and written words, but still did not constitute fully systematic methods of either phoneme awareness or code instruction (e.g., focusing only on initial phoneme identity is a low level of phoneme awareness, often grouped under an earlier stage of phonological awareness termed phonological sensitivity [Scarborough & Brady, 2002]). Consequently, while it may be productive to combine methods of instruction (Juel & Minden-Cupp, 2000; M. Lovett, Lacerenza, & Borden, 2000), this study does not adequately evaluate the value of systematic methods and illustrates that it is important to look beyond the labels when examining the efficacy of particular methods.

One of the insights from recent studies is that although various approaches to phonics enhance some literacy skills, more explicit, systematic methods of phonics instruction appear to facilitate more advanced code skills. Illustrating this are two studies that were carefully designed to match the instructional materials while varying the instructional methods. The first, conducted by de Graff, Bosman, Hasselman, and Verhoeven (2009), compared a systematic phonics approach with one that was nonsystematic. (A third group of children were in a nontreatment control condition.) Computer programs were used to teach the same 10 Dutch grapheme–phoneme correspondences (GPCs) to kindergarten students in the two experimental groups. Instruction in each of the phonics programs took place in fifteen 15-min sessions that were distributed over a period of 5 weeks. In the nonsystematic program, the sequence was not prespecified, the order of practice activities was chosen freely from a set of 10 different letter–sound and phonics activities, and the instruction did not gradually increase in difficulty. In contrast, in the systematic approach, children encountered a planned set of phonics-through-spelling and synthetic-phonics activities. Interestingly, both groups progressed to the same extent on letter–sound knowledge with both better than the control group. However, the systematic phonics group made significantly more progress than the other two groups on phoneme awareness, as well as on more advanced spelling and reading measures.

The second study, by Christensen and Bowey (2005), compared the efficacy of three programs: an orthographic rime (OR) program (i.e., word families), an approach focusing on GPC, and the regularly provided whole-language approach to teaching reading. The participants were children in their second year of schooling in elementary schools in Australia, described by the authors as being at an advanced beginner phase of reading acquisition. Two earlier studies failed to show effects based on the size of the orthographic unit (Haskell, Foorman, & Swank, 1992; Levy & Lysynchuk, 1997), but both were fairly brief (6 and 4 weeks in duration, respectively). The Christiansen and Bowey training program was implemented for 20 min per day for 14 weeks in small groups of six to eight children. The lessons in the OR and GPC conditions followed the same basic format, practicing the same number of words in each session and the same words across each of six modules of 10 lessons (8 lessons introducing a set of four new words and 2 review lessons). However, the words within sets for each program were presented in different orders and combinations so that the OR group had sets of rhyming words (e.g., top, mop, hop, and shop), whereas the corresponding GPC cohort had lists that did not contain any rhyming words (e.g., mat, hop, run, and shin). The results of this well-designed study showed significant superiority on interim and posttest measures for the OR and GPC groups over the classroom control group on nearly all of the reading and spelling assessments, consistent with the findings of the NRP meta-analysis. The point of particular interest to the present discussion is that groups of children receiving the two decoding programs did not differ statistically on the easier accuracy measures requiring reading or spelling the words that had been taught in the program and reading sentences. On the other hand, the GPC group had significantly better performance on the more demanding tasks. On measures of the accuracy and speed of reading transfer words with the same orthographic patterns as those taught in the programs, the GPC cohort tested significantly higher on accuracy and speed for the transfer words than both the OR and the nontreatment control groups. This last finding has important implications regarding the importance of explicit phonics approaches for building decoding skills that support abilities to read the large number of novel words that young readers encounter during reading, particularly as they reach the midelementary grades (Nagy & Anderson, 1984). Similar findings were found for the spelling measures, and the GPC group also performed significantly better than the other two groups on assessment of reading comprehension. In sum, the de Graff et al. (2009) and Christensen and Bowey studies are strong indicators that in designing experiments to compare methods of reading instruction, it is necessary, in addition to holding other design features constant, to have a sufficient range of outcome measures in order to be certain that the impact of instructional characteristics is adequately assessed. Further, the outcomes, along with those of the Johnston and Watson (2004) study, add evidence that choice of phonic methods is, indeed, consequential, with benefits associated with using synthetic methods at the grapheme–phoneme level.

Beyond First Grade

The NRP report cited stronger benefits from systematic, explicit code instruction in kindergarten and first grade than in the second through the sixth grades. Tellingly, documentation of teaching practices indicates that generally less time is spent on code instruction after first grade. For example, B. Foorman et al. (2006) reported that approximately 28% of the instruction during 90- to 120-min language arts periods in the first grade incorporated explicit code instruction, whereas only 14% of the language arts sessions in the second grade did so. A similar reduction of code instruction by half in the second grade also was noted by Connor, Morrison, and Underwood (2007). The prevailing assumption appears to be that it is more important to provide code instruction in first grade. However, for children who get off to a slow start, an examination of reading growth trajectories (Spira, Bracken, & Fischel, 2005) indicates an important role for instruction in the second grade, at least for struggling readers. Pointing to even broader significance, striking results obtained by Connor et al. indicate that classroom instructional practices in the second grade in phonics may make a significant impact on all students' reading development, not just those encountering difficulty. In this longitudinal study, 108 students were followed from the first through the third grade. The 2007 publication focused on first- and second-grade achievement and on the characteristics of classroom instruction. Connor et al. classified instruction along two dimensions, child managed versus teacher managed and code focused versus meaning focused. Child-by-instruction interactions were evident: (a) Students who entered first grade with weaker letter–word reading scores had stronger letter–word reading at the end of second grade when they had received more teacher-managed, code-focused instruction in both the first and second grades. (b) Students who entered first grade with stronger letter–word reading progress had better second-grade reading scores when they received less teacher-managed code instruction in the first grade (Connor, Morrison, & Katch, 2004), but more in the second grade. The latter pattern perhaps reflects a poor fit between the level of code instruction provided in the first grade for the advanced entering students, with a better match between the content of code instruction and the students' instructional level in the second grade. For this discussion, what is compelling is the dramatic difference in reading achievement for all students, hinging on whether they received direct instruction in phonics in the second grade. For the students who had started first grade with stronger letter–word skills, spending some time in second grade on teacher-managed, code instruction resulted in reading performance several years above grade level, whereas not having this instruction was linked with grade level achievement. For the students who began first grade with deficient letter–word knowledge, the data indicated they would reach grade level letter–word reading at the end of second grade only if they were in classes in which teacher-managed, code-focused instruction occurred during both the first and second grades. While more research on these issues would be helpful, these observational results point to the need to incorporate systematic, explicit instruction in code concepts in the second grade, and possibly beyond (Ganske, 2000; Gaskins, 2000; Henry, 2010).

Students Making Inadequate Progress in Learning to Read

A number of studies have documented significant gains in reading skills as a result of systematic, explicit phonics instruction for students who are not making good progress in learning to read (e.g., Hatcher, Hulme, & Snowling, 2004; Lovett et al., 2000, Vadasy & Sanders, 2008). In one investigation by McCandliss et al. (2003), the researchers' examined the students' decoding attempts prior to the intervention and identified a pattern of accurate decoding of the first grapheme of a word, followed by relatively worse performance on subsequent vowels and consonants, suggesting that the students (7–10 years of age) were not fully decoding the words. To address this problem, the intervention systematically focused attention over 20 sessions on each grapheme position within the word by a procedure of minimal pairing of words that differed only by a single grapheme (i.e., Beck's Word Building method [Beck, 1989]). In comparison to students assigned to a control group, those in the intervention group had greater improvements in decoding attempts at all grapheme positions and also had significantly greater improvements in standardized measures of decoding, reading comprehension, and phonological awareness.

Along similar lines, Blachman et al. (2004) reported the results of 8 months of intervention conducted with students in the second and third grades. During the sessions, Blachman and her team implemented a set of instructional activities that included sound-symbol instruction, manipulation of word structures using sound boards or scrabble tiles (e.g., changing *fan* to *fat* to *sat* to *sag*), fluency building for regular and irregular high-frequency words, oral reading practice with different types of text (controlled, trade books, and expository), and spelling/writing practice. In addition to the manipulation of graphemes on "sound boards" (a procedure similar to that used in the McCandless et al. study), Blachman et al. incorporated instruction on the six syllable types of English as a strategy to help students master vowel patterns, typically the most difficult part of beginning reading. The students in the treatment group made significantly greater gains than the students in the regular school-provided intervention program on numerous measures (real word reading, nonword reading, reading rate, passage reading, and spelling). These gains largely were maintained a year later when follow-up testing was conducted. The finding of significant improvement in spelling for treatment students is noteworthy; in the NRP, older poor readers were not found to have improved in spelling following phonics instruction. The mnemonics provided for the vowel syllable types and the associated understanding of contextual influences on vowel spelling may have played a role in this encouraging outcome.

Using other intervention programs, a study by Torgesen et al. (2001) also achieved impressive outcomes with struggling students beyond first grade. Torgesen et al. compared the outcomes of two types of intensive remedial instruction for children between 8 and 10 years of age who previously had been identified as learning disabled with serious weaknesses on word-level reading skills. It is important to point out that both forms of remediation contained explicit, systematic instruction on phonics, as well as other activities including reading connected text. A key part of what differed was the ratio of time allotted to phonics. In one approach, most of a session (85%) was spent on stimulating phonemic/articulatory awareness and building facility at decoding and encoding individual words, with a small portion of the time allotted to reading decodable text. In the second approach, 50% of the time was spent on activities involving meaningful text and only 20% on phonemic decoding and spelling (including phonetic rules and patterns), with additional time on reading sight words accurately and fluently. Despite substantial differences in duration, both methods targeted the grapheme–phoneme elements throughout words, rather than just rime units, and provided explicit instruction on spelling patterns in words. Interestingly, both instructional programs produced very large improvements in reading skills and student performance in each remained improved over a 2-year follow-up period. Torgesen et al. concluded "that within explicit 'structured language' approaches that follow sound instructional principles, there may be considerable latitude for arranging components of instruction according to teacher and student preference." (p. 56) (also see Mathes et al., 2005).

Studies with even older poor readers likewise have documented the benefits of addressing code weaknesses beyond the early grades. Bhattacharya and Ehri (2004) demonstrated that graphosyllabic instruction facilitated adolescent students' ability to decode novel words, providing a bridge to decoding multisyllabic structures. Using peer-mediated instruction that targeted both decoding and comprehension domains, Calhoon (2005) attained improved reading acquisition for middle school students. M. Lovett, Lacerenza, De Palma & Frijters (in press) documented robust gains with struggling readers in high school using a reading intervention program that incorporated word identification instruction together with the teaching of text structures and reading comprehension strategies. Two recent meta-analytic studies (Edmonds et al., 2009; Scammacca et al., 2007) likewise reported moderate effect size gains from word-level interventions with students in grades 6–12.

Relevant findings also are emerging from research investigating the RTI model with implementation of secondary and tertiary tiers of intervention, as needed, for students in regular classes who have been targeted as being at risk for reading problems (e.g., Coyne, Kame'enui, Simmons, 2001; B. Harn, Kame'enui, & Simmons, 2007; Kamps et al., 2008; McMaster, Fuchs, Fuchs, & Compton, 2005; O'Connor, Harty, & Fulmer, 2005). The findings indicate that more explicit, systematic methods of instruction, offered with greater intensity than in regular classroom instruction, result in improvements in basic literacy skills, with some students advancing to grade level performance. Research on the application of the RTI model in later grades is beginning to be done (e.g., Vaughn et al., 2010), though many issues remain concerning whether the conceptualization of RTI needs to be somewhat different (Fuchs, Fuchs, & Compton, 2010). It should be noted that thus far systematic, explicit phonics interventions with severely disabled readers generally succeed at narrowing the gap in reading problems, but not closing it (Torgesen, 2004). In addition, the breadth of reading weaknesses varies for different students, requiring differentiation of intervention and often multifaceted approaches (Fletcher et al., 2006; Leach, Scarborough, & Rescorla, 2003; also see Snowling (Chapter 6) and Catts and Adlof (Chapter 7)).

Other efforts likewise indicate the need to adjust the intensity of services to help students attain success. In an informal report of the steps implemented to raise reading achievement in a school district in Washington state (Fielding, Kerr, & Rosier, 2007), the authors reported that school personnel determined over a period of years that an inverse relationship holds between the amount of intervention required and how far behind students are: The further behind, the more intervention necessary to achieve catch-up growth. (This sensible approach runs counter to the common school practice of providing a fixed duration of intervention regardless of a student's extent of difficulty.) Researchers have verified that increasing the intensity of intervention in terms of the amount of time and/or the duration is beneficial (e.g., Al Otaiba, Schatschneider, & Silverman, 2005; Denton, Fletcher, Anthony, & Francis, 2006; B. A. Harn, Linan-Thompson, & Roberts, 2008; O'Connor, 2000). While agreeing with this general principle, a study by Simmons, Kame'enui, Harn, Coyne, Stoolmiller et al. (2007) linked the importance both of the content of remedial instruction and of the intensity of delivery. Using a randomized experimental design with three levels of intervention, Simmons et al. compared the effects of beginning reading interventions on early decoding, spelling, and phonemic awareness outcomes for 96 kindergartners who had been identified as at-risk for reading difficulty. The three instructional programs varied systematically along two dimensions, duration and instructional specificity. The outcomes indicated that more explicit instructional designs maximize the use of instructional time, attenuating the need to increase the duration of instruction.

More Than Phonics

The value of direct instruction on phonics that is explicit and systematic is ever more apparent after another 10 years of pertinent research since the NRP report. What is emerging as well is evidence that engaging students in processes of reading and writing, in addition to providing them with quality phonics instruction, is better than focusing solely on phonics. In 2004, Xue and Meisels reported the findings of a large sample of kindergarten children (n = 13,609) in 2690 classrooms from the base year of the Early Childhood Longitudinal Study. In the study, student reading performance was measured both with direct cognitive test scores and with indirect teacher ratings of children's language and literacy abilities. In addition, the teachers provided reports of their literacy instruction practices, rating how often they conducted particular curricular and instructional activities on a 6-point scale ranging from never to daily. This information led to two composite measures of instructional foci on phonics and integrated language arts. Xue and Meisels determined that the phonics approach was moderately, positively correlated with integrated language arts (r = .55). Further, they concluded that children performed better when both types of instruction were used more frequently and that the benefits were reciprocal: "Phonics is more effective when it is combined with integrated language arts activities in the classroom. Conversely, integrated language arts instruction works better in classrooms where phonics is also taught more frequently" (p. 219). (Also see Vadasy, Sanders, & Peyton, 2005). These observations echo those of Chall (1967) and the NRP report and fit with evidence from current instructional and intervention studies showing greater gains from multicomponent programs (e.g., Fletcher, Denton, Fuchs, & Vaughn, 2005; M. W. Lovett et al., 2005; M. Lovett et al., in press; Torgesen, 2005). A further source regarding the benefits of offering good instruction on both phonics and integrated language arts comes from observations of exemplary teachers and typical teachers in first-grade classrooms, as mentioned earlier (e.g., Pressley, 2006; Pressley et al., 2001).

CLOSING REMARKS

In the 10 years since the NRP released their conclusions regarding phonics instruction, developments in research have confirmed and extended the findings of the NRP. The sizeable body of research conducted in the intervening decade indicates that how phonics is taught matters: Systematic, explicit methods of code instruction are more effective than approaches that are less explicit (e.g., focusing on rime units; only using analogy techniques) and/or less systematic (e.g., incidental and unstructured methods). From the research that has accrued, normally achieving students, students at risk, and severely disabled readers all have been documented to benefit from systematic, explicit instruction, with variations in the intensity required. Likewise, research outcomes are pointing to the value of extending code-based instruction beyond first grade not only for struggling readers but also for those with stronger prowess in basic skills. Yet, whereas the studies conducted have supported use of a systematic, direct focus on grapheme–phoneme units, the amount of time devoted to this portion of the literacy curriculum varied widely. In addition, evidence is building that rather than solely providing quality code instruction, outcomes are superior when code instruction is accompanied by rich and varied literacy instruction with opportunities to read and write (e.g., Lyon & Weiser, 2009; Pressley, 2006).

Meanwhile, in educational settings, whether in public schools serving children or in higher education programs, current teacher practices and recommendations by leaders in literacy often represent adoption of an overtly neutral stance regarding phonics, emphasizing that no method is better than any other. At the same time, many educational leaders recommend the use of rime/analogy approaches rather than more fully systematic, explicit phonics instruction. Examination of textbook content and instructor knowledge for teacher education programs suggests that gaps pertaining to code instruction are not uncommon, contributing to inadequate preparation of future teachers to provide evidence-based literacy practices. Correspondingly, studies of teachers' knowledge of code concepts indicate that there still are marked discrepancies between the implications of research and teachers' knowledge base. Although fostering shifts in school practices and gains in student achievement require more than bolstering teacher knowledge (e.g., Smith & Brady, in preparation), this is a necessary ingredient. On the other hand, compatible with the growing research evidence, much of the education community already is endorsing the use of multifaceted literacy instruction (e.g., phonics, text reading, writing, fluency, and comprehension). With the appropriate balance, this approach results in beneficial literacy learning environments for students.

In moving forward, four challenges stand out. First, it will be important to overcome continued resistance in the education community to systematic, explicit phonics instruction and to undercut the claims that all methods of phonics instruction are equally effective. With supportive leadership from within the education field, it can be hoped that educators will become more aware of the additional wave of research since the NRP report and more accepting that direct teaching of the code is in the best interest of students. Perhaps the evidence that explicit instruction reduces the time it takes to launch successful readers will make it more palatable, particularly with the attendant message that doing so in the context of rich, comprehensive literacy instruction is optimal.

Second, teacher preparation programs will need to expand their curricula to build teacher expertise in code instruction (L. Moats, 2009; Stotsky, 2009). Recent research showed an interaction between teacher knowledge of code concepts and whether students benefited from instruction on phonics: When teachers had poor knowledge about phonics, more teaching about the code was detrimental and, when teachers had good knowledge, more teaching was beneficial (Piasta, Connor, Fishman, & Morrison, 2009). Further, programs will need to model quality integration of code instruction within comprehensive literacy curricula, rather than providing token support for systematic, explicit phonics.

Third, and central to the preceding two challenges, it will be important to provide clarification of what constitutes explicit, systematic instruction and of what kinds of activities achieve constructive synthetic methods. Prominent teacher resources on phonics instruction too often include many valuable complementary activities, but lack sufficient information regarding the content and procedures central to explicit, systematic methods (e.g., Cunningham, 2007; Pinnell & Fountas, 2003). The increasing research support for grapheme–phoneme instruction with sufficient systematic attention to the final and medial portions of words, not just the initial phoneme, needs to be conveyed to practitioners, as does the value of extending instruction to more advanced code concepts beyond first grade.

Fourth, despite the converging results from dozen more studies since the NRP report, numerous topics require further investigation, of course. Among these, more needs to be understood about the optimal duration and scope of instructional ingredients: The amount of time allocated to successful systematic, explicit phonics methods and the mix of instructional components varied widely across experimental studies/conditions leaving questions about the instructional requirements, and whether the aim should be confirming student mastery of components rather than specifying duration. Likewise, research on the benefits of advanced phonics instruction needs to be explored further: In addition to teaching letter–sound correspondences, how much attention to orthographic spelling patterns and morphological structures helps students gain mastery of the English writing system? What are the underlying weaknesses and instructional solutions for those children who are inadequate responders? What is the interplay between oral language development and ability to profit from code instruction?

While these and many other questions remain to be investigated; nonetheless, the research gains from the last 10 years have added to a coherent and consistent picture regarding the merit of systematic, explicit phonics instruction for normally developing readers and for those, younger and older, experiencing difficulty. Perhaps most important, the results from the growing scientific literature underscore the importance of ongoing research on reading instruction and that research can, and should, make a difference regarding educational practices.

REFERENCES

Adams, M. (1990). *Beginning to read: Thinking and learning about print*. Cambridge, MA: MIT Press.

Al Otaiba, S., Schatschneider, C., & Silverman, E. (2005). Tutor-assisted intensive learning strategies in kindergarten: How much is enough? *Exceptionality*, *13*(4), 195–208.

Au, K. H., & Raphael, T. E. (1998). Curriculum and teaching in literature-based programs. In T. E. Raphael, & K. H. Au (Eds.), *Literature-based instruction: Reshaping the curriculum* (pp. 123–148). Norwood, MA: Christopher-Gordon.

Beck, I. (1989). *Reading today and tomorrow* (Teachers' editions for grades 1 and 2). Austin, TX: Holt & Co.

Bhattacharya, A., & Ehri, L. (2004). Graphosyllabic analysis helps adolescent struggling readers read and spell words. *Journal of Learning Disabilities*, *37*(4), 331–348.

Blachman, B., Schatschneider, C., Fleltcher, J., Francis, D., Clonan, S., Shaywitz, B., et al. (2004). Effects of intensive reading remediation for second and third graders and a 1-year follow up. *Journal of Educational Psychology*, *96*(3), 444–461.

Bos, C., Mather, N., Dickson, S., Podhajski, B., & Chard, D. (2001). Perceptions and knowledge of preservice and inservice educators about early reading instruction. *Annals of Dyslexia*, *51*, 97–120.

Brady, S., Gillis, M., Smith, T., Liss-Bronstein, L., Lowe, E., Russo, E., et al. (2009). First grade teachers' knowledge of phonological awareness and code concepts: Examining gains from an intensive form of professional development. *Reading and Writing: An Interdisciplinary Journal*, *22*, 425–455.

Brady, S., & Moats, L. (1997). *Informed instruction for reading success: Foundations for teacher preparation* (Position Paper). Baltimore, MD: International Dyslexia Association.

Calhoon, M. B. (2005). Effects of a peer-mediated phonological skill and reading comprehension program on reading skill acquisition of middle school students with reading disabilities. *Journal of Learning Disabilities*, *38*(5), 424–433.

Cassidy, J., & Cassidy, D. (December 2009/January 2010). What's hot for 2010: 14th annual survey reveals some "crumbling pillars" of reading instruction. *Reading Today*, *27*(3), 1, 8, 9.

Catts, H. W., & Adlof, S. (2011). Phonological and other language deficits associated with dyslexia. In S. Brady, D. Braze, & C. Fowler (Eds.), *Explaining individual differences in reading: Theory and evidence*.

Chall, J. S. (1967). *Learning to read: The great debate*. New York: McGraw-Hill.

Christensen, C. A., & Bowey, J. A. (2005). The efficacy of orthographic rime, grapheme-phoneme correspondence, and implicit phonics approaches to teaching decoding skills. *Scientific Studies of Reading*, *9*(4), 327–349.

Cohen, J. (1988). *Statistical power analysis for the behavioral sciences* (2nd ed.). Mahwah, NJ: Lawrence Erlbaum.

Connelly, V., Johnston, R., & Thompson, G. B. (2001). The effect of phonics instruction on the reading comprehension of beginning readers. *Reading and Writing: An Interdisciplinary Journal*, *14*, 423–457.

Connor, C., Morrison, F., & Katch, E. L. (2004). Beyond the reading wars: The effect of classroom instruction by child interactions on early reading. *Scientific Studies of Reading*, *8*(4), 305–336.

Connor, C., Morrison, F., & Underwood, P. S. (2007). A second chance in second grade: The independent and cumulative impact of first and second grade reading instruction and students' letter-word reading skill growth. *Scientific Studies of Reading*, *11*(3), 199–233.

Coyne, M. D., Kame'enui, E. J., & Simmons, D. C. (2001). Prevention and intervention in beginning reading: Two complex systems. *Learning Disabilities Research and Practice*, *16*, 62–73.

Cunningham, A., Perry, K., Stanovich, K., & Stanovich, P. (2004). Disciplinary knowledge of K-3 teachers and their knowledge calibration in the domain of early literacy. *Annals of Dyslexia*, *54*, 139–168.

Cunningham, A., Zibulsky, J., Stanovich, K., & Stanovich, P. (2009). How teachers would spend their time teaching language arts: The mismatch between self-reported and best practices. *Journal of Learning Disabilities*, *42*, 418–430.

Cunningham, P. (2007). Best practices in teaching phonological awareness and phonics. In L. B. Gambrell, L. M. Morrow, & M. Pressley (Eds.), *Best practices in literacy instruction* (pp. 159–177). New York: Guilford.

Davis, L. H. (2000). The effects of rime-based analogy training on word reading and spelling of first-grade children with good and poor phonological awareness (Doctoral dissertation, Northwestern University). *Dissertation Abstracts International*, *61*, 2253A.

de Graff, S., Bosman, A. M. T., Hasselman, F., & Verhoeven, L. (2009). Benefits of systematic phonics instruction. *Scientific Studies of Reading*, *13*(4), 318–333.

Denton, C., Fletcher, J., Anthony, J., & Francis, D. (2006). An evaluation of intensive intervention for students with persistent reading difficulties. *Journal of Learning Disabilities*, *39*(5), 447–466.

Edmonds, M. S., Vaughn, S., Wexler, J., Reutebuch, C., Cable, A., Tackett, K. K., et al. (2009). A synthesis of reading interventions and effects on reading comprehension outcomes on older struggling readers. *Review of Educational Research*, *79*(1), 262–287.

Ehri, L., Nunes, S. R., Stahl, S., & Willows, D. (2001). Systematic phonics instruction helps students learn to read: Evidence from the National Reading Panel's meta-analysis. *Review of Educational Research*, *71*, 393–447.

Fielding, L., Kerr, N., & Rosier, P. (2007) *Annual growth for all students, catch up growth for those who are behind*. Kennewick, WA: The New Foundation Press.

Fletcher, J. M., Denton, C. A., Fuchs, L. S., & Vaughn, S. R. (2005). Multi-tiered reading instruction: Linking general education and special education. In J. Gilger, & S. Richardson (Eds.), *Research-based education and intervention: What we need to know* (pp. 21–43). Baltimore, MD: International Dyslexia Association.

Fletcher, J. M., Lyon, G. R., Fuchs, L. S., & Barnes, M. A. (2006). *Learning disabilities: From identification to intervention*. New York: Guilford.

Foorman, B., Schatschneider, C., Eakin, M., Fletcher, J., Moats, L., & Francis, D. (2006). The impact of instructional practices in Grades 1 and 2 on reading and spelling achievement in high poverty schools. *Contemporary Educational Psychology*, *31*(1), 1–29.

Foorman, B. F., Carlson, C., & Santi, K. L. (2007). Classroom reading instruction and teacher knowledge in the primary grades. In D. Haager, J. Klinger, & S. Vaughn (Ed.), *Evidence-based reading practices for response to intervention*. Baltimore, MD: Brookes Publishing.

Francis, D. (2008, June). *Reading First impact study: What have we learned and where do we go from here?* Paper presented at the annual meeting of the Institute of Education Science Research Conference, Washington, DC.

Fuchs, L. S., Fuchs, D., & Compton, D. L. (2010). Rethinking response to intervention at middle and high school. *School Psychology Review*, *39*(1), 22–28.

Gambrell, L. B., Morrow, L. M., & Pressley, M. (2007). *Best practices in literacy instruction*. New York: Guilford.

Gamse, B. C., Jacob, R. T., Horst, M., Boulay, B., & Unlu, F. (2008). *Reading First impact study: Final report* (NCEE 2008-4038). Washington, DC: U.S. Department of Education, Institute of Education Sciences, National Center for Education Evaluation and Regional Assistance.

Ganske, K. (2000). *Word journeys: Assessment-guided phonics, spelling and vocabulary instruction*. New York: Guilford.

Gaskins, I. W. (2000). *Word detectives program: 5th grade and above*. Media, PA: Benchmark Press.

Goodman, K. S. (1970). Reading: A psycholinguistic guessing game. In H. Singer, & R. B. Ruddell (Eds.), *Theoretical models and processes of reading* (pp. 259–272). Newark, DE: International Reading Association.

Goodman, K. S. (1993). *Phonics phacts*. Portsmouth, NH: Heinemann.

Haager, D., Klinger, J., & Vaughn, S. (Eds.) (2007). *Evidence-based reading practices for response to intervention*. Baltimore, MD: Brookes.

Harn, B., Kame'enui, E., & Simmons, D. C. (2007). The nature and role of the third tier in a prevention model for kindergarten students. In D. Haager, J. Klingner, & S. Vaughn (Eds.), *Evidence-based reading practices for response to intervention*. Baltimore, MD: Brookes.

Harn, B. A., Linan-Thompson, S., & Roberts, G. (2008). Intensifying instruction: Does additional instructional time make a difference for the most at-risk first graders? *Journal of Learning Disabilities*, *41*(2), 115–125.

Haskell, D. W., Foorman, B. R., & Swank, R. R. (1992). Effects of three orthographic/phonological units on first-grade reading. *Remedial and Special Education*, *13*, 40–49.

Hatcher, P. J., Hulme, C., & Snowling, M. J. (2004). Explicit phoneme training with phonic reading instructions helps young children at risk. *Journal of Child Psychology and Psychiatry*, *43*, 338–358.

Henry, M. (2010). *Unlocking literacy: Effective decoding and spelling instruction*. Baltimore, MD: Brookes.

Individuals with Disabilities Education Improvement ACT (IDEA) of 2004 (PL 108-446), U.S.C. §§ 1400 *et seq*.

International Reading Association. (1997). *The role of phonics in reading instruction*. A position statement of the International Reading Association. http://www.reading.org/Libraries/Position_Statements_and_Resolutions/ps1018_phonics.sflb.ashx

International Reading Association. (2002). *Evidence-based reading instruction: Putting the National Reading Panel Report into practice*. Newark, DE: International Reading Association.

Jeynes, W. H. (2008). A meta-analysis of the relationship between phonics instruction and minority elementary school student academic achievement. *Education and Urban Society*, *40*(2), 151–166.

Johnston, R. S., & Watson, J. E. (2004). Accelerating the development of reading, spelling and phonemic awareness skills in initial readers. *Reading and Writing*, *17*(4), 327–357.

Joshi, R. M., Binks, E., Graham, L., Ocker-Dean, E., Smith, D., & Boulware-Gooden, R. (2009). Do textbooks used in university reading education courses conform to the instructional recommendations of the National Reading Panel? *Journal of Learning Disabilities*, *42*, 458–463.

Joshi, R. M., Binks, E., Hougen, M., Dahlgren, M., Ocker-Dean, E., & Smith, D. (2009). Why elementary teachers might be inadequately prepared to teach reading. *Journal of Learning Disabilities*, *42*, 392–402.

Juel, C., & Minden-Cupp, C. (2000). Learning to read words: Linguistic units and instructional strategies. *Reading Research Quarterly*, *35*, 458–492.

Kamps, D., Abbott, M., Greenwood, C., Wills, H., Veerkamp, M., & Kaufman, J. (2008). Effects of small-group reading instruction and curriculum differences for students most at risk in kindergarten: Two-year results for secondary- and tertiary-level interventions. *Journal of Learning Disabilities*, *41*, 101–114.

Leach, J. M., Scarborough, H. S., & Rescorla, L. (2003). Late-emerging reading disabilities. *Journal of Educational Psychology*, *95*(2), 211–224.

Levy, B. A., & Lysynchuk, L. (1997). Beginning word recognition: Benefits of training by segmentation and whole word methods. *Scientific Studies of Reading*, *1*, 359–387.

Liberman, A. M. (1989). Reading is hard just because listening is easy. In C. von Euler (Ed.), *Wenner-Gren international symposium series: Brain and reading* (pp. 197–205). Hampshire: Macmillan.

Liberman, I. Y., & Liberman, A. M. (1990). Whole language vs. code emphasis: Underlying assumptions and their implications for reading instruction. *Annals of Dyslexia*, *40*, 51–76.

Lovett, M. W., Lacerenza, L., De Palma, M., & Frijters, J. C. (in press). Evaluating the efficacy of remediation for struggling readers in high school. *Journal of Learning Disabilities*.

Lovett, M., Lacerenza, L., & Borden, S. (2000). Putting struggling readers on the PHAST track: A program to integrate phonological and strategy-based remedial reading instruction and maximize outcomes. *Journal of Learning Disabilities*, *33*, 458–476.

Lovett, M. W., Lacerenza, L., Murphy, D., Steinbach, K. A., De Palma, M., & Frijters, J. C. (2005). The importance of multiple-component interventions for children and adolescents who are struggling readers. In J. Gilger, & S. Richardson (Eds.), *Research-based education and intervention: What we need to know* (pp. 67–102). Baltimore, MD: International Dyslexia Association.

Lyon, G. R., Fletcher, J. M., Shaywitz, S. E., Shaywitz, B. A., Torgesen, J. K., Wood, F. B., et al. (2001). Rethinking learning disabilities. In C. Finn, A. Rotherham, & C. Hokanson (Eds.), *Rethinking special education for a new century* (pp. 259–287). Washington, DC: Thomas B. Fordham Foundation and the Progressive Policy Institute.

Lyon, G. R., & Weiser, B. (2009). Teacher knowledge, instructional expertise, and the development of reading proficiency. *Journal of Learning Disabilities*, *42*, 475–480.

Mathes, P., Denton, C., Fletcher, J., Anthony, J., Francis, D., & Schatschneider, C. (2005). The effects of theoretically different instruction and student characteristics on the skills of struggling readers. *Reading Research Quarterly*, *40*, 148–182.

McCandliss, B., Beck, I. L., Sandak, R., & Perfetti, C. (2003). Focusing attention on decoding for children with poor reading skills: A study of the word building intervention. *Scientific Studies of Reading*, *7*, 75–104.

McCardle, P., & Chhabra, V. (Eds.). (2004). *The voice of evidence in reading research*. Baltimore, MD: Paul H. Brookes.

McCardle, P., Chhabra, V., & Kapinus, B. (2008). *Reading research in action: A teacher's guide for student success*. Baltimore, MD: Paul H. Brookes.

McCutchen, D., Abbott, R. D., Green, L. B., Beretvas, S. N., Cox, S., Potter, N. S., et al. (2002). Beginning literacy: Links among teacher knowledge, teacher practice, and student learning. *Journal of Learning Disabilities*, *35*, 69–86.

McMaster, K. L., Fuchs, D., Fuchs, L. S., & Compton, D. L. (2005). Responding to nonresponders: An experimental field trial of identification and intervention methods. *Exceptional Children*, *71*, 445–463.

Mitchell, K., Brady, S., Cutting, L., Carlo, M., Gutierrez, K., Lesaux, N., et al. (June 19, 2008). *Response to the Reading First impact study*. EducationNews.org http://www.ednews.org/articles/response-to-the-reading-first-impact-study.html, retrieval date on July 10, 2010.

Moats, L. (2007). *Whole language high jinks: How to tell when "scientifically-based reading instruction" isn't*. Washington, DC: The Thomas B. Fordham Institute. http://www.edexcellence.net/detail/news.cfm?news_id=367

Moats, L. (2009). Still wanted: Teachers with knowledge of language. *Journal of Learning Disabilities*, *42*, 387–391.

Moats, L. C. (1994). The missing foundation in teacher education: Knowledge of the structure of spoken and written language. *Annals of Dyslexia*, *44*, 81–102.

Morrow, L. M., & Tracey, D. H. (1997). Strategies used for phonics instruction in early childhood classrooms. *The Reading Teacher*, *50*, 644–651.

Nagy, W. E., & Anderson, R. C. (1984). How many words are there in printed English? *Reading Research Quarterly*, *19*, 304–330.

National Center for Education Statistics. (2007). *National assessment of educational progress*. http://nces.ed.gov/nationsreportcard/reading, retrieval date June 5, 2010.

National Institute of Child Health and Human Development. (2000). *Report of the National Reading Panel. Teaching children to read: An evidence-based assessment of the scientific research literature on reading and its implications for reading instruction: Reports of the subgroups* (NIH Publication No. 00-4754). Washington, DC: U.S. Government Printing Office.

National Research Council. (1998). C. E. Snow, M. S. Burns, & P. Griffin (Eds.) *Preventing reading difficulties in young children*. Washington, DC: National Academy Press.

No Child Left Behind Act of 2001, PL107-110, 115 Stat. 1425, 20 U.S.C. §§ 6301 *et seq.*

O'Connor, R. (2000). Increasing the intensity of intervention in kindergarten and first grade. *Learning Disabilities Research & Practice*, *15*, 43–54.

O'Connor, R., Harty, K., & Fulmer, D. (2005). Tiers of intervention in kindergarten through third grade. *Journal of Learning Disabilities*, *38*(6), 532–538.

Pearson, P. D., Raphael, T. E., Benson, V. L., & Madda, C. L. (2007). Balance in comprehensive literacy instruction: Then and now. In L. B. Gambrell, L. M. Morrow, & M. Pressley (Eds.), *Best practices in literacy instruction* (pp. 159–177). New York: Guilford Press.

Piasta, S., Connor, C., Fishman, B., & Morrison, F. (2009). Teachers' knowledge of literacy concepts, classroom practices, and student reading growth. *Scientific Studies of Reading*, *13*(3), 224–248.

Pinnell, G. S., & Fountas, I. C. (2003). *Phonics and word study lessons: K-3*. Portsmouth, NH: Firsthand, Heinemann.

Pressley, M. (2006). *Reading instruction that works: The case for balanced teaching* (3rd ed.). New York: Guilford.

Pressley, M., Wharton-McDonald, R., Allington, R., Block, C. C., Morrow, L., Tracey, D., et al. (2001). A study of effective Grade-1 literacy instruction. *Scientific Studies of Reading*, *5*, 35–58.

Rayner, K., Foorman, B., Perfetti, C., Pesetsky, D., & Seidenberg, M. (2001). How psychological science informs the teaching of reading. *Psychological Science in the Public Interest*, *2*, 31–74.

Risko, V., Roller, C., Cummins, C., Bean, R., Block, C., Anders, P., et al. (2008). A critical analysis of the research on reading teacher education. *Reading Research Quarterly*, *43*(3), 252–288.

RMC Research Corporation. (2007). *Alabama: How Reading First helps a state make the grade*. RMC Research Corporation, Portsmouth, NH. http://www.rmcportsmouth.com/documents/RMC_Alabama.pdf

Santa, C. M., & Hoien, T. (1999). An assessment of early steps: A reading program for early intervention. *Reading Research Quarterly*, *34*(1), 54–79.

Scammacca, N., Roberts, G., Vaughn, S., Edmonds, M., Wexler, J., Reutebuch, C. K., et al. (2007). *Interventions for adolescent struggling readers: A meta-analysis with implications for practice*. Portsmouth, NH: RMC Research Corporation, Center on Instruction. http://www.centeroninstruction.org/files/COI%20Struggling%20Readers.pdf

Scarborough, H. S., & Brady, S. A. (2002). Toward a common terminology for talking about speech and reading: A glossary of the "phon" words and some related terms. *Journal of Literacy Research*, *34*(3), 299–336.

Shankweiler, D., & Fowler, A. E. (2004). Questions people ask about the role of phonological processes in learning to read. *Reading and Writing: An Interdisciplinary Journal*, *17*, 483–515.

Simmons, D., Kame'enui, E., Harn, B., Coyne, M., Stoolmiller, M., Santoro, L., et al. (2007). Attributes of effective and efficient kindergarten reading intervention: An examination of instructional time and design specificity. *Journal of Learning Disabilities*, *40*(4), 331–347.

Smith, F. (1979). *Reading without nonsense*. New York: Teachers College.

Smith, F. (2003). *Unspeakable acts, unnatural practices*. Portsmouth, NH: Heinemann.

Smith, T., & Brady, S. *Beyond teacher knowledge: Examining the impact of teachers' attitudes on instruction*. Manuscript in preparation.

Snowling, M. (2011). Beyond phonological deficits: Sources of individual differences in reading disability. In S. Brady, D. Braze, & C. Fowler (Eds.), *Explaining individual differences in reading: Theory and evidence*.

Spear-Swerling, L., Brucker, P., & Alfano, M. P. (2005). Teachers' literacy-related knowledge and self-perceptions in relation to preparation and experience. *Annals of Dyslexia*, *55*, 266–296.

Spira, E. G., Bracken, S. S., & Fischel, J. E. (2005). Predicting improvement after first-grade reading difficulties: The effects of oral language, emergent literacy, and behavior skills. *Developmental Psychology*, *41*(1), 225–234.

Stahl, S. A. (1992). Saying the "p" word: Nine guidelines for exemplary phonics instruction. *The Reading Teacher*, *45*(8), 618–626.

Steiner, D., & Rozen, S. (2004). Preparing tomorrow's teachers: An analysis of syllabi from a sample of America's schools of education. In F. M. Hess (Ed.), *A qualified teacher in every classroom? Appraising old answers and new ideas* (pp. 119–148). Cambridge, MA: Harvard Education Press.

Stotsky, S. (2009). Licensure tests for special education teachers: How well they assess knowledge of reading instruction and mathematics. *Journal of Learning Disabilities*, *42*, 464–474.

Torgesen, J. K. (2004). Lessons learned from the last 20 years of research on interventions for students who experience difficulty learning to read. In P. McCardle, & V. Chhabra (Eds.), *The voice of evidence in reading research*. Baltimore, MD: Brookes Publishing.

Torgesen, J. K. (2005). Recent discoveries on remedial interventions for children with dyslexia. In M. J. Snowling, & C. Hulme (Eds.), *The science of reading: A handbook* (pp. 521–537). Oxford: Blackwell.

Torgesen, J. K., Alexander, A. W., Wagner, R. K., Rashotte, C. A., Voeller, K., Conway, T., et al. (2001). Intensive remedial instruction for children with severe reading disabilities: Immediate and long-term outcomes from two instructional approaches. *Journal of Learning Disabilities*, *34*, 33–58.

U.S. Department of Education, Office of Elementary and Secondary Education. (2002). *No child left behind*. Washington, DC.

U.S. Department of Education, Office of Special Education and Rehabilitative Services (2002). *A new era: Revitalizing special education for children and their families*. Washington, DC.

Vadasy, P. F., & Sanders, E. A. (2008). Code-oriented instruction for kindergarten students at risk for reading difficulties: A replication and comparison of instructional grouping. *Reading and Writing: An Interdisciplinary Journal*, *21*, 929–963.

Vadasy, P. F., Sanders, E. A., & Peyton, J. A. (2005). Relative effectiveness of reading practice or word-level instruction in supplemental tutoring: How text matters. *Journal of Learning Disabilities*, *38*(4), 364–380.

Vaughn, S., Cirino, P. T., Wanzek, J., Wexler, J., Fletcher, J. M., Denton, C. D., et al. (2010). Response to intervention for middle school students with reading difficulties: Effects of a primary and secondary intervention. *School Psychology Review*, *39*, 3–21.

Vellutino, F. R., Fletcher, J. M., Snowling, M. J., & Scanlon, D. M. (2004). Specific reading disability (dyslexia): What have we learned in the past four decades? *Journal of Child Psychiatry*, *45*(1), 2–40.

Wagstaff, J. M. (1997). Building practical knowledge of letter-sound correspondences: A beginner's word wall and beyond. *The Reading Teacher*, *51*, 298–304.

Walsh, K. (2006). *What teacher preparation programs aren't teaching, and what elementary teachers aren't learning*. Washington, DC: National Council on Teacher Quality.

Walton, P. D., Walton, L. M., & Felton, K. (2001). Teaching rime analogy or letter recoding reading strategies to prereaders: Effects on prereading skills and word reading. *Journal of Educational Psychology*, *93*(1), 160–180.

Walton, P. D., & Walton, L. M. (2002). Beginning reading by teaching in rime analogy: Effects on phonological skills, letter–sound knowledge, working memory and word-reading strategies. *Scientific Studies of Reading*, *6*, 79–115.

Wong-Ratcliff, M., Powell, S., & Holland, G. (2010). Effects of the Reading First program on acquisition of early literacy skills. *National Forum of Applied Educational Research Journal*, *23*(3), 1–14.

Xue, Y., & Meisels, S. J. (2004). Early literacy instruction and learning in kindergarten: Evidence from the Early Childhood Longitudinal Study—Kindergarten class of 1998–1999. *American Educational Research Journal*, *41*(1), 191–229.

5 The Phonological Hypothesis as a Valuable Framework for Studying the Relation of Dialect Variation to Early Reading Skills

Nicole Patton Terry
Georgia State University
and
Haskins Laboratories
Hollis S. Scarborough
Haskins Laboratories

The important contributions of phonological skills and knowledge to the process of learning to read are firmly established. The seminal insights of Shankweiler and his colleagues at Haskins Laboratories, referred to here as the phonological hypothesis, drew attention to the notion that the phonological component of language is most critical for reading acquisition, and that many reading difficulties in both young novice and older poor readers can be attributed to limitations in phonological skills, knowledge, and awareness. Over the past several decades, an abundance of empirical evidence has accrued in support of the phonological hypothesis as an explanatory model of reading acquisition and reading disabilities.

A hallmark of strong theories is their capacity to inspire corollary hypotheses that impel research along new paths. In this chapter, we describe how our approach to studying the relation of early reading to dialect variation has been fruitfully influenced by the phonological hypothesis and by past research on the phonological deficits that can underlie reading disabilities. We focus on two phonological factors, phonological awareness and phonological precision, discussing how weaknesses in each might contribute to explanations of the relationship between children's usage of nonmainstream speech patterns and their early reading achievement. Finally, we report a study in which we tested some differing hypotheses associated with these two explanations.

LANGUAGE VARIATION AND NONMAINSTREAM AMERICAN ENGLISH DIALECTS

Language variation is a general term that refers to the differences in language usage that are observed across different speakers, settings, and circumstances. Some language variation arises in response to regional or social pressures on language, and language varieties that are shared by a geographically or culturally defined group of speakers are called dialects of the language (Wolfram, Adger, & Christian, 1999; Wolfram & Schilling-Estes, 2006). In the United States, dozens of regional and social variants of English have been identified (Wolfram & Schilling-Estes). The spoken dialect that is most typical of formal contexts—and, notably, the one that adheres most closely to conventional written English—has been termed "school English" or "standard English" or "mainstream American English" (MAE). The numerous dialects that are used in everyday communication and in informal contexts are referred to as "vernacular" or "nonmainstream American English" (NMAE).

Speakers of different American dialects can usually understand one another quite readily. This is because NMAE dialects share a majority of their phonological, lexical, morphosyntactic, and pragmatic features with one another and with MAE. Indeed, dialects are differentiated by the frequency with which particular forms are used and the contexts in which they are produced, rather than just by whether specific features are produced or not produced. For instance, speakers of MAE and African American English (AAE) produce the regular present progressive affix in *running* as *runnin'* but the latter do so more frequently (Wolfram & Schilling-Estes, 2006). Sociolinguistic evidence has established firmly that NMAE dialects are not impoverished forms of English, but rather are complex alternative language systems that are as rule governed as MAE in their form, content, and use (Charity, 2008; Green, 2004; Gutiérrez-Clellen & Simon-Cereijido, 2007; Oetting & Garrity, 2006; Wolfram et al., 1999; Wolfram & Schilling-Estes, 2006).

Recent studies of language variation among children in the United States have yielded detailed descriptions of Southern American English (Oetting & McDonald, 2001), Creole English (Oetting & Garrity, 2006), Appalachian English (Garn-Nunn & Perkins, 1999), Latino English (Gutiérrez-Clellen & Simon-Cereijido, 2007), and AAE (Craig & Washington, 2006; Horton-Ikard & Miller, 2004; Pearson, Velleman, Bryant, & Charko, 2009) at young ages.

LANGUAGE VARIATION AND EARLY READING ACHIEVEMENT

Learning to read depends heavily on facility with spoken language, especially phonology. To acquire basic word recognition and decoding skills, young children must learn to map printed words onto their existing knowledge about the sounds of spoken words. It is thus reasonable to suppose that novice readers could be at a disadvantage if their spoken dialect differs substantially from the version of English that is represented in school texts. Consequently, it has long been hypothesized that language variation might contribute to the reading difficulties that are experienced by large numbers of disadvantaged and minority children, many of whom speak NMAE dialects (Charity, Scarborough, & Griffin, 2004; Labov, 1995; Terry, Connor, Thomas-Tate, & Love, 2010; Washington & Craig, 2001; Wolfram et al., 1999). Similarly, some recent international research has explored literacy gaps in relation to students' usage of Australian Aboriginal English, Spoken Arabic Vernacular, Hawaii Creole, and various dialects encountered in Sweden, Norway, Greece, and The Netherlands (Driessen & Withagen, 1999; Saiegh-Haddad, 2003; Siegel, 2007; Yiakoumetti, 2007).

In the United States, most studies have focused on the AAE dialect and its relation to literacy among African American students. Findings from early studies did not consistently or strongly support the hypothesized relationship between AAE usage and reading achievement, probably due to the aspects of their methodology (Washington & Craig, 2001). Recent investigations, however, have documented a substantial inverse relationship between children's production of AAE features in speech (as measured by sentence repetition, text reading, or discourse production) and their early literacy skills, including recognition of printed words, decoding of pseudo-words, text comprehension, and spelling (Charity et al., 2004; Connor & Craig, 2006; Kohler et al., 2007; Terry, 2006; Terry et al., 2010). For instance, Charity et al. reported substantial negative correlations between children's reading scores and their AAE feature usage during story imitation in large samples of African American students in kindergarten through second grade. Similarly, Craig and Washington (2004) observed that African American first through fifth graders who produced AAE features more frequently in spontaneous discourse tended to do less well on reading tests.

Reading achievement and AAE usage in this population are both known to vary, however, with the student's age, grade, gender, socioeconomic status (SES), and discourse context (Charity et al., 2004; Craig & Washington, 2004; Thompson, Craig, & Washington, 2004; Washington & Craig, 1998). It thus bears noting that the relationship between AAE usage and reading achievement remains substantial even after taking these factors into account (Charity et al.; Terry et al., 2010).

EXPLAINING THE RELATIONSHIPS BETWEEN NMAE USAGE AND READING ACHIEVEMENT

Two main hypotheses have been put forward to explain the association between using more NMAE features and achieving less well in reading. They postulate quite different explanatory mechanisms: (a) *linguistic interference* or *mismatches* between spoken and written language, and (b) a child's *linguistic awareness* and *flexibility* of feature usage in speech. Note that these are not mutually exclusive explanations. Thus, both the *interference/mismatch* and *awareness/flexibility* hypotheses about the role of dialect usage in reading acquisition could be valid, and each might account for the acquisition of different facets of the reading skill or may exert influence during different periods of development.

Both hypotheses focus on the role that dialect usage is posited to play in the child's acquisition of basic word recognition and decoding skills. To map knowledge of spoken words onto their printed forms, novice readers must discover and use the many regular correspondences between spellings (graphemes) and sounds (phonemes) of the language. Although dialects differ in every domain of language (phonology, morphology, syntax, semantics, and pragmatics), the phonological hypothesis and supporting evidence indicate that the phonological component is especially important for learning to read. In discussing the two hypotheses, therefore, we will focus mainly on the phonological domain.

Although developed primarily to explain reading difficulties of AAE-speaking students, the two hypotheses can reasonably be applied, we think, to children who speak other NMAE dialects that, like AAE, are phonologically distinct from MAE, are associated with low social status, and are not represented well by standard English orthography. In fact, Terry et al. (2010) found that the relation between NMAE usage and literacy skills was similar for African American and White children who spoke AAE and Southern American English. These findings suggest that the contribution of dialect differences to reading achievement may be similar across various NMAE dialects, regardless of the speaker's race or ethnicity.

Linguistic Interference/Mismatch Hypothesis

According to the *interference/mismatch* hypothesis, children who speak NMAE dialects experience greater interference between written and spoken language than do children whose oral dialects align more closely with printed spellings (Baratz, 1969; Goodman, 1969; Labov, 1995; Shuy, 1969; LeMoine, 2001). In languages like English, for which the writing system is not fully transparent, every novice reader will encounter some mismatches between written words and their spoken pronunciations. According to the interference/mismatch viewpoint, the frequency of mismatches is increased for NMAE speakers because their speech aligns more poorly with the spelling patterns of the words they are trying to read. For instance, a child who routinely reduces final consonant clusters (e.g., who says "tol" for *told*) might be puzzled by the presence of two letters rather than just one at the end of the printed word. Similarly, a child who produces stops that are realized as labiodentals in MAE (e.g., "dey" for *they*) might find it confusing that different graphemes (*th* and *d*) seem to be used to spell the same speech sound (e.g., the initial /d/s in "dey" and "dog"). Children who encounter many such mismatches are likely to find the learning of grapheme–phoneme correspondences to be a more complex and confusing task than children who encounter fewer mismatches.

According to this hypothesis, therefore, the NMAE speaker's difficulty in learning to read is directly related to the frequency with which mismatches occur between printed words and the way a child pronounces those words. The aforementioned relationship that has been consistently observed in past research—between the usage of nonmainstream features and difficulty in acquiring early reading skills—is thus consistent with this hypothesis (Charity et al., 2004; Terry, 2006; Terry et al., 2010).

Linguistic Awareness/Flexibility Hypothesis

An alternative explanation for the relationship has recently been put forth, stimulated by the emphasis on the facilitative role of phonological awareness and other metalinguistic skills in contemporary accounts of reading acquisition based on the phonological hypothesis. "Metalinguistic awareness" is the capacity to think intentionally about language rather than just to use it communicatively (Scarborough & Brady, 2002; Tunmer, Pratt, & Herriman, 1984). By the late preschool years, children typically exhibit their emerging metalinguistic skills in multiple language domains, including phonological awareness (understanding that spoken words consist of smaller elements of sound), lexical awareness (grasping the concept of the word as a constituent element of speech), and syntactic awareness (appreciating that sentences are comprised of systematically arranged words and phrases). Research within the phonological hypothesis framework has yielded considerable evidence that a beginning reader's level of metalinguistic awareness, especially in the phonological domain, is related robustly to progress in early reading, and that training in metaphonological skills facilitates early reading acquisition (Ehri et al., 2001; National Reading Panel, 2000; Scarborough, 1998).

Preschoolers also become aware that what one says, and how one says it, should take into account the setting and the listener(s). For example, 4-year-old African American children have been observed to produce fewer AAE features in formal than informal speech (Connor & Craig, 2006), suggesting that by the time they enter school, some are familiar with both the AAE and MAE dialects and their appropriateness in different settings. Young children also become cognizant of the differences between languages and between individual speakers of the same language, and are aware of their associations with cultural and racial differences (Hirschfield, 1989; Kuczaj & Harbaugh, 1982). These insights can be seen as a sign of nascent "dialect awareness" that is probably associated with the child's developing metalinguistic insight in other language domains. Indeed, negative correlations have been observed between AAE usage and linguistic awareness in beginning readers (Connor & Craig; Terry, 2006; Terry et al., 2010).

According to the linguistic *awareness/flexibility* hypothesis, the reading difficulties of children who speak NMAE dialects can be traced to a general insensitivity to language variation with regard to both structure and usage (Charity et al., 2004; Connor, 2008; Connor & Craig, 2006; Terry, 2006, 2008; Terry et al., 2010). Hence, children who produce many NMAE features in a context that presupposes MAE (e.g., taking a test or conversing with an unfamiliar adult at school) appear not to appreciate that a less colloquial register would be more appropriate, and thus may be demonstrating weak metalinguistic awareness in the pragmatic domain. This contextual inflexibility is likely to be an indication of a more general limitation in metalinguistic awareness that extends to other aspects of language, including phonological awareness.

According to this viewpoint, therefore, it is not the production of NMAE features itself that impedes the child's progress in learning to read. Rather, as the phonological hypothesis framework would posit, *any* child with limited linguistic awareness—regardless of dialect—is at increased risk for difficulty in early reading. The usage of NMAE features in speech is thus a marker of this other, more universal, risk factor for future academic difficulties.

METALINGUISTIC AWARENESS: PREDICTED RELATIONSHIPS WITH NMAE USAGE AND EARLY READING

The interference/mismatch and awareness/flexibility hypotheses are in disagreement with respect to the role of linguistic awareness. According to the former, the relationship of NMAE usage to reading is direct. That is, difficulty in mapping NMAE speech onto standard English orthography (which most closely represents MAE) is viewed as the main obstacle to learning to read for an NMAE-speaking novice reader. Although phonological awareness also may contribute to success in early reading (as is consistently found for MAE speakers), frequent NMAE production would be expected to affect the reading skill independently of this.

According to the linguistic awareness/flexibility hypothesis, the relationship of dialect to reading is indirect. Dialect variation among novice readers reflects differences in sensitivity to language that also would be evident on more conventional measures of metalinguistic skills, such as phonological awareness tests. Hence, it would be predicted that NMAE usage would correlate inversely with phonological awareness as well as with reading, and that the relationship between dialect and early reading skills would be mediated by phonological awareness.

Because the two hypothesized explanatory mechanisms are not mutually exclusive, it is possible that there could be both direct and mediated effects of speech variation on early reading, and thus that the predictions of both viewpoints would receive support. In our research, therefore, one question we addressed was whether the relationship of dialect variation to reading is mediated (fully or partially) by linguistic awareness.

PHONOLOGICAL REPRESENTATIONS OF WORD PRONUNCIATIONS BY NMAE SPEAKERS

According to the phonological hypothesis and the research in support of it, other aspects of phonological processing besides metalinguistic awareness can contribute to difficulties in learning to read. Several recent studies on the underpinnings of reading disabilities have examined the "precision" of young children's phonological representations of words. During the preschool years, children accumulate and store a wealth of information about the meanings and pronunciations of several thousand words, and the phonological representations of known words become more complete and well specified at the phonemic level (Fowler, 1991; Metsala & Walley, 1998). When the time comes to learn to read, this stored information is available to be mapped onto print. A novice reader whose phonological representations contain imprecise or incomplete information about how words are pronounced, therefore, would be at a disadvantage in learning to decode print.

Fowler and Swainson (2004) investigated this notion by asking first graders to judge the acceptability of puppets' pronunciations of familiar words (e.g., "popsicle" vs. "poksicle" vs. "potsicle"). Greater tolerance for multiple variants was exhibited by the poorer readers than the better readers, suggesting that the former were somewhat confused about precisely how the words should be pronounced. Similarly, in a longitudinal study of children at risk for dyslexia, reading outcomes in second grade were predicted by performance on a naming test in which kindergartners were encouraged to say familiar words with exaggerated clarity of pronunciation (Elbro, Borstrom, & Petersen, 1998). Furthermore, the precision of phonological representations has been correlated not just with reading skills but also with phonological awareness (Elbro et al.; Swan & Goswami, 1997a, 1997b).

With regard to children who speak NMAE dialects, Charity et al. (2004) noted that it cannot be assumed that their overt speech reflects everything that they know about the pronunciations of words. They reasoned that mismatches between print and speech will only be a major obstacle to cracking the reading cipher if there is also a mismatch between print and stored phonological representations of words. To date, however, no studies have previously addressed the question of how much NMAE speakers know about alternative pronunciations of words.

Phonological Representation of Words: Predicted Relationships to NMAE Usage and Early Reading Skills

The interference/mismatch and awareness/flexibility hypotheses differ in their assumptions about a child's stored knowledge of the phonological features of spoken words. The former presumes that lexical representations of word pronunciations coincide closely with overt speech for NMAE-speaking students, and thus that MAE features are not usually represented in their lexicons. Accordingly, a child who says "fas" for *fast* is assumed to be unaware of the presence of a final /t/ in the MAE pronunciation of the word, resulting in a mismatch when the letter *t* is encountered in reading.

In contrast, the awareness/flexibility hypothesis allows for the possibility that children's mental representations include more information than is evident from overt speech. That is, if a child who says "fas" knows that the word *fast* ends with an unrealized /t/, the presence of a printed *t* will not create a mismatch with stored knowledge. Hence, more generally, if a child who produces many NMAE features in speech has stored knowledge of the alternative MAE pronunciations that align better with print, then speech–print mismatches would be fewer, more easily resolved, and not likely to account for the relation between dialect differences and reading skill. The second major goal of our study was to investigate how NMAE and MAE features are represented phonologically in the mental lexicons of novice readers who vary widely in their spoken production of NMAE features.

METHOD

PARTICIPANTS

The sample included 55 typically developing children (25 boys and 30 girls) in prekindergarten and kindergarten whose ages ranged from 4.3 to 6.4 years ($M = 5.4$). All were native speakers of American English. The sample was racially and economically diverse, and included 26 (47.3%) White, 22 (40.0%) African American, 4 (7.3%) Latino, and 3 (5.5%) Asian American children.

The participants attended two elementary schools and associated preschools in an urban-fringe district in Connecticut. School reports indicated that the sites varied in the socioeconomic and racial diversity of the students. The percentage of students eligible for the federal free and reduced lunch programs was 6% at one school, which was located in a mainly middle-SES neighborhood, and 51% at the other, which served several middle and working class neighborhoods. Fewer minority students were enrolled at the middle-SES school (24%) than at the lower-SES school (67%).

MEASURES OF LANGUAGE VARIATION

By recruiting a mixed-race and mixed-SES sample from Northeastern United States, we expected to obtain considerable variation in the children's dialect usage, including phonological features of MAE, AAE, and several NMAE regional dialects (eastern New England, western New England, and New York City). Dozens of phonological and morphosyntactic features that are more characteristic of NMAE (especially AAE) dialects than MAE have been described in detail in many sources (e.g., Green, 2004; Labov, Ash, & Boberg, 2006; Washington & Craig, 2002; Wolfram & Schilling-Estes, 2006). In selecting the stimuli for our measures (see Appendix), we focused primarily on some NMAE features that are frequently produced in the region: reduction of final consonant clusters (e.g., "tol" in lieu of "told"); omission of postvocalic /r/ (e.g., "pahk" in lieu of *park*, "sistuh" in lieu of *sister*); realization of labiodental fricatives as other obstruents (e.g., "dis" in lieu of *this*; "wif" in lieu of *with*); devoicing of final stops (e.g., "bet" in lieu of *bed*); and substitution of the regular present progressive affix (e.g., "tryin" in lieu of *trying*).

Although phonological representations of words in the lexicon are not directly observable, researchers have designed several experimental measures to examine them indirectly (Elbro et al., 1998; Fowler & Swainson, 2004) and to assess the phonological skills of children who speak NMAE dialects (Charity et al., 2004; Rodekohr & Haynes, 2001). We adapted these approaches to assess children's usage of and knowledge about the phonological features of MAE and NMAE and the relation between them. Each task included dialect-sensitive items (i.e., words or pseudo-words with features that can be pronounced differently in NMAE than SAE) and two tasks also included dialect-neutral items (i.e., for which the pronunciation would be the same regardless of dialect). Tasks were presented on a laptop using Microsoft PowerPoint illustrations that, for the two tasks with spoken stimuli, included prerecorded audio clips that the examiner activated by clicking on-screen sound buttons. To insure accuracy of scoring, all sessions were audio recorded.

Sentence Imitation

Children's usage of MAE and NMAE features in their speech was measured with Charity et al.'s (2004) sentence imitation task. The child listened to a story spoken in MAE and was asked to repeat verbatim each sentence immediately after it was presented. While viewing the story's on-screen illustrations, the child heard audio clips of an adult White female MAE speaker reading 2 practice items and 15 test sentences, in which 18 phonological and 19 morphosyntactic dialect-sensitive items were embedded. The percentage of items on which the child produced an NMAE alternative rather than the MAE target was computed for each set, yielding a phonological score and a grammatical score.

Picture Naming: Conventional Versus Precision Instructions

To assess the knowledge of word pronunciations, differences between casual and deliberate speech were examined in a picture naming task that contrasted conventional naming instructions with requests for greater precision. On each of the 27 trials with dialect-sensitive stimuli (see Appendix), the child was first shown a picture of a common object and asked to say its name (conventional instructions). If the target word was not produced (e.g., *mask* was called "face"), the examiner prompted the child for an alternative. Then child was asked to say the word again "slowly and clearly" (precision instructions). The examiner modeled this with a practice item (*umbrella* pronounced as "ummm-BREL-luh") that all children were able to repeat in the same exaggerated manner. Similar tasks were used by Elbro et al. (1998) and Fowler and Swainson (2004) with 4- to 7-year-olds to examine the precision of pronunciations in relation to early reading skills.

For those items the child was able to name with the target word, the responses were scored for pronunciation. Each response was classified as the MAE pronunciation (e.g., "toothbrush"), as a correct NMAE alternative (e.g., "toofbrush"), or as a pronunciation that was not correct in either SAE or NMAE (e.g., "tooth-buss"). The percentage of each response type was computed for each type of instruction (i.e., conventional and precision).

Acceptability Judgments

Knowledge about alternative word pronunciations also was examined by asking the children to judge the acceptability of different pronunciations of 10 familiar dialect-sensitive words (see Appendix). A picture of the object was displayed above four robots that were "learning how to say words." The child was asked to listen carefully as each robot tried to name the picture, and to judge whether that robot's version was an "okay" way to say the word. After each variant had been judged, the next trial began with the display of a new picture. This task had to be terminated for two children who apparently could not understand the instructions.

Similar tasks were used by Elbro et al. (1998) and Fowler and Swainson (2004) to assess the precision of phonological representations of young children.

The four variant pronunciations were the MAE version (e.g., *breakfast*), two correct NMAE alternatives (e.g. *breakfas'* and *breffis*), and a version containing a speech error that was unrelated to dialect (e.g., *bweakfast*). The robots' voices were prerecorded by four adult speakers (two African American bidialectal NMAE-MAE speakers, one male and one female, and two White MAE speakers, one male and one female). One pronunciation per speaker was heard per trial, counterbalanced so that each child heard NMAE, MAE, and speech error pronunciations by all four robots. The percentage of pronunciations that were judged to be acceptable was scored for each stimulus type.

Pseudo-word Repetition

To assess encoding and reproduction of novel phonological sequences, many researchers have used pseudo-word repetition tasks (Brady, Poggie, & Rapala, 1989; Fowler & Swainson, 2004). Ours also was used to examine children's knowledge of the correspondences between SAE features and permissible AAE alternatives. Children were told that an on-screen robot wanted to teach them to "say robot words just like he does," and that they should listen carefully and try to imitate what was said. The 20 trials (see Appendix) included 10 dialect-sensitive items (e.g., "re-noy-tist") intermixed with 10 dialect-neutral items of similar phonological complexity (e.g., "de-bof-tidge"), which ranged from 3 to 5 syllables in length. Each dialect-sensitive item contained a targeted feature that could legitimately be pronounced differently in a real word by a NMAE speaker (e.g., the final consonant cluster /-st/). The corresponding dialect-neutral pseudo-word included a feature that could not be pronounced differently (e.g., the final consonant cluster /-dʒ/). The child's pronunciation of the targeted portion was scored as a verbatim reproduction; an appropriate substitution of a NMAE alternative for the MAE feature; or an incorrect repetition or omission of the feature. Percentages of response types were computed separately for dialect-sensitive and dialect-neutral items.

Measures of Early Literacy Skills

Two subtests of the *Woodcock-Johnson Tests of Achievement, Third Edition* (WJ3; Woodcock, McGrew, & Mather, 2001) were administered in standardized format. The *Letter–Word Identification* test was used to assess how well children could read aloud printed letters and words. The *Sound Awareness* test assesses phonological awareness by requiring the child to rhyme words and to manipulate sounds within words by deleting, adding, or reversing syllables and phonemes. Raw scores were converted to standard scores based on published norms.

Procedure

Each child was individually examined at school during three brief sessions within a 2-week period. Two female examiners, one African American and one White, each administered all tasks to approximately half of the participants; both used

MAE during testing sessions. For the three tasks with spoken responses, high percentages of agreement between two independent scorers were obtained: sentence imitation (95.6%), picture naming (98.3%), and pseudo-word repetition (86.4%).

RESULTS

We first divided the sample into subgroups of children who used relatively few versus many phonological NMAE features in speech, and then compared their performance on the experimental measures of language variation. In subsequent analyses, we applied regression methods to examine the relationships of children's early reading and phonological awareness skills to their production and stored knowledge of MAE and NMAE features. Prior to analysis, arcsine transformations were applied to percentage scores from the experimental measures. Preliminary analyses indicated no effect of the examiner's race on children's performance on any measures, so this variable was excluded.

Comparison of High- Versus Low-NMAE Subgroups

NMAE feature usage, as measured on the sentence imitation task, varied widely in this group of children, ranging from 0% to 93% ($M = 33.7$, $SD = 25.8$ for phonological scores and $M = 18.5$, $SD = 22.2$ for grammatical scores). Because phonology was the focus of our research questions, only the phonological scores from the sentence imitation task were used to create subgroups for analyses. The 25 children (4 White, 17 African American, 3 Latino, and 1 Asian American) who produced NMAE features on 30% or more of the items were assigned to the high-NMAE usage group ($M = 56.8\%$, $SD = 19.1$, range 31–93). The remaining 30 children (22 White, 5 African American, 1 Latino, and 2 Asian American) formed the low-NMAE group ($M = 14.4\%$, $SD = 9.6$, range 0–29). Given that the two sentence imitation scores correlated strongly with one another ($r = .79$), it is not surprising that the mean grammatical scores of these groups also differed (33.7% vs. 5.8%, respectively). Although age ranges were similar for the subsamples, the high-NMAE group was significantly younger, on average ($M = 5.3$ years, $SD = 0.6$, range 4.4–6.4), than the low-NMAE group ($M = 5.6$ years, $SD = 0.5$, range 4.3–6.4); hence, age was included as a covariate in all analyses of group differences. Separate one-way or two-way analyses of covariances (ANCOVA's) were used to compare group performance (summarized in Figure 5.1) on the picture naming and precision, acceptability judgments, and pseudo-word repetition tasks.

In the picture naming task, the children produced the target word for 83.6% of the pictures, indicating that the stimulus words were quite familiar. We first examined whether NMAE features were produced less often under "precision" than conventional naming instructions, particularly by the high-NMAE group. A 2 × 2 mixed model ANCOVA included instruction type as the within-subject repeated measure and group as the between-groups factor. There was a strong main effect of group, with the high-NMAE group producing more NMAE responses, $F(1, 52) = 20.757$, $p < .001$, $\eta_p^2 = .289$, but only weak and nonsignificant effects for instruction type,

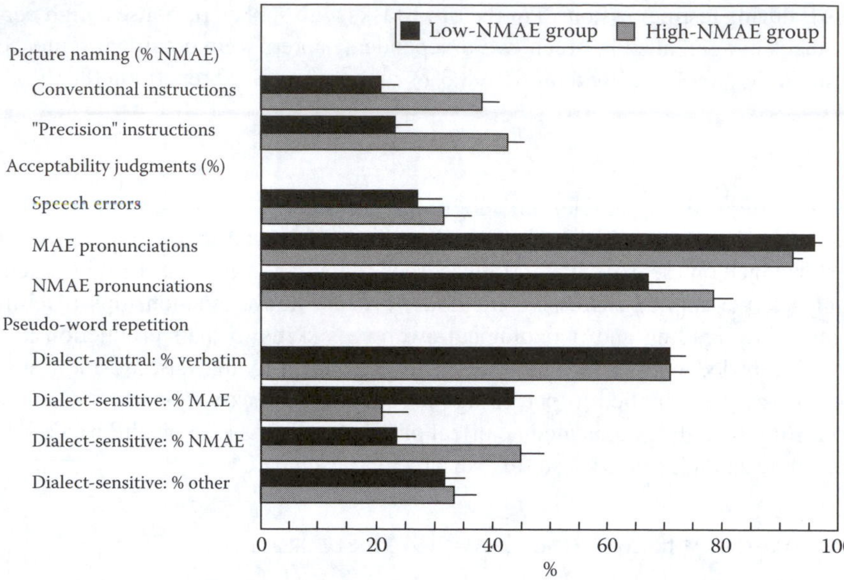

FIGURE 5.1 Comparison of the high-NMAE and low-NMAE dialect groups on their usage and knowledge of NMAE and MAE pronunciations of words. Mean age-adjusted percentages are plotted. The error bars extend 1 SE from the mean.

$F(1, 52) = 0.201$, $p = .656$, $\eta_p^2 = .004$, and for the interaction, $F(1, 52) = 0.554$, $p = .460$, $\eta_p^2 = .011$. Thus, asking children to pronounce known words more slowly and distinctly did not lead to production of more MAE features by the NMAE speakers.

On the acceptability judgments task, we examined whether the groups differed in their tolerance for alternative pronunciations of dialect-sensitive words. A 2 × 2 mixed model ANCOVA was carried out with stimulus type (MAE vs. NMAE variants) as the within-subject repeated measure and group as the between-groups factor. Main effects were weak for both group, $F(1, 50) = 0.197$, $p = .669$, $\eta_p^2 = .004$, and stimulus variants, $F(1, 50) = 0.124$, $p = .726$, $\eta_p^2 = .002$, but there was a substantial interaction effect, $F(1, 50) = 8.342$, $p = .006$, $\eta_p^2 = .143$. As can be seen in Figure 5.1, although both groups accepted nearly every MAE pronunciation and not quite as many NMAE items, this difference between stimulus types was larger for the low-NMAE than for the high-NMAE group.

On the pseudo-word repetition task, verbatim imitations of the dialect-neutral items were produced about equally often by the two groups, $F(1, 52) = 0.093$, $p = .762$, $\eta_p^2 = .001$, indicating that their ability to phonologically encode and reproduce novel stimuli was equivalent. For the dialect-sensitive items, a 2 × 2 mixed model ANCOVA with response type (verbatim vs. NMAE substitution) as the within-subject repeated measure yielded negligible main effects of group, $F(1, 52) = 0.623$, $p = .434$, $\eta_p^2 = .012$, and type of response, $F(1, 52) = 0.421$, $p = .510$, $\eta_p^2 = .008$. However, there was a strong interaction effect, $F(1, 52) = 16.617$, $p < .001$, $\eta_p^2 = .242$. As illustrated in Figure 5.1, the high-NMAE group's imitations included an NMAE substitution about twice as often as they contained a verbatim (MAE) reproduction of the targeted feature of the pseudo-word. For the low-NMAE group, this pattern of responding was reversed.

It bears noting that very few speech errors (less than 5% of responses) were made by either group on the picture naming task, and that on the acceptability judgments task, the pronunciations containing dialect-irrelevant speech errors were usually rejected, at similar rates, by both groups, $F(1, 50) = 0.405$, $p = .528$, $\eta_p^2 = .008$. Also, although both groups sometimes produced responses that were consistent with neither MAE nor NMAE, they did so with similar frequency (see Figure 5.1).

Summary scores were created such that higher values would reflect greater usage or knowledge of language variation. For the picture naming (combined) and pseudo-word repetition tasks, we computed the percentage of NMAE pronunciations out of the number of items on which either an NMAE or MAE pronunciation was used. For the judgment task, we computed the percentage of NMAE targets accepted out of the summed percentages for NMAE and MAE targets. All were reliably intercorrelated (median $r = .51$, range .31 –.74), so to simplify subsequent analyses, we created an overall dialect differences factor score that was based on a principal components analysis of the four phonological summary scores. This factor, which correlated with age ($r = -.33$, $p = .014$), was then regressed on age so that the age-adjusted residuals could be analyzed as the overall measure of a child's relative usage and knowledge of MAE versus NMAE features.

Relationships Between Dialect Differences and Early Literacy Skills

To examine word reading skill in relation to language variation, two regression analyses were conducted with Letter–Word Identification scores ($M = 107.6$, $SD = 10.2$) as the dependent measure, school as a surrogate for SES (entered first and accounting for 2% of the variance), and the age-adjusted dialect factor score as a predictor variable. In the second regression, Sound Awareness scores ($M = 109.9$, $SD = 14.4$) were also included as a predictor. The reading and awareness measures correlated with each other ($r = .57$, $p < .001$) and inversely with the dialect factor ($r = -.30$ and $-.42$, respectively, $p < .03$). Means for the high- and low-NMAE groups, respectively, were 104.1 ($SD = 13.9$) and 109.0 (10.1) for Letter–Word Identification, and 105.7 (14.0) and 113.3 (13.1) for Sound Awareness.

If there is a mediating effect of phonological awareness on the relation of NMAE usage to early reading skills, then the beta weight for the dialect variable should be greatly reduced when analyzed alongside phonological awareness (Baron & Kenny, 1986). This pattern was indeed obtained. In the first regression, the beta weight for dialect was –.292 ($p = .045$). In the second, with Sound Awareness included, the total R^2 increased from .094 to .308, and the beta weight for the dialect factor decreased to –.092. Similarly, this beta value decreased from –.252 to .002 when we repeated the regression analyses, but with the grammatical score from the sentence imitation task entered (after age-adjustment and arcsine transformation) in lieu of the dialect factor. All the regression results suggest that metalinguistic awareness fully mediated the relationships between dialect differences and early reading achievement.

DISCUSSION

Given the enormous scientific and practical value of the phonological hypothesis account of reading acquisition and reading disabilities, we were inspired to consider the relationship of dialect differences to reading in terms of two aspects of phonological processing that have been linked to early reading achievement: metalinguistic awareness and the precision of phonological representations. The results provided clear answers to the two main questions that we set out to address.

Are both NMAE and MAE features of words represented phonologically in the mental lexicons of novice readers who use many NMAE features in overt speech, or does lexical knowledge coincide closely with spoken pronunciations of words?

We compared picture naming, acceptability judgments, and pseudo-word repetitions for subgroups characterized by high versus low frequency of NMAE usage in sentence imitation. Not surprisingly, the children in the high-NMAE group produced many more NMAE features in their spoken responses on the naming and repetition tasks. On the judgment task, however, they almost always accepted MAE pronunciations of words in addition to the NMAE variants. Furthermore, the other subgroup, who consistently used few NMAE features in their own speech, also accepted both MAE and NMAE versions as "okay" ways to say familiar words. These findings, which are consistent with other recent results (Connor & Craig, 2006), suggest that knowledge of both dialects was strong and quite similar for our two groups, despite the marked differences in their patterns of overt speech. Moreover, it is striking that the high-NMAE group made mostly dialect-appropriate substitutions when imitating dialect-sensitive pseudo-words, in essence "translating" correctly from one dialect to the other. Doing so requires considerable knowledge about which MAE features have NMAE alternatives, and when it is permissible to produce them.

Although poorer readers have been shown to mispronounce familiar words and accept multiple pronunciations of words more frequently than better readers (Fowler & Swainson, 2004), these differences were not seen between our dialect groups. (Variability within each group suggests, of course, that some children in each group may have had relatively poor phonological precision.) The results are thus more compatible with the idea that on average, the phonological representations of NMAE speakers do not contain less adequate information about the ways words can permissibly be pronounced, and that the precision of their phonological representations is not responsible for their difficulties in reading acquisition. Rather, these youngsters appeared to know a great deal about alternative pronunciations of familiar words, and to know enough about MAE to enable a successful mapping of stored representations onto print.

It must also be emphasized that the speech and memory capabilities of the two groups were very similar. Both groups produced few speech errors during naming and usually rejected pronunciations that contained speech errors rather than dialect differences in the acceptability judgments task. This demonstrates that the children could readily distinguish legitimate MAE and NMAE pronunciations from wrong ones. Furthermore, the high- and low-NMAE speakers were nearly equally proficient at imitating the dialect-neutral pseudo-words verbatim, indicating that encoding and reproduction of novel phonological input was unimpaired.

Are dialect differences related directly to reading achievement, or is the link mediated (fully or partially) by phonological awareness?

As previously found by us and by others (Charity et al., 2004; Connor & Craig, 2006; Terry et al., in press), NMAE usage was correlated with word reading and phonological awareness skills in this sample of beginning readers. According to the interference/mismatch hypothesis, difficulty in mapping NMAE speech onto standard English orthography is the main obstacle to reading acquisition by NMAE-speaking children. Our regression analyses yielded no support for this direct relationship, however. Instead, phonological awareness fully mediated the contribution of dialect differences to the prediction of reading achievement. That is, the contribution of dialect variation to reading scores was negligible when phonological awareness was included as a predictor in the analyses. This finding is highly consistent with the linguistic awareness/flexibility hypothesis, which postulates that dialect variation among novice readers reflects more general differences in children's sensitivity to language variation.

The major findings thus converged in supporting the linguistic awareness/flexibility hypothesis about the relation between dialect variation and early reading skill. By the time children begin learning to read, it appears that those who have been exposed to multiple dialects have become quite knowledgeable about acceptable alternatives for pronouncing words, regardless of whether they produce all variants routinely in their speech in settings that presuppose MAE. By this age, many children also understand that the way one speaks should be flexibly adjusted so as to be contextually appropriate, and that using NMAE features may be perceived as inappropriate in school and other formal settings, including clinical tests and research tasks administered by an unfamiliar adult (Connor & Craig, 2006; Terry et al., in press). The observed correlation in our sample between dialect measures and phonological awareness thus suggests that children who do not produce predominantly MAE pronunciations in a research setting may have weaker metalinguistic skills than their classmates, probably not just in phonology but also in other domains of language.

Linguistic awareness has been shown to greatly facilitate learning to read. Children who realize that spoken words are made up of syllables and smaller sound elements (phonemes) can more readily appreciate how the orthographic system represents these aspects of language on the printed page. Whether or not they are speakers of NMAE dialects, novice readers who have not yet attained these insights will be at a disadvantage in learning to read. In light of this, the finding that phonological awareness fully mediated the relationship between NMAE usage and early reading skills is not surprising. Frequent NMAE production among beginning readers during formal contexts that call for MAE thus appears to be a marker for differences in awareness, rather than a direct influence on reading acquisition.

The foregoing conclusions must be interpreted with some caution, however. First, our racially and socioeconomically diverse sample was drawn from a single metropolitan area in the northeastern United States, so the findings might not generalize to other populations, particularly to children who encounter less linguistic diversity in their daily lives. The sample also consisted only of 4- to 6-year-old novice readers, and other factors probably contribute to reading difficulties of older NMAE-speaking children. For instance, instructional and motivational influences, and linguistic interference at the morphosyntactic and discourse levels, may be greater impediments to successful reading at older ages.

In summary, our findings suggest that using NMAE does not, in itself, place a child at risk for difficulty in learning to read. Rather, it may be an indication that a child has not developed the metalinguistic insights that underlie contextually appropriate flexibility of language usage and an appreciation of the phonological structure of words. We would also speculate that linguistic awareness would enable a bidialectal child to overcome confusion, if any is experienced, about which stored phonological representations are most closely mapped onto printed spellings. Nevertheless, the weak linguistic awareness signaled by inappropriate NMAE usage may be a source of difficulty in early reading acquisition. Fortunately, it is a risk factor than can readily be addressed through appropriate instruction.

Educational Implications

Several literacy instruction programs for students who speak NMAE dialects have been implemented in the United States and abroad (Fogel & Ehri, 2000; LeMoine, 2001; Siegel, 2007; Wheeler & Swords, 2006). Typically designed for upper elementary and older students, these programs mainly provide explicit teaching of MAE and its relation to NMAE through contrastive analysis activities and the provision of dialect-relevant reading materials. These programs have produced mixed, but generally positive, outcomes. As yet, however, there is insufficient evidence regarding the critical components of the instruction and the mechanisms that underlie student learning.

Our findings suggest that it would also be fruitful to provide instruction at the preschool and early elementary levels, and to focus on encouraging metalinguistic insight among young NMAE speakers in the phonological, lexical, syntactic, and pragmatic domains. Instruction could foster a greater appreciation that different people speak English differently, that language usage varies across settings, and that words and sentences contain smaller elements that can be isolated and manipulated. Appropriate activities might, for instance, include games and songs that promote phonological awareness and other metalinguistic insights, role playing with literature that uses different language styles, infusing contrastive analysis activities with discussions of contexts for language formality, and so forth. As literacy instruction with a print focus is introduced in the primary grades, the links between oral and written language can be scaffolded onto this foundation. According to the linguistic awareness hypothesis, this approach to early instruction would effectively support NMAE speakers in acquiring basic reading skills and would be of greater benefit than instructing them in MAE. Our results indicate that young AAE speakers already have receptive knowledge of MAE forms, and this receptive knowledge should be sufficient for acquiring reading skills, particularly if students are guided to exploit their stored knowledge appropriately. Fortunately, effective age-appropriate instruction to strengthen metalinguistic awareness (e.g., Brady, Fowler, Stone, & Winbury, 1994; Ehri et al., 2001) can benefit all novice readers, irrespective of differences in spoken dialect use.

CONCLUDING REMARKS

We have found the phonological hypothesis to be a valuable framework in which to study the relation of dialect variation to early reading skills. Our findings regarding the phonological representations and phonological awareness skills of beginning readers who varied in NMAE usage are highly consistent with the phonological hypothesis and quite inconsistent with the longstanding hypothesis that mismatches between overt speech and printed spellings are the main source of early reading difficulty in this population. Additional research on phonological skills and knowledge in relation to language variation is likely to deepen our understanding of how oral language relates to reading achievement, and to guide the design of improved instructional approaches for fostering metalinguistic and reading skills, especially for children who speak nonmainstream versions of English.

APPENDIX: ITEMS ON EXPERIMENTAL TASKS CREATED FOR THE STUDY

TABLE 5.A.1
Picture Naming Task

bed	bathtub	butterfly
broom	skateboard	pajamas
Mask	playground	stethoscope
Ghost	birthday cake	(corn) on the cob
scissors	(fire) hydrant	ironing (board)
flower	Handcuffs	(Ronald) McDonald
toothbrush	elephant	refrigerator
mushroom	basketball	helicopter
hanger	swimming (pool)	thermometer

Note: Targeted MAE forms with NMAE alternatives underlined. Some pictures were from the Boston Naming Test (Goodglass, Kaplan, & Weintraub, 1983).

TABLE 5.A.2
Acceptability Judgments Task

MAE Version	NMAE Versions		Speech Errors
goldfish	gol'fish	go'fish	goldfiss
bathroom	bafroom	bathroo'	bassroom
feather	fevver	feathuh	fezzer
candycane	cannycane	candyca'e	caddycane
breakfast	breakfas'	breffis	bwekfast
rockinghorse	rockin'horse	rockinghawse	rockerhorse
Gingerbread	gingerbret	ginge'bread	ginzerbread
Merry-go-round	merry-go-roun'	merry-go-rount	mewwy-go-round
salad dressing	salad dressin'	salat dressing	shalad dressing
jack-in-the-box	jack-in-de-box	jack-innuh-box	jack-in-the-bots

TABLE 5.A.3
Pseudo-word Repetition Task

Dialect Sensitive	Dialect Neutral
de-TOOV-ing	re-BING-ish
re-NOY-tist	de-BOF-tidge
AL-bo-NEETH	IM-po-MOOF
TIG-o-BUND	GAT-o-DUNK
DIN-zer-WEL-sher	WAN-chel-COY-bel
STRAD-yu-TISH-un	SPROG-yu-COSH-us
Co-ZECK-ing-flon	tu-VING-en-sham
DECK-a-DOTH-ity	BIT-a-BAFF-ity
UN-ca-NAY-buh-lind	IM-ba-LOO-duh-nance
FAVE-o-POFF-i-ter	SAZE-o-TESS-i-tin

Note: Stressed syllables are typed in uppercase. Targeted forms are underlined.

REFERENCES

Baratz, J. C. (1969). Teaching reading in an urban Negro school system. In J. C. Baratz & R. W. Shuy (Eds.), *Language differences: Do they interfere?* (pp. 92–116). Newark, DE: International Reading Association.

Baron, R. M., & Kenny, D. A. (1986). The moderator-mediator variable distinction in social psychological research: Conceptual, strategic and statistical considerations. *Journal of Personality and Social Psychology*, *51*, 1173–1182.

Brady, S. A., Fowler, A. E., Stone, B., & Winbury, N. (1994). Training phonological awareness: A study with inner-city kindergarten children. *Annals of Dyslexia*, *44*, 26–59.

Brady, S. A., Poggie, E., & Rapala, M. M. (1989). Speech repetition abilities in children who differ in reading skill. *Language & Speech*, *32*(2), 109–122.

Charity, A. H. (2008). African American English: An overview. *Perspectives on Communication Disorders and Sciences in Culturally and Linguistically Diverse Populations*, *15*, 33–42.

Charity, A. H., Scarborough, H. S., & Griffin, D. M. (2004). Familiarity with school English in African American children and its relation to early reading achievement. *Child Development*, *75*(5), 1340–1356.

Connor, C. M. (2008). Language and literacy connections for children who are African American. *Perspectives on Communication Disorders and Sciences in Culturally and Linguistically Diverse Populations*, *15*, 43–53.

Connor, C. M., & Craig, H. K. (2006). African American preschoolers' language, emergent literacy skills, and use of African American English: A complex relation. *Journal of Speech, Language, and Hearing Research*, *49*, 771–792.

Craig, H. K., & Washington, J. A. (2004). Grade related changes in the production of African American English. *Journal of Speech, Language, and Hearing Research*, *47*, 450–463.

Craig, H. K., & Washington, J. A. (2006). *Malik goes to school: Examining the language skills of African American students from preschool-5th grade*. Mahwah, NJ: Lawrence Erlbaum Associates.

Driessen, G., & Withagen, V. (1999). Language varieties and educational achievement of indigenous primary school pupils. *Language, Culture, and Curriculum*, *12*(1), 1–22.

Ehri, L. C., Nunes, S. R., Willows, D. M., Schuster, B. V., Yaghoub-Zadeh, Z., & Shanahan, T. (2001). Phonemic awareness instruction helps children learn to read: Evidence from the National Reading Panel's meta-analysis. *Reading Research Quarterly*, *36*(3), 250–287.

Elbro, C., Borstrom, I., & Petersen, D. K. (1998). Predicting dyslexia from kindergarten: The importance of distinctness of phonological representations of lexical items. *Reading Research Quarterly*, *33*, 36–61 .

Fogel, H., & Ehri, L. C. (2000). Teaching elementary students who speak Black English to write in standard English: Effects of dialect transformation practice. *Contemporary Educational Psychology*, *25*, 212–235.

Fowler, A. E. (1991). How early phonological development might set the stage for phoneme awareness. In S. Brady & D. P. Shankweiler (Eds.), *Phonological processes in literacy: A tribute to Isabelle Y. Liberman* (pp. 97–118). Hillsdale, NJ: Lawrence Erlbaum Associates.

Fowler, A. E., & Swainson, B. (2004). Relationships of naming skills to reading, memory, and receptive vocabulary: Evidence for imprecise phonological representations of words by poor readers. *Annals of Dyslexia*, *54*, 247–280.

Garn-Nunn, P. G., & Perkins, L. (1999). Appalachian English and standardized language testing: Rationale and recommendations for test adaptation. *Contemporary Issues in Communication Science and Disorders*, *26*, 150–159.

Goodglass, H., Kaplan, E. F., & Weintraub, S. (1983). *The Revised Boston Naming Test.* PA: Lea & Febiger.

Goodman, K. S. (1969). Dialect barrier to reading comprehension. In J. Baratz & R. W. Shuy (Eds.), *Language differences: Do they interfere?* (pp. 14–28). Newark, DE: International Reading Association.

Green, L. J. (2004). *African American English: A linguistic introduction*. Cambridge, U.K.: Cambridge University Press.

Gutiérrez-Clellen, V. F., & Simon-Cereijido, G. (2007). The discriminant accuracy of a grammatical measure with Latino English-speaking children. *Journal of Speech, Language, and Hearing Research*, *50*, 968–981.

Hirschfield, L. A. (1989). Discovering linguistic differences: Domain specificity and the young child's awareness of multiple languages. *Human Development*, *32*, 223–236.

Horton-Ikard, R., & Miller, J. (2004). It is not just the poor kids: The use of AAE forms by African-American school-aged children from middle SES communities. *Journal of Communication Disorders*, *37*(6), 467–487.

Kohler, C. T., Bahr, R. H., Silliman, E. R., Bryant, J. B., Apel, K., & Wilkinson, L. C. (2007). African American English dialect and performance on nonword spelling and phonemic awareness tasks. *American Journal of Speech-Language Pathology*, *16*, 157–168.

Kuczaj, S. A., II, & Harbaugh, B. (1982). What children think about the speaking capabilities of other persons and things. In S. A. Kuczaj, II (Ed.), *Language development: Vol. 2. Language, thought, and culture* (pp. 211–227). Hillsdale, NJ: Lawrence Erlbaum.

Labov, W. (1995). Can reading failure be reversed: A linguistic approach to the question. In V. L. Gadsden & D. A. Wagner (Eds.), *Literacy among African-American youth: Issues in learning, teaching, and schooling* (pp. 39–68). Cresskill, NJ: Hampton Press, Inc.

Labov, W., Ash, S., & Boberg, C. (2006). *Atlas of North American English: Phonology and phonetics*. Berlin: Mouton/de Gruyter.

LeMoine, N. R. (2001). Language variation and literacy acquisition in African American students. In J. L. Harris, A. G. Kamhi, & K. E. Pollock (Eds.), *Literacy in African American communities* (pp. 169–194). Mahwah, NJ: Lawrence Erlbaum Associates.

Metsala, J. L., & Walley, A. C. (1998). Spoken vocabulary growth and the segmental restructuring of lexical representations: Precursors to phonemic awareness and early reading ability. In J. L. Metsala & L. C. Ehri (Eds.), *Word recognition in beginning literacy* (pp. 89–120). Mahwah, NJ: Lawrence Erlbaum Associates.

National Reading Panel (2000). *Teaching children to read: Reports of the subgroups*. Washington, DC: National Institutes of Health.

Oetting, J., & Garrity, A. (2006). Variation within dialects: A case of Cajun marking within child SAAE and SWE. *Journal of Speech, Language, and Hearing Research*, *49*, 16–26.

Oetting, J., & McDonald, J. (2001). Nonmainstream dialect use and specific language impairment. *Journal of Speech, Language, and Hearing Research*, *44*, 207–223.

Pearson, B. Z., Velleman, S. L., Bryant, T. J., & Charko, T. (2009). Phonological milestones for African American English-speaking children learning mainstream American English as a second dialect. *Language, Speech, and Hearing Services in Schools*, *40*(3), 229–244.

Rodekohr, R. K., & Haynes, W. O. (2001). Differentiating dialect from disorder: A comparison of two processing tasks and a standardized language test. *Journal of Communication Disorders*, *34*, 255–272.

Saiegh-Haddad, E. (2003). Linguistic distance and initial reading acquisition: The case of Arabic diglossia. *Applied Psycholinguistics*, *24*, 431–451.

Scarborough, H. S. (1998). Early identification of children at risk for reading disabilities: Phonological awareness and some other promising predictors. In: B. K. Shapiro, P. J. Accardo, & A. J. Capute (Eds.), *Specific reading disability: A view of the spectrum* (pp. 75–119). Timonium, MD: York Press.

Scarborough, H. S., & Brady, S. A. (2002). Toward a common terminology for talking about speech and reading: A glossary of the "phon" words and some related terms. *Journal of Literacy Research*, *34*, 299–334.

Shuy, R. W. (1969). A linguistic background for developing beginning reading materials for Black children. In J. Baratz & R. W. Shuy (Eds.), *Language differences: Do they interfere?* (pp. 117–137). Newark, DE: International Reading Association.

Siegel, J. (2007). Creoles and minority dialects in education: An update. *Language and Education*, *21*(1), 66–86.

Swan, D., & Goswami, U. (1997a). Picture naming deficits in developmental dyslexia: The phonological representations hypothesis. *Brain and Language*, *46*, 334–353.

Swan, D., & Goswami, U. (1997b). Phonological awareness deficits in developmental dyslexia and the phonological representations hypothesis. *Journal of Experimental Child Psychology*, *66*, 18–41.

Terry, N. P. (2006). Relations between dialect variation, grammar, and early spelling skills. *Reading and Writing*, *19*, 907–931 .

Terry, N. P. (2008). Addressing African American English in early literacy assessment and instruction. *Perspectives on Communication Disorders and Sciences in Culturally and Linguistically Diverse Populations*, *15*, 54–61.

Terry, N .P., Connor, C. M., Thomas-Tate, S., & Love, M. (2010). Examining relationships among dialect variation, literacy skills, and school context in first grade. *Journal of Speech, Language, and Hearing Research*, *53*, 126–145.

Thompson, C. A., Craig, H. K., & Washington, J. A. (2004). Variable production of African American English across oracy and literacy contexts. *Language, Speech, and Hearing Services in Schools*, *35*, 269–282.

Tunmer, W. E., Pratt, C., & Herriman, M. L. (1984). *Metalinguistic awareness in children: Theory, research, and implications*. New York: Springer-Verlag.

Washington, J. A., & Craig, H. K. (1998). Socioeconomic status and gender influences on children's dialectal variation. *Journal of Speech, Language, and Hearing Research*, *41*, 618–626.

Washington, J. A., & Craig, H. K. (2001). Reading performance and dialectal variation. In J. L. Harris, A. G. Kamhi, & K. E. Pollock (Eds.), *Literacy in African American communities* (pp. 147–168). Mahwah, NJ: Lawrence Erlbaum Associates.

Washington, J. A., & Craig, H. K. (2002). Morphosyntactic forms of African American English used by young children and their caregivers. *Applied Psycholinguistics*, *23*, 209–232.

Wheeler, R. S., & Swords, R. (2006). *Code-switching: Teaching standard English in urban classrooms*. Urbana, IL: National Council of Teachers of English.

Wolfram, W., Adger, C. T., & Christian, D. (1999). *Dialects in schools and communities*. Mahwah, NJ: Lawrence Erlbaum Associates.

Wolfram, W., & Schilling-Estes, N. (2006). *American English* (2nd ed.). Malden, MA: Blackwell.

Woodcock, R., McGrew, K., & Mather, N. (2001). *Woodcock-Johnson Tests of Achievement* (3rd ed.). Rolling Meadows, IL: Riverside Publishing.

Yiakoumetti, A. (2007). Choice of classroom language in bidialectal communities: To include or to exclude the dialect? *Cambridge Journal of Education*, *37*(1), 51–66.

Part III

Sources of Individual Differences Beyond Phonological Deficits

6 Beyond Phonological Deficits

Sources of Individual Differences in Reading Disability

Margaret J. Snowling
University of York

During the past four decades, dyslexia research has been dominated by the phonological deficit hypothesis. According to this view, the causes of word-level reading impairments can be traced to deficits in language-based processes that are specialized for the processing of speech (Vellutino, Fletcher, Snowling, & Scanlon, 2004). The theoretical backdrop for this model, and indeed much of the evidence, can be attributed to the influential work of Shankweiler and his colleagues. From his earliest writings (e.g., Shankweiler, 1964), Shankweiler rejected the view that poor reading might be a consequence of a visual perceptual abnormality. Instead, recognizing the importance of phoneme segmentation and coding processes to typical reading development (Liberman & Shankweiler, 1991), he argued that, therein, is the problem of dyslexia. In short, dyslexia can be considered a phonological coding deficit that compromises the acquisition of the alphabetic principle (Byrne, 1998); in turn, this has downstream effects on decoding processes in reading, spelling, and to some extent grammatical processing (Shankweiler & Crain, 1986). Whereas in English the primary feature of dyslexia is a difficulty with reading and spelling accuracy, in transparent orthographies, the primary manifestation is a deficit in reading fluency, but in all cases phonological skills are impaired (Caravolas 2005, for a review). Within this model, the phonological deficit is necessary and sufficient to cause the reading impairment in dyslexia (Morton & Frith, 1995).

In recent years however, this view of dyslexia as a specific phonological deficit has come under scrutiny. From the perspective of developmental psychology, Thomas and Karmiloff-Smith (2002) have argued that even highly selective deficits in childhood have diffuse effects on developmental outcomes so that it would be unlikely for a phonological deficit to emerge in isolation. Relatedly, Plomin and Kovas (2005) have used evidence from behavior-genetics to argue that the effects of genes on behavior are general and hence shared genetic influences render specific developmental disorders unlikely. In a similar vein, Pennington (2006) and Bishop (2006) have argued that single deficit accounts (e.g., the phonological deficit account) are inadequate to explain developmental disorders; more specifically, Pennington (2006) has proposed that a causal model for dyslexia should incorporate deficits in phonology *together with* deficits in the speed of processing.

Outside of the domain of reading science, it is well established that pure disorders are rarely observed in childhood; rather, developmental disorders tend to co-occur (Caron & Rutter, 1991). The co-occurrence, or comorbidity, of disorders is important for both theoretical and practical reasons. Theoretically, comorbidity complicates causal reasoning, affects the classification of learning disorders, and, as a consequence, changes the educational implications that flow from "diagnosis." In this light, it is important to ask whether the findings that dyslexia frequently co-occurs with oral language impairments (McArthur, Hogben, Edwards, Heath, & Mengler, 2000) and also with attention deficit/hyperactivity disorder (ADHD) (Willcutt & Pennington, 2000) challenge the phonological deficit hypothesis. It is striking that there has been very little consideration of this issue from the perspective of cognition. In this chapter, therefore, we will consider dyslexia in the context of first ADHD and second specific language impairment (SLI) and ask what, if any role, do non-phonological processes play in determining reading development? Furthermore, do deficits in processes outside of the phonological module contribute to the risk of reading disability? We will begin by discussing findings from two laboratory studies in which we have contrasted dyslexia with ADHD and with SLI and then use these findings to argue that some of the classic features of dyslexia may be due to co-occurring disorders. We will then turn to a study of children at family risk of dyslexia who were followed from preschool through to adolescence to reveal continuities between reading impaired and unimpaired family members. Finally, we will propose that "dyslexia" should not be considered a category but rather as a developmental disorder that will be more or less handicapping depending on co-occurring conditions and also the environmental context.

DYSLEXIA AND ADHD

ADHD is a behavioral disorder characterized by impairments in attention and hyperactivity. According to Barkley (1997), the core deficit in ADHD is in behavioral inhibition associated with the disruption of executive functions. However, ADHD is heterogeneous, and there is suggestive evidence that the overlap with dyslexia may be due to symptoms of inattention rather than hyperactivity (Carroll, Maughan, Goodman, & Meltzer, 2005).

A growing body of evidence suggests that one of the primary deficits in ADHD is in temporal processing or timing (Smith, Taylor, Rogers, Newman, & Rubia, 2002; Toplak, Rucklidge, Hetherington, John, & Tannock, 2003). Furthermore, Castellanos and Tannock (2002) have proposed that such temporal processing deficits affect not only time perception but also, following Tallal (1980), speech perception and the development of phonological skills. However, the hypothesized causal link between impaired temporal processing and poor speech perception has been strongly challenged by the Haskins group (Mody, Studdert-Kennedy, & Brady, 1997). In this light, it seems possible that the co-occurrence of ADHD with dyslexia may have led to false causal reasoning. In short, both the popular hypothesis that dyslexia can be traced to temporal processing impairments (Klein & Farmer, 1995; Tallal, 1980), and clinical observations of phoneme awareness deficits in ADHD may in each case turn upon whether or not samples include cases of comorbid dyslexia and ADHD.

Gooch, Snowling, and Hulme (2010) investigated time perception and phonological skills in dyslexia and ADHD, comparing groups of such children with typically developing controls matched for age and nonverbal IQ. Children were classified as "dyslexic" if both their reading and spelling skills measured below a standard score of 85 (one standard deviation below the mean). Children with ADHD were either referred with a clinical diagnosis or were rated by parents and teachers as high on an ADHD rating scale. These children were then placed into one of the three subgroups depending upon whether or not they fulfilled the criteria for the other disorder; this procedure produced three clinical groups: pure dyslexia ($N = 17$), pure ADHD ($N = 19$), and a comorbid dyslexia–ADHD ($N = 25$). Importantly, the two dyslexia subgroups did not differ in the severity of their reading impairments and the two ADHD groups did not differ in the severity of their ADHD symptoms.

Each child participated in one or two sessions in the lab where they took part in a range of different tasks. For present purposes, we will focus on a test requiring time reproduction and a phoneme awareness task. From the phonological deficit hypothesis, we predicted that both groups of children with dyslexia would perform more poorly than children with ADHD-only on the phoneme awareness task. We also predicted that the children with ADHD would have problems in time estimation but hypothesized that the children with dyslexia-only would not.

The time reproduction test was simple. A blue square appeared on a color monitor for a period of time ranging between 2 and 10 s and when the square went off the child had to hold his or her finger down on a button to make a red square appear for the same amount of time for which he or she had observed the blue square appear. Each target time interval was presented twice and the length of time a child took to reproduce the target interval was recorded. The phoneme awareness task was phoneme deletion (McDougall, Hulme, Ellis, & Monk, 1994). In this task, the child heard a spoken monosyllabic nonword and was required to delete a specified phoneme. In all cases, deletion of the specified phoneme resulted in a word, for example, deleting the /b/ from /bais/ produces the word *ice*.

Figure 6.1a shows the absolute discrepancy between the participant's time reproduction and the interval presented (absolute error) for children in each of the four groups. The graph shows clearly that there is a significant effect of ADHD on time reproduction but no main effect of dyslexia: Children with attention disorders have more difficulty than those without attention disorders in reproducing intervals of time. Also of note is the observation that the comorbid group (dyslexia + ADHD) has the worst impairment in time perception (though not statistically greater than that of the ADHD group). Figure 6.1b shows the scores of the

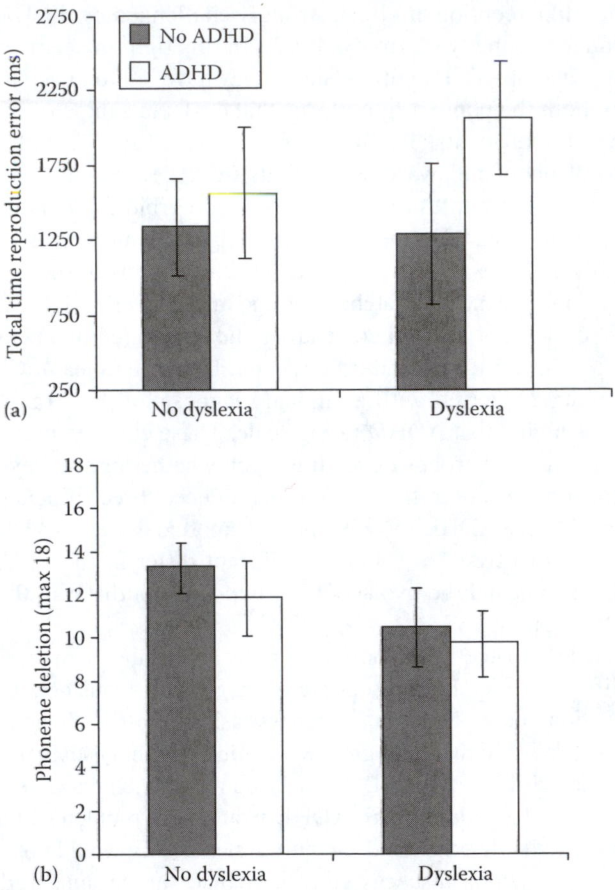

FIGURE 6.1 (a) Discrepancy between participants' time reproduction and the interval presented (absolute error) for children with ADHD, dyslexia, ADHD + dyslexia, and controls. (b) Scores on the phoneme deletion test for children with ADHD, dyslexia, ADHD + dyslexia, and controls.

four groups on the phoneme deletion test. Here the pattern is in direct contrast to the findings for time reproduction. There is a main effect of dyslexia on phoneme deletion but no significant effect of ADHD. Once again, there is a trend for the comorbid group to do least well.

The findings of this study are in line with the predictions of the phonological deficit hypothesis—it was the children with dyslexia who had problems with the phonological task. Thus, it seems likely that theoretical claims of temporal deficits in dyslexia (Klein & Farmer, 1995; Nicolson, Fawcett, & Dean, 1995) depend upon the presence of cases with comorbid ADHD in study samples. Likewise, clinical complaints of poor time management and organizational skills in dyslexia might be considered to be co-occurring features rather than behavioral symptoms of the reading disorder.

DYSLEXIA AND SPECIFIC LANGUAGE IMPAIRMENT

Specific language impairment (SLI) is a primary disorder of language development characterized by significant delays in oral language development with poor lexical learning and persistent difficulties with grammar (Bishop, 1997). The high risk of reading disorder in children with SLI is well documented (Catts, Fey, Zhang, & Tomblin, 1999; Snowling, Bishop, & Stothard, 2000) with some theorists arguing either that dyslexia is a less severe form of SLI or that they are comorbid disorders (Catts, Adlof, Hogan, & Ellis Weismer, 2005). However, SLI is a heterogeneous disorder (Conti-Ramsden, Botting, Simkin, & Knox, 2001; van Weerdenburg, Verhoeven, & van Balkom, 2006) making it difficult to evaluate such stark alternatives. A more fruitful approach to understanding the relationship between the two disorders is to focus directly on reading-related processes. With this in mind, Bishop and Snowling (2004) proposed a model of the relationship between dyslexia and SLI comprising two dimensions: phonological and non-phonological language skills. According to this model, the risk of decoding deficits in reading is carried by poor phonological skills, whereas the risk of reading comprehension impairments is associated with poor oral language beyond phonology (in vocabulary, grammatical, and pragmatic processes). Within the model, the less well developed the language skills on each dimension, the more severely impaired will be the associated component reading skill (decoding or comprehension).

Larkin and Snowling (2008) tested the hypothesis that children with dyslexia and SLI vary in the severity of their phonological impairment by focusing on spelling skills: Spelling errors are pervasive in the writing of children with dyslexia and also in children with SLI (Bishop & Clarkson, 2003). Broadly, two types of spelling problem can be observed: phonetic spelling, which reflects poorly developed knowledge of the orthography but in which the sound structure of words is portrayed correctly, and dysphonetic spelling, which reflects difficulty in reproducing the sound sequence of target words.

There were two clinical groups in this study: children with dyslexia and children with oral SLI. The groups were matched in age and in reading and spelling skill and compared with younger reading-level matched (RA-) controls; the children with dyslexia scored within the average range on a test of receptive vocabulary and just slightly below average on a test of sentence repetition. The children with SLI, in addition to their reading difficulties, had a poor level of vocabulary and had difficulties with sentence repetition. In addition to assessing spelling and writing skills, the children were administered a test of phoneme deletion like the one above in which they had to "take away" a sound from a set of consonant clusters, and a test of phonological memory requiring the repetition of nonwords that did not contain morphological constituents (Dollaghan & Campbell, 1998).

We proceeded to analyze the spelling errors that were made on regular and irregular words in the spelling list. Although the overall performance of the three groups on this test was the same, the children with SLI made fewer phonologically plausible spelling errors than the group with dyslexia; the latter performed at the level of the younger RA-controls. One possible reason for a child's difficulty in spelling phonetically is difficulty in segmenting words at the level of the phoneme. Contrary to this interpretation, the three groups performed equally well on the test of phoneme deletion. However, the groups did differ in phonological memory, with the SLI children showing the greatest deficit. The difficulties of the SLI group were more marked in writing and when they were required to spell multisyllabic words to dictation.

The findings of this study suggest that low levels of reading and spelling performance relative to chronological age in dyslexia and SLI are associated with poor phoneme awareness, indicative of the commonalities between the two disorders. However, qualitative analysis of spelling errors tells a different story with the two groups differing in the severity of their spelling errors and also in phonological memory resources. More generally, phonological memory appears to place a constraint on phonological spelling ability and is related to individual differences in the pattern of errors that are seen. It can be inferred that, when dysphonetic spelling errors are observed in dyslexia, they may be related to comorbid SLIs. A corollary of this finding is that dyslexia (as defined by a phonological deficit) can be observed both with and without broader language difficulties.

The data from our study also speak to an important theoretical hypothesis regarding the predictive relationship between phonological memory (as measured by nonword repetition) and vocabulary development (Baddeley, Gathercole, & Papagno, 1998; Gathercole & Baddeley, 1989). Figure 6.2 shows the relationship observed in our study between phonological memory (as measured by nonword repetition) and receptive vocabulary scores. Overall, there was a strong

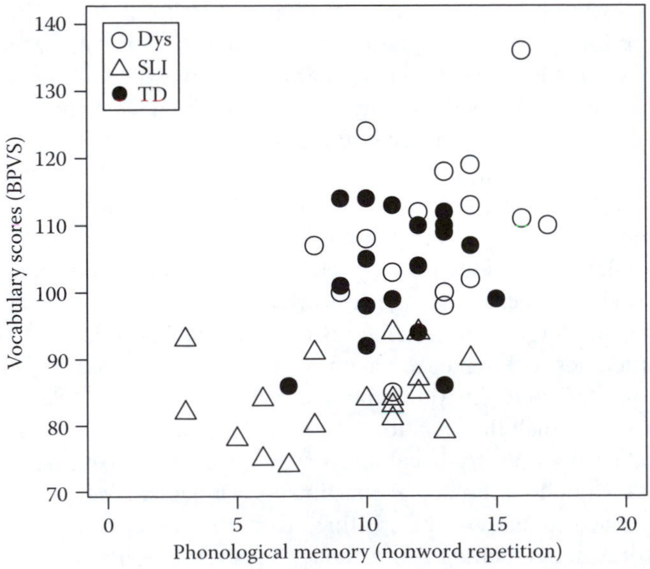

FIGURE 6.2 The relationship between phonological memory and receptive vocabulary scores in children with dyslexia, SLI, and typical reading development (TD).

relationship between phonological memory and vocabulary skills. However, it is striking that the relationship appears to hold for the children with dyslexia and the typically developing controls but not for those children with SLI. Among children with SLI, two subgroups can be discerned. In the lower left quadrant of the figure are a group of children with SLI who show poor phonological memory and poor vocabulary (in line with the causal hypothesis), and appear to conform to a more severe version of dyslexia. A second subgroup of children fall in the lower right of the figure—these children have good phonological memory but poor receptive vocabulary and might be considered to form a subgroup of children with SLI who are not on the dyslexia continuum. Arguably, it is children such as these who show the contrasting profile to dyslexia—they typically have good word-level reading and decoding skills but poor reading comprehension, and have been referred to as "poor comprehenders" (Nation, 2005).

In summary, there is heterogeneity in SLI: Some children with SLI fall on a continuum of skills with dyslexia, they have low phonological memory, poor phoneme awareness, and low vocabulary and they conform to what might be called an SLI-dyslexia subtype. Others show a more discrepant profile with high phonological memory and low vocabulary skills and resemble the SLI-poor comprehender subtype (Nation, Clarke, Marshall, & Durand, 2004). An important question for theories of reading development is what role is played by different oral language skills (phonology, vocabulary, and grammar) and in terms of dyslexia, what role do broader language difficulties play in determining reading outcomes?

Reading Outcomes in Children at Family Risk of Dyslexia

In order to consider the role of oral language and more specific phonological skills in the reading development of children with SLI and dyslexia, we now turn to a longitudinal prospective study of children at family risk of dyslexia (Gallagher, Frith, & Snowling, 2000; Snowling, Gallagher, & Frith, 2003; Snowling, Muter, & Carroll, 2007). The method here followed the pioneering study of Scarborough (1990) and was to recruit to the study children considered to be at high risk of dyslexia because they were born to a family in which there was at least one dyslexic parent. We also recruited 37 controls from typically literate families with no history of dyslexia. The two groups were matched for socioeconomic status. We followed the children in two phases. In the first phase of our study, children were seen at the ages of 4, 6, and 8 years and in the second phase, they were seen at 13 years.

Just before their fourth birthday, the children were given a large battery of oral language tests. For purposes of illustration we will focus here on one test of expressive language tapping vocabulary and grammatical skills and one test of phonological memory. The expressive language test was the Bus Story (Renfrew, 1969). On this test, children hear a story told with pictures and then have to use the pictures as prompts to retell the story; the measure is of the amount of information the children can convey. The nonword repetition test required the child to repeat the "names of strange animals" while posting their pictures into a box. At 6 years of age, a year after formal reading instruction began, the children were seen again to assess their language and reading-related skills. The battery of tasks included two tests of phonological awareness, a rhyme oddity task and a simple phoneme deletion task, together with tests of letter knowledge, reading, and spelling. At 8 years of age, we classified childrens' literacy outcomes to form three groups: children at family risk of dyslexia with a reading disorder (FR-RD), children at family risk of dyslexia without a reading disorder (FR-NR), and typically developing children (TDC). (A small group of controls ($N = 4$) were experiencing reading difficulties and these were excluded from the comparison.).

Figure 6.3 shows the performance of the three groups (FR-RD, FR-NR, and TDC) on the language tests at 4 and 6 years. Beginning with the test of expressive language given at age 4, the children who went on to have literacy problems (FR-RD) showed significant language delay, whereas family risk children who did not develop literacy problems (FR-NR) were indistinguishable from TDC. The findings from the expressive language test were replicated on tests of receptive and expressive vocabulary (not shown here). Performance on the nonword repetition test, also at age 4, revealed a different picture. On this test, both of the family risk groups were impaired, relative to controls. These data were puzzling in light of the phonological deficit hypothesis. If poor phonological memory is a risk factor for poor reading, then it was surprising to find that the two groups who differed in literacy outcome were each impaired on this task from the phonological domain.

Turning to the data from the tests of phonological awareness at age 6, as expected, the FR-RD group was impaired on both the rhyme oddity and phoneme deletion tests relative to controls. However, the FR-NR group's performance fell midway

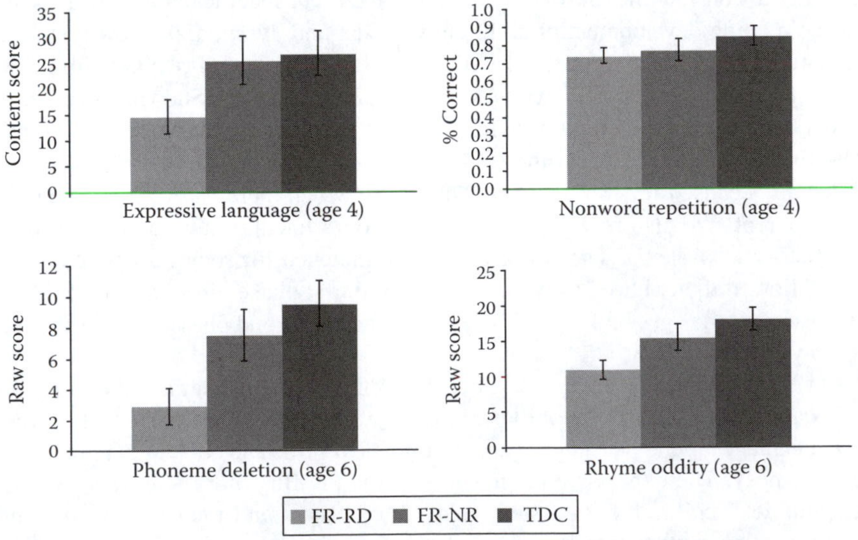

FIGURE 6.3 Performance on language tests at 4 and 6 years, grouped according to literacy outcome at 8 years (family risk-reading disorder, family risk-normal reader, and control).

between that of the FR-RD group and the TDC controls (an effect size of about .5). In short, the family risk "unimpaired" group showed mild deficits in phonological awareness; they also knew fewer letters than the age- and language-matched typically developing group. So why did they not succumb to reading problems? Here we proposed that the FR-NR group was "resilient" by virtue of their good vocabulary and broader oral language skills, allowing early compensation for the family risk of dyslexia (Nation & Snowling, 1998). In other words, good oral language might be a protective factor in children who are at high risk of dyslexia related to phonological deficits. Put another way, phonological deficits that presage literacy problems can be observed among children who carry a family risk, but whether or not they develop dyslexia depends on their wider language skills. Children who show poor phonology in the preschool years in the context of delayed language, a second risk factor, are more likely to develop a reading disorder than those who have poor phonology in the context of normal language development; within the model of Bishop and Snowling (2004) it is the group who carry two risk factors for literacy difficulties that are at higher risk of literacy impairment than those with only one risk factor. From a clinical perspective, children with two risk factors are more likely to reach the diagnostic threshold for dyslexia, though others may experience something akin to a "subclinical" form of the disorder.

If this characterization is correct, then it would not be surprising to find that the longer term outcome of children in the family risk group with normal reading at 8 years might be poor relative to peers—that is, the tendency to compensate early for phonological difficulties can be expected to come at a cost and may lead to a decline in the reading skill when the demands of literacy increase. Figure 6.4 shows the performance of the three groups of children on tests of exception word reading and reading fluency given at age 13. In terms of outcome in adolescence, children with two risk factors who were dyslexic at age 8 years continued to have significant difficulties on all literacy measures. Important, however, children who had only one risk factor were also doing less well than expected for their age and ability in reading, and their spelling was also weak. At this stage in their development, the FR-NR group conformed to what might be called the broader phenotype of dyslexia or compensated dyslexia (Ramus et al., 2003)—a kind of mild or partial version of the dyslexia phenotype, which, in childhood, does not reach the diagnostic threshold.

Together, these findings suggest that dyslexia is not as "specific" as was once thought. Although there is considerable evidence that poor phonological skills predict poor levels of reading in childhood (Bradley & Bryant, 1978; Muter, Hulme, Snowling, & Stevenson, 2004; Torgeson, Wagner, & Rashotte, 1994) and not wishing to downplay the importance of phonological deficits in the etiology of dyslexia, the current findings imply that it is important to think of "causes" of disorders not in absolute terms but as probabilistic (Hulme & Snowling, 2009). In this light, the influential phonological deficit hypothesis of dyslexia might be productively reframed to propose that children who have phonological deficits are at a high risk of reading impairment but that reading impairment is not inevitable in these children. Within this new formulation, the risk of dyslexia can be

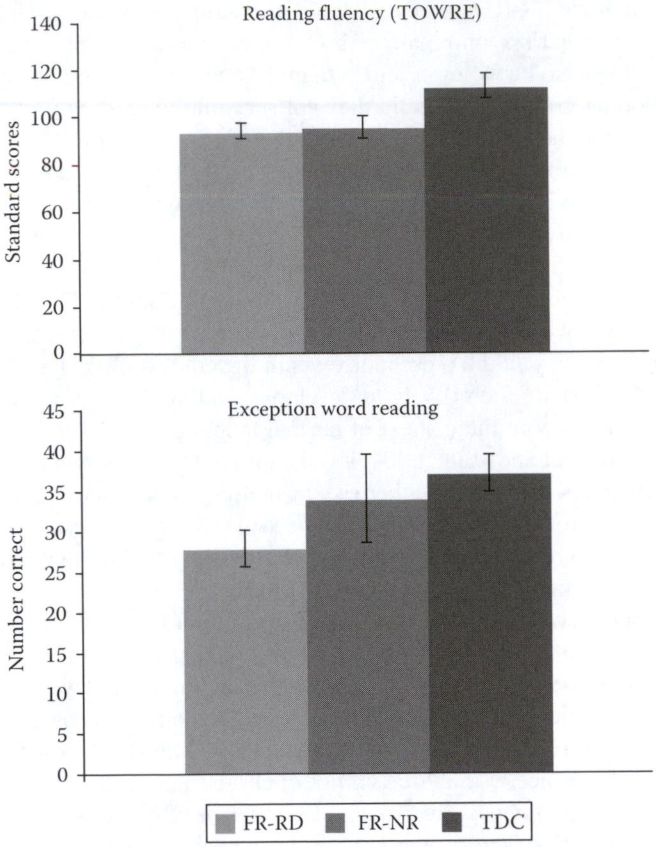

FIGURE 6.4 Performance on tests of exception word reading, reading fluency, and spelling (family risk-reading disorder, family risk-normal reader, and control).

moderated by within-child factors, such as well-developed language skills and good attentional resources (Snowling, 2008) as well as environmental conditions, such as early intervention. Moreover, the behavioral manifestations of dyslexia are likely to depend upon the language of learning (Paulesu et al., 2001).

In essence, the view that is espoused here is a dimensional rather than a categorical one that emphasizes continuous risk factors underpinning reading disorders. Figure 6.5 provides a schematic diagram to illustrate this idea. In the vertical columns, the diagram illustrates using circles the risk carried by three children (one in each row) on each of the two dimensions that underpin literacy (after Bishop & Snowling, 2004); the bolder the color of the circle, the greater the risk of impairment. In this diagram, the three children all have the same risk factor for dyslexia on the first dimension, phonology. In fact, they all have a phonological deficit. The three children differ in the risk expressed on the second dimension, language skills. The first child has good language (no risk). The second child has some expressive language difficulties (moderate risk). The third child

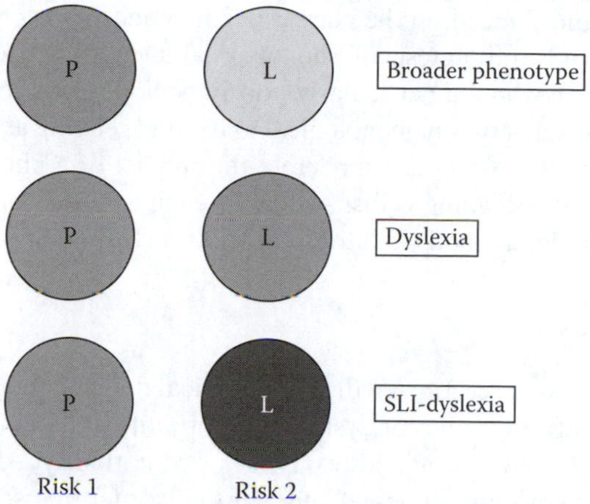

FIGURE 6.5 Schematic diagram to show a dimensional model of reading disorders in which outcome is determined through the interaction of continuous risk factors underpinning reading disorders.

has significant oral language difficulties (severe risk). If, as we hypothesize, the behavior manifestations of dyslexia associated with a given level of phonological impairment depend upon associated factors, then it can be inferred that the first child will show the broader phenotype of dyslexia, the second will show the classic dyslexia profile, and the third will show the dyslexia subtype of SLI. It is just such interactions between risk and protective factors that would be envisaged for a developmental disorder like dyslexia that depends upon the interaction of multiple genes acting through multiple environments (Rutter, 2006).

A CAUSAL MODEL OF DYSLEXIA

The phonological deficit hypothesis of dyslexia has survived many theoretical challenges throughout its long history. Amongst these have been theories purporting that the causes of dyslexia can be traced to low-level deficits in the magnocellular visual system (Lovegrove, Martin, & Slaghuis, 1986; Stein & Talcott, 1999), in auditory processing (Tallal, Miller, Jenkins, & Merzenich, 1997), or in the cerebellum (Nicolson, Fawcett, & Dean, 2001). However, it is reasonable to argue that the only positive longitudinal evidence is for a causal relationship between language and phonological skills and subsequent reading abilities, and, perhaps, therefore, these claims relate to other conditions that are frequently comorbid with dyslexia (e.g., Rochelle & Talcott, 2006). Notwithstanding this, data from prospective longitudinal studies of high-risk groups that are free of clinical biases highlight the fact that a phonological deficit may be necessary but not necessarily sufficient to cause dyslexia. Thus, in family-risk samples it is possible to find children with phonological deficits who are free of reading problems. In a similar vein, Bryant (1985) argued that there is not a necessary association between a phonological impairment and a poor reading outcome at the level of the individual child. Indeed, in the classic Bradley and Bryant (1983) study, 4% of children who did well on tests of phonological awareness became poor readers and 5% of those who did particularly poorly became good readers. Thus, the imperfect correlation between phonological skills and reading attainments leaves open the issue of factors that can moderate the impact of a phonological deficit on the development of reading skills. Arguably, such an issue can best be investigated using theoretically motivated training studies (Hulme & Snowling, 2009).

CONCLUSIONS

In this chapter, we have scrutinized the phonological deficit hypothesis of dyslexia in relation to data from studies of dyslexia comorbidity and of children at family risk of dyslexia. We have examined two types of comorbidity: ADHD (a disorder on a different dimension to dyslexia) and SLI (a disorder that shows continuities with dyslexia). In both cases, it was possible to find dissociations between the performance of children with pure dyslexia and children with comorbid forms. However, at the core of dyslexia were phonological deficits of likely causal significance. Indeed, the causal role of phonological deficits in the determination of literacy outcomes was observed in the "family-risk" study, but, in addition, the findings of this study suggest that non-phonological language skills may moderate its impact on reading development at least in the early school years.

More generally with regard to the concept of dyslexia, our findings are compatible with the view that this is a dimensional disorder with no clear boundaries between "dyslexic" and "not-dyslexic" (Pennington & Lefly, 2001). Furthermore, in line with multiple deficit theories, the risk of dyslexia is greater when a child presents with more than just a specific phonological deficit (Snowling, 2008).

To conclude, language and phonological skills are the foundations of literacy development. It is proposed that each can be selectively impaired rendering compensation possible, except in cases of severe disability. Moreover, when both language and phonological skills are deficient, pervasive literacy impairments are the usual outcome. It is heartening in this light that intervention programs that target language and phonological skills can be effective (Bowyer-Crane et al., 2008) though children with double deficits in language and phonology tend to show less good response to intervention (Duff et al., 2008). The contribution of Shankweiler in introducing the phonological deficit view has been seminal. The phonological deficit hypothesis remains a cornerstone of our understanding not only of the nature of reading disorders but also of how best to prevent them (Hindson et al., 2005). In the face of doubts about diagnostic categories to describe developmental disorders, the field is now poised to search for endophenotypes intermediate between genes and behavior (Bearden & Freimer, 2006). It is indubitable that phonological deficits are an endophenotype of dyslexia with a genetic basis; the legacy of the phonological deficit hypothesis is set to survive as a key casual explanation for dyslexia.

ACKNOWLEDGMENTS

This chapter was prepared with support from Wellcome Programme Grant 082036. Thanks to Susannah Witts for assistance.

REFERENCES

Baddeley, A., Gathercole, S., & Papagno, C. (1998). The phonological loop as a language learning device. *Psychological Review*, *105*, 158–173.

Barkley, R. A. (1997). Behavioral inhibition, sustained attention, and executive functions: Constructing a unifying theory of ADHD. *Psychological Bulletin*, *121*, 65–94.

Bearden, C. E., & Freimer, N. B. (2006). Endophenotypes for psychiatric disorders: Ready for primetime? *Trends in Genetics*, *22*, 306–313.

Bishop, D. V. M. (1997). *Uncommon understanding*. Hove: Psychology Press.

Bishop, D. V. M. (2006). Developmental cognitive genetics: How psychology can inform genetics and vice versa. *Quarterly Journal of Experimental Psychology*, *59*(7), 1153–1168.

Bishop, D. V. M., & Clarkson, B. (2003). Written language as a window into residual language deficits: A study of children with persistent and residual speech and language impairments. *Cortex*, *39*, 215–237.

Bishop, D. V. M., & Snowling, M. J. (2004). Developmental dyslexia and specific language impairment: Same or different? *Psychological Bulletin*, *130*, 858–888.

Bowyer-Crane, C., Snowling, M. J., Duff, F. J., Carroll, J. M., Fieldsend, E., Miles, J., et al. (2008). Improving early language and literacy skills: Differential effects of an oral language versus a phonology with reading intervention. *Journal of Child Psychology and Psychiatry*, *49*, 422–432.

Bradley, L., & Bryant, P. E. (1978). Difficulties in auditory organization as a possible cause of reading backwardness. *Nature*, *271*, 746–747.

Bradley, L., & Bryant, P. E. (1983). Categorizing sounds and learning to read—Causal connection. *Nature*, *301*, 419–421.

Bryant, P. E. (1985). Children's reading problems. In M. J. Snowling (Ed.), *Children's written language difficulties*. Windsor: NFER-Nelson.

Byrne, B. (1998). *The foundation of literacy: The child's acquisition of the alphabetic principle*. Hove: Psychology Press.

Caravolas, M. (2005). The nature and causes of dyslexia in different languages. In M. J. Snowling & C. Hulme (Eds.), *The science of reading: A handbook* (pp. 336–356). Oxford: Blackwell.

Caron, C., & Rutter, M. (1991). Comorbidity in child psychopathology: Concepts, issues and research strategies. *Journal of Child Psychology and Psychiatry*, *32*(7), 1063–1080.

Carroll, J., Maughan, B., Goodman, R., & Meltzer, H. (2005). Literacy difficulties and psychiatric disorders: Evidence for co-morbidity. *Journal of Child Psychology and Psychiatry*, *46*, 524–532.

Castellanos, F. X., & Tannock, R. (2002). Neuroscience of attention-deficit/hyperactivity disorder: The search for endophenotypes. *Nature Reviews Neuroscience*, *3*, 617–628.

Catts, H. W., Adlof, S. M., Hogan, T. P., & Ellis Weismer, S. (2005). Are specific language impairment and dyslexia distinct disorders? *Journal of Speech, Language, and Hearing Research*, *48*, 1378–1396.

Catts, H. W., Fey, M. E., Zhang, X., & Tomblin, J. B. (1999). Language basis of reading and reading disabilities: Evidence from a longitudinal investigation. *Scientific Studies of Reading*, *3*, 331–361.

Conti-Ramsden, G., Botting, N., Simkin, Z., & Knox, E. (2001). Follow-up of children attending infant language units: Outcomes at 11 years of age. *International Journal of Language & Communication Disorders*, *36*, 207–219.

Dollaghan, C., & Campbell, T. F. (1998). Nonword repetition and child language impairment. *Journal of Speech Language & Hearing Research*, *41*(5), 1136–1146.

Duff, F., Fieldsend, E., Bowyer-Crane, C., Hulme, C., Smith, G., Gibbs, S., et al. (2008). Reading with vocabulary intervention: Evaluation of an instruction for children with poor response to reading intervention. *Journal of Research in Reading*, *31*, 319–336.

Gallagher, A., Frith, U., & Snowling, M. J. (2000). Precursors of literacy-delay among children at genetic risk of dyslexia. *Journal of Child Psychology and Psychiatry*, *41*, 203–213.

Gathercole, S., & Baddeley, A. (1989). Evaluation of the role of phonological STM in the development of vocabulary in children: A longitudinal study. *Journal of Memory and Language*, *28*, 200–213.

Gooch, D., Snowling, M., & Hulme, C. (2010). Phonological skills, time perception and executive function in children with dyslexia and attention difficulties. *Journal of Child Psychology & Psychiatry*, online September 23, 2010, DOI: 10.1111/j.1469-7610.2010.02312.x

Hindson, B., Byrne, B., Fielding-Barnsley, R., Newman, C., Hine, D. W., & Shankweiler, D. (2005). Assessment and early instruction of pre-school children at risk for reading disability. *Journal of Educational Psychology*, *97*, 687–704.

Hulme, C., & Snowling, M. J. (2009). *Developmental disorders of language and cognition*. Oxford: Blackwell/Wiley.

Klein, R. M., & Farmer, M. E. (1995). Dyslexia and a temporal processing deficit: A reply to the commentaries. *Psychonomic Bulletin & Review*, *2*(4), 515–526.

Larkin, R. F., & Snowling, M. J. (2008). Phonological skills and spelling abilities in children with reading and language impairments. *International Journal of Language and Communication Disorders*, *43*, 111–124.

Liberman, I. Y., & Shankweiler, D. (1991). Phonology and beginning reading: A tutorial. In L. Rieben & C. A. Perfetti (Eds.), *Learning to read: Basic research and its implications* (pp. 3–17). Hillsdale, NJ: Erlbaum.

Lovegrove, W., Martin, F., & Slaghuis, W. (1986). The theoretical and experimental case for a visual deficit in specific reading disability. *Cognitive Neuropsychology*, *3*(2), 225–267.

McArthur, G. M., Hogben, J. H., Edwards, V. T., Heath, S. M., & Mengler, E. D. (2000). On the "specifics" of specific reading disability and specific language impairment. *Journal of Child Psychology and Child Psychiatry*, 41, 869–874.

McDougall, S., Hulme, C., Ellis, A. W., & Monk, A. (1994). Learning to read: The role of short-term memory and phonological skills. *Journal of Experimental Child Psychology*, *58*, 112–123.

Mody, M., Studdert-Kennedy, M., & Brady, S. (1997). Speech perception deficits in poor readers: Auditory processing or phonological coding? *Journal of Experimental Child Psychology*, *58*, 112–123.

Morton, J., & Frith, U. (1995). Causal modeling: A structural approach to developmental psychopathology. In D. Cicchetti & D. J. Cohen (Eds.), *Manual of developmental psychopathology* (pp. 357–390). New York: Wiley.

Muter, V., Hulme, C., Snowling, M. J., & Stevenson, J. (2004). Phonemes, rimes, vocabulary, and grammatical skills as foundations of early reading development: Evidence from a longitudinal study. *Developmental Psychology*, *40*, 663–681.

Nation, K. (2005). Children's reading comprehension difficulties. In M. J. Snowing & C. Hulme (Eds.), *The science of reading: A handbook* (pp. 248–266). Oxford: Blackwell.

Nation, K., Clarke, P., Marshall, C., & Durand, M. (2004). Hidden language impairments in children: Parallels between poor reading comprehension and specific language impairment? *Journal of Speech, Language, and Hearing Research*, *47*, 199–211.

Nation, K., & Snowling, M. J. (1998). Individual differences in contextual facilitation: Evidence from dyslexia and poor reading comprehension. *Child Development*, *69*(4), 996–1011.

Nicolson, R. I., Fawcett, A. J., & Dean, P. (1995). Time estimation deficits in developmental dyslexia: Evidence for cerebellar involvement. *Proceedings of the Royal Society of London: Biological Sciences*, *259*, 43–47.

Nicolson, R. I., Fawcett, A. J., & Dean, P. (2001). Developmental dyslexia: The cerebellar deficit hypothesis. *Trends in Neurological Sciences*, *24*, 508–511.

Paulesu, E., Demonet, J.-F., Fazio, F., McCrory, E., Chanoine, V., Brunswick, N., et al. (2001). Dyslexia: Cultural diversity and biological unity. *Science*, *291*, 2165–2167.

Pennington, B. F. (2006). From single to multiple deficit models of developmental disorders. *Cognition*, *101*, 385–413.

Pennington, B. F., & Lefly, D. L. (2001). Early reading development in children at family risk for dyslexia. *Child Development*, *72*, 816–833.

Plomin, R., & Kovas, Y. (2005). Generalist genes and learning disabilities. *Psychological Bulletin*, *131*(4), 592–617.

Ramus, F., Rosen, S., Dakin, S. C., Day, B. L., Castellote, J. M., White, S., et al. (2003). Theories of developmental dyslexia: Insights from a multiple case study of dyslexic adults. *Brain*, *126*, 1–25.

Renfrew, C. E. (1969). *The bus story: A test of continuous speech*. Headington: C. E. Renfrew.

Rochelle, K., & Talcott, J. (2006). Impaired balance in developmental dyslexia? A meta-analysis of contending evidence. *Journal of Child Psychology and Psychiatry*, *47*, 1159–1166.

Rutter, M. (2006). *Genes and behavior. Nature-nurture inter-play explained*. Oxford: Blackwell.

Scarborough, H. S. (1990). Very early language deficits in dyslexic children. *Child Development*, *61*, 1728–1743.

Shankweiler, D. (1964). Developmental dyslexia: A critique and review of recent evidence. *Cortex*, *1*, 53–62.

Shankweiler, D., & Crain, S. (1986). Language mechanisms and reading disorder: A modular approach. *Cognition*, *24*(1–2), 139–168.

Smith, A., Taylor, E., Rogers, J. W., Newman, S., & Rubia, K. (2002). Evidence for a pure time perception deficit in children with ADHD. *Journal of Child Psychology and Psychiatry and Allied Disciplines*, *43*(4), 529–542.

Snowling, M. J. (2008). Specific disorders and broader phenotypes: The case of dyslexia. *Quarterly Journal of Experimental Psychology*, *61*, 142–156.

Snowling, M. J., Bishop, D. V. M., & Stothard, S. E. (2000). Is pre-school language impairment a risk factor for dyslexia in adolescence? *Journal of Child Psychology and Psychiatry*, *41*, 587–600.

Snowling, M. J., Gallagher, A., & Frith, U. (2003). Family risk of dyslexia is continuous: Individual differences in the precursors of reading skill. *Child Development*, *74*(2), 358–373.

Snowing, M. J., Muter, V., & Carroll, J. M. (2007). Children at family risk of dyslexia: A follow-up in adolescence. *Journal of Child Psychology and Psychiatry*, *48*, 609–618.

Stein, J., & Talcott, J. (1999). Impaired neuronal timing in developmental dyslexia—The magnocellular hypothesis. *Dyslexia*, *5*, 59–77.

Tallal, P. (1980). Auditory temporal perception, phonics, and reading disabilities in children. *Brain and Language*, *9*, 182–198.

Tallal, P., Miller, S. L., Jenkins, W. M., & Merzenich, M. M. (1997). The role of temporal processing in developmental language-based learning disorders: Research and clinical implications. In B. A. Blachman (Ed.), *Foundations of reading acquisition and dyslexia: Implications for early intervention*. Mahwah, NJ: Lawrence Erlbaum Associates.

Thomas, M., & Karmiloff-Smith, A. (2002). Are developmental disorders like cases of brain damage? Implications from connectionist modelling. *Behavioral and Brain Sciences*, *25*, 727–788.

Toplak, M. E., Rucklidge, J. J., Hetherington, R., John, S. C. F., & Tannock, R. (2003). Time perception deficits in attention-deficit/ hyperactivity disorder and comorbid reading difficulties in child and adolescent samples. *Journal of Child Psychology and Psychiatry*, *44*(6), 888–903.

Torgeson, J. K., Wagner, R. K., & Rashotte, C. A. (1994). Longitudinal studies of phonological processing and reading. *Journal of Learning Disabilities*, *27*(5), 276–286.

van Weerdenburg, M., Verhoeven, L., & van Balkom, H. (2006). Towards a typology of specific language impairment. *Journal of Child Psychology and Psychiatry*, *47*, 176–189.

Vellutino, F. R., Fletcher, J. M., Snowling, M. J., & Scanlon, D. M. (2004). Specific reading disability (dyslexia): What have we learned in the past four decades? *Journal of Child Psychology and Psychiatry*, *45*(1), 2–40.

Willcutt, E. G., & Pennington, B. F. (2000). Comorbidity of reading disability and attention-deficit/hyperactivity disorder: Differences by gender and subtype. *Journal of Learning Disabilities*, *33*, 179–191.

7 Phonological and Other Language Deficits Associated With Dyslexia

Hugh W. Catts
University of Kansas
Suzanne Adlof
University of Pittsburgh

Over 30 years ago, Shankweiler, Liberman, and their colleagues at Haskins Laboratories introduced the phonological deficit hypothesis to account for the problems some children have in learning to read and spell (Liberman & Shankweiler, 1979; Shankweiler, Liberman, Mark, Fowler, & Fischer, 1979). Although others had offered somewhat similar proposals (e.g., Calfee, Chapman, & Venezky, 1972), the Haskins group was the first to fully articulate and investigate this view. They argued that individual differences in children's ability to learn to read and spell were the result of variability in children's representation of the speech codes on which written languages are based. In the years since, a large body of work has accumulated in support of this hypothesis. This work has shown that a phonological deficit can account for problems in learning to read in a variety of languages involving a variety of orthographies (Fletcher et al., 1994; Ho, Law, & Ng, 2000; H. Lyytinen et al., 2004; Stanovich & Siegel, 1994). Research has further revealed a neurological and genetic basis for individual differences in phonological processing ability* (Byrne et al., 2002; Simos, Brier, Fletcher, Bergman, & Papanicolauo, 2002).

Whereas a phonological deficit may underlie many reading problems, it is not the only language deficit associated with reading disabilities. Children with reading disabilities often have other language deficits involving limitations in vocabulary, grammar, and discourse (Catts, Fey, Zhang, & Tomblin, 1999; Gallagher, Frith, & Snowling, 2000; Scarborough, 1990). Early evidence of these deficits led Kamhi and me to argue for a language-based view of dyslexia (Kamhi & Catts, 1986). In that proposal, we highlighted the various language problems associated

* The term "phonological processing ability" is used in this chapter to refer to a category of cognitive abilities including those in phonological awareness, phonological memory, and rapid naming.

with difficulties in learning to read. However, our discussion of the specific relationships between a phonological deficit, other language problems, and reading disabilities was limited by a lack of relevant research. Since then, many investigations have examined more closely the language basis of reading disabilities (Catts, Adlof, Hogan, & Weismer, 2005; Gallagher, Frith, Snowling, 2000; P. Lyytinen, Poikkeus, Laakso, Eklund, & H. Lyytinen, 2001; Snowling, 2008). In this chapter, we review the results from a recently completed longitudinal investigation and discuss how other language deficits may be related to a phonological deficit and reading disabilities.

POSSIBLE RELATIONSHIPS

Figure 7.1 displays several possible relationships between language deficits and reading disabilities. Two types of reading disabilities are considered: poor comprehension and dyslexia. Dyslexia is a specific deficit in word reading, whereas poor comprehension refers to a specific difficulty in understanding printed text. Research shows that these difficulties may occur by themselves or in combination with each other (Aaron, Joshi, & Williams, 1999; Catts, Adlof, & Weismer, 2006; Catts, Hogan, & Adlof, 2005). It is now generally accepted that a phonological deficit is a primary cause of dyslexia (Lyon, Shaywitz, & Shaywitz, 2003). There is less agreement, however, concerning the relationship between reading disabilities/phonological deficit and other language deficits. For ease of presentation, the latter language deficits will be grouped under the category of language impairment (LI).

Figure 7.1 shows a link between a phonological deficit and dyslexia, which is the essence of the phonological deficit hypothesis. As noted above, considerable research indicates that a phonological deficit is the primary causal factor in dyslexia. Figure 7.1 also suggests that a phonological deficit may play an important role in an LI (Dollaghan & Campbell, 1998; Gathercole & Baddeley, 1990). According to this view, a phonological deficit causes a "bottleneck" in language processing that leads to downstream effects on the development of vocabulary and grammar. An extension of this view (e.g., the severity hypothesis) argues that the more severe the phonological deficit, the more likely a child will have both dyslexia and an LI (Kamhi & Catts, 1986; Tallal, Allard, Miller, & Curtiss, 1997).

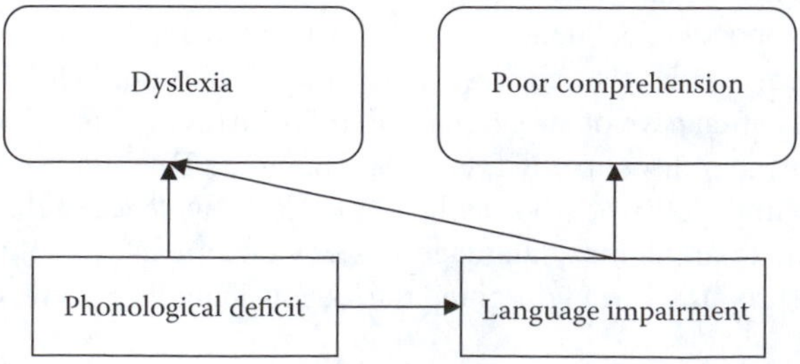

FIGURE 7.1 Possible relationships between a phonological deficit, language impairment (LI), dyslexia, and poor comprehension.

Less severe deficits lead to dyslexia alone. Figure 7.1 also indicates a possible link between an LI and dyslexia. According to this view, deficits in other aspects of language may be an additional causal factor in word reading problems in children with dyslexia. Finally, an LI may play an important causal role in poor comprehension. In other words, deficits in vocabulary and grammar could lead to significant problems in understanding connected text (Catts et al., 2006; Nation, Clarke, Marshall, & Durand, 2004).

RELEVANT FINDINGS

The results from a recent longitudinal investigation provide some useful data for evaluating the possible relationships shown in Figure 7.1. In this study, a large sample of children was followed from kindergarten through the 10th grade. The sample originally participated in an epidemiologic study of LIs in kindergarten children (Tomblin et al., 1997). The epidemiologic study examined the language and early literacy abilities of over 7000 kindergarten children selected in a representative manner from schools in Iowa and western Illinois. In the follow-up study, 604 of these children were ascertained, and their language, reading, and cognitive abilities were examined in second, fourth, eighth, and tenth grades. Because the focus of the follow-up study was children with LIs, the sample included a higher proportion of these children than would be found in a normative sample.

The results from this study provide relevant data for the examination of the relationships between a phonological deficit, an LI, and reading disabilities. One set of results is shown in Figure 7.2. This figure displays a scatter plot of kindergarten language ability and fourth-grade word reading achievement of all children in the study who had at least normal nonverbal cognitive abilities (N = 369).

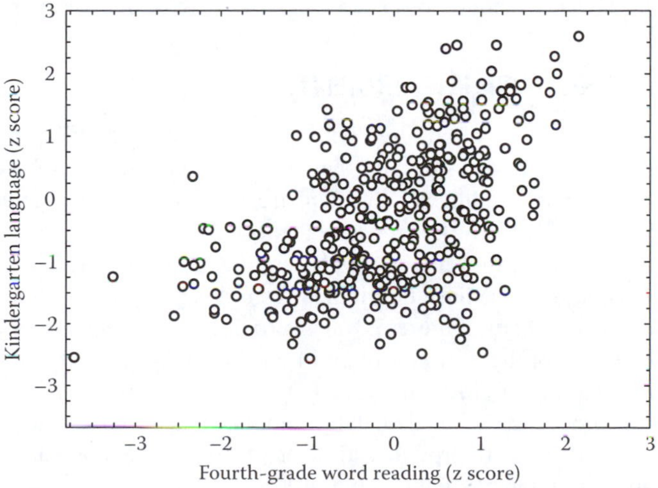

FIGURE 7.2 Scatter plot of kindergarten language ability and fourth-grade word reading achievement.

Also, because we are interested in how language abilities may impact reading and not the opposite relationship, we have chosen to plot kindergarten language ability. By focusing on kindergarten language ability, we limit the influence of word reading achievement on language ability. Children with reading disabilities read less often, and thus may not be able to take full advantage of the language learning opportunities that accompany reading experiences (Stanovich, 1986). This may, in turn, lead to the development of language problems during the school years (Share & Silva, 1987). Our estimate of kindergarten language ability was a composite measure based on the Test of Language Development 2: Primary (Newcomer & Hammill, 1988) and a narrative story task (Culatta, Page, & Ellis, 1983). Scores for each of the subtests of these measures were converted to z scores and combined to form an overall composite z score for language ability.

For ease of presentation, we limit our analysis of reading achievement to a single grade and plot fourth-grade word reading achievement. Similar results were obtained when we used word reading measures from other grades. Word reading was assessed by the Word Identification and Word Attack subtests of the Woodcock Reading Mastery Tests—Revised (Woodcock, 1987). Standard scores for each measure were converted to z scores and combined to form a composite z score for word reading.

The scatter plot shows a moderate relationship between kindergarten language ability and fourth-grade word reading achievement ($R = .50$). However, much of the strength of this relationship comes from data involving those with average or above average kindergarten language ability. Note that there is little relationship between kindergarten language ability and word reading achievement for those with poor language ability. If poor language is defined as performance that is at least 1 SD below the mean (<–1 z score), there appears to be as many children with poor language who are good word readers (>.25 z score or the 40th percentile) as there are those who are poor word readers (<–1 z score or the 16th percentile).

SPECIFIC LANGUAGE IMPAIRMENTS

In Figure 7.3, two groups of children with LIs are identified. Children with poor language ability (again, measured on the basis of kindergarten spoken language ability) and poor word reading achievement are referred to as having specific language impairment (SLI)+dyslexia, whereas those with poor language ability but normal word reading achievement are classified as SLI-only. SLI is appropriate in this context because we have eliminated from this analysis children who have broader cognitive deficits. Figure 7.3 also provides the weighted frequency of occurrence of each of these groups of children. The weighted frequency corrects for the over-sampling of children with LIs in the follow-up study. Also because our weighting procedure is based on data from the epidemiologic study (see Catts et al., 2005), it allows us to provide estimates of the expected prevalence of each of the groups within the population at large.

The estimated prevalence rates show that children with SLI are just as likely (if not slightly more so) to be normal word readers as they are to be poor word

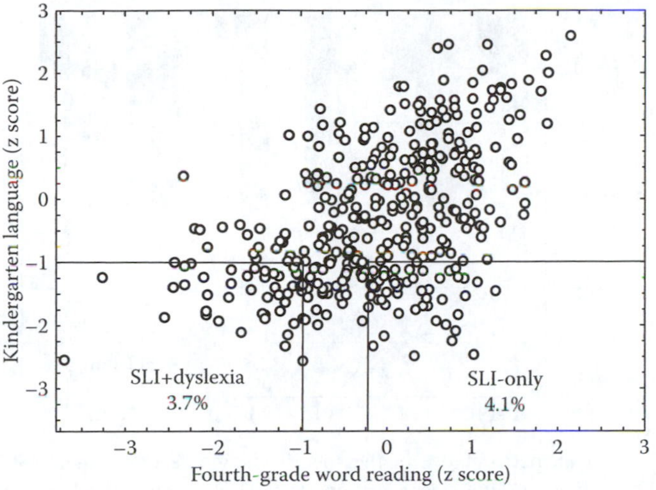

FIGURE 7.3 Scatter plot of kindergarten language ability and fourth-grade word reading achievement with specific language impairment (SLI)+dyslexia and SLI-only subgroups identified.

readers (i.e., dyslexia). Such a finding is problematic from the point of view that an LI is a cause of dyslexia. This is even more the case given that children with SLI-only did not differ significantly from those with SLI+dyslexia in the severity of their LI ($p > .05$, $d = .05$). Bishop, McDonald, Bird, and Hayiou-Thomas (2009) have reported similar findings in a recent comparison of SLI children with and without word reading deficits. Given that a large percentage of children with SLI in both studies developed normal word reading abilities despite their language deficits, it suggests that SLI is not by itself a likely causal factor in dyslexia.

Whereas we found that the SLI groups with and without dyslexia did not differ in language ability, they did differ in other important ways. Figure 7.4 displays the mean performances of each group on several kindergarten and second grade variables that have often been found to be related to reading achievement. Children with SLI-only performed significantly better than those with SLI+dyslexia on the letter identification subtest of the Woodcock Reading Mastery Tests—Revised (Woodcock, 1987; $p < .001$, $d = .92$). Such a finding is consistent with many other studies that have reported letter knowledge to be among the best early predictors of reading achievement (Scarborough, 1998; Schatschneider, Fletcher, Francis, Carlson, & Foorman, 2004). SLI groups also differed significantly on a measure of rapid naming of objects (Catts, 1993) administered in kindergarten ($p < .01$, $d = .67$) and second grade ($p < .01$, $d = .63$), with the SLI-only students permforming better. The latter result is in keeping with a recent finding by Bishop et al. (2009). They reported that the most apparent difference between SLI children with and without word reading deficits was the ability to name pictures and digits, rapidly.

We also administered a measure of phonological awareness in kindergarten and second grade. This measure, which was an adaptation of the one used by

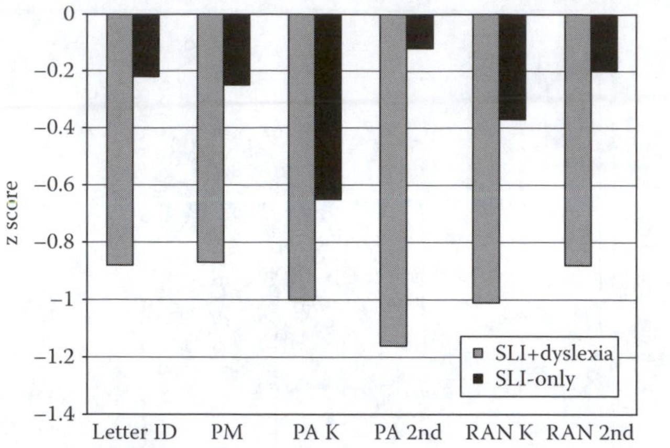

FIGURE 7.4 Mean performance of the specific language impairment (SLI)+dyslexia and SLI-only groups on letter identification (letter ID), phonological memory (PM) in kindergarten, and phonological awareness (PA), and rapid automatized naming (RAN) assessments in kindergarten and second grade.

Rosner and Simon (1979), involved syllable or phoneme deletion (Catts, 1993). As Figure 7.4 shows, children with SLI-only performed significantly better on this measure than those with SLI+dyslexia in both kindergarten ($p < .05$, $d = .50$) and second grade ($p < .001$, $d = 1.11$). Although groups differed significantly on this measure, it is important to note that the SLI-only subgroup actually showed a deficit on this measure in kindergarten.

In addition to the above measures, a nonword repetition task was administered in second grade. In this measure of phonological memory (Dollaghan & Campbell, 1998), children were required to repeat 16 spoken nonwords ranging from one to four syllables in length. The results indicated that phonological memory was closely related to word reading achievement in children with SLI. Specifically, children with SLI-only performed within the normal range in nonword repetition, and significantly better than children with SLI+dyslexia who performed poorly on this measure ($p < .01$, $d = .79$). These findings are consistent with the results of a twin study involving children with SLI (Bishop, 2001; Bishop, Adams, & Norbury, 2004). In that investigation, Bishop and her colleagues examined the genetic association between nonword repetition, overall language ability, and dyslexia in a sample of twins with a history of SLI. They found a significant genetic association (i.e., bivariate heritability) between nonword repetition and word reading deficits but no significant relationship between overall language ability (often used to index SLI) and reading deficits. It should be noted that the sample size for this study was relatively small, and thus the findings need replication. However, if the results hold, they provide further indication that it is deficits in phonological processing and not problems in other language abilities that are most closely related to the word reading deficits associated with dyslexia.

The results concerning nonword repetition in children with SLI also have implications for another relationship proposed in Figure 7.1. Recall, it was suggested that a phonological deficit may not only cause word reading problems but could be a primary causal factor for an LI. In fact, considerable attention has been paid in recent years to a link between a deficit in phonological processing and an LI (Bishop, North, & Donlan, 1996; Conti-Ramsden, Botting, & Faragher, 2001; Gathercole & Baddeley, 1990). For example, Gathercole and Baddeley (1990) have proposed that a specific deficit in the phonological loop component of working memory causes difficulties in semantic and syntactic development. Others have further argued that difficulty in nonword repetition may be a good phenotypic marker for SLI (Bishop et al., 1996; Conti-Ramsden et al., 2001).

Our result showing that children with SLI-only performed within the normal range in nonword repetition is problematic for the proposal of a close link between deficits in phonological memory and SLI. These results indicate that children with severe LIs and normal nonverbal cognitive abilities (i.e., SLI) can have essentially normal phonological memory. Bishop et al. (2009) also reported that children with SLI-only had phonological abilities in the normal range. A further finding from Bishop and colleagues (Adams & Bishop, 2002; Bishop, Adams, & Norbury, 2006) is even more troublesome for the view that a phonological deficit underlies SLI. This study compared twins with a history of SLI on measures of grammatical morphology and nonword repetition. They reported high heritability for both grammatical morphology and nonword repetition abilities; however, heritability of each of these skills was independent of the other. That is, the two abilities were not genetically related. This result is problematic because a deficit in grammatical morphology is considered by many to be the hallmark of SLI (Leonard, 1998; Rice, Tomblin, Hoffman, Richman, & Marquis, 2004). Given that grammatical morphology and nonword repetition are not genetically related, it is difficult to argue that a problem in phonological memory (as indexed by nonword repetition) is a primary factor in SLI.

Whereas our data did not support a relationship between an LI (i.e., SLI) and dyslexia, other data from our longitudinal study do show an association between these impairments and problems in reading comprehension. These data, reported by Catts, Fey, Tomblin, and Zhang (2002) and Catts, Bridges, Little, and Tomblin (2008) indicate that children with SLI are at a heightened risk for problems in reading comprehension. Also, examining this relationship from a different perspective, Catts et al. (2006) found that poor comprehenders (i.e., those with specific problems in reading comprehension) were characterized by a history of spoken language problems. In addition, approximately one-third of the poor comprehenders met the criteria for an LI in kindergarten (as seen in Nation et al., 2004).

DYSLEXIA

Another subgroup can be identified in the language by word reading scatter plot. As Figure 7.5 shows, these are children with deficits in fourth-grade word reading (z score < –1) but without deficits in kindergarten language ability (z score > –1).

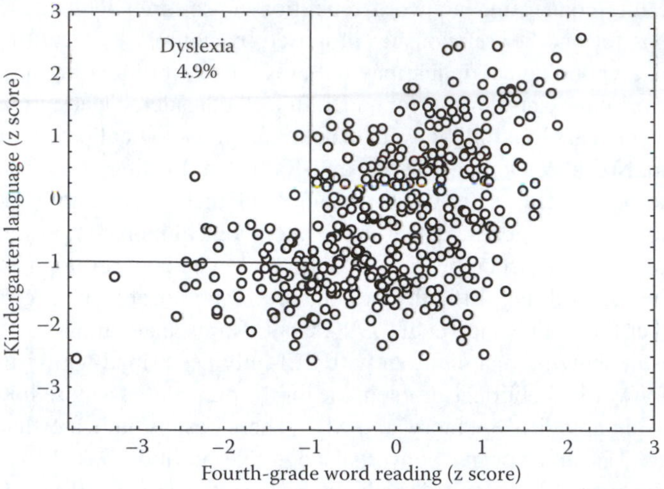

FIGURE 7.5 Scatter plot of kindergarten language ability and fourth-grade word reading achievement with the dyslexia subgroup identified.

This subgroup, referred to as children with dyslexia, had an estimated prevalence rate of 4.9% in our sample. According to the phonological deficit hypothesis, these children should have shown deficits on measures of phonological processing in kindergarten and second grade. This was generally the case. Children with dyslexia exhibited deficits in letter identification in kindergarten (z score = –.81) and phonological memory in second grade (z score = –.71). These deficits were comparable to those observed in children with SLI+dyslexia (z scores = –.88 and –.87, respectively). However, children with dyslexia had somewhat less severe deficits in phonological awareness in kindergarten (z score = –.66) and second grade (z score = –.88) than did children with SLI+dyslexia (z score = –1.00 and –1.16, respectively). These differences, however, were not significant ($p < .05$). Finally, children with dyslexia were found to have only mild deficits in rapid automatic naming in kindergarten (z score = –.42) and second grade (z score = –.36). The latter findings are somewhat surprising in the light of the large body of research indicating a strong relationship between rapid naming and word reading achievement. However, our rapid naming task employed colored objects. Studies have generally found that naming of colors or objects is less correlated with reading than naming of letters or numbers (Georgiou, Parrila, Kirby, & Stephenson, 2008; Wolf, Bally, & Morris, 1986). Nevertheless, individuals with dyslexia have been reported to have deficits in color/object naming (Denckla & Rudel, 1976; Vellutino, Scanlon, & Spearing, 1995). Perhaps, as we found in the present study, such deficits are more common among children with dyslexia and other LIs than those with dyslexia alone.

Whereas in the current analyses, children with dyslexia were categorized on the basis of poor word reading in the face of normal language abilities, few of these children had above average kindergarten language ability. Figure 7.5 shows that the majority of the children with dyslexia had what might be termed a mild LI (mean z score = –.51). The finding that children with dyslexia have mild spoken LIs is actually consistent with many other investigations (Gallagher et al., 2000; H. Lyytinen et al., 2004; Scarborough, 1990, 1991). Scarborough (1990), for example, found that children with a family history of dyslexia and a subsequent reading disability had mild deficits in semantics and syntax during the preschool years.

Shortly after introducing the phonological deficit hypothesis, Shankweiler and his colleagues also considered the possibility that children with dyslexia had deficits in other aspects of language. They acknowledged that some children with dyslexia showed difficulties in the comprehension and production of complex syntactic structures such as relative clauses. However, they proposed that these deficits actually resulted from poor phonological memory. In a series of studies, Shankweiler and his colleagues demonstrated that the syntactic abilities of children with dyslexia were no different from those of typical children when memory demands were reduced (Bar-Shalom, Crain, & Shankweiler, 1993; Mann, Shankweiler, & Smith, 1984; Shankweiler et al., 1995; Smith, Macaruso, Shankweiler, & Crain, 1989), thus supporting a phonological basis for some other language deficits.

Our results also suggest that at least a portion of the language problems that are found in children with dyslexia are the result of a deficit in phonological memory. Figure 7.6 shows the profile of performances of the children with dyslexia and SLI-only on the six language subtests administered in kindergarten.

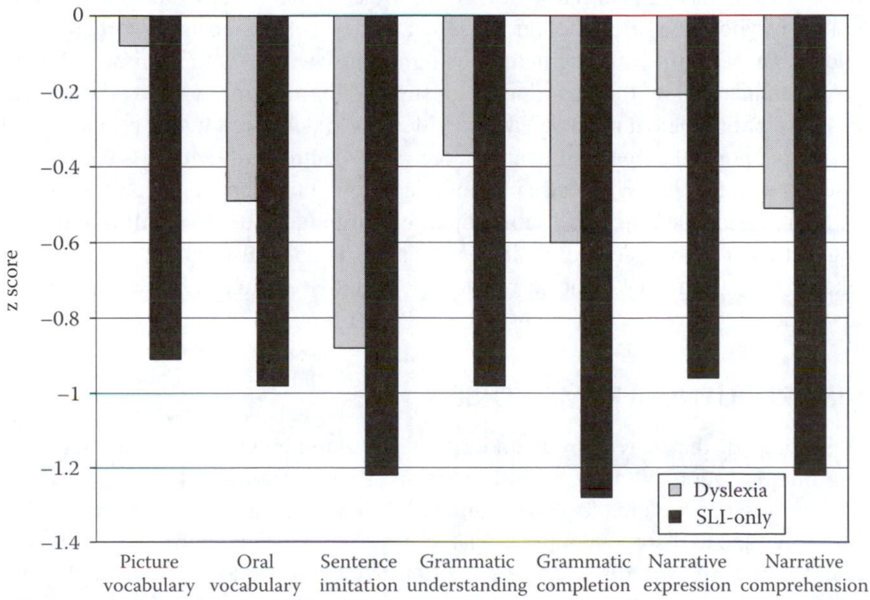

FIGURE 7.6 Mean performance of the dyslexia and specific language impairment (SLI)-only groups on language subtests in kindergarten.

Of course, differences between the groups are at least in part due to selection criteria. However, note that children with dyslexia show a very different profile of performances than those with SLI-only. The latter subgroup had a more even profile with somewhat comparable deficits across language tasks. Children in the dyslexic group, on the other hand, showed an uneven profile with near typical performance in some areas and mild to moderate deficits in others. Of particular relevance is that their lowest performance was on the sentence imitation task. Because this measure requires children to repeat sentences that increase in length and syntactic complexity, it is possible that a deficit in phonological memory may be partially responsible for the lowered performance.

Whereas some language problems in children with dyslexia can be explained on the basis of a phonological deficit, other language problems may go beyond phonology. Our results concerning children with SLI clearly show some independence between an LI and phonological deficits. That is, children with similar degrees of LI differed widely in phonological skills. Given this independence, it seems possible that we would find children with mild LIs (which do not meet requirements for SLI) who also have independent deficits in phonological processing and word reading ability (dyslexia).

EXPANDING THE MODEL

So far we have argued that a phonological deficit is the primary casual factor in dyslexia. A phonological deficit was observed in both children with dyslexia and those with SLI+dyslexia. However, if we look further in our data set, we find children who show a phonological deficit but who have normal word reading and language abilities. Specifically, using a conservative definition of a deficit, (performance below the mean of the dyslexia subgroup in phonological awareness and phonological memory), we can identify six children with a phonological deficit but normal language (mean z score = –.34) and word reading achievement (mean z score = .76). Whereas a phonological deficit may be the primary cause of dyslexia, the presence of this subgroup of children (admittedly small in number) suggests that a phonological deficit is not a sufficient cause. Other factors most likely impact whether or not a phonological deficit is manifested as a reading disability.

RISK-RESILIENCE FRAMEWORK

A framework that may help us understand the interaction of multiple factors in the manifestation of dyslexia is the risk-resilience framework (Rolf, Masten, Cicchetti, Nuechterlein, & Weintraub, 1990). This framework has been applied for some time to disorders of psychopathology, such as schizophrenia, depression, and bulimia. In such disorders, it has often been observed that individuals with very similar risk factors have very different outcomes. Some individuals seem to show resilience against even the strongest risk factors, whereas others do not. Researchers have sometimes explained these differences in resilience in terms of protective and vulnerability mechanisms (Rutter, 1990). Protective mechanisms are processes that reduce the impact of risk factors, whereas vulnerability mechanisms are those that intensify the impact. In most cases, protective and vulnerability mechanisms are the positive and negative poles of the same processes. Finally, according to this framework, protective/vulnerability mechanisms have their greatest impact in combination with risk factors. In other words, they serve as moderators of risk and have their impact primarily when risk factors are present. In the absence of risk, they have no impact or their impact is reduced considerably.

One protective/vulnerability mechanism that could moderate the effects of risk associated with a phonological deficit is instruction/intervention. That is, good instruction and/or well-tailored intervention might reduce the impact of a phonological deficit in at-risk children. Recent research provides both indirect and direct evidence of such moderation. For example, Connor and colleagues (Connor, Morrison, & Katch, 2004; Connor et al., 2009) found that teacher-managed, explicit code-focused instruction had a significant impact on first graders' reading skills. Furthermore, this impact was greater for poor readers than for good readers. More direct evidence of the moderation of a phonological deficit comes from the work of Foorman et al. (2003). In this study, researchers found that a prescriptive kindergarten curriculum that included phonological awareness instruction differentially raised the letter-naming and phonological awareness skills of the lowest performing students. Taken together, studies such as these indicate that instruction/intervention can impact risk associated with a phonological deficit.

Another possible protective mechanism that may interact with a phonological deficit is motivation or interest in reading. Less is currently known about how motivation or interest in reading could serve as a protective mechanism than is known in the case of instruction/intervention. There is a large body of research that documents a relationship between motivation/interest in reading and reading achievement (see Morgan & Fuchs, 2007, for a review). This work shows that good readers are more motivated to read and have more interest in reading than poor readers. This relationship, however, is bidirectional. Some studies document that early differences in reading achievement precede later differences in motivation/interest (Aunola, Leskinen, Onatsu-Arvilommi, & Nurmi, 2002; Chapman & Tunmer, 1997; Lepola, Salonen, & Vauras, 2000). On the other hand, investigations also show that early differences in motivation/interest can impact later reading achievement. For example, several studies have found that motivation/interest in reading during preschool or kindergarten is positively correlated with reading skills in first grade (Lepola et al., 2000; Salonen, Lepola, & Niemi, 1998). Whereas there is support for the causal role of motivation/interest in reading, studies have yet to show that this factor serves as a true protective/vulnerability mechanism that is operating differentially for at-risk versus not at-risk children. However, even if motivation/interest does not truly moderate the impact of a phonological deficit, it appears to be a factor that contributes to reading outcome, and therefore should be considered in causal models of reading disabilities.

SUMMARY

Considerable evidence has emerged in support of the phonological deficit hypothesis since it was first introduced by Shankweiler and his colleagues over 30 years ago. In this chapter, we considered how other language deficits are related to phonological deficits and dyslexia. Data from a longitudinal investigation suggested that LIs play little causal role in dyslexia. Some participants with an LI in kindergarten showed word reading difficulties (i.e., dyslexia) in fourth-grade, but many did not. These groups differed in phonological memory, phonological awareness, and rapid naming. Children with dyslexia but without a history of SLI also had deficits in phonological memory, phonological awareness, and to a lesser extent, rapid naming. We noted, however, that not all participants with a phonological deficit had dyslexia. A small group of children were found to have significant deficits in phonological processing but had normal word reading abilities. We argued that other factors may provide some at-risk children with the resilience to avoid reading disabilities.

REFERENCES

Aaron, P. G., Joshi, M., & Williams, K. A. (1999). Not all reading disabilities are alike. *Journal of Learning Disabilities*, *32*, 120–137.

Adams, C. V., & Bishop, D. V. M. (2002, July). *Genetic influences on verb morphology deficits in 6-year-old twins*. Poster presented at the joint conference of the International Association for the Study of Child Language and the Symposium for Research on Children with Language Disorders, Madison, WI.

Aunola, K., Leskinen, E., Onatsu-Arvilommi, T., & Nurmi, J. (2002). Three methods for studying developmental change: A case of reading skills and self-concept. *British Journal of Educational Psychology*, *72*, 343–364.

Bar-Shalom, E. G., Crain, S., & Shankweiler, D. (1993). A comparison of comprehension and production abilities of good and poor readers. *Applied Psycholinguistics*, *14*, 197–227.

Bishop, D. V. M. (2001). Genetic influences on language impairment and literacy problems in children: Same or different? *Journal of Child Psychology and Psychiatry*, *42*, 189–198.

Bishop, D. V. M., Adams, C. V., & Norbury, C. F. (2004). Using nonword repetition to distinguish genetic and environmental influences on early literacy development: A study of 6-year-old twins. *American Journal of Medical Genetics: Neuropsychiatric Genetics*, *129*, 94–96.

Bishop, D. V. M., Adams, C. V., & Norbury, C. F. (2006). Distinct genetic influences on grammar and phonological short-term memory deficits: Evidence from 6-year-old twins. *Genes, Brain and Behavior*, *5*(2), 158–169.

Bishop, D. V. M., McDonald, D., Bird, S., & Hayiou-Thomas, M. E. (2009). Children who read accurately despite language impairment: Who are they and how do they do it? *Child Development*, *80*, 593–605.

Bishop, D. V. M., North, T., & Donlan, C. (1996). Nonword repetition as a behavioral marker for inherited language impairment: Evidence from a twin study. *Journal of Child Psychology and Psychiatry*, *37*, 391–403.

Byrne, B., Delaland, C., Fielding-Barnsley, R., Quain, P., Samuelsson, S., Hoien, T., et al. (2002). Longitudinal twin study of early reading development in three countries: Preliminary results. *Annals of Dyslexia*, *52*, 49–74.

Calfee, R., Chapman, R., & Venezky, R. (1972). How a child needs to think to learn to read. In L. W. Greeg (Ed.), *Cognition in learning and memory*. New York: Wiley.

Catts, H. W. (1993). The relationship between speech–language impairments and reading disabilities. *Journal of Speech and Hearing Research*, *36*, 948–958.

Catts, H. W., Adlof, S. M., Hogan, T. P., & Weismer, S. E. (2005). Are specific language impairment and dyslexia distinct disorders? *Journal of Speech, Language and Hearing Research*, *48*(6), 1378–1396.

Catts, H. W., Adlof, S. M., & Weismer, S. E. (2006). Language deficits in poor comprehenders: A case for the simple view of reading. *Journal of Speech, Language, and Hearing Research*, *49*, 278–293.

Catts, H. W., Bridges, M. S., Little, T. D., & Tomblin, J. B. (2008). Reading achievement growth in children with language impairments. *Journal of Speech, Language, and Hearing Research*, *51*(6), 1569–1579.

Catts, H. W., Fey, M. E., Tomblin, J. B., & Zhang, X. (1999). Language basis of reading and reading disabilities. *Scientific Studies of Reading*, *3*, 331–361.

Catts, H. W., Fey, M. E., Tomblin, J. B., & Zhang, X. (2002). A longitudinal investigation of reading outcomes in children with language impairments. *Journal of Speech, Language, and Hearing Research*, *45*, 1142–1157.

Catts, H. W., Fey, M. E., Zhang, X., & Tomblin, J. B. (1999). Language basis of reading and reading disabilities: Evidence from a longitudinal investigation. *Scientific Studies of Reading*, *3*(4), 331.

Catts, H. W., Hogan, T. P., & Adlof, S. M. (2005). Developmental changes in reading and reading disabilities. In H. W. Catts, & A. G. Kamhi (Eds.), *Connections between language and reading disabilities* (pp. 50–71). Mahwah, NJ: Erlbaum.

Chapman, J. W., & Tunmer, W. E. (1997). A longitudinal study of beginning reading achievement and reading self-concept. *British Journal of Educational Psychology*, *67*, 279–291.

Connor, C., Morrison, F., & Katch, E. (2004). Beyond the reading wars: The effect of classroom instruction by child interactions on early reading. *Scientific Studies of Reading*, *8*, 305–336.

Connor, C. M., Piasta, S., Glasney, S., Schatschneider, C., Crowe, E., Underwood, P., et al. (2009). Individualizing student instruction precisely: Effects of child X instruction interactions on first grader's literacy development. *Child Development*, *80*, 77–100.

Conti-Ramsden, G., Botting, N., & Faragher, B. (2001). Psycholinguistic markers for specific language impairment (SLI). *Journal of Child Psychology and Psychiatry and Allied Disciplines*, *42*, 741–748.

Culatta, B., Page, J., & Ellis, J. (1983). Story retelling as a communicative performance screening tool. *Language, Speech, and Hearing Services in Schools*, *14*, 66–74.

Denckla, M. B., & Rudel, R. G. (1976). Rapid automatized naming (RAN): Dyslexia differentiated from other learning disabilities. *Neuropsychologia*, *14*, 471–479.

Dollaghan, C. A., & Campbell, T. F. (1998). Nonword repetition and child language impairment. *Journal of Speech, Language, and Hearing Research*, *41*, 1136–1146.

Fletcher, J. M., Shaywitz, S. E., Shankweiler, D. P., Katz, L., Liberman, I. Y., Stuebing, K. K., et al., (1994). Cognitive profiles of reading disability: Comparisons of discrepancy and low achievement definitions. *Journal of Educational Psychology*, *86*, 6–23.

Foorman, B., Chen, D., Carlson, C., Moats, L., Francis, D., & Fletcher, D. (2003). The necessity of the alphabetic principle to phonemic awareness instruction. *Reading and Writing*, *16*, 289–324.

Gallagher, A., Frith, U., & Snowling, M. J. (2000). Precursors of literacy delay among children at genetic risk of dyslexia. *Journal of Child Psychology and Psychiatry and Allied Disciplines*, *41*, 202–213.

Gathercole, S. E., & Baddeley, A. D. (1990). Phonological memory deficits in language disordered children: Is there a causal connection? *Journal of Memory and Language*, *29*, 336–360.

Georgiou, G. K., Parrila, R., Kirby, J. R., & Stephenson, K. (2008). Rapid naming components and their relationship with phonological awareness, orthographic knowledge, speed of processing, and different reading outcomes. *Scientific Studies of Reading*, *12*, 325–350.

Ho, C. S-H., Law, T. P-S., & Ng, P. M. (2000). The phonological deficit hypothesis in Chinese developmental dyslexia. *Reading and Writing: An Interdisciplinary Journal*, *13*, 57–79.

Kamhi, A. G., & Catts, H. W. (1986). Toward an understanding of developmental language and reading disorders. *Journal of Speech and Hearing Disorders*, *51*, 337–347.

Leonard, L. B. (1998). *Children with specific language impairment*. Cambridge, MA: MIT Press.

Lepola, J., Salonen, P., & Vauras, M. (2000). The development of motivational orientations as a function of divergent reading careers from pre-school to the second grade. *Learning and Instruction*, *10*, 153–177.

Liberman, I. Y., & Shankweiler, D. (1979). Speech, the alphabet, and teaching to read. In L. Resnick, & P. Weaver (Eds.), *Theory and practice in early reading* (pp. 109–134). Hillsdale, NJ: Lawrence Erlbaum.

Lyon, G. R., Shaywitz, S. E., & Shaywitz, B. A. (2003). A definition of dyslexia. *Annals of Dyslexia*, *53*, 1–14.

Lyytinen, H., Ahonen, T., Eklund, K., Guttorm, T., Kulju, P., Laakso, Marja-Leena, et al. (2004). Early development of children at familial risk for dyslexia: Follow-up from birth to school age. *Dyslexia*, *10*(3), 146–178.

Lyytinen, P., Poikkeus, Anna-Maija, Laakso, M. L., Eklund, K., & Lyytinen, H. (2001). Language development and symbolic play in children with and without familial risk for dyslexia. *Journal of Speech, Language, and Hearing Research*, *44*, 873–885.

Mann, V. A., Shankweiler, D., & Smith, S. T. (1984). The association between comprehension of spoken sentences and early reading ability: The role of phonetic representation. *Journal of Child Language*, *II*, 627–643.

Morgan, P., & Fuchs, D. (2007). Is there a bidirectional relationship between children's reading skills and reading motivation? *Exceptional Children*, *73*, 165–183.

Nation, K., Clarke, P., Marshall, C. M., & Durand, M. (2004). Hidden language impairments in children: Parallels between poor reading comprehension and specific language impairments? *Journal of Speech, Language, and Hearing Research*, *47*, 199–211.

Newcomer, P., & Hammill, D. (1988). *Test of language development—Primary* (2nd ed.). Austin, TX: Pro-Ed.

Rice, M. L., Tomblin, J. B., Hoffman, L., Richman, W. A., & Marquis, J. (2004). Grammatical tense deficits in children with SLI and nonspecific language impairment: Relationships with nonverbal IQ over time. *Journal of Speech, Language, and Hearing Research*, *47*, 816–834.

Rolf, J., Masten, A., Cicchetti, D., Nuechterlein, K., Weintraub, S. (1990). *Risk and protective factors in development of psychopathology*. Cambridge: Cambridge University Press.

Rosner, J., & Simon, D. P. (1971). The auditory analysis test. *Journal of Learning Disabilities*, *4*(7), 384–392.

Rutter, M. (1990). Psychosocial resilience and protective mechanisms. In J. Rolf, A. Masten, D. Cicchetti, K. Nuechterlein, & S. Weintraub, (Eds.), *Risk and protective factors in development of psychopathology* (pp. 181–214). Cambridge: Cambridge University Press.

Salonen, P., Lepola, J., & Niemi, P. (1998). The development of first graders' reading skill as a function of pre-school motivational orientation and phonemic awareness. *European Journal of Psychology of Education*, *13*, 155–174.

Scarborough, H. S. (1990). Very early language deficits in dyslexic children. *Child Development*, *61*, 1728–1743.

Scarborough, H. S. (1991). Early syntactic development of dyslexic children. *Annals of Dyslexia*, *41*, 207–220.

Scarborough, H. S. (1998). Early identification of children at risk for reading disabilities: Phonological awareness and some other promising predictors. In B. K. Shapiro, P. J. Accardo, & A. J. Capute (Eds.), *Specific reading disability: A view of the spectrum* (pp. 75–119). Timonium, MD: York Press.

Schatschneider, C., Fletcher, J. M., Francis, D. J., Carlson, C. D., & Foorman, B. R. (2004). Kindergarten prediction of reading skills: A longitudinal comparative analysis. *Journal of Educational Psychology*, *96*, 265–282.

Shankweiler, D., Crain, S., Katz, L., Fowler, A. E., Liberman, A. M., Brady, S. A., et al. (1995). Cognitive profiles of reading-disabled children: Comparison of language skills in phonology, morphology, and syntax. *Psychological Science*, *6*(3), 149–156.

Shankweiler, D., Liberman, I. Y., Mark, L. S., Fowler, C. A., & Fischer, F. W. (1979). The speech code and learning to read. *Journal of Experimental Psychology: Human Learning and Memory*, *5*, 531–545.

Share, D. L., & Silva, P. A. (1987). Language deficits and specific reading retardation: Cause or effect? *International Journal of Language & Communication Disorders*, *22*(3), 219–226.

Simos, P. G., Brier, J. L., Fletcher, J. M., Bergman, E., & Papanicolauo, A. C. (2002). Cerebral mechanisms involved in word reading in dyslexic children: A magnetic source imaging approach. *Cerebral Cortex*, *10*, 809–816.

Smith, S. T., Macaruso, P., Shankweiler, D., & Crain, S. (1989). Syntactic comprehension in young poor readers. *Applied Psycholinguistics*, *10*, 429–454.

Snowling, M. J. (2008). Specific disorders and broader phenotypes: The case of dyslexia. *The Quarterly Journal of Experimental Psychology*, *61*(1), 142–156.

Stanovich, K. E. (1986). Matthew effects in reading: Some consequences of individual differences in the acquisition of literacy. *Reading Research Quarterly*, *86*, 360–406.

Stanovich, K. E., & Siegel, L. S. (1994). The phenotypic performance profile of reading-disabled children: A regression-based test of the phonological-core variable-difference model. *Journal of Educational Psychology*, *86*, 24–53.

Tallal, P., Allard, L., Miller, S., & Curtiss, S. (1997). Academic outcomes of language impaired children. In C. Hulme, & M.J. Snowling (Eds.), *Dyslexia: Biology, cognition, and intervention* (pp. 167–181). London: Whurr.

Tomblin, J. B., Records, N., Buckwalter, P., Zhang, X., Smith, E., & O'Brien, M. (1997). Prevalence of specific language impairment in kindergarten children. *Journal of Speech, Language, and Hearing Research*, *40*, 1245–1260.

Vellutino, F. R., Scanlon, D. M., Spearing, D. (1995). Semantic and phonological coding in poor and normal readers. *Journal of Experimental Child Psychology*, *59*, 76–123.

Wolf, M., Bally, H., & Morris, R. (1986). Automaticity, retrieval processes, and reading: A longitudinal study of average and impaired readers. *Child Development*, *57*, 988–1000.

Woodcock, R. (1987). *Woodcock reading mastery tests—Revised*. Circle Pines, MN: American Guidance Service.

8 Phonology Is Critical in Reading

But a Phonological Deficit Is Not the Only Source of Low Reading Skill

Charles Perfetti
University of Pittsburgh

In the course of 30 years or so, the idea that reading words requires phonology has ascended from a minority view to one with such a substantial majority that it now amounts to a conventional wisdom. This sweeping change of opinion can be celebrated as a triumph of reading science. It can also provide a moment for reflection to consider the perils that come with being a comfortable majority. In what follows, I examine both the celebratory and the cautionary aspects of the ascendancy of phonology.

THE ASCENDANCE OF PHONOLOGY*

Skilled Adult Reading

Consider skilled word reading: In the 1970s, skilled reading was seen mainly as a matter of visually recognizing a familiar letter string as a word, whose access was said to be "direct" (Baron, 1977; Coltheart, 1978). The alternative route, by which letter strings were first converted to phoneme strings, was for unfamiliar words, and therefore more for young children than adults. And consider this observation about skilled reading of English from Frank Smith (1979): "We (fluent readers of English) … recognize words in the same way that fluent Chinese readers recognize the words of their nonalphabetic written language…" (p. 103 of second edition, 1985). Interesting here, in addition to the claim that English is read without phonology, is the use of Chinese as a benchmark writing system

* Reading research has used the term "phonology" loosely. In expressions such as "phonological awareness" and "prelexical phonology," researchers usually refer only to the phoneme level and not to the broader set of speech elements (e.g., syllabic stress, phrasal contours, and sentence prosody) that comprise phonology. I will use "phonological processes" to refer to the full range of phonology that may engage during reading, including phonemic processes.

for strictly visually reading, that is, reading without involvement of phonology. It turns out that even Chinese reading involves phonology, making the claim of parallels between Chinese and English empirically true in a way quite different from the original meaning of the 1979 statement by Smith. Nevertheless, I think that it turns out that Smith was partly right even in the way he intended.

The view that phonology is for children and is a backup route for adults reading unfamiliar words yielded over time to corrective research. The ascendancy of phonology came about through research that discovered phonological effects in word reading across a variety of tasks (with significant task differences). Among many experiments showing such effects were three lines of research that, at about the same time, made a strong case for phonology, specifically the role of phonemes in word identification: (a) brief exposure identification with masking and priming (Perfetti & Bell, 1991; Perfetti, Bell, & Delaney, 1988), (b) semantic category decisions (Van Orden, 1987), and (c) primed lexical decisions (Lukatela, G., Lukatela, K., & Turvey, 1993). Each of these lines of research produced multiple demonstrations that phonology plays a role in identifying a single word, in deciding whether a word fits a semantic category, or even just in deciding whether a letter string is a word.

To illustrate just the research from our backward masking experiments, Perfetti et al. (1988) presented subjects with a word for a brief subthreshold duration (e.g., 30 ms) followed by a pseudo-word mask, also for a short duration (30 ms), with a final pattern mask to terminate all letter string processing. The logic of the task was to expose the partial products of identification attempts. At subthreshold presentation, identification would be interrupted prior to completion by a following letter string mask, which would in turn would be interrupted by the final pattern mask. But if the mask contained letter overlap with the target, it could reinstate the letter information that was being interrupted. Similarly, if the mask contained phonemes that overlapped with the target, it could reinstate the phoneme information that was being interrupted by the mask, providing phonemic information was available prior to the interruption. In the key condition, a word written in all capital letters (*BAKE*) was followed by a lowercase pseudo-word homophone (*baik*) that reinstated its phonemes. This pseudohomophone mask condition was compared with a graphemic mask condition that was identical in its graphemic overlap with the word (*biak*). Compared with a control mask that shared no letters with the target, both the homophonic mask and the graphemic mask produced higher accuracy in identifying the word. Thus, the conclusion was that prior to the completion of word identification, phonemes, as well as graphemes, were partially activated and thus, could benefit from reinstatement from the mask. In a paradigm that presented the mask in a prime position, prior to the target, Perfetti and Bell (1991) found that identification accuracy for briefly presented targets grew as a function of orthographic priming and phonemic priming. Orthographic effects grew between 25 and 35 ms of prime exposure and purely phonemic effects (beyond orthographic effects) grew between 35 and 45 ms. Thus, as advertised in the title of the paper, phonemic effects can be observed within the first 40 ms of word identification. Time courses are relative to paradigms, and other tasks and measures produce different estimates. For example, in a recent ERP study, Ashby, Sanders, and Kingston (2009) found clear evidence for phoneme-level phonology effects at about 100 ms (an N170), again a pre-lexical effect within the masked priming procedure used.

Each of these lines of research, semantic category decisions and lexical decisions, as well as brief exposure identification, produced persuasive results and also created their own paradigm issues, prompting experiments that sometimes produced results less compatible with the assumption that all word reading includes prelexical activation of phonemes. For example, in the semantic category paradigm, which famously demonstrated homophonic confusions in category judgments (e.g., Flower: ROWS? Van Orden, 1987), additional experiments suggested that homophonic confusions might not be completely general, but restricted according to exemplar frequency and category breadth (Jared & Seidenberg, 1991). In the case of lexical decisions, experiments with clearly subthreshold presentations tended not to find "prelexical" phonological priming (Forster & Davis, 1984; but see Ashby et al., 2009).

The overall pattern of contrary results had the effect of suggesting limitations on the generalizations within a given task, rather than undermining the conclusion of pervasive phoneme-level phonology. Thus, the consensus that grew out of the aggregate research effort was that reading alphabetic writing involves phonology in the early stages of word reading, even in English with its spelling–pronunciation inconsistencies.

Adding to this research were studies with languages other than English showing phonological effects especially for shallower orthographies that have more consistent mapping between graphemes and phonemes (see Frost, 2005). The evidence across orthographies, including English, was persuasive enough to support what Frost (1998) termed the *strong phonological hypothesis*: that all word reading requires the engagement of phonological representations.

Reading Disability

Next consider views on the causes of reading disability. The early work on dyslexia seemed to point to a visual basis for developmental reading disorders. The very phrase "congenital word blindness" (Morgan, 1896) promoted by Hinshelwood (1917) conveys the visual basis of reading disorders. And although Orton's theory of dyslexia (Orton, 1928) was mainly about hemispheric specialization (i.e., the failure to have left hemisphere dominance was the hypothesized cause of disability), it was Orton's descriptions of the symptoms of dyslexia that drew attention. The "stephosymbolia" or twisted signs symptoms were observed in the letter reversals that came to be associated with a sort of popular image of dyslexia that implied a visual disorder. It is interesting, by the way, to consider that neuroimaging research suggests that Orton may have been more nearly correct on the theory of hemispheric specialization than on the defining symptom of dyslexia. Turkeltaub, Gareau, Flowers, Zeffiro, and Eden (2003) report a marked difference in laterality between more- and less-skilled children across temporal and frontal brain regions associated with word reading. Other imaging research has shown that these differences can be reduced with phonologically based training (Shaywitz et al., 2004; Simos et al., 2007).

As is clear from these imaging studies, phonological factors have ascended to central causal roles in explanations of dyslexia. The beginning of this ascendancy may be traced to Frank Vellutino's influential review of relevant research that included a strong critique of the visual theories (Vellutino, 1981). The case for a specifically phonological basis of dyslexia gained evidence from many sources that showed multiple phonological dimensions, including the importance of awareness of phonology (syllabic and phonemic) in learning to read (Bradley & Bryant, 1985; Liberman, Shankweiler, Fischer, & Carter, 1974; Stanovich, Cunningham, & Cramer, 1984). Beyond phonemic awareness was evidence showing weak phonological processes in low-skilled readers (e.g., Brady & Shankweiler, 1991; Snowling, Stackhouse, & Rack, 1986). This evidence grew across studies of groups of less-skilled readers that varied from well-defined dyslexics to "garden variety" poor readers. This evidence was sufficiently strong, and the issue of whether "true dyslexics" were different from garden variety poor readers was sufficiently important that Stanovich (1988) could propose a comprehensive and psychometrically coherent model that attributes the bulk of reading problems to a core phonological deficit that is accompanied by variable adaptations. Shankweiler and colleagues made much the same point: "Phonological deficits consistently accompany reading problems whether they occur in relatively pure form or in the presence of coexisting problems" (Shankweiler, Crain, & Katz, 1994, p. 2)

This conclusion of a core phonological deficit, based on experimental work, is reinforced by case studies of dyslexia. In an analysis of 16 dyslexia case studies, Ramus (2003) concluded that, although some patients had visual, cerebellar, or auditory problems, all 16 patients showed phonological deficits. Thus, the conclusions from behavioral studies of low-skilled readers, behavioral and imaging studies of dyslexics, and clinical studies converge on a core deficit in phonological representations or phonological processes. This does not mean that there are no other sources of reading problems; for example, contemporary visual deficit hypotheses have adherents and experimental results (Livingstone, Rosen, Drislane, & Galaburda, 1991; Stein & Walsh, 1997). But the ground has shifted so that the question has become not whether phonological deficits are a cause of disability, but whether there are any causes of dyslexia beyond phonological deficits or whether phonological deficits are the deepest level explanation (cf. auditory deficits or neural timing deficits) (e.g., Merzenich et al., 1996).

WHY IS PHONOLOGY SO IMPORTANT TO READING?

Phonology matters for reading because reading builds on language. If this is so, one then might wonder why phonology should be privileged over other levels of language, especially syntax and morphology. After all, syntax, morphology, and phonology are all part of the productive machinery of language, enabling it to code an infinity of messages through the combination of finite linguistic units.

Phonology is implicated so strongly because it is the level of language that provides the surface interface to written words. Graphic units map onto phonological units that can be phonemes (alphabetic writing) or syllables (either simple phonological syllables, as in Japanese Kana, or syllabic morphemes, as in Chinese). In the case of alphabetic writing, whether the orthography is shallow or deep, the basic units of writing are graphemes (consisting of one or more letters) that correspond to phonemes. Without sensitivity to the phonemic structure of language, and without word representations that include phonemes, there is a logical problem in mapping graphemes to phonemes.

It is important to be clear that this account does not claim that phonology is important only for alphabetic reading. When the focus was on English or other alphabetic orthographies, "phonology" tended to refer to the phoneme level, allowing the assumption that the importance of phonology (i.e., phonemes) was specifically about alphabetic reading. However, the discovery that reading a Chinese character also engages phonology (Perfetti & Zhang, 1991, 1995) demonstrated that the role of phonological factors in reading is highly general, probably universal. By now, there is substantial evidence that reading Chinese characters involves the activation of phonological representations, the spoken syllables that characters represent. (Some of this evidence is reviewed in Perfetti, Liu, and Tan (2005).) Phonology is not uniquely important for reading alphabets, although phonemes are. For once, it is appropriate to use the broad term "phonological processes" rather than "phonemic processes." To cover the broad universal character of phonology in reading, it is indeed *phonological* processes rather than merely phonemic processes that come into view. In the case of Chinese, the activated phonological unit in word reading is a syllabic form that includes non-segmental tone information (Spinks, Liu, Perfetti, & Tan, 2000). Phonemic knowledge is specifically important for reading alphabetic orthographies, whereas phonological knowledge is important for all types of reading systems. In addition, recent evidence suggests that a neglected aspect of phonology, syllabic stress, also plays a role in word reading (Ashby & Clifton, 2005).

Morphology: As Important as Phonology?

However, written word forms also represent morphemes, so we should expect morphosyntax to matter. Furthermore, morphology conditions lexical phonology, so that spellings may represent inflectional and derivational morphology more directly or more consistently than they do phoneme strings. English vowel alternation patterns in noun–adjective derivations (e.g., *nation* and *national*) illustrate the preservation of morpheme identity through spelling rather than pronunciation. Spelling also marks identity in bound morphemes affixes (e.g., *objection, protection*). Of course, spelling identity does not necessarily imply morpheme identity either in stems or affixes, so *mansion* and *revision* share a spelling but not a morpheme; *revision* and *omission* share a spelling and a morpheme, but the phoneme sequences that express the morpheme are different *(-zhun* vs. *shun*). *Omission* and *pollution* share a morpheme and pronunciation, but not a spelling.

These disassociations among morphemic, orthographic, and phonological components are subtle enough that skilled readers hardly notice them. But there is now substantial evidence that the morphemic status of a letter string—whether it is a morpheme or just a part of a word—affects written word identification across alphabetic orthographies (Feldman, Pnini, & Frost, 1995; Schreuder & Baayen, 1997). The issue for morphemic-based word identification is now strong enough that there is a corresponding issue for reading skill: that one source of reading problems is a morphemic processing deficit (Tsesmeli & Seymour, 2006). To the extent this is true, the question is whether such a deficit is primary, that is, independent of other problems, particularly phonology (Shankweiler et al., 1995).

One problem with the morphological deficit idea is that at least some of the evidence shows a surprisingly contrary result, namely, that both disabled and younger readers are more likely to show word reading benefits from morphemic constituents than are older and more skilled readers. Burani, Marcolini, De Luca, and Zoccolotti (2008) found clear evidence for this pattern in a study of Italian children's word reading, and Carlisle and Stone (2005) reported that in English, only younger readers showed a reading speed benefit for morphemically complex words compared with monomorphemes. Such a pattern suggests that morpheme constituents are available for younger and less able readers, and may provide a reading procedure to compensate for less-developed lexical and grapheme–phoneme strategies, which should be indifferent to the morphemic structure (Elbro & Arnbak, 1996).

There is an apparent contradiction between the general assumption that knowledge of morphemic structure is associated with skill in reading and the observation that skilled readers might use this knowledge less than disabled and younger readers. The solution may be that what is relevant is the aggregate of knowledge sources for word reading. Morphemic knowledge is one source, but there are three others that cohere around word knowledge: spelling, pronunciation, and meaning. (Notice that morpheme knowledge is similarly decomposable into spelling, pronunciation, and meaning.) In aggregate, these knowledge sources constitute lexical quality, the knowledge a reader has about a word. Accordingly, readers with generally low-quality lexical representations can have varying specific knowledge components about a word. In the case of a morphemically complex word, knowledge of a constituent morpheme may exceed knowledge at the word-as-a-whole level. Thus, a reader with generally low lexical quality may sometimes rely on morpheme knowledge to make up for weaknesses in other aspects of lexical knowledge. This possibility is consistent with the model of dual path word identification of Schreuder and Baayen (1997). A skilled reader can access a morphemically complex word through its constituent morphemes and through its whole lexical input. Highly familiar words can be accessed along the lexical path, whereas less familiar words can be accessed through a recognized morpheme constituent. Applied to the skill issue, a highly skilled reader can use high-quality representations for many words (i.e., representations that include detailed orthographic, phonologic, and semantic attributes), whereas a less skilled reader may benefit from using morpheme knowledge in reading many words of lower lexical quality.

Morphemes, as the basic form meaning units in language, are critical in the analysis of word knowledge and are functional as units in word reading. But because attention to morphology has traveled on the wake of an ascendant phonology, its importance has been a bit obscured. The importance of morphemic units in reading can be more readily seen in a writing system that elevates these units to greater prominence.

MORPHOLOGY, PHONOLOGY, AND ORTHOGRAPHY: A CROSS-WRITING SYSTEMS PERSPECTIVE

Relative to alphabetic writing, the high-contrast case is Chinese, which provides graphic units (characters and radicals) that correspond not to phonemes but to morphemes and syllables. The fact that characters correspond to spoken syllables as well as morphemes is critical, because it provides the basis for phonological processing in Chinese reading. Indeed, the role of phonology in reading Chinese characters is pervasive, instantiating the universal principle that writing systems are erected on language and not on conceptual objects directly. Although the pictographic nature of historically early Chinese writing reflects a competing correspondence principle of graph-to-concept, ultimately the full system evolved toward the universal language constraint that writing systems map language units. The general logic of writing systems—that their basic graphic units can correspond to language at the level of phonemes, syllables, and morphemes—compels corresponding units for reading procedures.

This logic was the basis for earlier hypotheses about reading units and reading development (Frith, 1985; Gleitman & Rozin, 1973) and has been an important part of the Universal Phonological Principle, which captures the observation that phonological units are immediately activated according to the units provided by the writing system (Perfetti, 2003). This logic is also the basis for the "psycholinguistic grain-size theory" of Ziegler and Goswami (2005), which adds the idea that the consistency of the mapping across written and language units affects the levels used, at least when the system provides multiple units (e.g., phoneme, syllable, and word or morpheme). Chinese writing, however, does not provide multiple levels systematically, and except for segmental and tonal cues provided by phonetic radicals, maps its written units to syllabic morphemes. Thus, in Chinese, unlike in other systems, reading procedures do not choose between a pronunciation unit and a meaning unit, they do both at once.

Here is the value of this perspective on the issue of whether morphemes are relevant in reading: If we are talking about a universal science of reading, morphemes have to be important. The question is how languages, which vary in their richness and expression of morphology, and writing systems, which vary in how directly basic writing units yield morphemes, modulate the role of morpheme units in reading. This question is difficult because of the tremendous variety among languages and writing systems in morphemic structures and their expressions, and it is beyond the scope of this chapter. However, for the present purpose, the simple point is that languages other than English make clearer the centrality of morphemes in reading. By hypothesis (now with considerable evidence), this is true in English as well, but it is not always as easy to see.

The Lexical Constituency Model (Perfetti, Liu et al., 2005) expresses the dual outcomes of reading a Chinese character, namely, that the orthographic input units (radicals) yield both phonological syllables and meaning-bearing morphemes through connections from character units to syllabic and morphemic units. The importance of the model for the present purpose is its implementation of two basic principles of reading: (a) phonology in reading is universal and (b) the implementation of phonology is specific to writing system and language constraints. The procedures that produce phonology in reading Chinese characters are not identical to those that produce phonology in alphabetic reading. For example, some priming studies that vary the onset of primes and targets show that phonological primes facilitate word identification at the same time point at which orthographic priming, which occurs earlier, turns to inhibition (Perfetti, et al., 2005). Such a result suggests that reading a Chinese character produces phonology (i.e., activates the corresponding syllable) only when the orthographic character is accessed, not before. This threshold-style processing, which places phonology at the point of lexical access and not prior to it, contrasts with alphabetic reading, which proceeds with rapid cascaded activation based on smaller units (graphemes to phonemes), allowing phonology to precede and contribute to lexical access. At the Chinese character access point, both the morpheme and the syllable connections to the character are available and can be accessed in parallel, with other factors determining the relative timing of meaning and pronunciation information.

Reading Problems Traced to Orthography and Morphology

This model of Chinese reading places orthographic and morphemic information in prominent positions (while maintaining an important, automatic role for phonology). The orthographic representation is the critical starting point for word identification universally; it may turn out to be important in Chinese reading disability in a way that exceeds its role in alphabetic reading. To be clear on this point, there is no reason to think that orthographic processing is not just as important in alphabetic reading; indeed the establishment of high-quality orthographic representations is the gateway to efficient reading. It is just that the importance of orthographic representations for reading ability has been obscured in English because of the well-demonstrated limitations placed by phonological processes. The way to understand the big picture here is to see that weak phonological processes have their effect in part by inhibiting the formation of quality orthographic representations. In alphabetic writing, orthography depends on phonology and in alphabetic reading, acquiring orthographic representations depends to some extent on being able to decode, to provide the phoneme strings that correspond to a word's letters (Share, 1995). In Chinese, by contrast, orthography depends on orthography. That is, the orthographic form in Chinese depends on graphic conventions that have evolved over centuries with only ad hoc connections to a word's phonology.

Given this analysis, it should come as no surprise that reading disability in Chinese may have causes beyond a phonological deficit. Again to be clear, a phonological deficit in Chinese will lead to a reading disability. However, a phonological disability might be more selective in its manifestations, more specific to phonological aspects of reading, less disabling to reading for meaning under circumstances in which a reader can gain sufficient practice in reading. Because Chinese characters are learned as graphic forms with strict compositional principles and no principled phonological aspects, the burden on learning is visual-motor memory. It is true, but irrelevant for the present argument, that children learn pinyin, an alphabet, before learning characters. This provides a phonological underpinning to reading in general (children learn that reading is about connecting print to spoken language) and to character reading in particular (as the character for a syllable replaces the pinyin for that syllable). But it does not alter the basic visual-motor learning required (motor, because children learn to write characters along with learning to read them).

The theoretical perspective sketched above has empirical support. Ho, Law, and Ng (2000) concluded that reading-disabled children have deficits in phonological processing, but only those who also have writing deficits. The idea that, in Chinese, reading depends on writing received confirmation from Tan, Spinks, Eden, Perfetti, and Siok (2005) in a study of Hong Kong children. They found a zero correlation between a phonemic odd-man-out task and beginning reading scores; similarly, syllable deletion was not correlated with beginning reading. What was correlated with beginning reading scores was copying performance on pseudocharacters ($r = .49$). Picture drawing performance showed a more modest correlation ($r = .23$) with reading. This pattern seems to suggest the importance of a specific orthographic form component that is measured by pseudocharacter copying. It is not just a cultural tradition that children in China spend their homework hours writing characters; the demands of recognizing hundreds of characters place a premium on a quality representation that is enhanced by practice at producing the character. There is even evidence that the perception of a character by adults is sensitive to the stroke orders used in production (Flores d'Arcais, Saito, & Kawakami, 1995). The big picture here is that the relative importance of lexical components (phonology, orthography, morphology) is shaped by the writing system and the specific orthography that implements the system, which cause writing-specific adaptations in learning to read. It is not that phonology is not important in Chinese reading. Indeed, not only is there ample evidence for automatic access of phonological information in character reading (e.g., Perfetti et al., 2005), beginning reading correlates with phonological awareness. However, in at least some of this research (Ho & Bryant, 1997; McBride-Chang & Kail, 2002), the relevant level of phonological awareness does not appear to be the phoneme, but the syllable. Beyond phonological awareness, at whatever level, the added demands of Chinese orthographic units, which have limited decomposability compared with alphabetic writing, require more ability at forming character-at-a-time representations through practice at reading and writing.

Universality and the Neural Basis of Reading

The idea that there is a universal phonological basis for reading and for reading disability comports with the assumption that there is a universal set of neural networks that underpin reading. This idea gains support from comparative studies of European alphabetic reading (Paulesu et al., 2000) and is captured in Paulesu et al.'s (2001) title *Dyslexia: Cultural diversity and biological unity.* The conclusion reflected evidence that the consistency of grapheme–phoneme mapping was reflected in the relative use of lexical and sublexical pathways in reading, and a corresponding variation in the expression of reading disability across different orthographies.

The existence of universal neural circuits for reading makes sense to the extent that visual, orthographic, phonological, and semantic components of word identification are universal. Meta-analyses of word reading studies show an alphabetic reading network that includes posterior visual regions (occipital areas and left mid-fusiform gyrus) for orthographic processes, temporal/parietal (superior temporal sulcus) and anterior areas (inferior frontal gyrus and sulcus/insula) for phonological processes, and both posterior (posterior temporal/anterior fusiform) and anterior regions (anterior portion of inferior frontal gyrus) for meaning (Bolger, Perfetti, & Schneider, 2005; Fiez & Petersen, 1998; Jobard, Crivello, & Tzourio-Mazoyer, 2003; Mechelli, Gorno-Tempini, & Price, 2003; Price, 2000; Turkeltaub, Eden, Jones, & Zeffiro, 2002).

This network may indeed be universal in general terms. Visual processing in any writing system involves occipital areas and the left fusiform gyrus is involved in visual word recognition for characters as well as for alphabetic words (Bolger et al., 2005). However, there also appear to be some writing-system-related variation. Perfetti et al. (2007) review this question, pointing out that with a growing body of imaging research in Chinese (Tan et al., 2001, 2003), the differences between Chinese and alphabetic reading have become impossible to ignore (see Tan, Laird, Li, & Fox, 2005, for a review and meta-analysis). Imaging results show more bilateral activation for Chinese in occipital and fusiform regions and more activation in a frontal area, the left middle frontal gyrus (LMFG), compared with alphabetic reading. Siok, Perfetti, Jin, and Tan (2004) further report that Chinese children who were poor in reading showed underactivation of the LMFG, compared with children who were skilled readers, and structural evidence suggests reduced mass of the LMFG for Chinese dyslexics (Siok, Niu, Jin, Perfetti, & Tan, 2008).

Studies of Chinese reading also find less involvement of the temporal-parietal region and the inferior frontal gyrus, compared with studies of alphabetic reading, where both are assumed to support phonological processes. It is possible that the LMFG is serving phonological processing in Chinese, but it also is possible that it is serving some other function (e.g., memory for character form). Its function is not clear, but its persistent appearance in imaging studies points to

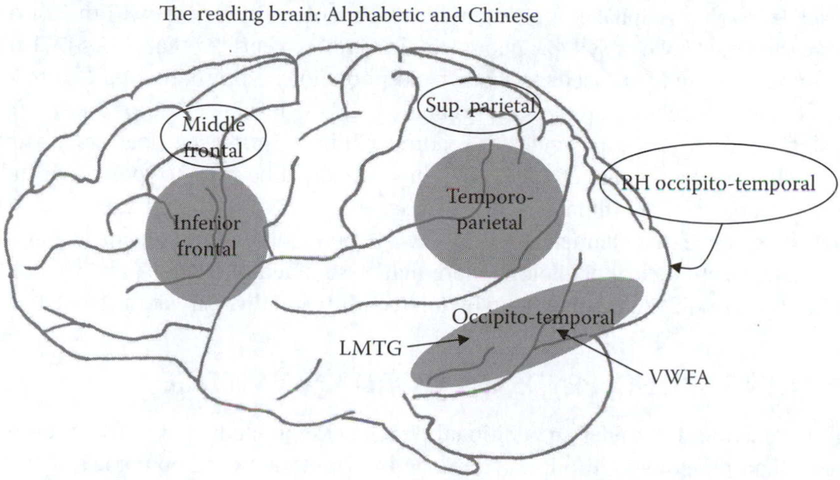

FIGURE 8.1 Schematic representation of left hemisphere reading networks highlighting areas identified for alphabetic reading (gray) and Chinese reading (based on Tan et al., 2005 and Bolger et al., 2005). Although there is evidence that part of this network is universal across writing systems, some differences between Chinese and alphabetic reading are highlighted. In particular, the frontal component for Chinese reading and Chinese dyslexia shows more involvement of the left middle frontal gyrus (labeled Middle frontal in the figure) and less for the inferior frontal gyrus. Chinese also shows less involvement of left temporal parietal areas and the left middle temporal gyrus (LMTG) and more for the superior parietal area (sup. parietal). Finally, the visual areas the visual word form area (VWFA) show more bilateral activation for Chinese (indicated by the label for the right hemisphere (RH) occipito-temporal region) as compared with the left hemisphere-dominant activation for an alphabetic system.

a routine and important role in character reading. (See Perfetti et al. (2007) for discussion of possible roles for the LMFG in reading.)

Thus, it appears that most imaging studies support a picture of Chinese reading that is illustrated in Figure 8.1, based on the Tan et al. (2005) meta-analysis. This shows that reading in Chinese recruits bilateral occipital-temporal areas and a frontal system that includes the LMFG, at least when phonology is involved. The frontal system for alphabetic reading, in contrast, makes greater use of the left inferior frontal cortex. There appears to be a universal reading network because orthographic, phonological, semantic, and morphosyntactic processes are part of word reading. (The last is little studied in single-word reading but becomes important in sentence reading.) An unexpected implication of some studies of bilingual reading is that the Chinese reading network may provide a general procedure for reading that can assimilate an alphabetic writing system, whereas the alphabetic network cannot be applied to Chinese (Perfetti et al., 2007).

To put these observations in the context of the main question about the role of phonological processes in reading, it is perfectly coherent and arguably true to conclude that phonology is universal in reading, whereas the implementation of phonology depends on the writing system. Theoretically, the incremental cascaded style of alphabetic phoneme-level phonology contrasts with the all-or-none threshold style of syllabic phonology in Chinese (Perfetti et al., 2005). These two complementary procedures both yield phonology as a routine part of reading. Further, a deficit in processing phonology at the level needed for the writing system leads to an impairment in reading Chinese, just as it does in reading English. The details matter, however. Thus, we should expect to see that visual-orthographic skill is important in Chinese, and it is. We should expect to see neural evidence that character reading involves phonology through cortical areas associated with lexical phonology more than assembled phonology, and we do. It should be possible to be impressed by universality and diversity at the same time.

READING SKILL DEPENDS ON WORD KNOWLEDGE

In this section, I consider an additional perspective on reading skill that requires more than phonology. It follows from one interpretation of phonological deficits (that such deficits are in the phonological system that serves spoken language) that reading disability implies a language disability. However, because reading requires using the phonological system in a new way with phonological units of limited accessibility being mapped to meaningless letters, reading may be the stressor that exposes a phonological deficit that can go undetected in spoken language. Either way, the phonological deficit hypothesis has a large scope: all difficulties in reading may be due to phonological deficits. The upward reach of the hypothesis was clearly expressed by Shankweiler (1989): "Difficulties at each level [the word, the sentence, the text] might stem from a deficit in phonological processing." This deficit was not about phonemic awareness, which came to be seen as just one symptom of a deeper phonological deficit, a point made very clearly by Liberman and Shankweiler (1991).

In the first part of this chapter, I reviewed some reasons to accept the centrality of phonology in explanations of reading disability, with other observable problems often secondary rather than primary causes. My point of departure is that, whereas the phonological deficit hypothesis is correct even with its large scope, it is not the end of the story. The scope of the phonological deficit hypothesis is parallel to the scope of the verbal efficiency hypothesis (Perfetti, 1985). The first traces problems in word knowledge and sentence and text comprehension to problems in phonological processes. The second traces problems in meaning and comprehension at the word, sentence, and text levels to word and subword processes that include phonology.

However, it is useful to qualify the upward implications of both theories. Neither verbal inefficiency nor phonological deficits are assumed to be the only cause of reading comprehension problems. One implication of any theory that postulates higher level consequences of lower level processing limitations is that identifying groups with comprehension problems in the absence of decoding or phonological problems requires stringent assessment of those lower level skills. This stringent assessment standard has not always been reached and much research that has claimed to identify higher level problems as causal has failed to do so because of this. However, there are now enough studies that have done more stringent assessments to allow the conclusion that there are both children and adults whose problems in reading are observable in the absence of phonological decoding problems. (See Nation (2005), for a review of such studies.)

Among the many other things that go wrong, knowledge of word meanings is a major candidate for a factor in reading skill beyond phonology. Beyond the obvious observation that it is difficult to understand a text that contains many words beyond the reach of the reader's vocabulary, the intertwining of word understanding and text understanding is a central part of reading. The general relation between vocabulary and comprehension is a strong one with reciprocal causation. (See Perfetti et al. (2005), for a review.)

Two large-scale studies with two different populations and writing systems suggest the power of word meaning knowledge relative to other factors. Protopapas, Sideridis, Simos, and Mouzaki (2007) studied a large sample ($n = 534$) of Greek children in Grades 2–4, taking measures of vocabulary, comprehension, fluency, and word and pseudo-word reading. The measures correlated in sensible ways over the age range. Especially interesting is that in a hierarchical regression analysis, the unique contribution of word reading to comprehension became negligible after vocabulary measures were entered, especially in the third and fourth grades. We can infer that the effects of word decoding on comprehension become lexically mediated, with word meanings more relevant than simple decoding. The authors' final structural model most consistent with the data showed vocabulary as a covariant of word reading accuracy and a direct cause of comprehension. Of course, Greek is a transparent orthography and this pattern of results and the model's causal pathways may reflect the relative ease of phonological decoding in a transparent orthography. But that is another way of expressing the argument made here: That when phonological decoding is mastered, problems in reading, both word reading and comprehension, become linked to low knowledge about word meanings.

Moreover, this important role for word knowledge is not restricted to transparent orthographies. Braze, Tabor, Shankweiler, and Mencl (2007) studied older readers (age 16–24) of English, using an array of assessments—phonological awareness, decoding, verbal working memory, listening comprehension, reading comprehension, word knowledge, and print experience. Whereas decoding was related to reading comprehension, an orally administered vocabulary test accounted for unique variance in reading comprehension even after listening comprehensions and decoding skill were accounted for. The differences between these two studies in reader ages and orthographies suggest that the role of word meanings in reading comprehension is quite robust beyond the beginning stages of reading.

None of this really surprises. We expect word meaning to be relevant, and no one has ever argued to the contrary. However, word meaning has not been afforded the same critical status as phonology and decoding, because one could argue that phonology and decoding were limiting factors in the acquisition of reading and, in turn, of word meanings. Therefore, one could assume that word meanings are secondary factors, whereas phonology and decoding (or maybe just phonology) are primary causes. However, although the logic of this view is correct as far as it goes, it leaves an incomplete picture. A reader who has acquired phonological decoding sufficient to decode an unfamiliar nonword can have a knowledge of word meanings (and word spellings) that is insufficient for many reading situations and thus costly to comprehension (e.g., Chall, Jacobs, & Baldwin, 1990). The consequences of low vocabulary knowledge can be a semantic deficit that affects not only comprehension, but, in English, the identification of words that are exceptional in their spelling–phoneme mappings (Nation & Snowling, 1998; Ricketts, Nation, & Bishop, 2007). Moreover, the use of word meanings may facilitate the acquisition of decoding skill. Sumutka, Brady, and Scarborough (2005) found that vocabulary knowledge supports the decoding of regularly spelled words when children first encounter them in print.

A general word knowledge perspective on reading skill is the lexical quality hypothesis (Perfetti, 2007; Perfetti & Hart, 2001), which claims that variation in the quality of individual word representations over phonological, orthographic, and semantic constituents has consequences for reading skill, including comprehension. Because phonology is a gateway to increasing lexical representations, it is reasonable to say that phonological representations and the phonological abilities that allow them are critical to word reading. However, it is equally clear that, with practice, orthographic representations of individual words are established and these become the gateways to highly skilled reading. If phonological decoding is the hallmark of basic word reading, the rapid use of orthographic patterns, including whole words, is the hallmark of fluent reading. The evidence that orthographic knowledge is related to reading skill has been around in one form or another for a long time (e.g., Katz, 1977; Mason & Katz, 1976) and supports the conclusion that orthographic knowledge makes a unique contribution to reading beyond phonological knowledge (Barker, Torgesen, & Wagner, 1992; Cunningham & Stanovich, 1990; Stanovich & West, 1989). However, the implications of this consistent result seem to have lost some visibility because of the attention given to phonological factors. Thus, even the unique role of orthographic knowledge is often termed "secondary" to the primary role of phonology (e.g., Share & Stanovich, 1995). Indeed, in the search for primary causes in complex causal chains, phonological processes deserve this primary status. However, to take seriously the results that show unique variance due to orthography, we must conclude that orthographic knowledge causes reading success. Of course, this is not a one-or-the-other issue. Orthographic and phonological knowledge both contribute to reading skill, and, as reviewed in the first section of this chapter, phonology continues to be part of word identification and a part of comprehension even in highly skilled reading. The acquisition of high-quality orthographic representations enables rapid lexical access with phonology.

Spelling is an indicator of the quality of orthographic representations, even though, of course, we can read words we cannot spell. Word reading skill depends on the refinement of word representations that add spelling knowledge to spoken word representations. Research on word reading skill has tended to ignore spelling. We are learning, however, that even among "good readers," differences in knowledge of word spellings leads to differences in word reading processes (Andrews, 2008).

CONCLUSION

Research leading to the ascendency of phonology as the critical component in learning to read and the major factor in dyslexia is one of the major achievements in reading science. The evidence that phonology continues to play a role in skilled adult reading and does so universally across writing systems is part of this achievement. The work of Shankweiler and his colleagues has been on the leading edge of this ascendency of phonology. The time has come to take a step back and appreciate the scope of this achievement, both as a scientific breakthrough and as a salubrious injection of scientific results into reading pedagogy and remediation. It is also a time to think about other parts of the reading puzzle. Phonology is universal in reading, but not uniformly implemented and certainly not reliant on universal units of language and writing. Ironically, the more universal procedures may have less to do with phonemes than with larger units of both speech and writing. What develops along with phonology is orthography, and in skilled reading, orthographic representations take on an increased role. Finally, word meanings and their associated morphological constituents are important in ways that go beyond phonology. Reading is above all dependent on word knowledge, including the spoken forms, written forms, meanings, and morphosyntactic structures of words. Although we have learned that acquiring this lexical knowledge depends significantly on a skilled phonological component, we have more to learn about the fuller story of word knowledge and skilled reading.

ACKNOWLEDGMENTS

The content of this chapter is shaped by research that has been supported at various times by grants to the author from programs of the National Science Foundation, the McDonnell Foundation, the Institute of Educational Sciences, and NICHD (Child Development & Behavior Branch).

REFERENCES

Andrews, S. (2008). Lexical expertise and reading skill. *Psychology of Learning and Motivation*, *49*, 249–281.

Ashby, J., & Clifton, C. E., Jr. (2005). The prosodic property of lexical stress affects eye movements during silent reading, *Cognition*, *96*, B89–B100.

Ashby, J., Sanders, L. D., & Kingston, J. (2009). Skilled readers begin processing subphonemic features by 80 ms during visual word recognition: Evidence from ERPs. *Biological Psychology*, *80*(1), 84–94.

Barker, T. A., Torgesen, J. K., & Wagner, R. K. (1992). The role of orthographic processing skills on five different reading tasks. *Reading Research Quarterly*, *27*(4), 334–345.

Baron, J. (1977). What we might know about orthographic rules. In S. Dornic (Ed.), *Attention and performance VI*. Hillsdale, NJ: Erlbaum.

Bolger, D. J., Perfetti, C. A., & Schneider, W. (2005). A cross-cultural effect on the brain revisited: Universal structures plus writing system variation. *Journal of Human Brain Mapping*, *25*(1), 83–91.

Bradley, L., & Bryant, P. E. (1985). *Rhyme and reason in reading and spelling*. Ann Arbor, MI: University of Michigan Press.

Brady, S., & Shankweiler, D. (Eds.). (1991). *Phonological processes in literacy. A tribute to Isabelle Liberman*. Hillsdale, NJ: Erlbaum.

Braze, D., Tabor, W., Shankweiler, D. P., & Mencl, W. E. (2007). Speaking up for vocabulary: Reading skill differences in young adults. *Journal of Learning Disabilities*, *40*(3), 226–243.

Burani, C., Marcolini, S., De Luca, M., & Zoccolotti, P. (2008). Morpheme-based reading aloud: Evidence from dyslexic and skilled Italian readers. *Cognition*, *108*(1), 243–262.

Carlisle, J. F., & Stone, C. A. (2005). Exploring the role of morphemes in word reading. *Reading Research Quarterly*, *40*, 428–449.

Chall, J. S., Jacobs, V. A., & Baldwin, L. E. (1990). *The reading crisis: Why poor children fall behind*. Cambridge, MA: Harvard University Press.

Coltheart, M. (1978). Lexical access in simple reading tasks. In G. Underwood (Ed.), *Strategies of information processing* (pp. 151–216). New York: Academic Press.

Cunningham, A. E., & Stanovich, K. E. (1990). Assessing print exposure and orthographic processing skill in children: A quick measure of reading experience. *Journal of Educational Psychology*, *82*(4), 733–740.

Elbro, C., & Arnbak, E. (1996). The role of morpheme recognition and morphological awareness in dyslexia. *Annals of Dyslexia*, *46*, 209–240.

Feldman, L. B., Pnini, T., & Frost, R. (1995). Decomposing words into their constituent morphemes. Evidence from English and Hebrew. *Journal of Experimental Psychology*, *21*, 947–960.

Fiez, J. A., & Petersen, S. E. (1998). Neuroimaging studies of word reading. *Proceedings of the National Academy of Sciences, USA*, *95*, 914–921.

Flores d'Arcais, G. B., Saito, H., & Kawakami, M. (1995). Phonological and semantic activation in reading kanji characters. *Journal of Experimental Psychology: Learning, Memory and Cognition*, *21*, 34–42.

Forster, K. I., & Davis, C. (1984). Repetition priming and frequency attenuation in lexical access. *Journal of Experimental Psychology: Learning, Memory, and Cognition*, *10*, 680–698.

Frith, U. (1985). Beneath the surface of developmental dyslexia. In K. E. Patterson, J. C. Marshall, & M. Coltheart (Eds.), *Surface dyslexia*. London: Erlbaum.

Frost, R. (1998). Towards a strong phonological theory of visual word recognition: True issues and false trails. *Psychological Bulletin*, *123*, 71–99.

Frost, R. (2005). Orthographic systems and skilled word recognition processes in reading. In M. J. Snowling & C. Hulme (Eds.), *The science of reading: A handbook* (pp. 269–271). Oxford: Blackwell Publishing.

Gleitman, L. R., & Rozin, P. (1973). Teaching reading by use of a syllabary. *Reading Research Quarterly*, *8*(4), 447–483.

Hinshelwood, J. (1917). *Congenital word-blindness*. London: H. K. Lewis.

Ho, C. S., & Bryant, P. (1997). Learning to read Chinese beyond the logographic phase. *Reading Research Quarterly*, *32*(3), 276–289.

Ho, C. S., Law, T. P., & Ng, P. M. (2000). The phonological deficit hypothesis in Chinese developmental dyslexia. *Reading and Writing*, *13*, 57–79.

Jared, D., & Seidenberg, M. S. (1991). Does word recognition proceed from spelling to sound to meaning? *Journal of Experimental Psychology: General*, *120*, 358–394.

Jobard, G., Crivello, F., Tzourio-Mazoyer, N. (2003). Evaluation of the dual route theory of reading: A meta-analysis of 35 neuroimaging studies. *Neuroimage*, *20*(2), 693–712.

Katz, L. (1977). Reading ability and single letter orthographic redundancy. *Journal of Educational Psychology*, *69*, 653–659.

Liberman, I. Y., & Shankweiler, D. (1991). Phonology and beginning reading: A tutorial. In L. Rieben & C. A. Perfetti (Eds.), *Learning to read: Basic research and its implications* (pp. 3–17). Hillsdale, NJ: Erlbaum.

Liberman, I. Y., Shankweiler, D., Fischer, F. W., & Carter, B. (1974). Explicit syllable and phoneme segmentation in the young child. *Journal of Experimental Child Psychology*, *18*, 201–212.

Livingstone, M. S., Rosen, G. D., Drislane, F. W., & Galaburda, A. M. (1991). Physiological and anatomical evidence for a magnocellular defect in developmental dyslexia. *Proceedings of the National Academy of Science USA*, *88*, 7943–7947.

Lukatela, G., Lukatela, K., & Turvey, M. T. (1993). Further evidence for phonological constraints on visual lexical access: TOWED primes FROG. *Perception & Psychophysics*, *53*, 461–466.

Mason, M., & Katz, L. (1976). Visual processing of nonlinguistic strings: Redundancy effects and reading ability. *Journal of Experimental Psychology: General*, *105*, 338–348.

McBride-Chang, C., & Kail, R. (2002). Cross-cultural similarities in the predictors of reading acquisition. *Child Development*, *73*, 1392–1407.

Mechelli, A., Gorno-Tempini, M. L., & Price, C. J. (2003). Neuroimaging studies of word and pseudoword reading: Consistencies, inconsistencies, and limitations. *Journal of Cognitive Neuroscience*, *15*(2), 260–271.

Merzenich, M. M., Jenkins, W. M., Johnston, P., Schreiner, C., Miller, S. L., & Tallal, P. (1996). Temporal processing deficits of language-learning impaired children ameliorated by training. *Science*, *271*, 77–81.

Morgan, W. P. (1896). A case of congenital word blindness. *The British Medical Journal*, 2, 1378.

Nation, K. (2005). Reading comprehension difficulties. In. M. J. Snowling & C. Hulme (Eds.), *The science of reading* (pp. 248–265). Oxford: Blackwell Publishing.

Nation, K., & Snowling, M. J. (1998). Semantic processing and the development of word recognition skills: Evidence from children with reading comprehension difficulties. *Journal of Memory and Language*, *39*, 85–101.

Orton, S. (1928). Specific reading disability—Strephosymbolia. *Journal of the American Medical Association*, *90*, 1095–1099.

Paulesu, E., Démonet, J-F., Fazio, F., McCrory, E., Chanoine, V., Brunswick, N., et al. (2001). Dyslexia: Cultural diversity and biological unity. *Science*, *291*, 2165–2167.

Paulesu, E., McCrory, E., Fazio, F., Menoncello, L., Brunswick, N., Cappa, S. F., et al. (2000). A cultural effect on brain function. *Nature Neuroscience*, *3*, 91–96.

Perfetti, C. A. (1985). Some reasons to save the grapheme and the phoneme [Commentary]. *Brain and Behavior Sciences*, *8*(4), 721–722.

Perfetti, C. A. (2003). The universal grammar of reading. *Scientific Studies of Reading*, *7*(1), 3–24.

Perfetti, C. A. (2007). Reading ability: Lexical quality to comprehension. *Scientific Studies of Reading*, *11*(4), 357–383.

Perfetti, C. A., & Bell, L. (1991). Phonemic activation during the first 40 ms of word identification: Evidence from backward masking and masked priming. *Journal of Memory and Language*, *30*, 473–485.

Perfetti, C. A., Bell, L., & Delaney, S. (1988). Automatic phonetic activation in silent word reading: Evidence from backward masking. *Journal of Memory and Language*, *27*, 59–70.

Perfetti, C. A., & Hart, L. (2001). The lexical bases of comprehension skill. In D. Gorfien (Ed.), *On the consequences of meaning selection* (pp. 67–86). Washington, DC: American Psychological Association.

Perfetti, C. A., Liu, Y., Fiez, J., Nelson, J., Bolger, D. J., & Tan, L.-H. (2007). Reading in two writing systems: Accommodation and assimilation in the brain's reading network. *Bilingualism: Language and Cognition*, *10*(2), 131–146. Special issue on "Neurocognitive approaches to bilingualism: Asian languages", P. Li (Ed.).

Perfetti, C. A., Liu, Y., & Tan, L. H. (2005). The lexical constituency model: Some implications of research on Chinese for general theories of reading. *Psychological Review*, *12*(11), 43–59.

Perfetti, C. A., & Zhang, S. (1991). Phonological processes in reading Chinese characters. *Journal of Experimental Psychology: Learning, Memory, and Cognition*, *17*, 633–643.

Perfetti, C. A., & Zhang, S. (1995). Very early phonological activation in Chinese reading. *Journal of Experimental Psychology: Learning, Memory, and Cognition*, *21*, 24–33.

Price, C. J. (2000). The anatomy of language: Contributions from functional neuroimaging. *Journal of Anatomy*, *197*, 335–359.

Protopapas, G. D., Sideridis, P. G., Simos, G., & Mouzaki, A. (2007). The development of lexical mediation in the relationship between text comprehension and word reading skills in Greek. *Scientific Studies of Reading*, *11*(3), 165–197.

Ramus, F. (2003). Developmental dyslexia: Specific phonological deficit or general sensorimotor dysfunction? *Current Opinion in Neurobiology*, *13*, 212–218.

Ricketts, J., Nation, K., & Bishop, D. (2007). Vocabulary is important for some but not all reading skills. *Scientific Studies of Reading*, *11*(3), 235–257.

Schreuder, R., & Baayen, R. (1997). How complex simplex words can be. *Journal of Memory and Language*, *37*, 118–139.

Shankweiler, D. (1989). How problems of comprehension are related to difficulties in decoding. In D. Shankweiler & I. Y. Liberman (Eds.), *Phonology and reading disability: Solving the reading puzzle* (pp. 35–68). Ann Arbor, MI: University of Michigan Press.

Shankweiler, D., Crain, S., & Katz, L. (April 1994). *Dissociation of children's language skills in reading disability: Deficits in phonological processing with sparing of syntax*. Unpublished paper based on presentation at the annual meeting of the AERA, New Orleans, April 5, 1994.

Shankweiler, D., Crain, S., Katz, L., Fowler, A. E., Liberman, A. M., Brady, S. A., et al. (1995). Cognitive profiles of reading-disabled children: Comparison of language skills in phonology, morphology, and syntax. *Psychological Science*, *6*(3), 149–156.

Share, D. L. (1995). Phonological recoding and self-teaching: Sine qua non of reading acquisition. *Cognition*, *55*, 151–218.

Share, D. L., & Stanovich, K. E. (1995). Cognitive processes in early reading development: Accommodating individual differences into a model of acquisition. *Issues in Education: Contributions from Educational Psychology*, *1*, 1–57.

Shaywitz, B., Shaywitz, S., Blachman, B., Pugh, K., Fulbright, R., Skudlarski, W., et al. (2004). Development of left occipito-temporal systems for skilled reading in children after a phonologically-based intervention. *Biological Psychiatry*, *55*(9), 926–933.

Simos, P. G., Fletcher, J. M., Sarkari, S., Billingsley, R. L., Denton, C., & Papanicolaou, A. C. (2007). Altering the brain circuits for reading through intervention: A magnetic source imaging study. *Neuropsychology*, *21*(4), 485–496.

Siok, W. T., Niu, Z., Jin, Z., Perfetti, C. A., & Tan, L. H. (2008). A structuralfunctional basis for dyslexia in the cortex of Chinese readers. *Proceedings of the National Academy of Sciences*, *105*(14), 5561–5566.

Siok, W. T., Perfetti, C. A., Jin, Z., & Tan, L. H. (2004). Biological abnormality of impaired reading constrained by culture: Evidence from Chinese. *Nature*, *431*, 71–76.

Smith, F. (1979). *Reading without nonsense*. New York: Teachers College Press.

Snowling, M. J., Stackhouse, J., & Rack, J. P. (1986). Phonological dyslexia and dysgraphia: A developmental analysis. *Cognitive Neuropsychology*, *3*, 309–339.

Spinks J. A., Liu, Y., Perfetti, C. A., & Tan, L. H. (2000). Reading Chinese characters for meaning: The role of phonological information. *Cognition*, *76*(1), B1–B11.

Stanovich, K. E. (1988). Explaining the differences between the dyslexic and the garden-variety poor reader: The phonological-core variable-difference model. *Journal of Learning Disabilities*, *21*(10), 590–604.

Stanovich, K. E., Cunningham, A. E., & Cramer, B. B. (1984). Assessing phonological awareness in kindergarten children. *Journal of Experimental Child Psychology*, *38*, 175–190.

Stanovich, K. E., & West, R. F. (1989). Exposure to print and orthographic processing. *Reading Research Quarterly*, *21*, 402–433.

Stein, J., & Walsh, V. (1997). To see but not to read; the magnocellular theory of dyslexia. *Trends Neuroscience*, *20*, 147–152.

Sumutka, B. M., Brady, S., & Scarborough, H. (June 2005). *The role of vocabulary knowledge in decoding new word meanings*. Presentation to the Society for the Scientific Study of Reading, Toronto.

Tan, L. H., Laird, A., Li, K., & Fox, P. T. (2005). Neuroanatomical correlates of phonological processing of Chinese characters and alphabetic words: A meta-analysis. *Human Brain Mapping*, *25*, 83–91.

Tan, L. H., Liu, H. L., Perfetti, C. A., Spinks, J. A., Fox, P. T., & Gao, J. H. (2001). The neural system underlying Chinese logograph reading. *NeuroImage*, *13*, 836–846.

Tan, L. H., Spinks, J. A., Eden, G., Perfetti, C. A., & Siok, W. T. (2005). Reading depends on writing, in Chinese. *Proceedings of the National Academy of Sciences*, *102*, 8781–8785.

Tan, L. H., Spinks, J. A., Feng, C. M., Siok, W. T., Perfetti, C. A., Xiong, J., et al. (2003). Neural systems of second language reading are shaped by native language. *Human Brain Mapping*, *18*, 158–166.

Tsesmeli, S. N., & Seymour, P. H. K. (2006). Derivational morphology and spelling in dyslexia. *Reading and Writing*, *19*, 587–625.

Turkeltaub, P. E., Eden, G. F., Jones, K. M., & Zeffiro, T. A. (2002). Meta-analysis of the functional neuroanatomy of single-word reading: Method and validation. *Neuroimage*, *16*(3 Pt 1), 765–780.

Turkeltaub, P. E., Gareau, L., Flowers, D. L., Zeffiro, T. A., & Eden, G. F. (2003). Development of neural mechanisms for reading. *Nature Neuroscience*, *6*(7), 767–773.

Van Orden, G. C. (1987). A ROWS is a ROSE: Spelling, sound, and reading. *Memory & Cognition*, *15*, 181–198.

Vellutino, F. R. (1981). *Dyslexia: Theory and research*. Cambridge, MA: MIT Press.

Ziegler, J., & Goswami, U. (2005). Reading acquisition, developmental dyslexia, and skilled reading across languages: A psycholinguistic grain size theory. *Psychological Bulletin*, *131*(1), 3–29.

Part IV

Unraveling the Biology of Reading and Reading Differences

9 Evaluating the Role of Phonological Factors in Early Literacy Development
Insights from Experimental and Behavior-Genetic Studies

Brian Byrne
University of New England

In this chapter, I offer an evaluation of the role that phonological factors play in reading acquisition and reading disability. The empirical bases for the exercise are both recent and not so recent, drawing on experimental studies by me and others that were completed some time ago, and from behavior-genetic studies of early literacy growth that are still ongoing. Together, the studies underpin four claims: (a) phonological factors play a role in explaining why, for all learners, learning to read and write is more challenging than learning to listen and talk; (b) factors based on morphology also may explain why learning to read challenges all children; (c) phonological factors, in the form of a phonological deficit, may be behind some children's continuing difficulty in learning to read, but they are not the only factors, and may be more minor than commonly accepted; and (d) factors based in learning processes also may explain special problems some children have in learning to read.

SPOKEN AND WRITTEN LANGUAGE

It is now well recognized that children learn to speak and understand with ease. They do so in the absence of formal or even informal instructions, despite the great complexity of the principles underlying language and the vast number of arbitrary associations (for vocabulary, most obviously) that need to be learned. Despite the existence of clinical conditions known collectively as *specific language impairment*, most children reach high levels of linguistic competence at an early age

(Crain, 1991; Crain & Thornton, 1998; Pinker, 1994). It is equally well recognized that, in contrast, learning to write and read is more labored, despite the fact that the principles and number of associations linking written to spoken forms are almost trivial compared to those operating in speech (i.e., for most alphabetic systems, a couple of dozen pairings between phonemes and the graphemes that stand in for them). With the possible exception of "hyperlexic" children, who seem to master decoding at a very early age and often without direct instruction (Nation, 1999), learning to read does not appear to happen spontaneously; it requires formal instruction, and it is not as broadly successful as learning to talk is (see I. Y. Liberman & A. M. Liberman, 1992, for an early account of some of these contrasts).

From certain standpoints, this contrast between learning to talk and learning to read is difficult to explain. If one accepts that spoken language and written language are cut from the same cloth, as it were, learning a visual code on a spoken form should not be more than one extra step once the spoken form is mastered. This is essentially the stance of "whole-language" theorists, who

> "believe that children learn to read and write *in the same way and for the same reason* that they learn to speak and listen. That way is to encounter language in use as a vehicle for communicating meaning.... Children are in no more need of being taught to read than they are of being taught to listen" (K. S. Goodman & Y. M. Goodman, 1979, pp. 138–140, italics added).

Or, if one accepts that children, like humans in general, are adept at detecting and learning patterns, learning the visual code should also present little in the way of challenge. This view underpinned an early influential approach to reading instruction (Bloomfield & Barnhart, 1961) that recommended presenting words arranged in families, like *hand*, *band*, and *sand*, in the expectation that the regularities between letters and sounds would be noticed and learned with the construction of a "sight vocabulary" of this kind.

From both of these perspectives, whole-language and the Bloomfield and Barnhart (1961) "linguistic" approach, difficulties that children might experience in learning to read could be attributed to defective methods of instruction and not to an inherent difference between spoken and written language. Whole language could, and did, criticize directing the child's attention away from meaning to sounds, or as one spokesman put it, "breaking whole (natural) language into bite-size, abstract little pieces" (Goodman, 1986, p. 7). Phonics, in other words, was a distraction. In Bloomfield and Barnhart's system, attention *should* be paid to printed words ("a linguistic system of teaching reading separates the problem of the study of word-form from the study of word-meaning," p. 9), but in available teaching materials "[t]hese forms are usually presented in a hit-or-miss fashion dependent upon the content of the various stories..." (p. 10).

The proposition that spoken and written forms of language are equally natural has been subject to searching examination and found wanting. For instance, I. Y. Liberman and A. M. Liberman (1992) catalogued certain facts that fly in the face of this claim: only a minority of languages exist in written form; written language emerged only in the last few thousand years, in contrast to speech, presumably as old as the species; all spoken languages employ a single principle for constructing utterances, combining a few dozen meaningless segments to form an infinite number of words and sentences, whereas writing selects from a range of different strategies (representing phonemes, syllables, moras, morphemes, etc.). So we will not pursue this equivalence claim further. But the idea that children are pattern detectors and that this can be put to good effect in learning to read if only the material is arranged appropriately cannot be so readily dismissed. In fact, at the time, in a letter to Clarence L. Barnhart, the great psychologist Thorndike applauded the Bloomfield and Barnhart program, endorsing the basic principle that connections between print and meaning would come as a by-product of the training without resorting to "old so-called phonic methods…" (Bloomfield & Barnhart, 1961, p. 12). And there exist many lines of evidence demonstrating pattern detection in the absence of direct instruction. An example with a long history is the body of research on artificial grammar learning in children and adults, where participants implicitly learn how surface forms, such as pseudo-words, map onto rule-based grammars (e.g., Byrne & Davidson, 1985; Moeser, 1977; Moeser & Olson, 1974; Reber, 1967). Pattern learning for novel visual forms in word identification also can be shown for adults (Brooks, 1977).

IMPLICIT INDUCTION OF ORTHOGRAPHY–PHONOLOGY MAPPINGS: TESTING THE LIMITS

Despite the evidence for implicit pattern detection and acquisition in humans, it is an open question as to whether the process operates freely and automatically in all domains. In fact, and of particular relevance in the current context, there is evidence that adults and children are *not* adept at learning the pattern relating graphic forms to phonological ones if the phonological structures are at a fine-grained level. Byrne (1984) and Byrne and Carroll (1989) created an artificial orthography that represented the subphonetic features of voicing and place, as in Figure 9.1A. In a series of experiments, adult participants overlearned the

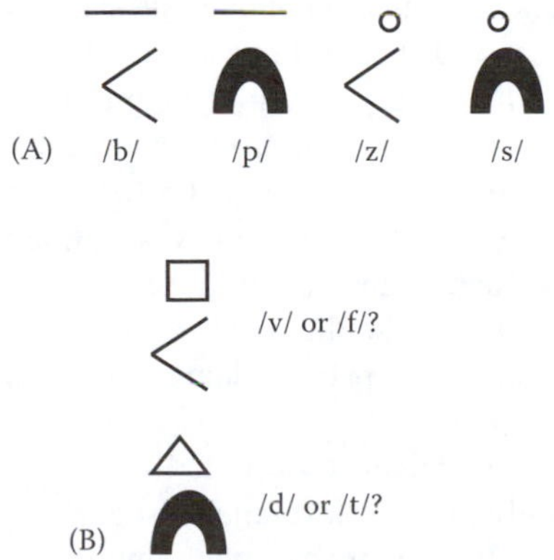

FIGURE 9.1 (A) Artificial orthography representing the subphonetic features of voicing and place. (B) Example of transfer items.

associations between the "letters" and their phonemes and were then tested for transfer to partially new forms, such as those in Figure 9.1B. Transfer could only be successful for those subjects who had detected, consciously or unconsciously, the mapping of the voicing distinction onto its distinctive graphic elements. Very few subjects were successful. Even lengthy exposure to the novel orthography, consisting of 3200 learning trials, generated no detectable understanding of the basic structure of the orthography despite subjects being able to "read" the symbols quickly and without error. Control experiments showed that failure was not due simply to the cognitive demands of substituting new graphic forms in place of old ones (letters) for phonological structures. Other experiments showed that explicit instruction in the relevant phonological structures, namely, the voicing contrast between pairs like /z/ and /s/, and /b/ and /p/, was sufficient for some subjects to fathom the mapping of the orthography onto the phonology as evidenced by successful transfer, whereas others required even more explicit instruction before they could transfer successfully in the test items. But the primary point is that induction of the orthography's relation to phonology was not an automatic consequence of systematic exposure to the pairings and successful acquisition of them. It was as if the learning process was blind to the underlying structural relations (Byrne, 1992a).

Adults are one case, children quite possibly another. To check, I conducted a series of experiments following the training-to-transfer paradigm with children prior to formal reading instruction (Byrne, 1992b). Phonemes were the target level of phonology and normal letters were the graphic forms for most of the experiments. The basic setup was to teach preschoolers who lacked relevant letter knowledge to read their first words in pairs and test for transfer, as in Figure 9.2. To learn the word pairs, the children would have had to focus on the distinctive letters, F and B, and use them to discriminate the two words, *fat* and *bat*. It would thus be a small cognitive step, it would seem, to figure out that F and B also stood for the "sounds" that discriminated the words. The children did successfully learn to pronounce the printed words in about 10 min of training, but, as in the adult experiments using subphonemic features, failed at the transfer stage. Control studies showed that children of this tender age *could* succeed in transfer tasks with graphic representation of language if the linguistic unit was above the phoneme. For instance, learning symbols that represented components of compounds like *bus-stop* and *doorstop* was a secure basis for transfer to pairs like *busman* and *doorman*. The syllable, too, was a phonological unit over which pattern detection was possible. Thus, for children, it was the phoneme that proved to be the point in the phonological hierarchy at which pattern detection for graphic representation failed.

	fat	*bat*
fun	/fʌn/ or /bʌn/	
bin	/fɪn/ or /bɪn/	

FIGURE 9.2 Example of words to be learned and transfer items for experiments with preliterate children.

These experiments by no means tested the limits; more extensive training might have uncovered successful induction of the grapheme–phoneme mapping. But in fact in some experiments, the children *were* pushed harder; they were asked to learn two pairs, such as *fat* and *bat*, and *fin* and *bin* (Byrne, 1992b). Not all of the preschool children could learn quadruples like these, evidence that the learning was a serious challenge, but the children who did so were still unable to succeed at transfer. Of course, none of these experimental studies approached the recommended density of training in the Bloomfield and Barnhart (1961) method, but they do constitute a kind of proof of principle that for novice readers acquisition of letter–phoneme links is not an automatic by-product of acquiring systematic word-level links.

THE PHONETIC MODULE

The groundbreaking work of the speech scientists affiliated with the Haskins Laboratories furnished an answer to the question of why certain levels of phonology appeared off-limits to the processes of induction. The explanation lay in the nature of the speech code, in the proposition that speech was not properly conceived of as a string of sounds but as set of overlapping ("coarticulated") gestures grounded in motor production (A. M. Liberman, Cooper, Shankweiler, & Studdert-Kennedy, 1967; A. M. Liberman & Mattingly, 1985; Studdert-Kennedy, 1998). Further and importantly, conscious access to these gestural elements was not required for speech because humans possess a phonetic module that automatically and subconsciously parses the acoustic signal (A. M. Liberman & Mattingly). Consequently, a graphic code that has as its basic currency the speech elements to which linguists give the name *phoneme* (and more fine-grained elements, as the experiments with adults outlined above suggest) will present a challenge to the learner because s/he does not need to be aware, in advance, of these very elements—they are part of the cognitive subconscious (Rozin, 1976). (In contrast to the phoneme, the larger unit of the syllable has more "weight," and is more open to conscious consideration, as the early emergence of a sense of rhyme suggests [Gipstein, Brady, & Fowler, 2000].) The phonetic module is, on this view, part of our linguistic inheritance, the thing that makes speech a fast and reliable means of signaling in a system that is built on the meaningless particle, the phoneme (Byrne & Liberman, 1999; A. M. Liberman, 1999; Shankweiler, 1999). The whole explanatory package was neatly summed up in A. M. Liberman's (1989) apt phrase that *reading is hard just because listening is easy*. That insight was and remains, in my view, a core contribution of this group to our modern understanding of literacy development:

> Children faced with the task of learning to read in an alphabetic script cannot be assumed to understand that letters represent phonemes because awareness of the phoneme as a linguistic object is not part of their easily accessible mental calculus, and because its existence is obscured by the physical properties of the speech stream.

The evidence for the motor theory of speech perception is both substantial and complex, and beyond the scope of this chapter. The independent evidence for the child's lack of conscious access to the phonemic elements of speech is equally substantial but straightforward. A seminal article was published over three decades ago in the *Journal of Experimental Child Psychology* (I. Y. Liberman, Shankweiler, Fischer, & Carter, 1974) describing children's inability to segment words into their phonemic (but not syllabic) constituents, and since then there have been many independent verifications of the lack of "phonemic awareness" (PA) in the preliterate child and in some older individuals who carry persistent reading and spelling difficulties (see Snowling & Hulme, 2005, for recent surveys of this literature, and other issues to do with the science of literacy).

A ROLE FOR MORPHOLOGY IN EARLY ENCOUNTERS WITH PRINT

Despite the convincing results about a role for PA in early and later literacy development, it remained true that young children *could* learn to think about phonemes, as evidenced by word games like "I spy." In various experiments, we showed that even preschoolers could be taught to recognize that words can begin and end with the same phoneme, as in *boy* and *ball*, and *pot* and *hit* (Byrne & Fielding-Barnsley, 1989). Once this insight was in place, many children could recruit it as a basis for simple acts of decoding when combined with relevant letter knowledge (Byrne & Fielding-Barnsley, 1989, 1991, 1993). Why, then, was learning to read word groups like *fat bat fin bin* such a poor basis for discovering phoneme identity and the ways that letters represent phonemes? Was something else blinding the children to discovery of the alphabetic principle?

At the time, interesting observations were emerging about a possible role for meaning in young children's early negotiations with the world of print. For example, children wanted long words to belong to long things and short words to short things (Levin & Korat, 1993; Lundberg & Tornéus, 1978). Or, once a child decided that a letter like C stood for a word like *chicken* the plural *chickens* could be represented by CCC… (Ferreiro, 1986). Even judgments about phonology might revolve around meaning, as in the case of a preschooler who affirmed that *tiger* and *clown* began with the same sound because they were both in the circus, or the one whose only correct rhyme judgment was for *plane* and *train*, because both took you places (Byrne, 1998). Could an orientation to meaning be obscuring the phonological basis for alphabetic orthography? In a series of experiments, I demonstrated that this was a distinct possibility (Byrne, 1996).

Perhaps the one that is the most transparent example of the findings from these experiments is as follows: I taught preschoolers with no relevant letter knowledge to discriminate pairs of printed words like *small* and *smaller* and *fat* and *fatter*, and tested for transfer by presenting pairs like *cold* and *colder*, and *mean* and *meaner*, asking the child which said which. Transfer was successful on average. But with pairs like *corn* and *corner*, and *post* and *poster*, transfer failed. The difference, of course, is that in pairs such as *cold* and *colder*, the distinguishing element, *er*, represents both a morphological and a phonological structure, whereas in pairs such as *corn* and *corner*, it is just phonological. It appeared that morphology acted as an attractor for the young learners, blinding them to the fact that the letter group also stood in for a syllable. The same results emerged for the letter *s*, which in *cats* (vs. *cat*) is a morphological as well as a phonological site, but in *purs* ("purse" vs. *pur*, "purr") has only a phonemic role. Children could transfer to the *cat/cats* contrast successfully having learned to read pairs like *book/books*, but not to the *pur/purs* contrast.

Writing systems that systematically represent a particular level of speech, say the phoneme, also systematically represent higher levels, say the morpheme. So it is *correct* to characterize alphabetic writing as morphological as well as phonemic, and children whose first hypothesis is that print elements stand in for morphemes are not in error, they are just incomplete in their analysis. Recovering from this correct but incomplete hypothesis is akin to the classic problem in learnability as posed in language acquisition—what kinds of information will be needed if learners start with the wrong hypothesis (Pinker, 1979, 1990). Pinker argues that in language the problem is finessed by setting initial hypotheses of the grammar to undergenerate utterances, with the result that recovery can be driven by positive evidence. His stance is that negative evidence (e.g., correction of ungrammatical utterances) is not systematically available to the language learner, and hence the interplay of initial hypotheses about the grammar and adjustments to them to accommodate the facts of language must be arranged to use only positive evidence (evidence that something *can* be said in a particular way). Overgeneration requires correction, which is not available, Pinker argues.

Whatever the learning architecture is for printed as opposed to spoken language, there is evidence that young readers may not easily recover from the morphological (or more generally, meaning driven) hypothesis about the nature of print. Here is a revealing quotation from an adult reminiscing about his history as a failed reader, collected by Johnston (1985):

> I had learned symbols...1 and 2 and 3...so I wanted that for five-letter words... I had this idea I was going to know just by looking...But there is no way you could possibly take all the words in the dictionary and just learn them by sight... (p. 157).

So the story so far is that apprentice readers will not automatically discover the alphabetic principle merely by learning to read alphabetic writing, because its phonological basis is normally invisible, encased within the phonetic module. But its *morphological* basis may be highly visible, leading to a correct but incomplete analysis of the relation between speech and print. This analysis may continue to be accepted because it continues to be true, even though, in time, learning print sequences for all of the morphemes of the language becomes overwhelming.

THE SPECIAL CASE OF ENGLISH: A PERFECT STORM?

Note that the processes that I have been outlining would in principle apply to *any* alphabetic writing system—they all code phonemes, and they are all morphological as well as phonological. But I propose that English creates special problems. The apparently unruly nature of the orthography, the existence of many words that do not follow straightforward one-to-one mapping of letter onto phoneme, may undermine the resolve of teachers to teach reading as if it were an exercise in alphabetic decoding. And teachers may not have such a resolve in the first place. We know that some do not because they have been trained to avoid explicit instruction in the alphabetic principle (Goodman, 1986; Shankweiler & Fowler, 2004). This in turn has been in part based on the conviction that reading cannot be done this way anyway, precisely because of the existence of irregular words like *the, once, one, was, were, there*.... So we may have the beginnings of a perfect storm—children *ill* equipped to discover, all by themselves, the alphabetic nature of English writing, the same children *well* equipped, all by themselves, to discover its morphemic nature, and a teacher who advertently or inadvertently fosters the morphemic hypothesis and obscures the phonemic one, leading to children trapped in an initially successful strategy but one that will eventually leave them floundering (Byrne, Freebody, & Gates, 1992). The apprentice readers in Spain or Germany or Italy or Finland are better served by their teachers because they, in turn, are better served by their versions of the alphabet—teachers teach reading as a decoding exercise right from the start, because they easily *can* (Seymour, 2005).

INTERIM SUMMARY

Phonological factors play a substantial role in the early stages of literacy development. Children, by the time they start school, are perfectly good speakers of language. Part of their competence is ownership of a phonetic module that automatically attends to the very complex task of recovering the linguistic units that are smeared across the speech stream's acoustic signal and identifying, from them, the words and sentences that carry meaning. A writing system that requires breaking into the phonetic module to discover its basic mapping, at least at the level of the phoneme for the alphabet, is challenging to all children. But complicating the picture further is another tendency, based also on the fundamental nature of language as the way we convey meaning, and that is a drive to find a relatively direct mapping of meaning onto orthographic form. Initial success in that mission can trap learners into sticking with a learning strategy that ultimately proves overwhelming. The nature of English as a quasi-regular writing system, combined with teaching strategies that eschew direct attention to the phonemic basis of the orthography, may exacerbate this trajectory. In a nutshell, phonology is a something of a distractor when it comes to acquiring alphabetic literacy, and morphology is a tempting attractor.

THE PHONOLOGICAL DEFICIT HYPOTHESIS

There is a second way in which phonological factors may affect the course of reading acquisition, through selective impairment in aspects of phonology in some children. This impairment undermines the development of PA, and, in turn, undermines development of decoding, spelling, and the growth of fast and accurate word-specific recognition, thus leaving these children as struggling readers. This hypothesis will be familiar to readers of this chapter, and so it needs little in the way of elaboration.

There are several types of data that support the hypothesis. One is correlational—the established relationship between measures of phonological sensitivity and literacy skill. One subtype of correlational data is predictive, with measures taken prior to or on the cusp of reading instruction predicting subsequent reading development. Among the tasks that can be used with such young children are rhyme detection, alliteration, and various blending and elision exercises (what word does *m* and *at* make? say *tin* without saying *t*). Scarborough (1998) has summarized such studies and reported a median correlation of .42 between the PA tasks and later reading growth. The other subtype of correlational evidence is concurrent correlation between PA and literacy levels in older children and adults. Sometimes, such studies employ cross-lagged correlational methods and/or structural equation modeling to help unravel the causal direction of the relationships. A useful summary of earlier work is in Stanovich (1992), and of more recent research in Bowey (2005). The other, and most convincing, kind of evidence is experimental, where advances in reading are shown to be contingent on training in phonological awareness (some of the many examples: Bradley & Bryant, 1983; Byrne, Fielding-Barnsley, & Ashley, 2000; Elbro & Petersen, 2004; Hindson et al., 2005; Lundberg, Frost, & Petersen, 1988; see Bus & van IJzendoorn, 1999; Ehri et al., 2001, for meta-analyses). Since these studies show positive effects of phonological training on reading acquisition, it is reasonable to assume that children who are hampered in attaining insights into phonological structure will likewise be hampered in reading development.

There is thus a convergence of correlational and experimental evidence favoring the phonological deficit hypothesis of reading difficulties, a convergence first identified as critical by Bradley and Bryant (1983). Despite this, however, there remain some questions surrounding the interpretation of the data. Correlations are not sure signs of causal connections, as is universally acknowledged. Further, it is known that tasks based on the phonology of words can be affected by knowledge of the spelling patterns of words (Ehri, 2005; Morais & Kolinsky, 2005; Polich, McCarthy, Wang, & Donchin, 1983), so a concurrent correlation between literacy levels and phonological awareness in older children could be driven in part by the literacy levels themselves. Even in preschool children, there is evidence that embryonic knowledge of letters and words can precede, and possibly, underpin embryonic phonological awareness. Apart from this matter of bidirectionality between the two variables, there is the in-principle possibility of a common influence operating on both. We will explore this possibility in more detail for preschool children later.

Experimental studies seem immune from much in the way of criticism in establishing causal relations, but this immunity depends on what exactly is being claimed. If they are seen as offering unambiguous support for a casual role for phonological awareness in learning to read, they need to have been carefully constructed so that only phonological awareness is being trained. Castles and

Coltheart (2003) critiqued this body of research (e.g., work by Blachman, Ball, Black, & Tangel, 1994; Brady, Fowler, Stone, & Winbury, 1994; Lundberg et al., 1988) and concluded that this requirement has not always been met. Letters and other aspects of print might be included in the training, for example (but see Hulme, Snowling, Caravolas, & Carroll, 2005).

In view of a degree of uncertainty attending the phonological deficit hypothesis, other sources of evidence that converge on existing bodies of data and afford the prospect of helping settle the residual questions would be valuable. I suggest that data collected within a genetically sensitive paradigm can play such a role, so we will turn to studies of this sort.

TWIN STUDIES OF EARLY LITERACY DEVELOPMENT

Twins provide a "natural experiment" that is useful for tracing the roles of genes and aspects of the environment on variation in human characteristics. Identical (monozygotic) twins share all of their genes, whereas fraternal (dizygotic) share about half of their segregating genes (genes that make people different). If variation in a trait is largely determined by genetic differences, monozygotic twins within a pair will be very similar to each other and dizygotic twins about half as similar. If, in contrast, the environment that twins share (e.g., developing in the same prenatal environment, being brought up in the same house, sharing the family socioeconomic status, or going to the same school) is the major determinant of variation, within a pair the twins will be highly similar to each other, irrespective of zygosity. Finally, if neither genes nor shared environment play a major role in determining variation for the trait, members of a twin pair will be no more alike that two individuals selected at random. Quantitative methods based on these three limiting situations generate estimates of genetic, shared environmental, and unique environmental influence by partitioning the total variation into these three components (Plomin, DeFries, McClearn, & McGuffin, 2008).

Using these methods, several groups have been decomposing variance in reading and related skills in young children and adolescents into its genetic and environmental components (e.g., Byrne et al., 2005, 2006, 2007; Harlaar, Dale, & Plomin, 2007; Harlaar, Spinath, Dale, & Plomin, 2005; Keenan, Betjemann, Wadsworth, DeFries, & Olson, 2006; Petrill et al., 2007; Samuelsson et al., 2005, 2007, 2008; Willcutt et al., 2007). The broad picture is of substantial genetic influence on early literacy skills, along with weak to modest effects of shared environment and modest unique environment influence (which also includes measurement error). Data on preschool twins show that the precursor skill of phonological awareness is around 60% heritable (Byrne et al., 2002; Samuelsson et al., 2005, 2007). Equally heritable are rapid naming (colors and objects) and verbal memory. Early (preschool) print knowledge is more affected by the home and/or preschool environment, with estimates around 65% of variance explained and with the influence of genes limited to about 25%. Once in school, reading and spelling show substantial effects of genes, along with low to modest shared environment effects (Byrne et al.; Harlaar et al.).

These univariate estimates are interesting in their own right, but they do not inform the question we have been addressing, of the status of the phonological deficit hypothesis. It does not matter whether the major source of variance in phonological awareness is genetic or environmental, the resulting effects on reading could be the same. But multivariate analyses of the same data can contribute to this question. It can do so for several reasons. One is that multivariate analyses can point to the existence of any common factors that might underlie the relationship between two variables. We can ask, for example, whether the phenotypic relation known to exist between letter knowledge and phonological awareness is due to both sharing the same genes. Another reason is that longitudinal multivariate analyses help trace the etiological path across development. We can ask, for example, whether the genes that are known to influence preschool levels of phonological awareness also are involved in kindergarten levels of reading ability. If they turned out not to be linked with kindergarten reading achievement, the case that a genetically influenced deficit in PA can hamper reading development would be less convincing. We now turn to some of these analyses.

MULTIVARIATE BEHAVIOR-GENETIC ANALYSES

There are several ways to model mutivariate data in twin research. The one we report here is known as the Cholesky decomposition model (Neale, Boker, Xie, & Maes, 2002). It can be thought of as similar in principle to hierarchical regression, where the effects of an independent variable on a dependent variable are assessed after the effects of another correlated predictor are taken into account. In Figure 9.3, X and Y are measured variables, and A, C, and E are latent variables representing genetic, shared environment, and unique environment factors, respectively. Path a_{11} represents the genetic influence on X, and a_{21} represents the genetic influence on Y that is shared with X. Path a_{22} represents the genetic influence on Y that is independent of the genetic influence on X; similarly, for the C and E factors and paths. Any of the paths can be zero, and significance tests can be conducted on the values. So, this method permits an assessment of genetic, shared environment, and nonshared environment influences that are common to two or more measured variables, as well as those same influences that are specific to each measured variable. Multivariate approaches can also be couched in terms of genetic, shared environment, and nonshared environment correlations among measures, or the degree to which individual differences on different measures share the same genetic and environmental influences.

What, then, have we learned from the study of twins about variation in PA, its relation to other variables that are implicated in literacy development and its relation to literacy itself? First, and as stated earlier, when assessed prior to the start of school, the considerable variation in PA, assessed using tasks such as rhyme and phoneme identity recognition, blending, and elision, is substantially under the influence of genes, at around 60% of the variance (Byrne et al., 2006; Samuelsson et al., 2005). Second, multivariate analysis of the preschool data shows that some of the genes are shared with those affecting print knowledge (letter names, awareness of words vs. pictures, etc.) and some are specific to PA (Samuelsson et al.). This immediately

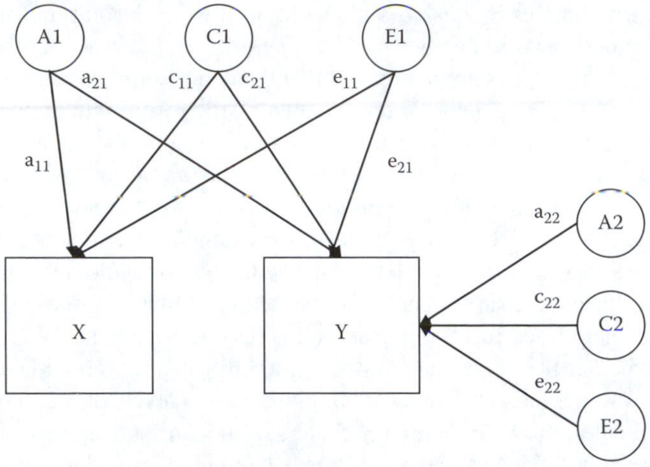

FIGURE 9.3 Cholesky decomposition model shown for one member of a twin pair for two measured variables. Measured variables are represented by rectangles and latent variables by circles. Paths a_{11}, c_{11}, and e_{11} represent additive genetic, shared environment, and unique environment factors that influence variable X. Paths a_{21}, c_{21}, and e_{21} represent additive genetic, shared environment, and unique environment factors that variable Y shares with variable X. Latent variables A2, C2, and E2 represent additive genetic, shared environment, and unique environment factors contributing to variance in variable Y after the contributions of A1, C1, and E1 have been taken into account.

tells us that part of the correlation between letter knowledge and PA is driven by common genes. As it turns out, those same common genes also affect other variables that we measured in preschool, namely, rapid naming and general verbal ability. This makes them candidates for what Plomin and Kovas (2005) refer to as "generalist genes," or genes of wide effect. Third, the PA-specific genes do *not* in turn contribute to variation in school-level word reading skill, at least in the first three school years. Only the genes that PA shares with print knowledge, the generalist genes, show up as influential in later word identification (Byrne et al., 2005, 2006). Figure 9.4 shows the Cholesky model for preschool and kindergarten, with just the A matrix included. Reading, as measured by the test of word recognition efficiency (TOWRE; Torgesen, Wagner, & Rashotte, 1999), was affected by the genes that print and PA shared in preschool—see the paths from factor A1. But the genetic source that was specific to PA, factor A2, did not load on kindergarten reading—the loading of .03 from factor A2 to kindergarten reading was insignificant, statistically and psychologically. (Although we do not show the Cholesky model for shared and unique environment components here, factors C2 and E2 do not load on PA, meaning that PA is not subject to environmental effects that are specific to it.) Fourth, however, the PA-specific genes *do* contribute in a modest way to reading comprehension in Grade 2 (but not to word-level skills). In recent analyses (Byrne, Coventry, Olson, Samuelsson, Corley, Willcutt et al., 2009), factor A2 of Figure 9.4, the one that loads specifically on PA, accounts for 5% of the variance in Grade 2 reading comprehension, but its loading on Grade 2 word reading and spelling is nonsignificant.

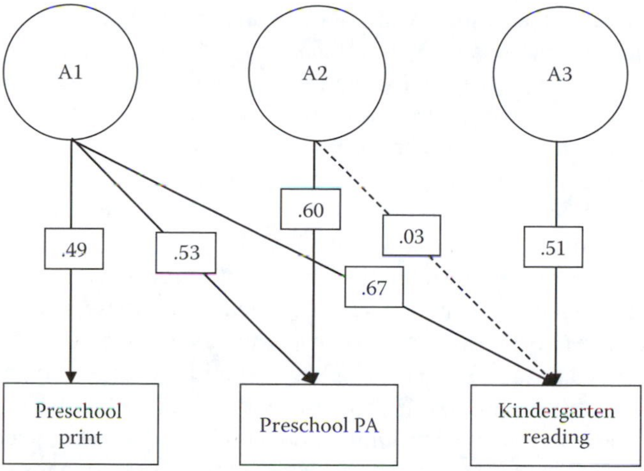

FIGURE 9.4 Cholesky model of additive genetic factor loadings for preschool print knowledge and PA, and kindergarten reading.

To summarize, PA at preschool is substantially heritable, with about 36% (=$.60^2$; see Figure 9.4) of its variance being attributable to genes that are specific to it, with the remainder of its genetic variance, 28% (=$.53^2$), shared with print knowledge. However, the PA-specific genetic source does not appear to be among the determinants of word reading in the early school years, though it does play a small role in reading comprehension by Grade 2. Only genes that PA shares with print knowledge affect word reading skills in those years. Thus, the predictive power of preschool PA for school-level word identification is largely due to its genetic correlation with letter knowledge and other aspects of print familiarity. This is not the pattern one would expect if deficiencies in PA had the *unique* power to undermine word recognition. The genetic correlation with comprehension *may* be the pattern one might expect from a variant hypothesis that the *tasks* used to assess PA share method variance with acts of reading comprehension, possibly due to similar demands on executive functions (Ramus & Gayaneh, 2008). This is speculation, of course, but *something* has to be modified in the broad-brush phonological deficit hypothesis to account for the surprising isolation of its specific genes from subsequent word-level reading (and spelling, for that matter). In the next section, I suggest how the behavior-genetic data might contribute to that modification.

A ROLE FOR A LEARNING PARAMETER

Recall that the "generalist" genes identified in our preschool analysis, the genetic factor that affects general verbal ability, print awareness, PA, and rapid naming, made the most substantial contribution to kindergarten word recognition (Byrne et al., 2006). Recall, too, that it has generally been found that letter and print knowledge is the single best preschool predictor of literacy development in the first few years (Foulin, 2005; Scarborough, 1998), better then verbal ability, PA, and rapid naming.

If letter knowledge, then, can be seen as the signature task for the phenotype that this genetic factor influences, we might justifiably consider its core processes as a way of characterizing the phenotype. I suggest that learning letter names is an example of long-term learning, particularly associative learning. Even by 4–5 years, the letter names that children do know are established in long-term memory. So the genes that affect how efficiently a child fixes memory traces for environmentally available information may be playing a role in early literacy development.

Other data support this view. Snowling, Gallagher, and Frith (2003) studied children at risk for severe reading disability and favored an account focusing on deficiencies in associative learning, characterized by slowness in learning verbal material such as nursery rhymes. Two intervention studies, one with a sample of unselected preschoolers (Byrne et al., 2000) and one with preschoolers at risk for reading disability because of a family history of such problems (Hindson et al., 2005), are relevant. In these, how *quickly* the children responded to the intervention and the final *outcome level* they achieved in postinstruction tests of PA (the ability being taught) were dissociable though correlated. It was the rate of learning rather than outcome level that best predicted future literacy growth, though level did add to variance explained.

The twin study I have been describing provides further, direct evidence supporting a role for the genetics of learning efficiency in literacy development (Byrne et al., 2008). In Grade 2, we challenged those children with an orthographic learning task, modeled on Share (1999), in which the children read novel words in short texts and subsequently were tested for spelling accuracy. An example is the word *laif* (which could be spelt, e.g., *lafe*). We also assessed decoding skill when the children read the stories containing the test items and we tested the spelling of real words using the WRAT-R Spelling subtest (Jastak & Wilkinson, 1984).

The multivariate model for the A matrix is presented in Figure 9.5. There is just one genetic factor that affects all variables (though the path of A3 to spelling, represented with a dashed line because the loading of .45 is not statistically significant, is likely to prove significant as the sample size increases in this ongoing study). Consistent with the model's single, reliable genetic source, the genetic correlation between orthographic learning and decoding was .97, between orthographic learning and spelling was .95, and between decoding and spelling was .85. We interpreted this pattern of results as follows:

> We favor a parsimonious account of this pattern which posits as basic a genetically determined learning rate factor, most directly tapped by orthographic learning in our study. According to our hypothesis, this factor has, historically, influenced both spelling knowledge and decoding skill in the children in our sample. Thus, spelling is one of the "crystallized" products of this factor. So, too, is decoding skill, reflecting prior responsiveness to learning opportunities, abundant in the school contexts in which children in the sample operate. In brief, this is a common genetic factor model with one of our variables, orthographic learning, as the most direct measure of that factor and the other variables, spelling achievement and decoding skill, as products of its prior operation (Byrne et al., 2008, p. 17).

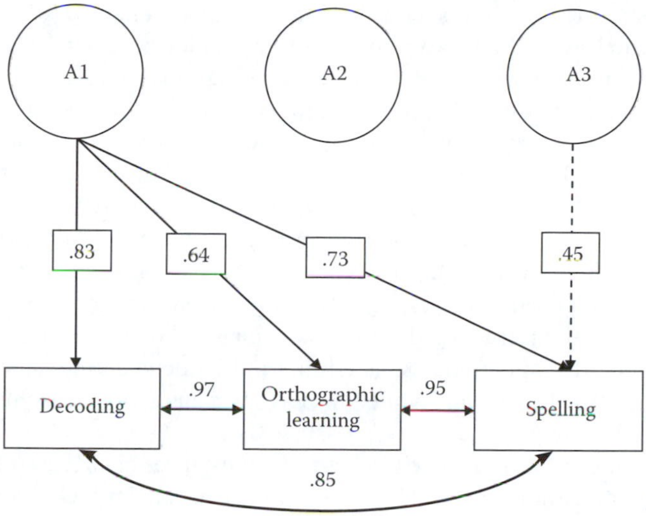

FIGURE 9.5 Cholesky model of additive genetic factor loadings for decoding, orthographic learning, and spelling. Latent variable A2 loads negligibly and nonsignificantly on orthographic learning and spelling and hence no path is represented. Values on double-headed arrows are the genetic correlations between the variables.

Assuming that this account has merit, there is a lot more to discover about the role of longer term learning in reading development. For example, if there is a genetically influenced learning efficiency factor, how broad is its scope? In Byrne et al. (2008), we showed that it was not coincidental with nonverbal IQ (Block Design, in our study), though there was a modest genetic correlation of .42 between nonverbal IQ and orthographic learning. But whether the learning parameter is constrained narrowly, say to mapping speech onto print, or applies to a wider range of domains is unknown, though work is continuing on this question with the twin data.

Whatever its scope, a genetic factor that affects the efficiency with which long-term associations are established could underlie many literacy-relevant variables: rate of letter name learning (Foulin, 2005); learning new spelling patterns (Reitsma, 1983); reaching word recognition levels that support highly automatized reading, including in languages with transparent orthographies (Ehri, 2005; Wimmer & Goswami, 1994); performance on PA tasks where orthographic knowledge plays a role (Ehri; Seidenberg & Tanenhaus, 1979); and vocabulary (Stromswold, 2001). PA is generally thought of as understanding a principle rather than as a set of learned associations, but on some accounts memorized instances lead to abstractions that foster further generalization (Hintzman, 1986), affording a possible role for genes that affect how readily the instances are learned.

I am not implying that an account that posits a role for the efficiency with which material is lodged in long-term memory in explaining reading ability can supplant other theories, such as the phonological deficit hypothesis as traditionally envisaged. If, for example, a child cannot conceive of words segmented into their phonemic constituents, learning to read an alphabetic script certainly is going to suffer. Or, perhaps more likely, if a child cannot efficiently integrate segmented and nonsegmented phonology for words, as proposed by Paulesu et al. (1996) in their "disconnection" model of dyslexia, learning to read, and actual reading performance when decoding is required, will likewise suffer. (Segmented phonology, according to Paulesu et al., is tapped by tasks like rhyming, which require access to sub-word phonological structures. Nonsegemented phonology is in play when whole words are the objects of attention, as in mentally retrieving the name of a pictured object, letter, etc.) There is, in addition, the voluminous research literature documenting deficiencies in reading-disabled children and adults in short term and working memory and in other executive processes.

Again, however, there is much to learn. For instance, biological processes in short- and long-term memory are not fully independent (Kandel, 2006), so it is conceivable that genetic variations that affect one also affect the other. Further, the concept of long-term working memory (Kintsch & Rawson, 2005) opens an avenue whereby deficiencies in long-term storage could undermine performance in what otherwise appears to be a short-term memory task. A goal for research is to gain a clearer picture of the genetics of all of these processes in their own right and of the ways they bear on literacy development.

SUMMARY

Phonological factors play an important role in literacy development. Scripts that map onto language at the level of the phoneme require that children acquire a grasp of segmental phonology at the appropriate level of awareness. This level is neither part of their inborn language capacity not does it appear to come for free with exposure to examples of alphabetic script, even when examples are arranged so as to make the mapping as transparent as possible. A helping hand in the form of instruction is needed. But that instruction has to overcome another obstacle, a focus on word meaning on the part of the child and a consequent attempt to forge links between print and language around meaning. Phonology, therefore, is part, but only part, of the story about a child's early understanding of the nature of alphabetic orthography. As a kind of postscript, I suggested that reading instruction for English, in particular, might be a place where the relative invisibility of phonological structure and the relative visibility of morphological structure might conspire to obscure the fundamental nature of alphabetic orthography, especially in the hands of a teacher whose training has discouraged attention to "bite-size, abstract little pieces."

When it comes to differences among young learners in how soon and how well they master the arts of reading and spelling, we see a substantial role for genetic variation. The question then turns to figuring out what the genes are for. We don't know the answer, but what does seem clear is that those that affect PA independently of other precursors of reading, such as letter knowledge, have a limited role, and not the one most expected, namely, underpinning the growth of decoding and efficient word identification. What also seems clear is that genes that affect the efficiency with which literacy-relevant material is committed to memory in a stable way have a role in influencing reading outcomes. That, too, will only be part of the story. Given that the story is incomplete, and given all of the independent evidence about phonological factors in literacy growth, they will, and ought to, continue to be an important focus in the broad research agenda to understand how all children learn to read and why some find it a more challenging assignment than others.

REFERENCES

Blachman, B. A., Ball, E. W., Black, R. S., & Tangel, D. M. (1994). Kindergarten teachers develop phoneme awareness in inner-city, low-income classrooms: Does it make a difference? *Reading and Writing: An Interdisciplinary Journal*, *6*, 1–18.

Bloomfield, L., & Barnhart, C. L. (1961). *Let's read: A linguistic approach*. Detroit, MI: Wayne State University Press.

Bowey, J. A. (2005). Predicting individual differences in learning to read. In M. Snowling & C. Hulme (Eds.), *The science of reading: A handbook* (pp. 155–172). Oxford: Blackwell.

Bradley, L., & Bryant, P. E. (1983). Categorizing sounds and learning to read—A causal connection. *Nature*, *301*, 419–421.

Brady, S., Fowler, A., Stone, B., & Winbury, N. (1994). Training phonological awareness: A study with inner-city kindergarten children. *Annals of Dyslexia*, *44*, 26–59.

Brooks, L. R. (1977). Visual pattern in fluent word identification. In A. S. Reber & D. L. Scarborough (Eds.), *Toward a psychology of reading*. Hillsdale, NJ: Lawrence Erlbaum Associates.

Bus, A. G., & van IJzendoorn, M. H. (1999). Phonological awareness and early reading: A meta-analysis of experimental training studies. *Journal of Educational Psychology*, *91*, 403–414.

Byrne, B. (1984). On teaching articulatory phonetics via an orthography. *Memory & Cognition*, *12*, 181–189.

Byrne, B. (1992a). Experimental psychology and real life: The case of literacy acquisition. In J. Alegria, D. Holander, J. Morais, & M. Radeau (Eds.), *Analytic approaches to human cognition* (pp. 169–182). Amsterdam: North Holland.

Byrne, B. (1992b). Studies in the acquisition procedure for reading: Rationale, hypotheses, and data. In P. B. Gough, L. C. Ehri, & R. Treiman (Eds.), *Reading acquisition* (pp. 1–34). Hillsdale, NJ: Lawrence Erlbaum Associates.

Byrne, B. (1996). The learnability of the alphabetic principle: Children's initial hypotheses about how print represents spoken language. *Applied Psycholinguistics*, *17*, 401–426.

Byrne, B. (1998). *The foundation of literacy: The child's acquisition of the alphabetic principle*. Hove: Psychology Press.

Byrne, B., & Carroll, M. V. (1989). Learning artificial orthographies: Further evidence of a nonanalytic acquisition procedure. *Memory & Cognition*, *17*, 311–317.

Byrne, B., Coventry, W. L., Olson, R. K., Hulslander, J., Wadsworth, S., DeFries, J. C., et al. (2008). A behavioral-genetic analysis of orthographic learning, spelling, and decoding. *Journal of Research in Reading*, *31*, 8–21.

Byrne, B., Coventry, W. L., Olson, R. K., Samuelsson, S., Corley, R., Willcutt, E. G., et al. (2009). Genetic and environmental influences on aspects of literacy and language in early childhood: Continuity and change from preschool to Grade 2. *Journal of Neurolinguistics*, *22*, 33–49.

Byrne, B., & Davidson, E. (1985). On putting the horse before the cart: Exploring conceptual bases of noun order via acquisition of a miniature artificial language. *Journal of Memory and Language*, *24*, 377–389.

Byrne, B., Delaland, C., Fielding-Barnsley, R., Quain, P., Samuelsson, S., Hoien, T., et al. (2002). Longitudinal twin study of early reading development in three countries: Preliminary results. *Annals of Dyslexia*, *52*, 49–73.

Byrne, B., & Fielding-Barnsley, R. (1989). Phonemic awareness and letter knowledge in the child's acquisition of the alphabetic principle. *Journal of Educational Psychology*, *81*, 313–321.

Byrne, B., & Fielding-Barnsley, R. (1991). Evaluation of a program to teach phonemic awareness to young children. *Journal of Educational Psychology*, *83*, 451–455.

Byrne, B., & Fielding-Barnsley, R. (1993). Evaluation of a program to teach phonemic awareness to young children: A 1-year follow-up. *Journal of Educational Psychology*, *85*, 104–111.

Byrne, B., Fielding-Barnsley, R., & Ashley, L. (2000). Effects of preschool phoneme identity training after six years: Outcome level distinguished from rate of response. *Journal of Educational Psychology*, *92*, 659–667.

Byrne, B., Freebody, P., & Gates, A. (1992). Longitudinal data on the relations of word-reading strategies to comprehension, reading time, and phonemic awareness. *Reading Research Quarterly*, *28*, 141–151.

Byrne, B., & Liberman, A. M. (1999). Meaninglessness, productivity and reading: Some observations about the relationship between the alphabet and speech. In J. Oakhill & R. Beard (Eds.), *Reading development and the teaching of reading: A psychological perspective* (pp. 157–173). Oxford: Blackwell.

Byrne, B., Olson, R. K., Samuelsson, S., Wadsworth, S., Corley, R., DeFries, J. C., et al. (2006). Genetic and environmental influences on early literacy. *Journal of Research in Reading*, *29*, 33–49.

Byrne, B., Samuelsson, S., Wadsworth, S., Hulslander, J., Corley, R., DeFries, J. C., et al. (2007). Longitudinal twin study of early literacy development: Preschool through grade 1. *Reading and Writing: An Interdisciplinary Journal*, *20*, 77–102.

Byrne, B., Wadsworth, S., Corley, R., Samuelsson, S., Quain, P., DeFries, J. C., et al. (2005). Longitudinal twin study of early literacy development: Preschool and kindergarten phases. *Scientific Studies of Reading*, *9*, 219–235.

Castles, A., & Coltheart, M. (2003). Is there a causal connection from phonological awareness to learning to read? *Cognition*, *91*, 77–111.

Crain, S. (1991). Language acquisition in the absence of experience. *Behavioral and Brain Sciences*, *14*, 597–650.

Crain, S., & Thornton, R. (1998). *Investigations in universal grammar: A guide to experiments on the acquisition of syntax and semantics*. Cambridge, MA: MIT Press.

Ehri, L., Nunes, S. R., Willows, D. M., Schuster, B. V., Yaghoub-Zadeh, Z., & Shanahan, T. (2001). Phonemic awareness instruction helps children learn to read: Evidence from the National Reading Panel's meta-analysis. *Reading Research Quarterly*, *36*, 250–287.

Ehri, L. C. (2005). Development of sight words: Phases and findings. In M. Snowling & C. Hulme (Eds.), *The science of reading: A handbook* (pp. 135–154). Oxford: Blackwell.

Elbro, C., & Petersen, D. K. (2004). Long-term effects of phoneme awareness and letter sound training: An intervention study with children at risk for dyslexia. *Journal of Educational Psychology*, *96*, 660–670.

Ferreiro, E. (1986). The interplay between information and assimilation in beginning literacy. In W. H. Teale & E. Sulzby (Eds.), *Emergent literacy: Writing and reading*. Norwood, NJ: Ablex.

Foulin, J. N. (2005). Why is letter-name knowledge such a good predictor of learning to read? *Reading & Writing: An Interdisciplinary Journal*, *18*, 129–155.

Gipstein, M., Brady, S., & Fowler, A. (2000). Questioning the role of syllables and rimes in early phonological awareness. In M. Masland (Ed.), *Early identification and remediation of reading disability* (2nd ed., pp. 179–216). Parkton, MD: York Press.

Goodman, K. S. (1986). *What's whole in whole language: A parent-teacher guide*. Portsmouth, NH: Heineman.

Goodman, K. S., & Goodman, Y. M. (1979). Learning to read is natural. In L. B. Resnick & P. A. Weaver (Eds.), *Theory and practice of early reading* (Vol. 1, pp. 137–154). Hillsdale, NJ: Lawrence Erlbaum Associates.

Harlaar, N., Dale, P. S., & Plomin, R. (2007). From learning to read to reading to learn: Substantial and stable genetic influence. *Child Development*, *78*, 116–131.

Harlaar, N., Spinath, F. M., Dale, P. S., & Plomin, R. (2005). Genetic influences on word recognition abilities and disabilities: A study of 7-year-old twins. *Journal of Child Psychology and Psychiatry*, *46*, 373–384.

Hindson, B. A., Byrne, B., Fielding-Barnsley, R., Newman, C., Hine, D., & Shankweiler, D. (2005). Assessment and early instruction of preschool children at risk for reading disability. *Journal of Educational Psychology*, *94*, 687–704.

Hintzman, D. L. (1986). Schema abstraction in a multiple-trace memory model. *Psychological Review*, *93*, 411–428.

Hulme, C., Snowling, M., Caravolas, M., & Carroll, J. (2005). Phonological skills are (probably) one cause of success in learning to read: A comment on Castles and Coltheart. *Scientific Studies of Reading*, *9*(4), 351–365.

Jastak, S., & Wilkinson, G. S. (1984). *The Wide Range Achievement Test-Revised: Administration manual*. Wilmington, DE: Jastak Associates.

Johnston, P. H. (1985). Understanding reading disability. *Harvard Educational Review*, *55*, 153–177.

Kandel, E. (2006). *In search of memory: The emergence of a new science of mind*. New York: W. H. Norton.

Keenan, J. M., Betjemann, R. S., Wadsworth, S. J., DeFries, J. C., & Olson, R. K. (2006). Genetic and environmental influences on reading and listening comprehension. *Journal of Research in Reading*, *29*, 79–91.

Kintsch, W., & Rawson, K. A. (2005). Comprehension. In M. Snowling & C. Hulme (Eds.), *The science of reading: A handbook* (pp. 209–226). Oxford: Blackwell.

Levin, I., & Korat, O. (1993). Sensitivity to phonological, morphological, and semantic cues in early reading and writing in Hebrew. *Merrill-Palmer Quarterly*, *39*, 213–232.

Liberman, A. M. (1989). Reading is hard just because listening is easy. In C. von Euler (Ed.), *Wenner-Gren international symposium series: Brain and reading* (pp. 197–205). Hampshire: Macmillan.

Liberman, A. M. (1999). The reading researcher and the reading teacher need the right theory of speech. *Scientific Studies of Reading*, *3*, 95–111.

Liberman, A. M., Cooper, F. S., Shankweiler, D. P., & Studdert-Kennedy, M. (1967). Perception of the speech code. *Psychological Review*, *74*, 431–461.

Liberman, A. M., & Mattingly, I. G. (1985). The motor theory of speech perception revised. *Cognition*, *21*, 1–36.

Liberman, I. Y., & Liberman, A. M. (1992). Whole language versus code emphasis: Underlying assumptions and their implications for reading instruction. In P. B. Gough, L. C. Ehri, & R. Treiman (Eds.), *Reading acquisition* (pp. 343–366). Hillsdale, NJ: Lawrence Erlbaum Associates.

Liberman, I. Y., Shankweiler, D., Fischer, F. W., & Carter, B. (1974). Explicit syllable and phoneme segmentation in the young child. *Journal of Experimental Child Psychology*, *18*, 201–212.

Lundberg, I., Frost, J., & Petersen, O. (1988). Effects of an extensive program for stimulating phonological awareness in preschool children. *Reading Research Quarterly*, *23*, 263–284.

Lundberg, I., & Tornéus, M. (1978). Nonreaders' awareness of the basic relationship between spoken and written words. *Journal of Experimental Child Psychology*, *25*, 404–412.

Moeser, S. D. (1977). Semantics and miniature artificial languages. In J. Macnamara (Ed.), *Language learning and thought*. New York: Academic Press.

Moeser, S. D., & Olson, A. J. (1974). The role of reference in children's acquisition of a miniature artificial language. *Journal of Experimental Child Psychology*, *17*, 204–218.

Morais, J., & Kolinsky, R. (2005). Literacy and cognitive change. In M. Snowling, & C. Hulme (Eds.), *The science of reading: A handbook* (pp. 188–203). Oxford: Blackwell.

Nation, K. (1999). Reading skills in hyperlexia: A developmental perspective. *Psychological Bulletin*, *125*(3), 338–355.

Neale, M. C., Boker, S. M., Xie, G., & Maes, H. H. (2002). *Mx: Statistical modeling* (6th ed.). Richmond, VA: Virginia Commonwealth University.

Paulesu, E., Frith, U., Snowling, M., Gallagher, A., Morton, J., Frackowiak, R. S. J., et al. (1996). Is developmental dyslexia a disconnection syndrome? Evidence from PET scanning. *Brain*, *119*, 143–157.

Petrill, S. A., Deater-Deckard, K., Thompson, L. A., Schatschneider, C., DeThorne, L. S., & Vandenbergh, D. J. (2007). Longitudinal genetic analyses of early reading: The Western Reserve Reading Project. *Reading and Writing: An Interdisciplinary Journal*, *20*, 127–146.

Pinker, S. (1979). Formal models of language learning. *Cognition*, *7*, 217–283.

Pinker, S. (1990). Language acquisition. In D. N. Osherson & H. Lasnik (Eds.), *Language: An invitation to cognitive science* (Vol. 1, pp. 199–241). Cambridge, MA: MIT Press.

Pinker, S. (1994). *The language instinct: The new science of language and mind*. London: Penguin.

Plomin, R., DeFries, J. C., McClearn, G. E., & McGuffin, P. (2008). *Behavioral genetics* (5th ed.). New York: Worth.

Plomin, R., & Kovas, Y. (2005). Generalist genes and learning disabilities. *Psychological Bulletin*, *131*, 592–617.

Polich, J., McCarthy, G., Wang, W. S., & Donchin, E. (1983). When words collide: Orthographic and phonological interference during word processing. *Biological Psychology*, *16*, 155–180.

Ramus, F., & Gayaneh, S. (2008). What phonological deficit? *Quarterly Journal of Experimental Psychology*, *61*, 129–141.

Reber, A. S. (1967). Implicit learning of artificial grammars. *Journal of Verbal Learning and Verbal Behavior*, *6*, 855–863.

Reitsma, P. (1983). Printed word learning in beginning readers. *Journal of Experimental Child Psychology*, *75*, 321–339.

Rozin, P. (1976). The evolution of intelligence and access to the cognitive unconscious. In J. Sprague & A. N. Epstein (Eds.), *Progress in psychobiology and physiological psychology* (Vol. 6, pp. 245–280). New York: Academic Press.

Samuelsson, S., Byrne, B., Olson, R. K., Hulslander, J., Wadsworth, S., Corley, R., et al. (2008). Response to early literacy instruction in the United States, Australia, and Scandinavia: A behavioral-genetic analysis. *Learning and Individual Differences*, *18*, 289–295.

Samuelsson, S., Byrne, B., Quain, P., Wadsworth, S., Corley, R., DeFries, J. C., et al. (2005). Environmental and genetic influences on prereading skills in Australia, Scandinavia, and the United States. *Journal of Educational Psychology*, *97*, 705–722.

Samuelsson, S., Byrne, B., Wadsworth, S., Corley, R., DeFries, J. C., Willcutt, E., et al. (2007). Genetic and environmental influences on prereading skills and early reading and spelling development in the United States, Australia, and Scandinavia. *Reading and Writing: An Interdisciplinary Journal*, *20*, 51–75.

Scarborough, H. S. (1998). Early detection of children at risk for reading disabilities: Phonological awareness and other promising predictors. In B. K. Shapiro, P. J. Accardo, & A. J. Capute (Eds.), *Specific reading disability: A view of the spectrum* (pp. 75–119). Timonium, MD: York Press.

Seidenberg, M. S., & Tanenhaus, M. K. (1979). Orthographic effects on rhyme monitoring. *Journal of Experimental Psychology: Human Learning and Memory*, *5*, 546–554.

Seymour, P. H. K. (2005). Early reading development in European orthographies. In M. Snowling & C. Hulme (Eds.), *The science of reading: A handbook* (pp. 296–315). Oxford: Blackwell.

Shankweiler, D. (1999). Words to meanings. *Scientific Studies of Reading*, *3*, 113–127.

Shankweiler, D., & Fowler, A. E. (2004). Questions people ask about the role of phonological processes in learning to read. *Reading and Writing: An Interdisciplinary Journal*, *17*, 483–515.

Share, D. L. (1999). Phonological recoding and orthographic learning: A direct test of the self-teaching hypothesis. *Journal of Experimental Child Psychology*, *72*, 95–129.

Snowling, M. J. & Hulme, C. (Eds.). (2005). *The science of reading: A handbook*. Oxford: Blackwell.

Snowling, M. J., Gallagher, A., & Frith, U. (2003). Family risk of dyslexia is continuous: Individual differences in the precursors of reading skill. *Child Development*, *74*, 358–373.

Stanovich, K. E. (1992). Speculation of the causes and consequences of individual differences in early reading acquisition. In P. B. Gough, L. C. Ehri, & R. Treiman (Eds.), *Reading acquisition* (pp. 307–342). Hillsdale, NJ: Lawrence Erlbaum Associates.

Stromswold, K. (2001). The heritability of language: A review and meta-analysis of twin, adoption and linkage studies. *Language*, *77*, 647–723.

Studdert-Kennedy, M. (1998). The particulate origins of language productivity: From syllable to gesture. In J. Hurford, M. Studdert-Kennedy, & C. Knight (Eds.), *Approaches to the evolution of language: Social and cognitive bases* (pp. 202–221). Cambridge, MA: Cambridge University Press.

Torgesen, J., Wagner, R., & Rashotte, C. A. (1999). *A Test of Word Reading Efficiency (TOWRE)*. Austin, TX: PRO-ED.

Willcutt, E., Betjemann, R., Wadsworth, S, Samuelsson, S., Corley, R., DeFries, J. C., et al. (2007). Preschool twin study of the relation between attention-deficit/hyperactivity disorder and prereading skills. *Reading and Writing: An Interdisciplinary Journal*, *20*, 103–125.

Wimmer, H., & Goswami, U. (1994). The influence of orthographic consistency on reading development: Word recognition in English and German children. *Cognition*, *51*, 91–103.

10 Genetic and Environmental Influences on Phonological Abilities and Reading Achievement

Richard Olson
University of Colorado

INTRODUCTION

Investigators associated with the Colorado Learning Disabilities Research Center (CLDRC) have been exploring genetic and environmental influences on reading and related skills since 1979. From the beginning, our selection of measures and theoretical framework has been strongly influenced by the phonological deficit hypothesis. Thus, we are deeply grateful to Don Shankweiler and his colleagues for their pioneering theoretical and empirical contributions that emphasized the importance of phonological skills in learning to read. Their generous consultation on the development of our initial test battery supported our inclusion of several experimental measures of phonological awareness and decoding that have played an important role in our behavior-genetic and intervention research over the past 30 years. This chapter provides an overview of results from the CLDRC that largely support the phonological deficit hypothesis and also suggest the need for some revision of the hypothesis and its implications for intervention.

I will begin the chapter with a discussion of good and poor readers' use of phonological processes in memory and reading that is at least partly separable from their precision in phonological processing. The second section reviews results from our recent longitudinal analyses of reading growth from age 10 to 16 showing its lack of relation to substantial individual differences in phonological skills that remain after controlling for reading level. The third section focuses on results from our computer-based intervention studies showing that poor readers' performance on phonological processing tasks can be substantially improved through direct instruction, though the unique benefit of direct instruction in phonological skills compared to accurate reading practice on the computer for growth in word recognition varies with reading grade and is of short duration. The fourth and main section of the chapter reviews the evidence from twins for genetic and environmental influences on phonological awareness and decoding skills and their correlation with word reading and reading comprehension. The final concluding section reviews the broad implications of our research and offers some amendments to the phonological deficit hypothesis as a causal model from phonological awareness to word recognition to reading comprehension. These amendments involve a distinction between explicit phonological awareness that can be taught, and less malleable implicit phonological processes.

DISTINGUISHING GOOD AND POOR READERS' USE VERSUS PRECISION IN PHONOLOGICAL PROCESSING

Phonological Confusion in Memory of Good and Poor Readers

One of the most interesting early studies conducted in support of the phonological deficit hypothesis was an exploration of good and poor readers' memory for lists of letters that contained rhyming versus non-rhyming items (I. Y. Liberman, Shankweiler, A. M. Liberman, Fowler, & Fischer, 1977; Shankweiler, Liberman, Mark, Fowler, & Fischer, 1979). Previous research had shown that lists of rhyming items were more difficult to recall than non-rhyming lists in unselected samples of young children (Conrad, 1971), presumably because the phonological overlap among the rhyming items led to phonological confusion in memory. Shankweiler et al. hypothesized that the rhyming effect might be diminished in poor compared to good readers because the poor readers' phonological processing deficit would be associated with less use of phonological codes in memory. In fact their results seemed to support this hypothesis: The rhyming deficit was significantly smaller in poor compared to good readers in the second grade.

We were interested in using the rhyming effect in our behavior-genetic study of reading disability across a broader age range, so we conducted a follow-up study of the rhyming confusion effect in good and poor readers from 8 to 17 years of age (Olson, Davidson, Kliegl, & Davies, 1984). We adapted the method of Mark, Shankweiler, Liberman, and Fowler (1977) that measured error responses to rhyming foils in a surprise memory test of words that subjects had orally read from a list. We were quite surprised to find that contrary to the results from Mark et al., our good and poor reader groups were not significantly different in their errors to the rhyming foils. However, our age range and sample size were large enough to detect a significant age by reading group interaction for rhyme confusion: Younger poor readers exhibited fewer rhyming errors compared to younger good readers, but older poor readers exhibited more rhyming errors compared to older good readers. This surprising result indicated that rhyming errors may not be a straightforward index of the use of phonological codes in memory, because it would imply that older good readers use phonological representations in memory less than older poor readers. We hypothesized that both good and poor readers rely on phonological representations in memory but that they differ in the precision of those representations. Thus, the more precise phonological representations of older good readers, particularly for the consonant codes that distinguished the rhyming items, led to less phonological confusion between rhyming foils and memory list items. This view is consistent with the more recent work by Elbro and colleagues who have shown that good and poor readers differ in the precision of their phonological representations (Elbro, Borstrom, & Petersen, 1998).

The Regularity Effect in Word Reading for Good and Poor Readers

The idea that poor readers make less use of phonological processing than do good readers was extended to word reading by Barron (1980). He reported that children who were good readers responded more rapidly to orthographically regular words (i.e., words with spellings that map in a regular way to phonological forms) compared to irregular or exception words (i.e., words such as *pint*, whose word body neighbors, such as *hint*, have differently pronounced word bodies), while poor readers did not show this difference, presumably because they were recognizing words by sight without the use of sub-lexical phonological processing. This interesting result led us to further examine the regularity effect in good and poor readers for possible use in our behavior-genetic studies. However, we found a similar regularity effect for good and poor readers across a broad age range, suggesting that both groups *were* relying on phonological processes in reading (Olson, Kliegl, Davidson, & Foltz, 1985), though perhaps the poor readers were less *able* in this as reflected in their higher error rates for reading words and nonwords. Equivalent regularity effects in good and poor readers have been replicated in a number of subsequent studies reviewed by Metsala, Stanovich, and Brown (1998). So, as with good and poor readers' similar use of phonological processes in memory, it seems that good and poor readers may also be similar in their use of phonological processing in reading words. However, in the following section we will see that the poor readers are less accurate in phonological processing of speech and print than would be expected from their level of word reading skill, and this may support a causal role for phonological deficits in reading disability.

Reading-Level-Match Group Comparisons of Good and Poor Readers' Phonological Processing

While good and poor readers may often be similar in their *reliance on* phonological processing as indexed by memory tasks and the regularity effect, Snowling (1981) demonstrated that poor readers' *accuracy* in decoding nonwords was significantly lower than their ability to read words. She did this by matching older poor readers with younger good readers on a measure of printed word recognition and then compared the two groups' nonword reading accuracy. In spite of the groups' matched level of printed word recognition, the older poor-reader group was significantly lower in their accuracy for reading multisyllabic nonwords.

Snowling extended the comparison to the repetition of orally presented multisyllabic nonwords and found a similar accuracy deficit for the poor-reader group. Thus, as a group, the poor readers had unique phonological processing deficits both in reading and in speech, and consistent with Shankweiler et al. (1979). Snowling argued that these deficits played a causal role in reading disability.

Snowling's (1981) group results have been replicated in our laboratory (Friend & Olson, 2008; Olson, 1985; Olson, Wise, Conners, Rack, & Fulker, 1989), and meta-analyses have shown that most other reading-level-match comparisons of good- and poor-reader groups' reading English show similar poor-reader group deficits (Rack, Snowling, & Olson, 1992). However, it is important to note that while effect sizes may approach 1 standard deviation of difference between the older poor- and younger good-reader groups' phonological skills, there are many poor readers whose phonological skills exceed the average for good readers at the same level of reading ability, just as there are many good readers whose phonological skills are below the average for the poor readers in reading-level-match comparisons. I will discuss the evidence for this reading-independent variance in phonological skills and its implications for the phonological deficit hypothesis in the next two sections.

VARIATION IN PHONOLOGICAL AWARENESS AND DECODING SKILL INDEPENDENT FROM READING SKILL

A strict phonological deficit hypothesis might suggest that all poor readers should be uniquely deficient in their phonological skills, and that the substantial within-group variance for phonological skills in reading-level-match comparisons is simply due to measurement error. However, the results of two studies show that this within-group variance in phonological skills that is independent from reading ability is reliable. The first study by Scarborough, Ehri, Olson, and Fowler (1998) explored the phonological awareness of older children and adults who were good readers. They found across several samples that there were reliable phonological awareness deficits among some of the good readers.

The second study was recently completed by Hulslander, Olson, Willcutt, and Wadsworth (in press). This study modeled the variance in phonological awareness, phonological decoding (nonword reading skill), and word reading skills in a large sample ($N = 324$) that included poor and normal-range readers from the CLDRC. The children were initially tested on multiple measures of their word recognition, phonological awareness, and phonological decoding skills at mean age 10 years. Then they were followed up with the same measures at mean age 16. With multiple measures of each skill, we were able to model latent traits for the skills to improve reliability. With the longitudinal follow-up, we were able to assess the stability and reliability of the latent traits across the 6-year testing interval. The measures of phonological awareness, phonological decoding, and word recognition used in the Hulslander et al. study were the same as those used in our previously discussed reading-level-match studies and in the intervention and behavior-genetic studies that will be discussed later in the chapter, so they are briefly described here.

We developed two experimental measures of phonological awareness in language that were sensitive to individual differences across the broad age range of the CLDRC twin sample. Our *Phoneme Deletion* task (Olson, Forsberg, Wise, & Rack, 1994) was based on earlier work by Bruce (1964). The task consisted of 6 practice and 40 test trials presented via a CD player in which the participant repeated a nonword and was then asked to say it again, deleting a specified phoneme to form a real word ("say prot—now say prot without the /r/"). Participants were given 2 s for repetitions and 4 s for deletions, as signaled by a warning tone on the CD. Raw data for this task consist of percent correct scores. Our second experimental measure of phonological awareness, *Phoneme Segmentation and Transposition* (Olson et al., 1989), required participants to play a word game similar to "Pig Latin" where they take the first phoneme off the front of a word, move it to the end of the word, and add a long "a" sound. A percent correct score was calculated for the 45 test items.

Our experimental measures of phonological decoding in reading were also developed to reliably measure individual differences across the broad age and reading ability range of our twin sample. The *Phonological Choice* task consisted of 60 items requiring participants to select which of three printed nonwords would sound like a real word (beal *bair* rabe) (Olson et al., 1994). The *Oral Nonword Reading* task consisted of reading 45 one-syllable (ter, strale) and 40 two-syllable (vogger, strempick) nonwords aloud (Olson et al.). Percent correct scores were calculated for each task.

Our two measures of word reading included the experimental Timed Word Recognition Test (Olson et al., 1994), and the Peabody Individual Achievement Test Word Recognition (Dunn & Markwardt, 1970; Markwardt, 1989). The Timed Word Recognition Test consists of words presented on a computer screen in order of increasing difficulty, as assessed in an independent sample. Responses are considered correct only when the correct pronunciation of the word is initiated within 2 s of stimulus onset. Testing continues through a list of 182 items until the participant fails to answer 10 of the last 20 items correctly within the time limit or the end of the list is reached. Raw scores are based on the last word read. The Peabody Individual Achievement Test Word Recognition task presents words of increasing difficulty in rows across a page. The participant reads the words aloud in sequence until five of the last seven items are missed or the end of the list is reached.

Four results from the Hulslander et al. (in press) study with these measures are of particular interest. First, the latent-trait longitudinal-stability correlations for the children's reading ($r = .98$), phonological awareness ($r = 1.0$), and phonological decoding ($r = .93$) skills standardized at each test occasion were remarkably high. Second, there was significant variance in subjects' phonological awareness and phonological decoding latent traits at mean ages 10 and 16 that was independent from their word recognition latent trait. Third, the longitudinal latent trait stability correlations for word reading independent variance were significant for phonological awareness (r = 1.0) and phonological decoding (r = .78), so it might be expected that individual differences in these important reading-related phonological skills would have a significant influence on growth in word recognition across the test interval. The fourth and most important result was that this longitudinally reliable variance in phonological awareness and decoding that was independent from word recognition at mean age 10 had virtually no influence on individual differences in word-recognition growth from mean age 10 to mean age 16 (respective R^2 = .0001 and .0004). Of course, it is difficult to predict any independent variance in word reading at time 2 after controlling for word reading at time 1 when the longitudinal stability correlation for the word reading latent trait was .98, although the children's full-scale IQ score at time 1 adjusted for time 1 word reading level was able to do so at a very modest but statistically significant level in our large sample (R^2 = .006).

So what do the Hulslander et al. (in press) results have to say about the phonological deficit hypothesis? They certainly question a completely direct causal link from phonological awareness skill to word reading ability. However, there is no question that there is a close association between phonological awareness and word reading ability. Hulslander et al. provided some of the strongest evidence to date for the strength of that association through their latent trait modeling. To wit: latent trait correlations at initial and final test respectively were .85 and .82 between word recognition and phonological awareness, .93 and .90 between word recognition and phonological decoding, and .95 and .91 between phonological awareness and phonological decoding. Proponents of a strict causal link from phonological awareness to phonological decoding to word reading might feel supported by these high latent trait correlations, but such correlations may arise at least partly from some underlying third factor. The need to consider third factor accounts of the correlations between phonological processes and reading will be further supported by results from our intervention studies reviewed in the next section.

INTERVENTION FOR DEFICITS IN PHONOLOGICAL SKILLS AND READING

Our research on interventions for reading disabilities beginning in the mid-1980s was partly motivated by reactions to our early reports of genetic influences on reading disability (DeFries, Fulker, & LaBuda, 1987) and deficits in phonological skills (Olson et al., 1989). Some people concluded from our behavior-genetic results that environmental intervention for the remediation of reading disability would be pointless because it was genetically determined. (Of course that was a misinterpretation of our results, but it kindled our interest in developing a strong intervention to counter this mistaken view.) As I will explain more thoroughly in the next section on genetics, even when population estimates of genetic influence are high, they may only imply a limited range of environmental influence in the sampled population. For example, extraordinary environmental interventions for genetically influenced disorders such as myopia (eye glasses) and diabetes (insulin supplements) can often resolve those disorders. The field of dyslexia has often been offered such simple and straightforward treatments (e.g., read with colored lenses, warm oil in the ear, eye movement training, and balancing exercises), but none of these treatments has been supported in well-controlled research studies. In contrast, the early work of Shankweiler and colleagues clearly showed that phonological skills were important in early reading development, and educational studies had clearly shown that direct instruction in grapheme–phoneme correspondences in first-grade reading instruction supported more rapid early reading development than "whole-language" approaches that relied more on children to induce those correspondences from print exposure (Bond & Dykstra, 1967; Chall, 1967). Therefore, it seemed clear to us that an intervention for reading disability should pay particular attention to improving phonological skills in children with reading disability. (The other person implied by "us" is my former graduate student and long time colleague, Dr. Barbara Wise.)

The second reason Barbara and I decided to develop an intervention for reading disability was the emergence in 1985 of a high quality synthetic speech engine named "Dectalk" made by Digital Equipment Corporation that could be interfaced with microcomputers. We initially designed a simple program to present stories on the computer screen wherein children with dyslexia in grades 3–6 could target words with a mouse and have them highlighted and pronounced at the same time. This allowed the children to read material that was more advanced than what they could read without synthetic speech assistance. We demonstrated that feedback for difficult words in the stories was far more effective in promoting learning of those words compared to reading the stories without feedback and attempting to guess difficult words (Olson, Foltz, & Wise, 1986). This may seem an obvious result, but it countered the claims of some extreme "whole-language" advocates that guessing difficult words from first letter sounds and context would lead to better growth in reading (K. S. Goodman & Y. M. Goodman, 1979). The "whole-language" approach was dominant in the Boulder Colorado schools during the 1980s and early 1990s, so this evidence was needed to convince teachers that our computer program would provide greater benefits for reading development than guessing difficult words from context. As a result, we gained permission to further explore the benefits of synthetic speech feedback for children with reading disabilities in the Boulder schools.

Our next step was to explore the benefits of segmenting targeted words on the computer screen with speech support for the segments to better develop the children's phonological decoding skills and ultimately make them less dependent on computer speech support. We compared three groups of poor readers in the lower 10% of their class who read stories on the computer for a half hour each day: One group had targeted words highlighted and spoken as whole words, one group had targeted words highlighted and spoken in syllable units, and one group had regular targeted words highlighted and spoken in onset and rime units. A fourth control group remained in their regular reading or language arts classroom. We hypothesized that the segmented feedback conditions would lead to greater growth in phonological decoding skills and perhaps in word reading skills as well. The results of an initial small study seemed to support the hypothesis: There was a significantly greater gain in phonological decoding (but not in standardized measures of word recognition) for the onset-rime segmentation condition compared to the syllable and whole word conditions. All three feedback conditions gained more in word reading and decoding than the untreated control group (Wise et al., 1989). Encouraged by these preliminary results, we trained a much larger sample for a longer time with subjects randomly assigned to the three segmentation conditions and an untreated control group. Though all three feedback groups improved more in phonological decoding and word recognition than the untreated control group, we were surprised to find no significant differences between the three feedback conditions (Olson & Wise, 1992). However, we noted that pretest phoneme awareness was positively related to reading and decoding gains across all the conditions, so this led to our next series of studies that included training in phoneme awareness.

Our training of phoneme awareness was based partly on the articulatory training methods developed by Lindamood and Lindamood (1975) that seemed consistent with the motor theory of speech perception and the importance of articulatory gestures that was proposed by A. Liberman, Cooper, Shankweiler, and Studdert-Kennedy (1967). The Lindamood and Lindamood program helps children understand the distinctions between phonemes by training them to feel and recognize in pictures the articulatory movements that are associated with the different phonemes. We consulted with Pat Lindamood to adapt some of the articulatory exercises for small group activities and for presentation as computer games, and we developed computer programs for practice in the spelling and phonological decoding of nonwords. I will briefly summarize the results of two studies that included training in articulatory awareness and phonological decoding exercises. Then I will discuss what I think the implications are for the phonological deficit hypothesis and intervention for reading disabilities.

The first study compared two groups of second to fifth graders who received 50–60 half-hour training sessions over a semester. The phonological analysis (PA) group ($N = 109$) included seven small-group hours using the articulatory training methods developed by Lindamood and Lindamood (1975). About half of their individual time on the computer was devoted to exercises to support phoneme awareness and phonological decoding while the other half was spent reading stories on the computer with targeted unfamiliar multisyllabic words segmented into syllables and regular single-syllable words segmented into onsets and rimes for orthographic and speech feedback. Irregular ("special") words were not segmented. The other accurate-reading-in-context (ARC) group ($N = 91$) spent 22 computer hours reading stories with speech feedback and seven small-group hours practicing the Palinscar and Brown (1984) comprehension strategies while reading together. Both experimental groups answered multiple choice comprehension questions every five to nine pages and reviewed targeted words at the end of each session (Wise, Ring, and Olson, 2000). Pretests, midtests, and posttests were given before, during, and at the end of training. Follow-up tests were given 1 and 2 years after the end of training for a subset of the generally younger subjects who remained in their elementary schools and available for testing.

At the end of training, the ARC condition showed significantly greater growth in time-limited word recognition, and the PA condition showed significantly greater growth in phoneme awareness, phonological decoding, and untimed word recognition. There were no significant group differences in spelling or reading comprehension. However, there were significant interactions with grade level: The PA condition yielded better results for untimed word reading and spelling for children in grades 2 and 3, while the ARC condition yielded greater gains in all measures of word reading and spelling for children in grades 4 and 5. We were surprised by this result, since the poor readers in grades 4 and 5 who were trained in the PA condition showed significant end-of-training advantages in phoneme awareness and phonological decoding over the fourth and fifth graders in the ARC condition. Yet the ARC fourth and fifth graders were superior in word reading and spelling at the end of training. We were also surprised by the results from follow-up tests of the mostly younger subjects who were tested 1 and 2 years after the end of training: The PA condition tended to maintain its significant superiority in phoneme awareness and phonological decoding, but there were no significant group differences in word recognition at follow-up. It is possible that the differential gains in phonological awareness and decoding at the end of 29 hr of training, though they were large in effect size and statistical significance and trained close to normal levels in the PA group, were still not sufficiently strong to transfer to lasting differences in reading and spelling 1 or 2 years after training. However, similar null results from a one-on-one tutoring study with longer training (88 hr) have led Torgesen et al. (2001) to conclude that we still don't know how to connect remedied phonological skills in third- to sixth-grade poor readers to more rapid growth in fluent reading.

Our second study focused on the importance of articulatory awareness training in our PA training condition (Wise, Ring, & Olson, 1999). One of the conditions was similar to the PA training condition of Wise et al. (2000) that included 7 hr of training in articulatory awareness. Another condition replaced the time devoted to articulatory awareness training with practice in organizing block patterns to represent changes in spoken phoneme sequences, manipulating graphemes to correspond to phoneme changes in nonwords and words spoken by the computer, spelling words spoken by the computer, and practicing the reading of nonwords. The group trained in articulatory awareness also practiced with these programs, but for less time due to their work with small-group articulatory awareness activities. Both groups read stories on the computer for part of their training time, which totaled 40 hr in half-hour sessions. To our surprise, at the end of training and in 1-year follow-up tests, there were no significant group differences for gains in phoneme awareness, phonological decoding, or word reading measures. We were pleased that both conditions yielded substantial gains compared to a regular reading classroom control group for phoneme awareness (effect sizes = 0.92–1.73), phonological decoding (effect size = 1.46), and word recognition (effect size = 0.73–0.98), but the presence or absence of training in articulatory awareness had no significant influence on these effect sizes.

A study by Castiglioni-Spalten and Ehri (2003) is sometimes cited as supporting the unique benefit of articulatory awareness training in nonreaders, but in fact there was no significant advantage for reading from articulatory awareness training in that study either. While I still find the A. Liberman et al. (1967) motor theory of speech perception to be a compelling account of how we represent the overlapping phonemes in speech, it does not seem that training children's conscious awareness of articulatory gestures and their related phonemes yields any unique advantage for the remediation of phonological and reading deficits in second- to fifth-grade children, or in nonreaders.

Now I will summarize what I think the results of training studies have to say about the phonological deficit hypothesis and its relevance for education. First, there is no question that direct instruction in grapheme–phoneme correspondence for beginning readers leads to more rapid growth in reading in the early grades compared to less direct instruction, and we have known this for a long time (Bond & Dykstra, 1967; Chall, 1967). The results of our remedial training studies are consistent with this research by showing initial advantages in short-term growth for accurate word reading and spelling for poor readers in the second and third grades whose initial deficits on our phonological measures were largely remediated. However, the unique benefits of direct instruction and phonological training in beginning reading programs and in the remediation of reading disability in the early grades are time limited. This was noted by Bond and Dykstra when they found significant benefits for direct instruction in the first grade that did not last beyond grade 3. Similarly, Wise et al. (2000) found that phonological training for second- and third-grade poor readers yielded greater untimed reading and spelling gains at the end of training compared to accurate reading practice, but this advantage was not significant at 1- and 2-year follow-up assessments. Thus, for both beginning readers in grade 1 and poor readers in the early grades, remediating the "phonological deficit" has unique short-term benefits but limited or no long-term benefits for reading development beyond less direct instruction or accurate reading practice. For older poor readers in the fourth and fifth grades, it appears that even in the short term there is no unique benefit from phonological remediation, because they improved more from accurate reading practice. Of course, the initial level of phonological skill and reading rather than grade may be the critical variable for our differential treatment effects by grade, but we were not able to separate the effects of grade from reading level.

So do these results challenge the phonological deficit hypothesis? I think they do, at least to some extent, if the phonological deficit is operationally defined by performance on measures of phonological awareness and decoding. Our training studies show that phonological skills and reading level can be dissociated, and the longitudinal study by Hulslander et al. (in press) has shown that this reliable dissociation exists in the general population. The resolution of this apparent conflict with the phonological deficit hypothesis may require a reevaluation of the operational definition of phonological awareness that has been based on behavioral measures of that construct. I will return to this issue at the end of the chapter after exploring the genetic and environmental etiology of phonological skills and their relations to reading skills.

GENETIC AND ENVIRONMENTAL INFLUENCES ON PHONOLOGICAL ABILITIES AND READING ACHIEVEMENT

In this section we are shifting from specific measured environmental influences embodied in the training studies to a more abstract assessment of the contribution of environment and genes to individual differences and deficits in phonological skills and related reading skills. We do this by contrasting within-pair similarities for identical twins and within-pair similarities for fraternal twins. If differences in genes were the only influence on individual differences in a behavior, the expected correlation would be 1.0 for identical twins because they are derived from the same sperm and egg (i.e., they are monozygotic or MZ twins) and share the same genes. The expected correlation for fraternal twins would be .5 because they are derived from two different sperm and egg combinations (i.e., they are dizygotic or DZ twins) and they share half of their segregating genes on average, the same as ordinary siblings (Plomin, DeFries, McClearn, & McGuffin, 2008).

Of course genes are not the only influence on behavioral variation. Behavior-genetic studies of twin pairs that share their home environment are able to simultaneously estimate the proportion of variance in the population that is due to environmental influences shared by the twins in their homes and schools, environmental influences not shared by the twins (i.e., different peers, accidents, different teachers, measurement error), and genetic influences. The non-shared environmental influences are estimated as 1—the MZ correlation, since MZ twins share the same genes and home environment. So, for example, an MZ correlation of .9 would yield a non-shared environment estimate (e^2) of .1 or 10% of the variance. Genetic influence is estimated as twice the difference between the MZ and DZ correlations, so an MZ r of .9 and a DZ r of .6 would yield a genetic estimate (h^2) of .6. Shared environment (c^2) can be estimated as $1 - (h^2 + e^2)$, yielding a c^2 estimate of .3. These three estimates total 100% of the population variance. Most behavior-genetic research models the variance–covariance matrices for MZ and DZ twins instead of simply computing correlation differences to derive these estimates (Neale, Boker, Xie, & Maes, 2002).

Investigators in the CLDRC have focused primarily on the genetic and environmental etiology of group deficits in reading and related skills. This requires a somewhat different statistical approach from the estimates described in the previous paragraph for individual differences in the population, because the genetic and environmental etiology of extreme group performance (i.e., reading disability) could differ from that of individual differences in reading across the normal range (DeFries & Fulker, 1985, 1988). For our analyses of group deficits, we select twin pairs that include at least one twin (the proband) that meets some extreme selection criterion, usually about 1.5 standard deviation units from the mean of a control group of twin pairs wherein both members were above this selection criterion and had no school history of reading difficulty. Then we observe the average regression of the co-twins of the MZ and DZ probands toward the mean of the control group. With appropriate scaling of the regression scores, the MZ and DZ co-twin regression means can be viewed as group correlations and analyzed in a similar fashion as the population correlations described in the previous paragraph (Purcell & Sham, 2003). To distinguish these extreme-group estimates of genetic and environmental influences from the estimates for individual differences in the population, we add the g subscript for genetic h_g^2, shared environment c_g^2, and non-shared environment e_g^2.

Gayán and Olson (2001) analyzed the genetic and environmental etiology of group deficits in phonological awareness and phonological decoding with measures the same as those previously described in the study by Hulslander et al. (in press). The genetic, shared environment, and non-shared environment estimates for phoneme deletion ($h_g^2 = .72$, $c_g^2 = .15$, $e_g^2 = .13$) and phoneme transposition ($h_g^2 = .69$, $c_g^2 = .11$, $e_g^2 = .20$) revealed that genes were the main influence on these deficits. Genetic influence was also strong for deficits in oral nonword reading ($h_g^2 = .71$, $c_g^2 = .18$, $e_g^2 = .12$) and phonological choice ($h_g^2 = .60$, $c_g^2 = .28$, $e_g^2 = .12$), our two measures of phonological decoding. Genetic influence somewhat less strong but still is substantial for a composite measure of word recognition ($h_g^2 = .54$, $c_g^2 = .39$, $e_g^2 = .06$). Thus, there is a strong biological basis for the difficulties that poor readers have with phonological skills, and the effects of environmental factors are relatively weak. But keep in mind that the estimates of environmental and genetic influences are only averages across twin pairs that are dependent on the environmental range in our sample. The training studies of Wise et al. (1999, 2000) and others have shown powerful effects on poor readers' phonological skills and word recognition. If there were wide variation in such training within our twin sample, say half were well trained and half were not, the estimates of environmental influence would rise and estimates of genetic influence would fall.

Gayán and Olson (2001) also explored the bivariate genetic correlations between their measures. This was done by selecting probands on one variable and observing co-twin regression on a second variable. This procedure yielded an estimate of the degree to which group deficits in a pair of variables were caused by the same genes. We found very high genetic correlations with word recognition for oral nonword reading ($r_g = .99$) and phonological choice ($r_g = .97$) measures of phonological decoding. Thus, the genes that influence deficits in word recognition are virtually the same genes that influence deficits in phonological decoding. This was not the case for the genetic correlations between word recognition and phoneme deletion ($r_g = .67$) or phoneme transposition ($r_g = .70$) measures of phonological awareness, though the genetic overlap was also significant. Similar genetic correlations were found between the measures of phonological decoding and phonological awareness. Thus, whereas deficits in word reading and the phonological decoding of nonwords are very tightly linked at a genetic level, phonological awareness has a significant amount of genetic influence that is independent from the genetic influences on reading words and nonwords.

Gayán and Olson (2003) found a similar pattern of genetic influences and correlations when they combined the selected and control group samples from the CLDRC to model genetic and environmental influences on individual differences in latent traits for word recognition, phonological decoding, and phoneme awareness across the normal range. Genetic influences were somewhat stronger for individual differences compared to the previously discussed group deficits on individual measures. Individual differences in latent traits for word recognition ($h^2 = .85$, $c^2 = .04$, $e^2 = .11$), phonological decoding ($h^2 = .85$, $c^2 = .04$, $e^2 = .11$), and phoneme awareness ($h^2 = .85$, $c^2 = .04$, $e^2 = .11$) were strongly influenced by genes. Also, the pattern of results for genetic correlations was similar to what Gayán and Olson (2001) found for group deficits: For individual differences, the genetic correlation was .97 between the latent traits for word recognition and phonological decoding, but a significantly lower genetic correlation of .75 was found between word recognition and phonological awareness.

The strong genetic influences on individual differences in word recognition and phonological decoding reported by Gayán and Olson (2003) are quite consistent with those from our studies of first- and second-grade twins' nonword reading and word reading efficiency (Byrne et al., 2007, 2008). Byrne (Chapter 9) summarizes these results, and he also comments on some interesting results from our assessment of the twins' phonological awareness in preschool and their later reading ability. We found that the genes for phonological awareness that were shared with preschool print knowledge carried through to later word recognition in kindergarten, but the larger genetic influence on phonological awareness that was independent from preschool print knowledge did not, though it did account for a small amount of genetic variance in reading comprehension in grade 2. Byrne suggested that the preschool measures of phonological awareness may be influenced by working memory and other cognitive processes that are important for reading comprehension but less so for word recognition. Gayán and Olson did not include reading comprehension in their analyses, but they did include full-scale IQ. The genetic correlation between the phonological awareness latent trait and IQ (.56) was significant, and the genetic influence it shares with IQ may account for part of the genetic variance in phonological awareness influencing reading comprehension that was independent from word recognition. Further research is needed to isolate the specific cognitive skills involved in measures of phonological awareness that account for its unique relation to reading comprehension.

Since the Gayán and Olson (2001, 2003) papers were published, we have collected additional data on reading comprehension and related skills in our CLDRC sample. Analyses of the relations between phoneme awareness and reading comprehension are planned, and a paper has been published on the genetic and environmental relations between word recognition, reading comprehension, and listening comprehension (Keenan, Betjeman, Wadsworth, DeFries, & Olson, 2006). I will briefly discuss the background and results of this paper that relate to the phonological deficit hypothesis.

Keenan et al. (2006) noted some of the early strong claims of a direct causal pathway from phonological awareness to word recognition to reading comprehension (A. Liberman, Shankweiler, Fisher, & Carter, 1974; Perfetti, 1985; Shankweiler, 1989). Keenan et al. also noted evidence that has accumulated in recent years to support at least a partial dissociation between decoding and reading comprehension problems that was recognized in Hoover and Gough's (1990) "simple model" of reading. The "simple model" says that reading comprehension is a product of skill in decoding and skill in listening comprehension. Since then a number of studies have confirmed that listening comprehension accounts for independent variance in reading comprehension after decoding, although tests of reading comprehension differ in the amount of independent variance associated with listening comprehension (Cutting & Scarborough, 2006; Keenan, Betjemann, & Olson, 2008).

To understand the genetic and environmental etiology of reading comprehension, Keenan et al. (2006) conducted a behavior-genetic analysis of individual differences in word recognition, listening comprehension, and reading comprehension with twins from 8 to 18 years of age in the CLDRC. The Cholesky decomposition procedure described by Byrne (Chapter 9) was used to compute the genetic and environmental influences on the variables and on their correlations. Genetic influences were significant for all three variables (word recognition $h^2 = .65$; listening comprehension $h^2 = .51$; reading comprehension $h^2 = .51$). After controlling for genetic influences on word recognition, the remaining genetic variance in listening comprehension was significantly related to genetic influences on reading comprehension. Together, word recognition and listening comprehension accounted for all of the genetic influence on reading comprehension, confirming a genetic basis for the "simple model." Common environment influences were nearly all shared by the variables, and non-shared environmental influences were largely measure specific, suggesting the influence of measurement error. The independent genetic influence from listening comprehension on reading comprehension can be understood by comparing the genetic correlations between the variables. The genetic correlation between word recognition and reading comprehension was substantial ($r_g = .83$). In contrast, the genetic influence on listening comprehension was only modestly correlated with genetic influence on word recognition ($r_g = .37$), but strongly correlated with genetic influences on reading comprehension ($r_g = .80$).

I will conclude this section by briefly mentioning one final result from behavior-genetic analyses before summarizing the implications of our research for the phonological deficit hypothesis. Byrne et al. (2008) conducted a behavior genetic study of second graders' learning of nonword spellings that were embedded in stories that they read. The method and results are clearly described by Byrne (Chapter 9), so I will simply note that children's orthographic learning of nonword spellings was genetically influenced by virtually the same genes that influenced their ability to decode the nonwords in the stories and to spell words on a standardized test of spelling. Byrne et al. also noted previous research showing that preschoolers' learning rate for phoneme awareness in a training program was a better predictor of later reading skills than their final level of phoneme awareness (Byrne, Fielding-Barnsley, & Ashley, 2000). Thus, a learning rate parameter may be fundamental to the difficulties many children have with phonological awareness and reading, an idea that is implied in the general construct of "learning disabilities." The specificity of the learning rate parameter that was linked to orthographic learning, decoding, and spelling remains to be determined. The low genetic correlation between word recognition and listening comprehension in the study by Keenan et al. (2006) suggests that genetic influences on individual differences in learning rates for print-speech associations may be partly independent from genetic influences on oral language.

IMPLICATIONS OF OUR RESEARCH FOR THE PHONOLOGICAL DEFICIT HYPOTHESIS

The last chapter that I wrote on the phonological deficit hypothesis was in honor of Ingvar Lundberg (Olson, 2002). Ingvar had also been strongly influenced by Don Shankweiler and his colleagues at Haskins, and this influence lead to Ingvar's seminal paper on preschool training of phonological awareness and its benefits for early reading development (Lundberg, Frost, & Peterson, 1988). My contribution to the volume in honor of Ingvar was titled "Phoneme awareness and reading, from the old to the new millennium." My main conclusion was that the research on beginning reading instruction and our research on phonological remediation for reading disabilities suggested that there must be a third factor underlying the correlation between phonological awareness and reading ability. I wrote the following in my conclusion.

> A third possibility is that there could be a general processing problem in disabled readers that constrains growth in phoneme awareness and other reading processes independently, and in different ways at different stages of reading development (Wesseling & Reitsma, 2000). Progress in slow but accurate reading at beginning alphabetic stages of learning may be more closely linked to children's explicit awareness of phonemes. Later fluent reading and spelling, particularly of a deep orthography such as English, may be more dependent on other processes that are also constrained by a deeper third factor which is ultimately responsible for the correlation between early phoneme awareness and later reading. If a third factor does independently constrain growth in phoneme awareness and other reading-related skills, the remediation of deficits in phoneme awareness might not significantly diminish the constraints of that third factor on the other correlated reading skills. Scarborough (2001) has commented on a similar third-factor issue in the correlation between preschool speech/language impairments and later reading problems: "Preschool training that successfully ameliorates early speech/language impairments is not effective in reducing such children's risk for later reading problems, as it ought to be if those language weaknesses are a causal impediment to learning to read." A major challenge for the new millennium is to understand the nature of this third factor (p. 116).

On further reflection, I don't completely agree with Scarborough and some of my earlier thinking that the causal role of preschool speech/language impairments in later reading disabilities is ruled out by the remediation studies, and I don't think that is the necessary implication of our failure to show any unique benefits of phonological remediation in children past the third grade. My current thought is that while children with deficits in phonological awareness and decoding can improve in those skills as we measure them in our intervention studies, our measures may not be sensitive to the continuing underlying deficits in the automatic application of those skills in reading.

As I noted at the end of the last section, Byrne et al. (2008) and Byrne (Chapter 9) have proposed a general constraint on learning rate for phonological skills from preschool studies and for orthographic learning from the second-grade study. Learning rate could be a third factor underlying the slow growth in reading and related skills such that improving phonological awareness has limited influence on other untrained skills in the causal chain from phonological awareness to decoding to reading comprehension implied by the phonological deficit hypothesis. However, a general deficit in learning rate does not imply an absolute constraint on achievement level. For example, children with genetically compromised learning rate for phonological skills and word recognition might achieve normal or even superior levels of word recognition and reading comprehension if they compensate with extraordinarily high levels of reading practice, while their phonological skills and often their spelling may lag behind (Olson, 2004). Such differences in reading practice could contribute to the partial dissociation between phonological skills and reading ability in the population that have been found by Scarborough et al. (1998) and Hulslander et al. (in press).

It also now seems likely that there is at least some biologically based dissociation between efficiency in the associative memory systems of the posterior cortex linked to automatic word recognition that are described by Diehl, Frost, Mencl, and Pugh (Chapter 11), and the executive functions of the frontal lobes involved in complex reading comprehension (Speer, 2006). The partial dissociation of brain systems associated with word recognition and reading comprehension could underlie the genetic influence on listening and reading comprehension that is partly independent from genetic influence on phonological decoding and word recognition (Keenan et al., 2006). This genetic dissociation is most apparent when reading comprehension is measured with lengthy passages whose memory and understanding depend more on subjects' active building of situation models (Betjemann, Keenan, DeFries, & Olson, in review).

In summary, the phonological deficit hypothesis has motivated much of our research on the genetic and environmental etiology of reading disabilities and on our studies of specific methods for their remediation. The results of our research suggest the need for two important general qualifications of the hypothesis. The first qualification is that there likely are third-variable influences on the correlations between phoneme awareness, word decoding, and reading comprehension. The second is that there is evidence from our behavior genetic studies for partially independent genetic influences on word recognition and reading comprehension. Both of these qualifications have important implications for the etiology and remediation of reading disabilities and for individual differences in reading ability across the normal range. Putting aside these qualifications, it is likely that we would have been much less successful in our behavior-genetic and training studies without the early influence on our research from the phonological deficit hypothesis of Don Shankweiler and his colleagues.

ACKNOWLEDGMENTS

I am deeply grateful for the invaluable support of my colleagues in the Colorado Learning Disabilities Research Center, including Brian Byrne, John DeFries, Janice Keenan, Bruce Pennington, Shelley Smith, Sally Wadsworth, Erik Willcutt, and Barbara Wise. The research reported in my authored papers has been supported by grant numbers HD 27802, HD 38526, HD 11683, HD 22223, and HD11681-3 from the National Institutes of Health, and grants DP0663498 and DP0770805 to Brian Byrne from the Australian Research Council. I also would like to acknowledge the invaluable contributions of the twins and their families to our behavior-genetic research.

REFERENCES

Barron, R. W. (1980). Visual and phonological strategies in reading and spelling. In U. Frith (Ed.), *Cognitive processes in spelling* (pp. 195–215). New York: Academic Press.

Betjemann, R. S., Keenan, J. M., DeFries, J. C., & Olson, R. K. (in press). Choice of reading comprehension test influences the outcomes of genetic analyses. *Scientific Studies of Reading.*

Bond, G. L., & Dykstra, R. (1967). The cooperative research program in first-grade reading instruction. *Reading Research Quarterly*, *2*, 5–142.

Bruce, D. J. (1964). The analysis of word sounds by young children. *British Journal of Psychology*, *34*, 158–170.

Byrne, B., Coventry, W. L., Olson, R. K, Hulslander, J., Wadsworth, S., DeFries, J. C., et al. (2008). A behavior-genetic analysis of orthographic learning, spelling, and decoding. *Journal of Research in Reading*, *31*, 8–21.

Byrne, B., Fielding-Barnsley, R., & Ashley, L. (2000). Effects of preschool phoneme identity training after six years: Outcome level distinguished from rate of response. *Journal of Educational Psychology*, *92*, 659–667.

Byrne, B., Samuelsson, S., Wadsworth, S., Hulslander, J., Corley, R., DeFries, J. C., et al. (2007). Longitudinal twin study of early literacy development: Preschool through grade 1. *Reading and Writing: An Interdisciplinary Journal*, *20*, 77–102.

Castiglioni-Spalten, M., & Ehri, L. (2003). Phonemic awareness instruction: Contribution of articulatory segmentation to novice beginners reading and spelling. *Scientific Studies of Reading*, *7*, 25–52.

Chall, J. (1967). *Learning to read: The great debate*. New York: McGraw Hill.

Conrad, R. (1971). The chronology of the development of covert speech in children. *Developmental Psychology*, *5*(3), 398–405.

Cutting, L. E., & Scarborough, H. S. (2006). Prediction of reading comprehension: Relative contributions of word recognition, language proficiency, and other cognitive skills can depend on how comprehension is measured. *Scientific Studies of Reading*, *10*, 277–299.

DeFries, J. C., & Fulker, D. W. (1985). Multiple regression analysis of twin data. *Behavior Genetics*, *15*, 467–473.

DeFries, J. C., & Fulker, D. W. (1988). Multiple regression analysis of twin data: Etiology of deviant scores versus individual differences. *Acta Geneticae Medicae et Gemellologiae: Twin Research*, *37*, 205–216.

DeFries, J. C., Fulker, D. W., & LaBuda, M. C. (1987). Evidence for a genetic aetiology in reading disability of twins. *Nature*, *329*, 537–539.

Dunn, L. M., & Markwardt, F. C. (1970). *Peabody individual achievement test.* Circle Pines, MN: American Guidance Service.

Elbro, C., Borstrom, I., & Petersen, D. K. (1998). Predicting dyslexia from kindergarten: The importance of distinctness of phonological representations of lexical items. *Reading Research Quarterly*, *33*, 36–60.

Friend, A., & Olson, R. K. (2008). Phonological spelling and reading deficits in children with spelling disabilities. *Scientific Studies of Reading*, *12*, 90–105.

Gayán, J., & Olson, R. K. (2001). Genetic and environmental influences on orthographic and phonological skills in children with reading disabilities. *Developmental Neuropsychology*, *20*(2), 487–511.

Gayán, J., & Olson, R. K. (2003). Genetic and environmental influences on individual differences in printed word recognition. *Journal of Experimental Child Psychology*, *84*, 97–123.

Goodman, K. S., & Goodman, Y. M. (1979). Learning to read is natural. In L. B. Resnick & P. A. Weaver (Eds.), *Theory and practice of early reading* (Vol. 1, pp. 137–154). Hillsdale, NJ: Lawrence Erlbaum Associates.

Hoover, W. A., & Gough, P. B. (1990). The simple view of reading. *Reading and Writing*, *2*, 127–160.

Hulslander, J., Olson, R. K., Willcutt, E. G., & Wadsworth, S. J. (2010). Longitudinal stability of reading-related skills and their prediction of reading development. *Scientific Studies of Reading*, *14*(2), 111–136.

Keenan, J. M., Betjemann, R. S., & Olson, R. K. (2008). Reading comprehension tests vary in the skills they assess: Differential dependence on decoding and oral comprehension. *Scientific Studies of Reading*, *12*(3), 281–300.

Keenan, J. M., Betjemann, R., Wadsworth, S. J., DeFries, J. C., & Olson, R. K. (2006). Genetic and environmental influences on reading and listening comprehension. *Journal of Research in Reading*, *29*, 75–91.

Liberman, A., Cooper, F., Shankweiler, D., & Studdert-Kennedy, M. (1967). Perception of the speech code. *Psychological Review*, *75*, 431–461.

Liberman, A., Shankweiler, D., Fisher, F. W., & Carter, B. (1974). Explicit syllable and phoneme segmentation in the young child. *Journal of Experimental Child Psychology*, *18*, 201–212.

Liberman, I. Y., Shankweiler, D., Liberman, A. M., Fowler, C. A., & Fischer, F. W. (1977). Phonetic segmentation and recoding in the beginning reader. In A.S. Reber & D. L. Scarborough (Eds.), *Toward a psychology of reading*: *The proceedings of the CUNY conferences* (pp. 207–225). New York: Erlbaum.

Lindamood, C., & Lindamood, P. (1975). *Auditory discrimination in depth.* Columbus, OH: MacMillan/McGraw Hill.

Lundberg, I., Frost, J., & Petersen, O. (1988). Effects of an extensive program for stimulating phonological awareness in preschool children. *Reading Research Quarterly*, *23*, 263–284.

Mark, L. S., Shankweiler, D., Liberman, I. Y., & Fowler, C. A. (1977). Phonetic recoding and reading difficulty in beginning readers. *Memory & Cognition*, *5*, 623–629.

Markwardt, F. C., Jr. (1989). *Peabody individual achievement test-revised.* Circle Pines, MN: American Guidance Service.

Metsala, J. L., Stanovich, K. E., & Brown, G. D. A. (1998). Regularity effects and the phonological deficit model of reading disabilities: A meta-analytic review. *Journal of Educational Psychology*, *90*(2), 279–293.

Neale, M. C., Boker, S. M., Xie, G., & Maes, H. H. (2002). *Mx: Statistical modeling* (6th ed.). Richmond, VA: Virginia Commonwealth University.

Olson, R. K., Forsberg, H., Wise, B., & Rack, J. (1994). Measurement of word recognition, orthographic, and phonological skills. In G.R. Lyon (Ed.), *Frames of reference for the assessment of learning disabilities: New views on measurement issues* (pp. 243–277). Baltimore, MD: Paul H. Brookes.

Olson, R. K. (1985). Disabled reading processes and cognitive profiles. In D. Gray & J. Kavanagh (Eds.), *Biobehavioral measures of dyslexia* (pp. 215–244). Parkton, MD: York Press.

Olson, R. K. (2002). Phoneme awareness and reading, from the old to the new millenium. In E. Hjelmquist & C. von Euler (Eds.), *Dyslexia and literacy: A tribute to Ingvar Lundberg* (pp. 100–116). London: Whurr Publishers.

Olson, R. K. (2004). Genes, environment, and the components of the reading process. *Perspectives*, *30*(3), 6–9.

Olson, R. K., Davidson, B. J., Kliegl, R., & Davies, S. E. (1984). Development of phonetic memory in disabled and normal readers. *Journal of Experimental Child Psychology*, *37*, 187–206.

Olson, R. K., Foltz, G., & Wise, B. (1986). Reading instruction and remediation with the aid of computer speech. *Behavior Research Methods, Instruments, and Computers*, *18*, 93–99.

Olson, R. K., Kliegl, R., Davidson, B. J., & Foltz, G. (1985). Individual and developmental differences in reading disability. In G. E. MacKinnon & T. G. Waller (Eds.), *Reading research: Advances in theory and practice* (Vol. 4, pp. 1–64). New York: Academic Press.

Olson, R. K., & Wise, B. W. (1992). Reading on the computer with orthographic and speech feedback: An overview of the Colorado Remedial Reading Project. *Reading and Writing: An Interdisciplinary Journal*, *4*, 107–144.

Olson, R. K., Wise, B., Conners, F., Rack, J., & Fulker, D. (1989). Specific deficits in component reading and language skills: Genetic and environmental influences. *Journal of Learning Disabilities*, *22*, 339–348.

Palinscar, A. S., & Brown, A. L. (1984). Reciprocal teaching of comprehension-fostering and comprehension-monitoring activity. *Cognition and Instruction*, *2*, 117–175.

Perfetti, C. A. (1985). *Reading ability*. New York: Oxford University Press.

Plomin, R., DeFries, J. C., McClearn, G. E., & McGuffin, P. (2008). *Behavioral genetics* (5th ed.). New York: Worth.

Purcell, S., & Sham, P. C. (2003). A model-fitting implementation of the DeFries-Fulker model for selected twin data. *Behavior Genetics*, *33*, 271–278.

Rack, J. P., Snowling, M. J., & Olson, R. K. (1992). The nonword reading deficit in developmental dyslexia: A review. *Reading Research Quarterly*, *27*(1), 28–53.

Scarborough, H. S. (2001). Connecting early language and literacy to later reading (dis) abilities: Evidence, theory, and practice. In S. Neuman & D. Dickinson (Eds.), *Handbook for early literacy Research* (pp. 97–110). New York: Guilford Press.

Scarborough, H. S., Ehri, L. C., Olson, R. K., & Fowler, A. E. (1998). The fate of phonemic awareness beyond the elementary school years. *Scientific Studies of Reading*, *2*, 115–142.

Shankweiler, D. (1989). How problems of comprehension are related to difficulties in decoding. In D. Shankweiler & I. Y. Liberman (Eds.), *Phonology and reading disability: Solving the reading puzzle*. Ann Arbor, MI: University of Michigan Press.

Shankweiler, D., Liberman, I. Y., Mark, L. S., Fowler, C. A., & Fischer, F. W. (1979). The speech code and learning to read. *Journal of Experimental Psychology: Learning, Memory, and Cognition*, *5*, 531–545.

Snowling, M. J. (1981). Phonemic deficits in developmental dyslexia. *Psychological Research*, *43*, 219–234.

Speer, N. (2006). Text comprehension processes in the brain. *Dissertation Abstracts International: Section B: The Sciences and Engineering*, *67*(2-B), 1177.

Torgesen, J., Alexander, A., Wagner, R., Voeller, K., Conway, T., & Rose, E. (2001). Intensive remedial instruction for children with severe reading disabilities: Immediate and long-term outcomes from two instructional approaches. *Journal of Learning Disabilities*, *34*, 33–58.

Wesseling, R., & Reitsma, P. (2000). The transient role of explicit phonological recoding for reading acquisition. *Reading and Writing: An Interdisciplinary Journal*, *13*, 313–336.

Wise, B. W., Olson, R. K., Anstett, M., Andrews, L., Terjak, M., Schneider, V., et al. (1989). Implementing a long-term computerized remedial reading program with synthetic speech feedback: Hardware, software, and real-world issues. *Behavior Research Methods, Instruments, and Computers*, *21*, 173–180.

Wise, B. W., Ring, J., & Olson, R. K. (1999). Training phonological awareness with and without attention to articulation. *Journal of Experimental Child Psychology*, *72*, 271–304.

Wise, B. W., Ring, J., & Olson, R. K. (2000). Individual differences in gains from computer-assisted remedial reading with more emphasis on phonological analysis or accurate reading in context. *Journal of Experimental Child Psychology*, *77*, 197–235.

11 Neuroimaging and the Phonological Deficit Hypothesis

Joshua John Diehl
Haskins Laboratories
and
University of Notre Dame
Stephen J. Frost and W. Einar Mencl
Haskins Laboratories
Kenneth R. Pugh
Haskins Laboratories
and
University of Connecticut

Neuroimaging technology has provided researchers with access to the brain on multiple dimensions, including anatomy and functional activity. Advances in this technology have vastly improved our knowledge of the neural circuitry related to reading, and the role of phonological processing in reading skill. The phonological deficit hypothesis (PDH; I. Y. Liberman, Shankweiler, & A. M. Liberman, 1989; Shankweiler & Crain, 1986; Shankweiler et al., 1995) is a theory that posits deficits in phonological processing; connecting phonemes to letters is the core deficit of reading disability (RD). In this chapter, we present an overview of what imaging tells us about the reading circuit in the brain. We then take a look at the history of neuroimaging research on skilled and impaired reading, and examine how the PDH has facilitated the progression of knowledge in this area. Finally, we address current and future directions of research, including emerging research on precursors to reading skills and deficits, cross-cultural studies, and reading interventions.

THE READING CIRCUIT

The neural structures and functions involved in skilled reading and the acquisition of that skill (hereafter "the reading circuit") have been outlined in several reviews (Frost, Landi, Mencl, Sandak, Fulbright, Tejada, et al., 2009; Pugh, Mencl, Jenner, et al., 2000; Pugh, Sandak, Frost, Moore, & Mencl, 2005; Vellutino, Fletcher, Snowling, & Scanlon, 2004). Here, we provide a brief summary of these findings.

There appear to be three major components in the reading circuit: (a) an anterior system primarily in the posterior portion of the inferior frontal gyrus, (b) a posterior dorsal system in temporo-parietal cortex, and (c) a posterior ventral system in occipito-temporal cortex and adjacent areas. Systematic research suggests that each of these areas has a specialized role in the reading process. The anterior system is tuned to syntactic and phonological processing in reading, and is hypothesized to be particularly important for speech-motor coding and learning new words (T. T. Brown et al., 2005; Church, Coalson, Lugar, Petersen, & Schlaggar, 2008; Pugh, Mencl, Shaywitz, et al., 2000; Pugh et al., 1996). The posterior dorsal system, which includes posterior portions of the superior temporal gyrus (Wernicke's area) and extends into the angular and supramarginal gyri in the inferior parietal lobule, is important for learning to read new words. Its specific functions appear to involve mapping orthography onto phonology and binding them together with semantic features (Price, Winterburn, Giraud, Moore, & Noppeney, 2003). The posterior ventral system includes extrastriate areas, portions of the middle and inferior temporal gyrus, and a left inferior occipito-temporal/fusiform region known as the visual word form area (Cohen & Dehaene, 2004; Cohen et al., 2000, 2002). Engagement of this area appears to be a late-developing signature for skilled and fluent word identification (B. A. Shaywitz et al., 2002; S. E. Shaywitz et al., 2003).

Research has shown that these areas are differently engaged by the act of reading as a function of reader skill and the presence/absence of RD. Skilled readers tend to have lateralized left hemisphere activity on reading tasks (see Pugh et al., 1996, among many others). Beginning readers appear to rely on the anterior and posterior dorsal systems more heavily, whereas skilled readers rely on the posterior ventral system when presented with familiar material (T. T. Brown et al., 2005; Church et al., 2008; B. A. Shaywitz et al., 2002; S. E. Shaywitz et al., 2003). In contrast, it is reported that individuals with RD tend to exhibit underactivation of the left hemisphere posterior structures compared to non-impaired controls and to exhibit right hemisphere and frontal activation, perhaps reflecting compensation for deficient phonological processing (Pugh, Mencl, Shaywitz, et al., 2000; Rippon & Brunswick, 2000; S. E. Shaywitz et al.). Individuals with RD also fail to show a developmental trend of increased specialization of the ventral left hemisphere areas for print (B. A. Shaywitz et al.)

In general, the areas in the brain that have been implicated in reading show significant overlap with traditional left-lateralized language areas (such as Broca's area and Wernicke's area). More specifically, reading performance (behaviorally and neurally) reflects the difficulties of phonological processing, which has long been thought to play a crucial role in RD. In the following section, we describe how neuroimaging has further underscored the importance of phonological processing in reading. Moreover, we highlight how the advancement in our knowledge of how printed material is processed in the brain has been facilitated by the PDH and the methodological paradigms driven by it.

HISTORICAL PERSPECTIVE ON NEUROIMAGING AND THE READING CIRCUIT

In order to understand how neuroimaging and the PDH have mutually influenced each other, it is important to put the current state of research and theory in a historical context. This section tracks the relationship between the PDH and our understanding of the neural processes involved in reading through several decades of methodological developments in neuroimaging.

Theories That Predate Neuroimaging

Behavioral research over the past few decades has consistently emphasized the importance of phonological processing for reading skill acquisition (I. Y. Liberman et al., 1989; Shankweiler & Crain, 1986; Shankweiler et al., 1995; Vellutino et al., 2004). From both neurobiological and sociocultural perspectives, it is not surprising (but also not inevitable) that spoken language has primacy over written language, both in time of development and in utilization (A. M. Liberman, 1992; Schlaggar & McCandliss, 2007). Spoken language is mastered naturally by almost all individuals without direct instruction, but reading skill is more variable, with failure occurring in significant numbers of children within every language community that has a written form. Moreover, written language is essentially the spoken language written down; alphabetic writing systems represent phonological language forms. Successful reading requires a mastery of the internal phonological structure of language in relation to the orthography (i.e., the alphabetic principle; I. Y. Liberman et al.). Therefore, it follows that deficits in phonological systems that support spoken language would also affect an individual's ability to learn to read. Similarly, it is likely that neurobiological systems for reading rely on existing areas that support the spoken language abilities that have previously developed.

At about the time neuroimaging was emerging as a useful tool, there were a number of theories of the mechanisms underlying reading disorders based on behavioral findings. These theories included (but were not limited to) ones that hypothesized deficits in auditory discrimination (Tallal, Miller, & Fitch, 1993), motor timing (Wolff, Cohen, & Drake, 1984), verbal working memory (Hulme & Roodenrys, 1995), visual processing and the magnocellular deficit hypothesis (Eden, VanMeter, Rumsey, Maisog, & Zeffiro, 1996), and phonological awareness and the PDH (Goswami & Bryant, 1990; I. Y. Liberman et al., 1989; Shankweiler & Crain, 1986). Deficits in phonological awareness were the most consistent findings across research groups and often constituted the strongest single predictor of literacy acquisition (Fletcher et al., 1994; Goswami & Bryant; Shankweiler et al., 1995; Share, Jorm, Maclean, & Matthews, 1984; Stanovich & Siegel, 1994). Thus, it was argued that reading deficits were primarily a result of a general weakness in phonological processing (Olson, Wise, Connors, & Rack, 1990; Shankweiler et al.; Vellutino & Scanlon, 1991; Wagner, Torgesen, Laughon, Simmons, & Rashotte, 1993); however, debate continued as to whether this deficit might be a downstream consequence of some other underlying factor.

Neuroanatomy

Early Anatomical Discoveries: Soft Signs, Lesions, and Postmortem Discoveries

Even before neuroimaging methods became widely used, it was thought that neurological abnormalities were present in RD (see Vellutino et al., 2004, for a review). One type of evidence came from clinical indications, or "soft signs," of neurological dysfunction, including perceptual difficulties and motor clumsiness, among others (Vellutino et al.). There were also established associations between reading impairment and specific aspects of phonological processing such as poor retention of phonological information in verbal working memory (Brady, 1991; Shankweiler, Liberman, Mark, Fowler, & Fischer, 1979).

Before neuroimaging, the postmortem examination of individuals with brain damage was one of the only available methods for understanding the neurobiology of normal and impaired cognitive functioning. Some individuals with focal brain lesions displayed dissociations of reading abilities from other skills, and this led to early hypotheses about what brain regions might be involved in RD (Vellutino et al., 2004). Based on such data, Dejerine (1891) was one of the first to report that lesions in the angular gyrus might be related to the reading deficits in individuals with acquired dyslexia. Later, Hinschelwood (1917) conjectured that the same area might be related to developmental dyslexia.

Early postmortem studies revealed neuroanatomical atypicalities in the brains of individuals with reading difficulties. One region of interest was the planum temporale of the left temporal lobe, an area thought to support aspects of language functioning. In non-impaired adults, postmortem examination revealed that the planum temporale area tended to be larger in the left hemisphere (Geschwind & Levitsky, 1968). Individuals with dyslexia, however, usually did not show this asymmetry (and in some cases showed a reversal of asymmetry), a finding that seemed to implicate language-related structures in reading (Galaburda, Sherman, Rosen, Aboitiz, & Geschwind, 1985; Humphreys, Kaufmann, & Galaburda, 1990). Recently, Galaburda (2006) has used postmortem histological findings to argue that individuals with RD may have a congenital abnormality of brain structure, possibly as a result of errors in neuronal migration, which precedes reading (and perhaps) language development (e.g., Galaburda & Cestnick, 2003). For a review of findings beyond those highlighted in this section, see Galaburda (2006).

Anatomical Neuroimaging

Neuroimaging has provided a new tool for probing the neuroanatomy of individuals with neurodevelopmental disorders. Magnetic resonance imaging (MRI) allows the examination of brain structures in vivo. Findings from MRI studies of individuals with RD were more mixed than the early postmortem research. For example, although some postmortem studies had found a reversal of asymmetry in the planum temporale, some MRI studies on RD found left hemisphere–right hemisphere symmetry (Hynd, Semrud-Clikman, Lorys, Novey, & Eliopulos, 1990; Larsen, Høien, Lundberg, & Odegarrd, 1990), some found no differences

(Rumsey et al., 1997; Schultz et al., 1994), whereas others replicated the post-mortem findings of the increased right hemisphere size (Hynd et al.). Studies that examined cortical differences in the corpus callosum and temporo-parietal areas were also inconsistent, and even when differences between individuals with RD and non-impaired controls were present, the differences were relatively small (Pennington, 1999; Schultz et al.; Vellutino et al., 2004). Still, a growing number of studies have found structural differences between individuals with and without RD that show a pronounced overlap with regions identified as being important for reading, including temporo-parietal (Brambati et al., 2004; W. E. Brown et al., 2001), inferior frontal (W. E. Brown et al.; Eckert et al., 2003), and (less consistently) occipito-temporal sites (Kronbichler et al., 2008).

Some recent studies have suggested that individual differences in anatomy might predict reading and oral language impairments (Leonard, Eckert, Givens, Berninger, & Eden, 2006). Recently, Hoeft et al. (2007) used voxel-based morphometry to measure gray and white matter structure, and found that the presence of greater gray matter density in the right fusiform gyrus and greater white matter density in the left superior temporal and inferior parietal regions predicted later decoding ability. Although the findings summarized here are intriguing, it is as yet unclear why the pattern of morphological differences is inconsistent across studies. See Eckert (2004) and Leonard et al. (2001) for reviews.

The use of diffusion tensor imaging (DTI) has shown promise as an approach to examining white matter tracts. Results from a number of studies using DTI have indicated that individuals with dyslexia have less white matter development in left hemisphere, language-related areas, including reduced myelination in left temporo-parietal regions that are implicated in language processing (Beaulieu et al., 2005; Klingberg et al., 2000; Niogi & McCandliss, 2006). A study of a group of children with a range of reading abilities, Deutsch et al. (2005) showed that white matter volume in the left hemisphere was positively correlated with reading performance. Furthermore, Dougherty et al. (2007) have used DTI data to show that interhemispheric connectivity in the temporal-collosal pathway was positively correlated with phonemic awareness.

Neuroanatomical research has provided insight into the neural basis of reading in RD. The most consistent finding demonstrates group differences in areas traditionally thought to be devoted to language. Recent technological advances, including DTI, will be important for identifying major neuroanatomical differences that could be a signature of RD.

Functional Neuroimaging

Over the past decade, there has been a growing interest in online measures of brain function in order to achieve better understanding of the neural circuitry involved in reading. The expectation was that functional neuroimaging would enable identification of cortical networks related to reading. The identification of cortical networks was especially important for understanding RD because reading theories had developed to a level of complexity that involved interactive processes and networks of activity that would not necessarily be confined to a specific area (Horwitz, Rumsey, & Donohue, 1998; Pugh, Mencl, Shaywitz, et al., 2000). Two main classes of functional neuroimaging techniques have emerged. The first is based on electrophysiological indicators of brain activity, including electro-encephalography (EEG) and magneto-encephalography (MEG). The second is based on hemodynamic measures of brain activity and includes functional MRI (fMRI) and positron emission tomography (PET).

Electrophysiological Imaging

Electrophysiological measures of brain activity, starting with EEG, were among the first measures to allow researchers to associate behavior with neural responses. These measures have the advantage of possessing fine-grained temporal resolution, which is particularly important for exploring the dynamic nature of reading and language processing. They do, however, lack the spatial resolution of fMRI or PET. EEG, and more recently MEG, have proven to be sensitive to the temporal progression of activity in language-specific areas even with simple language tasks (e.g., Breier, Simos, Zouridakis, & Papanicolaou, 1998; Papanicolaou et al., 1999; Simos et al., 1999).

Nonetheless, electrophysiological studies (EEG, MEG, and evoked response potentials) have provided support for the involvement of core-language areas in RD, particularly areas involved in phonological processing. In one study, children with dyslexia did not engage or were much slower to engage the temporo-occipital region when passively viewing words, whereas controls showed pronounced activation (Salmelin, Service, Kiesila, Uutela, & Salonen, 1996). When the task targeted phonological processing, group differences in neural activity became most pronounced (Duffy, Denckla, Bartels, & Sandini, 2004; Spironelli, Penolazzi, & Angrilli, 2008; Spironelli, Penolazzi, Vio, & Angrilli, 2006). For example, when both phonological and visual processing were measured separately, individuals with RD showed increased frontal activity only during the phonological task, and also showed a right hemisphere shift in parieto-occipital activity in both tasks when compared to controls (Rippon & Brunswick, 2000). This provides further support for left hemisphere dysfunction, and right hemisphere compensation for this deficit. There are also several studies that have found differences in intra- and interhemispheric coherence (Arns, Peters, Breteler, & Verhoeven, 2007; Leisman & Ashkenazi, 1980; Sklar, Hanley, & Simmons, 1972), although the involvement of specific cortical areas or regions is often difficult to interpret. Other studies have examined activation patterns relative to subtypes of RD, although the delineation and categorization of subtypes is a matter of significant debate (Arns et al.).

Although electrophysiological methods show great sensitivity to temporal changes in processing, one disadvantage is the lack of spatial sensitivity of these measures, which is why electrophysiological studies often refer to hemispheres and quadrants rather than specific neural structures or functional areas. By contrast, hemodynamic measures of neural activity tend to have good spatial resolution and poor temporal resolution, and the presence of these complementary strengths/limitations accentuates the need for both measures. Still, electrophysiological data provide compelling and replicated evidence for the role of language areas in the left hemisphere in reading tasks, and reduced activity patterns in these areas during tasks that specifically tax phonological processing in individuals with RD. For findings from electrophysiological research in addition to those we have highlighted in this section, see recent reviews (Goswami, 2008; Pammer, 2009).

Hemodynamic Measures of Neural Activity

The earliest hemodynamic measure of neural activity was PET. It involves the injection of a radioactive tracer, which emits gamma rays as the result of neural metabolic activity as a signal of the functional involvement of brain areas. PET provided the first opportunity for researchers to isolate neuroanatomical areas engaged during specific cognitive tasks. (e.g., Fox & Mintun, 1989; Mintun, Fox, & Raichle, 1989; Petersen, Fox, Posner, Mintun, & Raichle, 1989; Petersen, Fox, Snyder, & Raichle, 1990). The advent of fMRI, which does not require a tracer, made it possible, with a noninvasive procedure, to detect the location and magnitude of activity with better spatial resolution than PET (Constable, McCarthy, Allison, Anderson, & Gore, 1993; Ogawa, Lee, Nayak, & Glynn, 1990; Ogawa et al., 1992; B. A. Shaywitz et al., 1995). As with all functional imaging measures, task design is crucial to the relevance of fMRI findings to inferences about brain–behavior connections that researchers are attempting to make. One approach is cognitive subtraction, which involves using a series of tasks thought to differ minimally on a single characteristic of interest. The "cognitive subtraction" of the results of one task from the results of another putatively isolates the neural activity related to the desired behavior. Cognitive subtraction provides strong evidence for localization of function. In this section, we highlight some of the major findings in this area, focusing on how methodology has shaped the way we understand the processing of printed material in skilled and impaired readers. For the purposes of this chapter, we focus mainly on the work that is directly relevant to the PDH.

An important step in understanding neural markers for reading disorder was the identification of the cortical regions functionally involved in reading. Although early fMRI studies found group differences in left hemisphere activation between individuals with RD and controls (Rumsey et al., 1992; Wood, Flowers, Buchsbaum, & Tallal, 1991), the cortical regions involved in specific aspects of word reading—orthographic, phonological, and lexical–semantic processing—were not identified until later (Pugh et al., 1996). Initial studies attempting to localize component processes utilized a series of hierarchical subtractions (see Table 11.1). For example, by subtracting activation for a visuospatial task from activation for a task involving both visuospatial and orthographic processing, Pugh et al. were able to isolate a unique activation for orthographic processing in lateral extrastriate cortex. They also found that phonological processing for both real words and nonwords engaged the inferior frontal gyrus as well as temporal regions. Lexical–semantic processing was found to engage middle and superior temporal gyri. The results of Pugh

TABLE 11.1
Model for Functional Neuroimaging Studies of Dyslexia to Allow for Comparisons Between Orthographic, Lexical–Semantic, and Phonological Processes

Condition Levels	Task Demands[a]	Stimulus Example
1. Visuospatial	Identify whether two line patterns are the same or different	Same = *N/* and *N/* Different = */N* and *N/*
2. Visuospatial + orthographic	Identify whether two consonant strings are the same or different, where capitalization is the differentiating characteristic	Same = bbCb and bbCb Different = bbCb and bBcb
3. Visuospatial + orthographic + phonological[b,c]	Identify whether two single letters rhyme	Same = B and C Different = B and F
4. Visuospatial + orthographic + phonological[d]	Identify whether two pseudo-words rhyme	Same = lete and jeat Different = lete and jiff
5. Visuospatial + orthographic + phonological + semantic	Identify whether two words are in the same semantic category	Same = corn and rice Different = corn and cart

[a] Participant pushed a button for every pair that was the same visually (1 and 2), rhymed (3 and 4), or was in the same semantic category (5). Children were told not to respond if stimulus did not meet these criteria.

[b] This component was not used until S. E. Shaywitz et al. (1998).

[c] This component places a smaller demand on orthography, in comparison to #4.

[d] This component places a greater demand on orthography, in comparison to #3.

et al. have been replicated in MEG using the same cognitive subtraction method (Breier, Simos, Zouridakis, & Papanicolaou, 1999) and PET (Herbster, Mintun, Nebes, & Becker, 1997).

An important methodological advance was the application of brain–behavior analyses. For example, Pugh et al. examined correlations between task-dependent BOLD activation and a behavioral measure of phonological processing (Pugh et al., 1997). Participants had performed a lexical decision task outside of the MRI scanner, providing behavioral measures of sensitivity to grapheme–phoneme regularity (a marker of phonological processing). These findings were then analyzed with previously collected brain activation patterns from fMRI using the paradigm in Table 11.1. Individual differences in lexical decision performance were found to correlate with the magnitude of left-lateralized activation in the inferior frontal gyrus. Specifically, an increased regularity effect was associated with more nearly bilateral activity, and participants who were less sensitive to the regularity effect exhibited more left-lateralized activation. This finding confirmed the role of the inferior frontal gyrus in phonological processing.

As the neural signature for skilled reading became better understood, the next step was to identify how these areas were disrupted in adults with developmental reading disorders (S. E. Shaywitz et al., 1998). S. E. Shaywitz et al. argued that inconsistencies in previous functional imaging studies (Eden et al., 1996; Flowers, Wood, & Naylor, 1991; Gross-Glenn et al., 1991; Paulesu et al., 1996; Rumsey et al., 1992, 1997; Salmelin et al., 1996) were the result of a methodology that measured multiple overlapping reading processes, failing to systematically isolate each of the components. S. E. Shaywitz et al. used a design similar to that of Pugh et al. (1996) but added a letter rhyme identification task to the paradigm (level #3, see Table 11.1) to examine further the role of orthography in reading. They found that adults with dyslexia failed to engage posterior cortical structures (Wernicke's area, angular gyrus, occipito-temporal cortex) and tended to over-engage anterior structures (e.g., inferior frontal gyrus and related areas), and importantly that group differences in these areas increased as the demands for phonological processing became greater. These findings have held up fairly well in subsequent studies (e.g., Brunswick, McCrory, Price, Frith, & Frith, 1999; Rumsey et al., 1997).

Shaywitz et al. then extended their findings to a large cross-sectional sample of RD and non-impaired children aged 7–17 years, looking at developmental changes in the reading circuit (B. A. Shaywitz et al., 2002). The paradigm in Table 11.1 was used, although case matching for single letters was used rather than letter strings. Brain activation was correlated with chronological age to examine development, and also with reading skill (after age was covaried). Increases in reading skill were associated with increased specialization for print of the ventral left hemisphere occipito-temporal areas, which indicated that this area is important for skilled reading. Children with RD tended to have greater activation in frontal areas (left and right inferior frontal gyrus) than non-impaired children, especially as they grew older. This study was one of the first to provide empirical support for the long-held idea that developmental and acquired dyslexia had similar neural disruptions. It also suggested the possibility of neurodevelopmental changes in RD indicating that there may be plasticity in the brain that is amenable to intervention. Recent studies have shown similar results that support the role of temporo-parietal regions and lateral frontal regions in printed word learning in children and temporo-occipital (visual word form area) regions in skilled reading in several different types of reading paradigms (e.g., T. T. Brown et al., 2005; Church et al., 2008). Moreover, findings indicate that there are divergent neurodevelopmental patterns in individuals with RD, some of whom have persistent reading difficulties, and others that show marked improvement in reading skill (S. E. Shaywitz et al., 2003).

In addition to isolating the language-related areas involved in skilled and disabled reading, studies have also highlighted relationships between phonological awareness and patterns of brain activity during both language and reading tasks. Frost, Landi et al. (2009) examined the relationship between phonological awareness and brain activation patterns in children aged 6–10 years, both for print and for speech. Individual differences in behavioral measures of phonological awareness were correlated with activation differences for modality (print vs. speech) and pronounceability (printed pseudo-words vs. consonant strings) in several language-related areas, particularly the superior temporal gyrus. The findings showed that greater phonological awareness was associated with activation by print of areas primarily active for speech, and, further, that the response to print in speech areas was selective; these were activated by phonologically well-structured print tokens but not by unpronounceable consonant strings. The findings underline the importance of phonological processing in early reading development and suggest that differences in the magnitude of activation in speech areas may serve as an early predictor of reading outcome (cf. Turkeltaub, Lynn, Flowers, Zeffiro, & Eden, 2003).

In total, this series of studies suggests that neural systems involved in reading are subject to systematic developmental change in both typical and atypical development, and that phonological awareness is linked to neural activity in reading and language tasks, highlighting its importance for the development of skill in reading. Children rely chiefly on phonological processing mechanisms in anterior and temporo-parietal regions when they are first learning to read, and that phonological processing appears to play a role in the development of a left hemisphere occipito-temporal region that is important for skilled reading (Pugh et al., 2001). A fuller account of the neural signature of RD will require focus not only on within-region group differences, but also on group differences in patterns of interregional correlations or functional connectivity (Friston, 1994; Horwitz, 1994; Horwitz et al., 1992; McIntosh & Gonzalez-Lima, 1994; Pugh, Mencl, Shaywitz, et al., 2000) to determine how these putative reading areas interact with each other during the processing of text.

An appreciation for the interaction between brain regions, or functional connectivity, involved in reading will allow a deeper understanding of RD (Pugh, Mencl, Shaywitz, et al., 2000). Functional connectivity is typically measured as correlations in activation levels among brain regions during a task. Horwitz et al. (1998), using PET, were the first to note disruptions in functional connectivity in adults with dyslexia between areas traditionally thought to be involved in reading (left angular gyrus, visual association areas, and Wernicke's area), although it was unclear whether the reduced connectivity was specific to areas associated with reading, or part of a more global deficit in connectivity.

Pugh, Mencl, Shaywitz, et al. (2000) asked directly whether differences in connectivity could be derived from predictions derived from the PDH. Using the paradigm in Table 11.1 to compare adults with RD and non-impaired readers, Pugh et al. found that connectivity in adults with RD was deficient only on tasks that relied on phonological assembly. For example, non-impaired readers displayed robust functional connectivity on all tasks, but the RD group demonstrated functional connectivity only on the letter-case and single-letter rhyming tasks, which did not require complex phonological assembly. Reduced left hemisphere functional connectivity was found only when phonological processing was important (e.g., nonword rhyming vs. semantic category judgment). Importantly, the

RD group appeared to show increased right hemisphere activation in homologous structures, suggesting a rightward compensatory shift in neural engagement.

In another study using a line judgment task, a nonword rhyming task, and a semantic category judgment task (levels 1, 4, and 5 in Table 11.1), a group of adults with persisting RD was compared to a group who were poor readers as children but had improved with age and to a non-impaired group of adults (S. E. Shaywitz et al., 2003). An interesting developmental pattern emerged. Similar to Pugh, Mencl, Shaywitz, et al. (2000), the results indicated that the RD group who had shown improvement in reading abilities tended to show connectivity between left hemisphere ventral (temporo-occipital) region and right hemisphere regions typically associated with working memory, whereas the non-impaired group showed the expected left hemisphere connectivity between reading areas. This suggested that readers who had improved (but were not skilled readers) were relying on compensatory strategies for poor basic reading skills, possibly involving working memory, instead of the typical phonologically based processing networks. In addition, persistently poor readers failed to activate posterior regions associated with learning new words when presented with pseudo-words. This contrasts with the pattern displayed by skilled readers, who show strong connections between the left occipito-temporal (visual word form area) region and Broca's area, and weak connections between areas thought to be involved in word learning (e.g., left angular gyrus and Broca's area, T. T. Brown et al., 2005; Church et al., 2008; S. E. Shaywitz et al., 2003).

Intervention as an Experiment

Several studies have shown that phonologically based interventions for individuals with RD can lead to improvements in reading skill and concomitant changes in brain activation patterns to more closely resemble those of individuals with normal reading skills (Simos et al., 2002; Temple et al., 2003). Furthermore, the effects of phonologically mediated reading intervention have been shown to remain stable one year post-intervention (B. A. Shaywitz et al., 2004). Varying the treatment conditions within subjects can also be used to test questions relating to the PDH. In a word learning study on a normative sample, Sandak et al. (2004) investigated the relative efficacy of phonological, orthographic, and semantic cues. Participants were instructed to attend to one of the three cue types when attempting to learn pseudo-words. Findings indicated that phonological and semantic cues similarly facilitated learning as indexed through behavioral (accuracy) measures. However, words acquired through phonologic or semantic training yielded distinct brain activation patterns. Phonological training supported increased sensitivity of the visual word form area to the phonological structure of words, whereas semantic training was associated with greater bilateral activation in superior and medial temporal gyri, regions that are involved in the formation and recall of semantic representations. Both training regimens were effective in the remediation of RDs, but each acted on a distinct system that was important for skilled reading. This study highlights the mutually supporting roles of well-designed treatment studies for understanding basic neural mechanisms in reading and, for evaluating changes resulting from the treatment of neurodevelopmental reading disorders.

Summary of Neuroimaging Findings

In sum, neuroanatomical and functional neuroimaging studies using a variety of techniques have been important for understanding the role of phonological processing in reading, and also for creation of a neurological model of the relationship between phonological processing and reading, including disabled reading. Skilled and impaired readers have contrasting developmental patterns of activation and connectivity. Impaired readers show frontward and rightward shifts in activation, relative to skilled readers, a finding that suggests less reliance on phonological processing and more on visual processing or other right hemisphere–based faculties. A crucial point is that progress would not have been made in these research areas without the development of neurobehavioral paradigms that could be replicated across studies, across research groups, and across populations.

CURRENT AND FUTURE DIRECTIONS

Several ongoing areas of research will be crucial to improving our knowledge of reading disabilities. These include further investigations of (a) the role that phonological awareness and phonological deficits play in initial reading acquisition, (b) determining what cross-linguistic studies can tell us about the PDH, and (c) determining how we can improve reading interventions and, at the same time, how treatment studies can experimentally test the PDH.

Although most current research on reading development uses cross-sectional designs, there is a need to examine development longitudinally with integrated brain and behavior designs. First, a major question in the field that requires longitudinal study is to identify the behavioral and neurobiological preconditions for successful literacy acquisition. It will be important to examine children at risk for reading failure using research designs that relate multiple levels of analysis through time, including behavior, genetics, neuroanatomy, neurochemistry, and neurocircuitry. Second, we know that phonemic awareness scores reflect reading readiness, but how do children with higher reading readiness differ in initial brain organization? Recent research reviewed in this chapter suggests that children who are developing normally in phonological skills utilize brain systems specialized for spoken language processing to process visual graphemes (e.g., Frost, Sandak, Mencl, Landi, Rueckl, Katz et al., 2009; Petersson, Reis, Askelöf, Castro-Caldas, & Ingvar, 2000; Petersson, Silva, Castro-Caldas, Ingvar, & Reis, 2007). What are the preconditions that allow phonological processing systems acquired for spoken language to adapt to different (but related) forms of communication (as in printed language)?

Cross-linguistic research affords comparisons between systems of writing that differ in orthographic depth (i.e., the ease by which a reader can access pronunciation from spelling) in order to determine what aspects of RD are universal and what aspects might be culturally driven. Important, research has found substantial overlap in the neural signature for skilled and impaired reading across languages (Paulesu et al., 2000, 2001). Still, there may be language-specific differences that arise from the complexity of the mapping between phonology and orthography for a given language (although see Bergmann & Wimmer, 2008, for different findings). For example, research is starting to show that for readers of Mandarin Chinese (where the writing system lacks direct phoneme-to-grapheme mappings) orthographic processing is more important for the development of skilled reading than for English readers (Tan, Spinks, Eden, Perfetti, & Siok, 2005). Moreover, Chinese readers who have RD show differences in frontal activation but do not show the differences in posterior activation seen in readers of alphabetic writing systems with RD (Siok, Niu, Jin, Perfetti, & Tan, 2008). This indicates that different writing systems can tax different brain systems based on the amount and kind of phonological processing the writing system requires. Future research that looks at writing systems with varying orthographic depth can further illuminate the relationship of phonological processing to reading acquisition by allowing researchers to explore the implications of variation in the phoneme-to-grapheme correspondence.

Some of the most socially valuable research currently being conducted relates to intervention for reading disorders. One significant question is whether or not remediation can work by normalizing the developmental trajectory, and if these changes can be measured by changes in neural activity. Additionally, can treatment of phonological skills such as phonological awareness improve outcomes in children at risk for reading disorders when initially learning to read? Also, do different treatments work better for different brain "subtypes"?

Although the PDH's influence on our understanding of skilled and impaired reading is profound, it is important to pay attention to other sources of variation that may interact with phonological processing to interfere with the normal acquisition of reading skill. In a recent article, Pugh et al. (2008) found that factors known to facilitate reading performance (e.g., imageability of word, frequency of occurrence, repetition of exposure) led to decreased activation in reading-related areas in non-impaired readers, but resulted in *increased* activation for these sites in individuals with RD. The study confirmed that these facilitative factors were helpful to both groups in supporting word reading accuracy, yet they generated different neural activity between groups. Specifically, in children with RD these tasks activated neural areas associated with reading, suggesting that the reading circuit may be intact but poorly trained. Stated differently, even when the phonological systems are activated, learning and consolidation may pose additional problems for individuals with RD.

It is important to investigate potential compensatory strengths that individuals with RD might possess (Geschwind & Galaburda, 1987; Winner, 2000). There are many clinical and anecdotal reports of visual processing strengths in individuals with dyslexia (see Gilger & Hynd, 2008; Winner). Unfortunately, there are very few published research studies in this area, and results have not been consistent in finding visual processing strengths among RD individuals (e.g., Bannatyne, 1971; Winner et al., 2001). Still, there are experimental data that suggest a compensatory shift in favor of visual-spatial processing for some individuals with language and reading disability (von Karolyi, Winner, Gray, & Sherman, 2003), or indications that visual-spatial information is processed differently in this population (Riccio & Hynd, 1996). This is an area where neuroimaging studies could provide unique insight into the neural underpinnings of these putative visual processing differences. It is an area that merits further exploration.

GENERAL SUMMARY

Neuroimaging techniques have allowed our field to make tremendous strides in understanding skilled and impaired reading. In particular, when this technology has been exploited with sound methodology to probe subcomponents of reading, the result has been consistent support for the centrality of phonological processing in reading, and the importance of phonological deficits in RD. Important areas for future research include longitudinal studies of children at risk for RD, cross-linguistic studies using writing systems that exploit phonology in different ways including different phoneme-to-grapheme correspondences, treatment studies, and studies looking at general resources of learning and consolidation, which, in addition to the phonological processing, could influence reading skill. It will be especially important to take a multilevel-analysis approach that incorporates genetics, neuroanatomy, neurochemistry, and neurocircuitry, and also to combine the strengths of the different neuroimaging techniques. Finally, it will be important to better understand differences between individuals and subgroups of children with RD in order to identify more accurately the factors that lead to different developmental trajectories and more effective treatments.

ACKNOWLEDGMENTS

This work was supported in part by NICHD Grant HD01994 to Carol Fowler, HD 048830 to Kenneth R. Pugh, and the Alexander Brown and James Hudson Brown-Coxe Fellowship through the Yale School of Medicine to Joshua John Diehl.

REFERENCES

Arns, M., Peters, S., Breteler, R., & Verhoeven, L. (2007). Different brain activation patterns in dyslexic children: Evidence from EEG power and coherence patterns for the double-deficit theory of dyslexia. *Journal of Integrative Neuroscience*, *6*, 175–190.

Bannatyne, A. (1971). *Language, reading, and learning disabilities: Psychology, neuropsychology, diagnosis, and remediation*. Springfield, IL: Charles C. Thomas.

Beaulieu, C., Plewes, C., Paulson, L. A., Roy, D., Snook, L., Concha, L., et al. (2005). Imaging brain connectivity in children with divers reading ability. *Neuroimage*, *25*, 1164–1173.

Bergmann, J., & Wimmer, H. (2008). A dual-route perspective on poor reading in a regular orthography: Evidence from phonological and orthographic lexical decisions. *Cognitive Neuropsychology*, *25*, 653–676.

Brady, S. A. (1991). The role of working memory in reading disability. In S. A. Brady & D. P. Shankweiler (Eds.), *Phonological processes in literacy: A tribute to Isabelle Y. Liberman* (pp. 129–151). Hillsdale, NJ: Erlbaum.

Brambati, S. M., Termine, C., Ruffino, M., Stella, G., Fazio, F., Cappa, S. F., et al. (2004). Regional reductions of gray matter volume in familial dyslexia. *Neurology*, *63*, 742–745.

Breier, J. I., Simos, P. G., Zouridakis, G., & Papanicolaou, A. C. (1998). Relative timing of neuronal activity in distinct temporal lobe areas during a recognition memory task for words. *Journal of Clinical and Experimental Neuropsychology*, *20*, 782–790.

Breier, J. I., Simos, P. G., Zouridakis, G., & Papanicolaou, A. C. (1999). Temporal course of regional brain activation associated with phonological decoding. *Journal of Clinical and Experimental Neuropsychology*, *21*, 465–476.

Brown, T. T., Lugar, H. M., Coalson, R. S., Miezin, F. M., Petersen, S. E., & Schlaggar, B. L. (2005). Developmental changes in human cerebral functional organization for word generation. *Cerebral Cortex*, *15*, 275–290.

Brown, W. E., Eliez, S., Menon, V., Rumsey, J. M., White, C. D., & Reiss, A. L. (2001). Preliminary evidence of widespread morphological variations of the brain in dyslexia. *Neurology*, *56*, 781–783.

Brunswick, N., McCrory, E., Price, C., Frith, C. D., & Frith, U. (1999). Explicit and implicit processing of words and pseudowords by adult developmental dyslexics: A search for Wernicke's Worschatz? *Brain*, *122*, 1901–1917.

Church, J. A., Coalson, R. S., Lugar, H. M., Petersen, S. E., & Schlaggar, B. L. (2008). A developmental fMRI study of reading and repetition reveals changes in phonological and visual mechanisms over age. *Cerebral Cortex*, *18*, 2054–2065.

Cohen, L., & Dehaene, S. (2004). Specialization within the ventral stream: The case for the visual word form area. *Neuroimage*, *22*, 466–476.

Cohen, L., Dehaene, S., Naccache, L., Lehricy, S., Dehaene-Lambertz, G., Henaff, M., et al. (2000). The visual word form area: Spatial and temporal characterization of an initial stage of reading in normal subjects and posterior split-brain patients. *Brain*, *123*, 291–307.

Cohen, L., Lhericy, S., Chochon, F., Lerner, C., Rivard, S., & Dehaene, S. (2002). Language-specific tuning of visual cortex? Functional properties of the visual word form area. *Brain*, *125*, 1054–1069.

Constable, R. T., McCarthy, G., Allison, T., Anderson, A. W., & Gore, J. C. (1993). Functional brain imaging at 1.5 T using conventional gradient echo MR imaging techniques. *Magnetic Resonance Imaging*, *11*, 451–459.

Dejerine, J. (1891). Sur un cas eccite verbale avec agraphie, suivi d'autopsie. *C.R. Societe du Biologie*, *43*(43), 197–201.

Deutsch, G. K., Dougherty, R. F., Bammer, R., Siok, W. T., Gabrieli, J. D., & Wandell, B. A. (2005). Children's reading performance is correlated with white matter structure measured by diffusion tensor imaging. *Cortex*, *41*, 354–363.

Dougherty, R. F., Ben-Shachar, M., Deutsch, G. K., Hernandez, A., Fox, G. R., & Wandell, B. A. (2007). Temporal-callosal pathway diffusivity predicts phonological skills in children. *Proceedings of the National Academy of Sciences*, *104*, 8556–8561.

Duffy, F. H., Denckla, M. B., Bartels, P. H., & Sandini, G. (2004). Dyslexia: Regional differences in brain electrical activity by topographic mapping. *Annals of Neurology*, *7*(5), 412–420.

Eckert, M. (2004). Neuroanatomical markers for dyslexia: A review of dyslexia structural imaging studies. *The Neuroscientist*, *10*, 362–371.

Eckert, M., Leonard, C. M., Richards, T. L., Aylward, E. H., Thomson, J., & Berninger, V. (2003). Anatomical correlates of dyslexia: Frontal and cerebellar findings. *Brain, 126*, 482–494.

Eden, G. F., VanMeter, J. W., Rumsey, J. M., Maisog, J., & Zeffiro, T. A. (1996). Abnormal processing of visual motion in dyslexia revealed by functional brain imaging. *Nature, 348*, 66–69.

Fletcher, J., Shaywitz, S. E., Shankweiler, D. P., Katz, L., Liberman, I. Y., Stuebing, K. K., et al. (1994). Cognitive profiles of reading disability: Comparisons of discrepancy and low achievement definitions. *Journal of Educational Psychology, 86*, 6–23.

Flowers, D. L., Wood, F. B., & Naylor, C. E. (1991). Regional cerebral blood flow correlates of language processes in reading disability. *Archives of Neurology, 48*, 637–643.

Fox, P. T., & Mintun, M. (1989). Noninvasive functional brain mapping by change-distribution analysis of averaged PET images of H215O tissue activity. *Journal of Nuclear Medicine, 30*, 141–149.

Friston, K. J. (1994). Functional and effective connectivity: A synthesis. *Human Brain Mapping, 2*, 56–78.

Frost, S. J., Landi, N., Mencl, W. E., Sandak, R., Fulbright, R. K., Tejada, E. T., et al. (2009). Phonological awareness predicts activation patterns for print and speech. *Annals of Dyslexia, 59*, 78–97.

Frost, S. J., Sandak, R., Mencl, W. E., Landi, N., Rueckl, J. G., Katz, L., et al. (Eds.). (2009). *Mapping the work reading circuitry in skilled and disabled readers*. New York: Taylor & Francis.

Galaburda, A. M. (2006). Advances in cross-level research. In G. D. Rosen (Ed.), *The dyslexic brain: New pathways in neuroscience discovery* (pp. 329–354). New York: Psychology Press.

Galaburda, A. M., & Cestnick, L. (2003). Developmental dyslexia. *Revista de neurologia, 36*(Suppl. 1), S3–S9.

Galaburda, A. M., Sherman, G. F., Rosen, G. D., Aboitiz, F., & Geschwind, N. (1985). Developmental dyslexia: Four consecutive patients with cortical anomalies. *Annals of Neurology, 18*, 222–233.

Geschwind, N., & Galaburda, A. M. (1987). *Cerebral lateralization*. Cambridge, MA: MIT Press.

Geschwind, N., & Levitsky, W. (1968). Human brain: Left-right asymmetries in temporal in temporal speech region. *Science, 161*, 186–187.

Gilger, J. W., & Hynd, G. W. (2008). Neurodevelopmental variation as a framework for thinking about the twice exceptional. *Roeper Review: A Journal on Gifted Education, 30*(4), 214–228.

Goswami, U. (2008). Reading, dyslexia, and the brain. *Journal of Educational Research, 50*, 135–148.

Goswami, U., & Bryant, P. E. (1990). *Phonological skills and learning to read*. Hillsdale, NJ: Erlbaum.

Gross-Glenn, K., Duara, R., Barker, W. W., Loewenstein, D., Chang, J. Y., Yoshii, F., et al. (1991). Positron emission tomographic studies during serial word reading by normal and dyslexic adults. *Journal of Clinical and Experimental Neuropsychology, 13*, 531–544.

Herbster, A., Mintun, M., Nebes, R., & Becker, J. (1997). Regional cerebral blood flow during word and nonword reading. *Human Brain Mapping, 5*, 84–92.

Hinschelwood, J. (1917). *Congenital word blindness*. London: H.K. Lewis.

Hoeft, F., Ueno, T., Reiss, A. L., Meyler, A., Whitfield-Gabrieli, S., Glover, G., et al. (2007). Prediction of children's reading skills using behavioral, functional, and structural neuroimaging measures. *Behavioral Neuroscience, 121*, 602–613.

Horwitz, B. (1994). Data analysis paradigms for metabolic-flow data: Combining neural modeling and functional neuroimaging. *Human Brain Mapping*, *2*, 112–122.

Horwitz, B., Grady, C. L., Haxby, J. V., Ungerleider, L. G., Schapiro, M. B., Mishkin, M., et al. (1992). Functional associations among human posterior extrastriate brain regions during object and spatial vision. *Journal of Cognitive Neuroscience*, *4*, 311–322.

Horwitz, B., Rumsey, J. M., & Donohue, B. C. (1998). Functional connectivity of the angular gyrus in normal reading and dyslexia. *Proceedings of the National Academy Sciences*, *95*, 8939–8944.

Hulme, C., & Roodenrys, S. (1995). Practitioner review: Verbal working memory development and its disorders. *Journal of Child Psychology and Psychiatry*, *36*, 373–398.

Humphreys, P., Kaufmann, W. E., & Galaburda, A. M. (1990). Developmental dyslexia in women. *Annals of Neurology*, *28*, 727–738.

Hynd, G. W., Semrud-Clikman, M., Lorys, A. R., Novey, E. S., & Eliopulos, D. (1990). Brain morphology in developmental dyslexia and attention deficit/hyperactivity disorder. *Archives of Neurology*, *47*, 919–926.

Klingberg, T., Hedehus, M., Temple, E., Salz, T., Gabrieli, J. D., Moseley, M. E., et al. (2000). Microstructure of temporo-parietal white matter as a basis for reading ability: Evidence from diffusion tensor magnetic resonance imaging. *Neuron*, *25*, 493–500.

Kronbichler, M., Wimmer, H., Staffen, W., Hutzler, F., Mair, A., & Gunther, L. (2008). Developmental dyslexia: Gray matter abnormalities in occipitotemporal cortex. *Human Brain Mapping*, *29*, 613–625.

Larsen, J. P., Høien, T., Lundberg, I., & Odegarrd, H. (1990). MRI evaluation of the size and symmetry of the planum temporale in adolescents with developmental dyslexia. *Brain and Language*, *39*, 289–301.

Leisman, G., & Ashkenazi, M. (1980). Aetiological factors in dyslexia: IV. Cerebral hemispheres are functionally equivalent. *International Journal of Neuroscience*, *11*, 157–164.

Leonard, C. M., Eckert, M., Givens, B., Berninger, V., & Eden, G. F. (2006). Individual differences in anatomy predict reading and oral language impairments in children. *Brain*, *129*, 3329–3342.

Leonard, C. M., Lombardino, L. J., Mercado, L. R., Browd, S. R., Breier, J. I., & Agee, O. F. (2001). Anatomical risk factors for phonological dyslexia. *Cerebral Cortex*, *11*, 148–157.

Liberman, A. M. (1992). The relationship of speech to reading and writing. In R. Frost & L. Katz (Eds.), *Orthography, phonology, morphology, and meaning* (pp. 167–178). North Holland: Elsevier.

Liberman, I. Y., Shankweiler, D., & Liberman, A. M. (1989). The alphabetic principle and learning to read. In D. S. I. Y. Liberman (Ed.), *Phonology and reading disability: Solving the reading puzzle.* Research Monograph Series. Ann Arbor, MI: University of Michigan Press.

McIntosh, A. R., & Gonzalez-Lima, F. (1994). Structural equation modeling and its application to network analysis of functional brain imaging. *Human Brain Mapping*, *2*, 2–22.

Mintun, M. A., Fox, P. T., & Raichle, M. E. (1989). A highly accurate method of localizing regions of neuronal activation in the human brain with positron emission tomography. *Journal of Cerebral Blood Flow and Metabolism*, *9*, 96–103.

Niogi, S. N., & McCandliss, B. D. (2006). Left lateralized white matter microstructure accounts for individual differences in reading ability and disability. *Neuropsychologia*, *44*, 2178–2188.

Ogawa, S., Lee, T. M., Nayak, A. S., & Glynn, P. (1990). Oxygenation-sensitive contrast in magnetic resonance image of rodent brain at high magnetic fields. *Magnetic Resonance Medicine*, *14*, 68–78.

Ogawa, S., Tank, D. W., Menon, R., Ellerman, J. M., Kim, S. G., Merkle, H., et al. (1992). Intrinsic signal changes accompanying sensory stimulation: Functional brain mapping with magnetic resonance imaging. *Proceedings of the National Academy of Sciences, 89*, 5951–5955.

Olson, R. K., Wise, B., Connors, F., & Rack, J. (1990). Organization, heritability, and remediation of component word recognition and language skills in disabled readers. In T. H. Carr & B. A. Levy (Eds.), *Reading and its development: Component skill approaches* (pp. 261–322). New York: Academic Press.

Pammer, K. (2009). What can MEG neuroimaging tell us about reading? *Journal of Neurolinguistics, 22*, 266–280.

Papanicolaou, A. C., Simos, P. G., Breier, J. I., Zouridakis, G., Willmore, L. J., Wheless, J. W., et al. (1999). Magnetoencephalographic mapping of the language specific cortex. *Journal of Neurosurgery, 90*, 85–93.

Paulesu, E., Démonet, J.-F., Fazio, F., McCrory, E., Chanoine, V., Brunswick, N., et al. (2001). Dyslexia: Cultural diversity and biological unity. *Science, 291*, 2165–2167.

Paulesu, E., Frith, U., Snowling, M. J., Gallagher, A., Morton, J., Frackowiak, R. S. J., et al. (1996). Is developmental dyslexia a disconnection syndrome? Evidence from PET scanning. *Brain, 119*, 143–157.

Paulesu, E., McCrory, E., Fazio, F., Menoncello, L., Brunswick, N., Cappa, S. F., et al. (2000). A cultural effect on brain function. *Nature Neuroscience, 3*, 91–96.

Pennington, B. F. (1999). Dyslexia as a neurodevelopmental disorder. In H. Tager-Flusberg (Ed.), *Neurodevelopmental disorders* (pp. 307–330). Cambridge, MA: MIT Press.

Petersen, S. E., Fox, P. T., Posner, M. I., Mintun, M., & Raichle, M. E. (1989). Positron emission tomographic studies of the processing of single words. *Journal of Cognitive Neuroscience, 1*, 153–170.

Petersen, S. E., Fox, P. T., Snyder, A. Z., & Raichle, M. E. (1990). Activation of extrastriate and frontal cortical areas by visual words and word-like stimuli. *Science, 249*, 1041–1044.

Petersson, K. M., Reis, A., Askelöf, S., Castro-Caldas, A., & Ingvar, M. (2000). Language processing modulated by literacy: A network analysis of verbal repetition in literate and illiterate subjects. *Journal of Cognitive Neuroscience, 12*, 364–382.

Petersson, K. M., Silva, C., Castro-Caldas, A., Ingvar, M., & Reis, A. (2007). Literacy: A cultural influence on functional left-right differences in the inferior parietal cortex. *European Journal of Neuroscience, 26*, 791–799.

Price, C. J., Winterburn, D., Giraud, A. L., Moore, C. J., & Noppeney, U. (2003). Cortical localization of the visual and auditory word form areas: A reconsideration of the evidence. *Brain and Language, 86*, 272–286.

Pugh, K. R., Frost, S. J., Sandak, R., Landi, N., Rueckl, J. G., Constable, R. T., et al. (2008). Effects of stimulus difficulty and repetition on printed word identification: An fMRI comparison of nonimpaired and reading-disabled adolescent cohorts. *Journal of Cognitive Neuroscience, 20*, 1146–1160.

Pugh, K. R., Mencl, W. E., Jenner, A. R., Katz, L., Frost, S. J., Lee, J. R., et al. (2001). Neurobiological studies of reading and reading disability. *Journal of Communication Disorders, 34*, 479–492.

Pugh, K. R., Mencl, W. E., Jenner, A. J., Katz, L., Lee, J. R., Shaywitz, S. E., et al. (2000). Functional neuroimaging studies of reading and reading disability (developmental dyslexia). *Mental Retardation and Developmental Disabilities Review, 6*, 207–213.

Pugh, K. R., Mencl, W. E., Shaywitz, B. A., Shaywitz, S. E., Fulbright, R. K., Skudlarski, P., et al. (2000). The angular gyrus in developmental dyslexia: Task-specific differences in functional connectivity in posterior cortex. *Psychological Science, 11*, 51–56.

Pugh, K. R., Sandak, R., Frost, S. J., Moore, D., & Mencl, W. E. (2005). Examining reading development and reading disability in English language learners: Potential contributions from functional neuroimaging. *Learning Disabilities Research & Practice*, *20*, 1–24.

Pugh, K. R., Shaywitz, B. A., Constable, R. T., Shaywitz, S. E., Skudlarski, P., Fulbright, R. K., et al. (1996). Cerebral organization of component processes in reading. *Brain*, *119*, 1221–1238.

Pugh, K. R., Shaywitz, B., Shaywitz, S. E., Shankweiler, D., Katz, L., Fletcher, J., et al. (1997). Predicting reading performance from neuroimaging profiles: The cerebral basis of phonological effects in printed word identification. *Journal of Experimental Psychology: Human Perception and Performance*, *23*, 299–318.

Riccio, C. A., & Hynd, G. W. (1996). Neuroanatomical and neurophysiological aspects of dyslexia. *Topics in Language Disorders*, *16*, 1–13.

Rippon, G., & Brunswick, N. (2000). Trait and state EEG indices of information processing in developmental dyslexia. *International Journal of Psychophysiology*, *36*, 151–165.

Rumsey, J. M., Andreason, P., Zametkin, A. J., Aquino, T., King, C., Hamburger, S. D., et al. (1992). Failure to activate the left temporoparietal cortex in dyslexia: An oxygen 15 positron emission tomographic study. *Archives of Neurology*, *49*, 527–534.

Rumsey, J. M., Nace, K., Donohue, B., Wise, D., Maisog, J. M., & Andreason, P. (1997). A positron emission tomographic study of impaired word recognition and phonological processing in dyslexic men. *Archives of Neurology*, *54*, 562–573.

Salmelin, R., Service, E., Kiesila, P., Uutela, K., & Salonen, O. (1996). Impaired visual word processing in dyslexia revealed with magnetoencephalography. *Annals of Neurology*, *40*, 157–162.

Sandak, R., Mencl, W. E., Frost, S. J., Rueckl, J. G., Katz, L., Moore, D., et al. (2004). The neurobiology of adaptive learning in reading: A contrast of different training conditions. *Cognitive, Affective, & Behavioral Neuroscience*, *4*, 67–88.

Schlaggar, B. L., & McCandliss, B. D. (2007). Development of neural systems for reading. *Annual Reviews of Neuroscience*, *30*, 475–503.

Schultz, R. T., Cho, N. K., Staib, L. H., Kier, L. E., Fletcher, J. M., Shaywitz, S. E., et al. (1994). Brain morphology in normal and dyslexic children: The influence of sex and age. *Annals of Neurology*, *35*, 732–742.

Shankweiler, D., & Crain, S. (1986) Language mechanisms and reading disorder: A modular approach. *Cognition*, *24*, 139–168.

Shankweiler, D., Crain, S., Katz, L., Fowler, A. E., Liberman, A. M., Brady, S. A., et al. (1995). Cognitive profiles of reading-disabled children: Comparison of language skills in phonology, morphology, and syntax. *Psychological Science*, *6*, 149–156.

Shankweiler, D., Liberman, I. Y., Mark, L. S., Fowler, C. A., & Fischer, F. W. (1979). The speech code and learning to read. *Journal of Experimental Psychology: Human Learning and Memory*, *5*, 531–545.

Share, D., Jorm, A., Maclean, R., & Matthews, R. (1984). Sources of individual differences in reading acquisition. *Journal of Educational Psychology*, *76*, 1309–1324.

Shaywitz, B. A., Shaywitz, S. E., Blachman, B., Pugh, K. R., Fulbright, R., Skudlarski, P., et al. (2004). Development of left occipito-temporal systems for skilled reading following a phonologically-based intervention in children. *Biological Psychiatry*, *55*, 926–933.

Shaywitz, B. A., Shaywitz, S. E., Pugh, K., Constable, T., Skudlarski, P., Fulbright, R., et al. (1995). Sex differences in the functional organization of the brain for language. *Nature*, *373*, 607–609.

Shaywitz, B. A., Shaywitz, S. E., Pugh, K. R., Mencl, W. E., Fulbright, R. K., Skudlarski, P., et al. (2002). Disruption of posterior brain systems for reading in children with developmental dyslexia. *Biological Psychiatry*, *52*, 101–110.

Shaywitz, S. E., Shaywitz, B. A., Fulbright, R. K., Skudlarski, P., Mencl, W. E., Constable, R. T., et al. (2003). Neural systems for compensation and persistence: Young adult outcome of childhood reading disability. *Biological Psychiatry*, *54*, 25–33.

Shaywitz, S. E., Shaywitz, B. A., Pugh, K. R., Fulbright, R. K., Constable, R. T., Mencl, W. E., et al. (1998). Functional disruption in the organization of the brain for reading in dyslexia. *Proceedings of the National Academy of Sciences*, *95*, 2636–2641.

Simos, P. G., Breier, J. I., Maggio, W. W., Gormley, W., Zouridakis, G., Willmore, L. J., et al. (1999). Atypical language representation: MEG and intraoperative stimulation mapping correlations. *Neuroreport*, *10*, 139–142.

Simos, P. G., Fletcher, J. M., Bergman, E., Breier, J. I., Foorman, B. R., Castillo, E. M., et al. (2002). Dyslexia-specific brain activation profile becomes normal following successful remedial training. *Neurology*, *58*, 1203–1213.

Siok, W. T., Niu, Z., Jin, Z., Perfetti, C. A., & Tan, L. H. (2008). A structural-functional basis for dyslexia in the cortex of Chinese readers. *Proceedings of the National Academy of Sciences*, *105*, 5561–5566.

Sklar, B., Hanley, J., & Simmons, W. W. (1972). An EEG experiment aimed toward identifying dyslexic children. *Nature*, *240*, 414–416.

Spironelli, C., Penolazzi, B., & Angrilli, A. (2008). Dysfunctional hemispheric asymmetry of theta and beta EEG activity during linguistic tasks in developmental dyslexia. *Biological Psychiatry*, *77*, 123–131.

Spironelli, C., Penolazzi, B., Vio, C., & Angrilli, A. (2006). Inverted EEG theta lateralization in dyslexic children during phonological processing. *Neuropsychologia*, *44*, 2814–2821.

Stanovich, K. E., & Siegel, L. S. (1994). Phenotypic performance profile of children with reading disabilities: A regression-based test of the phonological-core variable-difference model. *Journal of Educational Psychology*, *86*, 24–53.

Tallal, P., Miller, S. L., & Fitch, R. H. (1993). Neurobiological basis of speech: A case for the preeminence of temporal processing. *Annals of the New York Academy of Sciences*, *682*, 27–47.

Tan, L. H., Spinks, J. A., Eden, G. F., Perfetti, C. A., & Siok, W. T. (2005). Reading depends on writing, in Chinese. *Proceedings of the National Academy of Sciences*, *102*, 8781–8785.

Temple, E., Deutsch, G. K., Poldrack, R. A., Miller, S. L., Tallal, P., Merzenich, M. M., et al. (2003). Neural deficits in children with dyslexia ameliorated by behavioral remediation: Evidence from functional MRI. *Proceedings of the National Academy of Sciences*, *100*, 2860–2865.

Turkeltaub, P. E., Lynn, G., Flowers, D. L., Zeffiro, T. A., & Eden, G. F. (2003). Development of neural mechanisms for reading. *Nature Neuroscience*, *6*, 767–773.

Vellutino, F. R., Fletcher, J. M., Snowling, M. J., & Scanlon, D. M. (2004). Specific reading disability (dyslexia): What have we learned in the past four decades? *Journal of Child Psychology and Psychiatry*, *45*, 2–40.

Vellutino, F. R., & Scanlon, D. M. (1991). The preeminence of phonologically basked skills in learning to read. In S. A. Brady & D. P. Shankweiler (Eds.), *Phonological process in literacy: A tribute to Isabelle Y. Liberman* (pp. 237–252). Hillsdale, NJ: Erlbaum.

von Karolyi, C., Winner, E., Gray, W., & Sherman, G. F. (2003). Dyslexia linked to talent: Global visual-spatial ability. *Brain and Language*, *85*, 427–431.

Wagner, R. K., Torgesen, J. K., Laughon, P., Simmons, K., & Rashotte, C. A. (1993). Development of young readers' phonological processing abilities. *Journal of Educational Psychology*, *85*, 83–103.

Winner, E. (2000). The origins and ends of giftedness. *American Psychologist*, *55*, 159–169.

Winner, E., von Karolyi, C., Malinsky, D., French, L., Seliger, C., Ross, E., et al. (2001). Dyslexia and visual-spatial talents: Compensation vs. deficit model. *Brain and Language*, *76*, 81–110.

Wolff, P. H., Cohen, C., & Drake, C. (1984). Impaired motor timing in specific reading retardation. *Neuropsychologia*, *22*, 587–600.

Wood, F., Flowers, L., Buchsbaum, M., & Tallal, P. (1991). Investigation of abnormal left temporal functioning in dyslexia through rCBF, auditory evoked potentials, and positron emission tomography. *Reading and Writing*, *3*, 379–393.

Author Index

C

D

E

H

I

J

N

O

P

Q

R

S

T

U

V

W

X

Y

Z

Subject Index

O

P

S

T

V

W